FREEDOM LOST

A HISTORY OF NEWSPAPERS, JOURNALISM, AND PRESS CENSORSHIP IN AUSTRALIA

ROBERT PULLAN

First published 2020 by:
Australian Academic Press Group Pty. Ltd.
Samford Valley QLD 4520, Australia
www.australianacademicpress.com.au

Copyright © 2020 Robert Pullan.

Copying for educational purposes
The *Australian Copyright Act 1968* (Cwlth) allows a maximum of one chapter or 10% of this book, whichever is the greater, to be reproduced and/or communicated by any educational institution for its educational purposes provided that the educational institution (or the body that administers it) has given a remuneration notice to Copyright Agency Limited (CAL) under the Act.
For details of the CAL licence for educational institutions contact:
Copyright Agency Limited, 19/157 Liverpool Street, Sydney, NSW 2000.
E-mail info@copyright.com.au

Production and communication for other purposes
Except as permitted under the Act, for example a fair dealing for the purposes of study, research, criticism or review, no part of this book may be reproduced, stored in a retrieval system, or transmitted in any form or by any means electronic, mechanical, photocopying, recording or otherwise without prior written permission of the copyright holder.

 A catalogue record for this book is available from the National Library of Australia

Freedom Lost: A history of newspapers, journalism, and press censorship in Australia

ISBN 9781925644388   (paperback)
ISBN 9781925644395   (hardback)

Publisher: Stephen May
Cover design: Luke Harris, Working Type Studio
Typesetting: Australian Academic Press
Printing: Lightning Source

For the journalists, every last one of us, yesterday, today and tomorrow.

And to my partner, Merrilyn Walton, whose love and generosity made it possible.

Freedom Lost: A history of newspapers, journalism, and press censorship in Australia.

Contents

Acknowledgements ....

About the author...

Chapter 1   What happened **1**

Chapter 2   Lightning Strikes..**7**

    1803–1817 The first Australian editor, **George Howe**, edits *The Sydney Gazette and New South Wales Advertiser* under Governors Phillip King and Lachlan Macquarie.

Chapter 3   News in Leg-irons **23**

    1821–1829 **Robert Howe**; *The Sydney Gazette, New South Wales Advertiser* and *The Australian Magazine*, Dr William Redfern's horsewhip, Samuel Terry and the Bank of New South Wales; W.C.Wentworth and the Court of Quarter Sessions.

Chapter 4   The Vagabond Free Press **29**

    1824–1827 **Robert Wardell**, *The Australian*; Governor Thomas Brisbane, Chief Justice Francis Forbes, Earl Bathurst, John and Hannibal Macarthur, Governor Ralph Darling, Attorney General Saxe Bannister, Archdeacon Thomas Scott, Henry Dumaresq.

Chapter 5   Duelling with Authority **41**

    1826–1827: **Edward Smith Hall**, *The Monitor*; **Robert Howe**, *The Sydney Gazette* and *New South Wales Advertiser*; **Robert Wardell**, *The Australian*; **Lawrence Hynes Halloran**, *The Gleaner*; Governor Ralph Darling, Chief Justice Francis Forbes, Attorneys General Saxe Bannister, William Moore and Alexander Baxter; Under Secretaries Richard Hay and Robert Wilmot Horton.

Chapter 6   The Hobart Press Musket **59**

    1816–1888 **Andrew Bent, Henry Emmett** and **Evan Thomas**, *The Hobart Town Gazette, Southern Reporter* and *Van Diemen's Land Advertiser*; Governors Thomas Davey, William Sorrell and George Arthur; **Terry Howe**, *The Tasmanian and Port Dalrymple Advertiser*; **Robert Lathrop Murray, James Ross**, *The Colonial Times*; **Gilbert Robertson**, *The Colonist* and *The True Colonist*; Chief Justice John Lewes Pedder; Attorney General Joseph Gellibrand; **John Charles** and **George Davies** and *The Mercury*.

v

Freedom Lost: A history of newspapers, journalism, and press censorship in Australia.

Chapter 7   Sedition in a Prison 79

1828–1831 **Edward Hall**, *The Monitor* and *The Sydney Monitor*, Archdeacon Thomas Scott, **Atwell Hayes** and *The Australian*, the **Rev. Ralph Mansfield** and *The Sydney Gazette*; Governor Ralph Darling, Chief Justice Francis Forbes, Justice James Dowling, Attorney General Alexander Baxter.

Chapter 8   'I shot the doctor for your benefit' 89

1834: **Robert Wardell** is murdered.

Chapter 9   Faith 95

1835–1851: **John Dunmore Lang**, *The Colonist*, *The Colonial Observer* and *The Press*; **Edward O'Shaunessy**, and **William Watt**, *The Sydney Gazette*; **Henry Parkes**, *The Empire*.
1931–2009: **Frank Devine**, *The Weekend News* and *The Australian*.

Chapter 10   Port Phillip Press Partisans 113

1829–1840 **John Pascoe Fawkner**, *The Melbourne Advertiser* and *The Port Phillip Patriot* and *Melbourne Advertiser*; **Thomas Strode** and **Phillip Arden**, *The Port Phillip Gazette*; **George Cavenagh**, *Port Phillip Herald*.

Chapter 11   Port Phillip Patriot Partiality 133

1838–1845 **William Kerr, John Duerdin, John Curtis, Edward Wilson** and *The Melbourne Argus*; **Edmund Finn, George Cavenagh**, Magistrate Edward St John and *The Port Phillip Herald*; Superintendent Charles Joseph La Trobe; *The Port Phillip Patriot*; *Melbourne Daily News*.

Chapter 12   King David's Duty 147

1827–1908: **Ebenezer** and **David Syme**, *The Age*; **G.F.H.Schuler, Alfred Deakin**, special correspondent for the *London Morning Post*; *The Herald*, *The Morning Herald*, **George Dill** and **Hugh George**, *The Argus*; Speight v Syme.

Chapter 13   News Under the Sun 167

1846–1891: **James Swan, Arthur Lyon, William Wilkes, Theophilus Pugh, Thomas Stephens**, Attorney General Ratcliffe Pring and *The Moreton Bay Courier*; *The Courier 1861–1864*, *The Queensland Guardian 1860–1868*; *The Brisbane Courier* from June 1864; **Gresley Lukin; George Wight** and *The Queensland Guardian*.

Chapter 14   Inflammatory Justice 179

1841–1842: Justice John Willis, **John Fawkner** and **William Kerr**, *The Port Phillip Patriot 1839–1845*; **George Cavenagh, George Arden**, *Port Phillip Gazette* and *Settlers' Journal*; Police Magistrate Frederick St John; Justice John Walpole Willis.

Chapter 15   Ned Kelly and Montague Grover 185

1888–1914: **Monty Grover** on *The Age,* *The Boomerang,* *The Argus* and *The Sun News-Pictorial.*

Chapter 16   The Tabloid School 195

1884–1923 **John, Ada** and **Ezra Norton**, the *Evening News, Truth, Daily Mirror, The Sun,* **Jack Muir.**

Chapter 17   News and Lies: The Capricornia School 209

1873–1996: **Richard Wells, William Bednall, Charles Kirkland, George Mayhew, Louis Solomon, Joseph Skelton, Frederick Thompson,** and *The Northern Territory Times;* **Jessie Litchfield,** first Australian woman editor, **R.D.Beresford** and the *North Australian;* Administrator, John Anderson Gilruth; Justice David Bevan; **Michaael O'Halloran** and *The Northern Standard;* **Lieut. Alex Baz** and *The Sunday Army News;* **Jim Bowditch** and *The Northern Territory News.*

Chapter 18   The Black Swan 231

1829–1993: **Charles Macfaull** and *The Perth Gazette* and *Western Australian Journal;* **Frances Lochee** and *The Inquirer;* **John Winthrop Hackett, Charles Harper, Griff Richards, Jim Macartney, Paul Haslluck** and *The West Australian.*

Chapter 19   The Act of Creation 249

1895–1949: revolution: news on page one; the world's first labor daily, **Jack Lang** and *The Daily Post;* **Alfred Deakin** and *The Age;* **Hugh Denison** and *The Sun;* **Hugh D. McIntosh, Robert Clyde Packer** and *The Sunday Times;* **James Joynton Smith, Claude McKay,** *Smith's Weekly* and *The Daily Guardian.*

Chapter 20   The Press in Utopia 269

1836–1973: **George Stevenson, Robert Thomas** and *The South Australian Gazette* and *Colonial Register;* **John Brown, Charles Mann** and *The Southern Australian;* Resident Commissioner *James Hurtle Fisher* and Governor Sir *John Hindmarsh;* **John Stephens,** *The Adelaide Observer;* **John Henry Barrow, Langdon Bonython, Catherine Spence, King O'Malley,** Prime Minister *Billy Hughes,* **Lloyd Dumas,** *The Advertiser.*

Chapter 21   Style, Stereos, Seers 283

Acknowledgements

In keeping the wolf from the door a grant from the Literature Board of the Australia Council was invaluable; my thanks to my peers who deemed the project original and worth supporting. Thanks to Laurie Muller and UQP for the contract and advance — though it didn't work out, it surely helped. In a project that has taken too long, 25 years actually, what I learned from students — this is the way things go — helped more than they and I knew. From the beginning my dear partner Merrilyn Walton sometimes thought I was mad but put up with me anyway and sustained me with her great heart and energy. My friends Matthew Blake and Wendy Beckett gave me years of a collegial office, which batted away cabin fever. My colleagues in the newsroom of The West Australian, when it was a good paper, taught me the fundamentals, particularly Peter Ewing, Leo Johnston, Don Smith and my friends and flatmates Zoltan Kovacs and Kim Lockwood. To Stephen May — good on you.

About the author

Robert Pullan, born in Kalamunda, WA, worked as a newspaper journalist in Perth, Melbourne, Canberra, Sydney and New York from 1966 and has freelanced in Sydney from 1979. His books include Guilty Secrets: Free Speech and Defamation in Australia. He taught journalism at the University of Technology, Sydney, Macleay College and Broadmeadows TAFE and served 28 years on the board of the Australian Society of Authors.

Chapter 1

What happened?

Because it begins as idea, news is limitless. Nothing in the universe — fire, flood, sub-atomic particles, poetry, the beginning of time — is beyond its scope. No universal theory of newspapers — let alone Australian newspapers — has been written and this is not an attempt, or a theory. In practice the limits of the newsroom imposed by time, talent, budgets and law are as strict as the convict boundaries of the lash and sandstone cell. Within those limits the *printer's devil*, traditionally responsible for error since Europeans suspected the craft of associating with Satan, is always hyperactive.

The British settlers brought with them the common law, one of the civilizers of human history, to govern power, authority, life, death and civility. When nyungars were making song-lines in the western desert a thousand years before, the British judges who preceded common-law applied trial by ordeal, reasoning that an innocent accused forced to clutch a red-hot poker would be spared burns, spared agony, by the merciful intervention of Almighty God. By 1803 the reasoning had evolved in subtlety, but George Howe, teacher and storyteller, founding editor of *The Sydney Gazette and New South Wales Advertiser*, could publish nothing without Government approval, an arrangement he believed ideal because he thought truth was what emerged from the sands of time sifted by an Anglican God, the English Crown and the law which he and most of his readers violated to earn their passage to Sydney.

Journalism is philosophy, (one of Lachlan Murdoch's early academic interests), because only time stops the questions though philosophers say 'take your time' and journalists 'are you on deadline?' Even the perpetual boundary of the reader's boredom is porous because, myth says, a great reporter can make anything interesting to anyone. In logic, the boundary of news is the limit of human understanding. In reality, it is the boundary of readers' understanding.

Still, when HMS Beagle sailed into Sydney Harbour on 12 January 1836, with Charles Darwin, aboard with a story, evolution by natural selection, which would shake the foundations of the known, perhaps the biggest story in history, while the Beagle was reported 7533 times in newspapers from Adelaide to Hobart, not a single journalist reported the great scientist.

No theory answers the question *what causes newspapers?* Today in the early years of the digital revolution even the future of ink and paper are dicey. Arthur Sulzberger Jr, chairman and publisher of *The New York Times,* said on 8 September 2010 the paper would not be printed from a date 'to be decided'. As newsrooms, circulations, revenues and journalists shrink and bankruptcies grow, some professionals, including some on the *Times*, say the best information system in the history of the world might mean the end not just of publishing companies, but 'news itself'. From the beginning the most intriguing and mysterious fundamental has been the psychological core of the journalist, particularly the editor-proprietor, including portions of ideology, stability, intellectual and imaginative capacity often mysterious to the self which possesses them. The young Rupert Murdoch who talked into the Adelaide night with Clyde Cameron about the future of man evolved into a reactionary oligarch who caused crime waves among the journalists News Limited employed in London a half century later. The driven young Rupert appointed brilliant communist-voting Adrian Deamer to edit *The Australian*, then with circulation, sales and revenue thriving under Deamer's flair, a capitalist model of press success, sacked him a few years later specifically because he was too progressive.

In my final year at law school I entered journalism by chance in November 1966 through a scheme devised by Jim Macartney, managing director of West Australian Newspapers, the most gifted west-coast journalist of his generation. After reporting from Melbourne, Canberra and Sydney for the West, from New York for the Herald and Weekly Times group, and a brief stint on *The Bulletin* where my colleagues included the promising youngsters Bob Carr and Malcolm Turnbull, I wrote this history convinced that press freedom evolved and expanded since the convict years only to discover to my surprise and dismay that this is not the case. I've only known one newspaper proprietor intimately, my law-school friend Robert Holmes aCourt, whose intense desire for privacy concealed his drive for media influence from, among others, himself. 'My sole interest is in trading profitably,' he told me. Among editors and proprietors, as among all journalists, including Prime Minister Malcolm Turnbull and his predecessor Tony Abbott, the cast of characters is immense: poets, drunks, gunmen, preachers, reformers and reactionaries. The story is one of the keys to human growth and learning and the news story one of the keys to democratic accountability, itself a concept too dangerous to be uttered in public at the start of the (British) Australian experiment.

Near the beginnings of the thought processes that led to scholarship, science, news and newsrooms, Aristotle, noting that poets' pernicious ravings had the capacity to turn young minds away from truth, deduced that rationality required state supervision of the transmission of words. Censorship. Reinforcing Aristotle's reasoning, much later applied in the theories of a former European correspondent for the *New York Herald Tribune*, Karl Marx, was the anxiety about free speech that manifests itself in the abuse inflicted on Julian Assange.

The tension between love and fear that censors human communication appears historically tenacious, world-wide and self-harming. Why is it, when hornets, bees and ants exchange information as best they can to optimal advantage, that the most intelligent animal falls short of insects? A short answer is that ants don't have parliaments. But since words on pages have made science, history, law and religion possible, it seems profoundly paradoxical for humanity to invent and enforce censorship and sanctify ignorance.

In *Freedom on the Fatal Shore* (1988) the prolific, subtle, insightful Melbourne historian John Hirst dealt quite simply with an evident contradiction of freedom — editors repeatedly jailed — quite simply: he ignored it. You can't do that, as cadets are routinely told, in journalism.

In evolving from a press secretly censored because government was too afraid of the consequences of freedom either to permit it or to deny it openly, Australian newspapers mirrored the country's evolution from a foreign jail on the edge of the unknown to a progressive industrial democracy, contributing the secret 'kangaroo ballot' to world mechanisms of accountability and enabling women to vote 16 years before the British and 18 before the new world in the U.S.

At the peak of newspaper influence in 1923 when twenty-one proprietors owned twenty-six capital-city daily newspapers in a population of 5.7 million — less than one-quarter of 2019's 25 million — print monopolised communication and only the lowly billboard competed for advertisers' money. Print penetration was *90 times* what it is in 2019. Commercial radio broadcasting started in September 1923, commercial television in September 1956; the internet's evolution from a U.S. defence and academic information-sharer in 1965 to a universal web made an equivalent start date logically impossible. Hopes for information-communication, its capacity to teach and heal, end ignorance and enhance love, for which Julian Assange and Edward Snowden suffered, expanded into optimism as social media turned us all into journalists, broadcasters, teachers and philosophers.

Anxiety remained contagious. The Australian Communication and Media Authority in March 2009 secretly censored — blocked — 2395 websites, Wikileaks reported. Two centuries after a conservative British General censored a conservative Sydney founding editor, a Labor communications minister, Senator Stephen Conroy, censored the Internet as it started to transform the world.

What were and are the limits of press influence? The 'red republican' editor Dr John Dunmore Lang thought in April 1835 that 'the press was the most powerful engine Almighty God ever enabled man to use.' In my first weeks in journalism Fred Morony, a West editor with an historical sense, told me that the conscription plebiscites of 1916 and 1917 had been supported by every capital city daily in the country.

With the world war dominating news and Australia's survival at stake no-one was indifferent. The national 'no' majority increased from 73,000 in 1916 to 176,000 in 1917. 'Some influence,' Fred said. He had a point, especially since, as we will see, Prime Minister Billy Hughes inspired editors not to report anti-conscription rallies; news was patriotically censored. *Sydney Morning Herald* associated editor Charles Brunsdon Fletcher's candor in a memo to Geoffrey Fairfax was recorded by Fairfax historian Gavin Souter: 'We are to be our own censors in everything affecting the referendum … it would be well to shut down on all resolutions of anti-conscription meetings, as they were generally violent and mostly intended to do harm.'

Why can't we read what we want? The censor within says: because you are not worthy, too ignorant to understand. Or, it might aid the enemy. Or, the subconscious whispers, we do not know what's good for us.

'Is Google Making Us Stupid?' *The Atlantic Monthly* asked on 1 July 2008, and a year later: 'Is Google Making Us Smart?' Religious leaders after Gutenberg feared print would undermine church authority because people reading the Gospels without the help of priests might misunderstand; they might not know what the priests knew the gospels meant; believers thought the gag an educator.

By 2015 printers that could print houses in China were old news. As printing teeth crowns and skull bones became routine, Monash University researchers developed a three-dimensional jumbo-jet printer, opening the door, Professor Ian Smith, Vice-Provost for research said, to printers in operating theatres developing body parts as needed while the operation proceeds.

As the Internet shapes mass psychology to favour instant access to everything, the capacity to achieve this access is shrinking as news jobs disappear and newsrooms, journalists, editors and newspapers diminish. The Abbott Government's legislation to retain telephone metadata involved an old journalist Prime Minister with another, his successor Malcolm Turnbull, as Minister for Communication — legally and with the support of the Australian Labor Party — making off-the-record telephone conversation practically impossible, and a central tool of journalism useless. As we will see, it could be 1826.

But as we apply the best information system since time began to enhance science, scholarship, history, poetry and love, the blue kookaburra of optimism is still laughing in the ghost gums and on screens in urban kitchens, cafes and offices, poised to mock ring-barkers and hunt the brown snake …

Professor Neil Gershenfeld, director of the Centre for Bits and Atoms at the Massachusetts Institute of Technology, said in an Edge lecture on 9 February 2015 that 'the most exciting work on digital fabrication' — computer-directed manufacture — 'is the creation of life from scratch.' The God-machine! Professor Andy Dong, engineering innovation specialist at Sydney University told me: 'Two years ago we would have laughed at that. We're not laughing now …'

From 5 March 1803 our newspapers had a part in distributing our stories second only to conversation. Since we first encounter the story as fairy tale when we're being formed as toddlers, and the story is a central learning device, factual newspaper yarns have a part in making us. Perhaps in time with the help of the quantum computer we will transcend our fear and retain our skepticism, even save ourselves. As we'll see, it's a hope with a past. The Irish poet Evan Thomas hoped in 1824 to make *The Hobart Town Gazette* 'a beacon placed by divine graciousness on the awfully perilous coast of human frailty.' But between idea and action fell a shadow …

Freedom Lost: A history of newspapers, journalism, and press censorship in Australia.

Chapter 2

Lightning Strikes

1803–1817 The first Australian editor, **George Howe**, edits *The Sydney Gazette and New South Wales Advertiser* under Governors Phillip King and Lachlan Macquarie.

The function of the press in society is to inform, but its role is to make money.
A.J.Leibling, The Press, New York 1981

March 5, 1803. Mocked as 'Happy George' because he suffers depression, George Howe, a West Indian creole, starts the first print experiment in 60,000 years to shape conversation and power in the island continent, publishing *The Sydney Gazette and New South Wales Advertiser*. The first fleet brought a wooden hand-screw press but no printer from England in 1788. The press accumulated cobwebs, dust and rat dung, used briefly for government orders and handbills, till the lottery of Howe's life brought the mechanical miracle of print to the edge of the unknown. For Howe, sentenced to death after he robbed a haberdashery six years earlier, the paper spells out his governing principle: *Thus, We Hope to Prosper*. The inner George, securely indifferent to influence and power, is a man for the money.

Born in 1769 on the West Indian island of St Kitts — his father Thomas, the government printer, published a bi-weekly newspaper — George served an apprenticeship, went to London, worked on *The Times* and was convicted at the Warwick court on 25 March 1797 of robbing a haberdashery. Mr Justice Heath sentenced him to death.

After a Midland Circuit judge cut the sentence to life transportation, Howe boarded the *Royal Admiral* for Sydney with his wife Mary and infant son Robert among 300 passengers including twelve missionaries and four Frenchmen, two vignerons and two prisoners-of-war.

Typhoid killed 43 during the voyage via Rio de Janiero and Mary, heavy with pregnancy, died near the equator. The *Admiral* creaked in Sydney Cove in November 1800; Governor Phillip King appointed the 'ingenious' Howe Government Printer and early in 1803 gave him permission to publish the *Gazette*. No trust was implied: Colonial Secretary William Chapman scrutinized page proofs as Government Censor. When anxiety moved him to censor the proofs himself, Howe said, King would sometimes 'without rhyme or reason' strike out words, a column, even a page. Howe wept.

As a government-sponsored storyteller to 7,000 potential readers in 1803 — half the settlers are illiterate and fewer than a thousand are free — progressives find him contemptible, a stenographer beneath notice, while to military conservatives he becomes the Aesop of Sydney Cove, the first editor's priorities being God, King and the status quo. His muscular forearms power a wooden screw-press little advanced in the 350 years since Gutenberg and his prodigious energy delivers the paper to readers by foot, pontoon and horse-cart as far as the Hawkesbury River —50 kilometres. A consummate multi-tasker, he is skilled in language and analysis for reporting and editing, has the exactitude of eye for proof-reading, memory and scepticism for fact-checking and the front of a frontier salesman to enhance circulation.

A newspaper published with the Government, prepared in an office at the back of Government House and secretly censored by the Governor's secretary, journalism structurally unable to question the status quo, established a precedent. The bias was invisible.

Howe's wealthiest advertisers, merchants and traders, depended on Government favours. He hustled for advertisements and begged subscribers to pay up. The Government took most of page one with orders and notices for which it paid nothing. The slogan 'Thus, We Hope to Prosper' was also a rebellion. In his ambition to pay his way George was challenging both the Governor, whose support was essential, and the readers, many of them convicts who defined themselves both by the distance they kept from authority and the rancid scepticism with which they read every word in the *Gazette*. As the lash and noose sought deterrence, Howe started a tradition of journalism dictated by authority because he could do no other, but while so ironed, remained a storyteller.

None of the personas in the inner George — reporter, printer, sandalwood dealer, poet, father, lover, teacher — asks '*why?*' of the way things are. 'We open no channel to political discussion or personal animadversion; information is our only purpose,' he wrote in the first issue. Conservative by instinct, temperament and heart, he wishes, hopes and works to make his voice echo authority. Clear that the press is about money — 'Thus We Hope to Prosper' is the logo — he believes deeply in the Christian trinity, father, son and Holy Ghost and perhaps still more profoundly in a secular trio, the Government, the printing press and the status quo. Happy George is happy with the way things are. Though the paper is 'Published by Authority' and many, conmen and clergy alike, read it because they must — government orders are a must — Howe's first gift is as storyteller.

For the first issue he finds a new angle on the ancient English practice of wife-selling. Since the ratification of the Treaty of Peace with France in March 1802 wives have been publicly exhibited for sale in Manchester. The good ones, 'being scarce, brought a great price' but ordinary wives sold for next to nothing. Magistrates, 'suppressed the growing evil and restored the Fair Sex to their ORIGINAL value.' Source: an unidentified English paper. How the magistrates achieved this Howe does not report, but he thinks wife-selling as disgraceful as it is immoral. The Sydney press started as a preacher.

On 7 January 1810 Howe reports the first story about the *Gazette*. A thunderstorm rages as he reads proofs, preparing the paper for press on late Saturday afternoon; six children play in the lower office.

Suddenly lightning bursts in the door, fractures chimneys, scatters type and reduces a wall to powder. Howe, flung backwards, staggers upright, thinking he is engulfed in smoke then realises it's mortar dust. A ball of plasma the size of a man's hand, fiery, stinking, hissing, veers around the office at walking pace.

Bruised, astonished, they are otherwise unhurt.

Howe sets a half-column story for page two. He is indebted to Divine Protection and guesses the mixed-metal type attracted the bolt. The story omits the disorienting thunderclap and the plasma's stench and hiss. He beats up no 'near-death' near-misses, tells his handful of subscribers among the colony's 11,950 people of his 'heavy expenses' and inadequate revenue and begs them once again to pay up.

Government shapes newspapers which shape government: the London papers setting standards to which Sydney journalists could only aspire were all in the pay of political factions. Extortion was integral to newspaper culture. 'Journalism was synonymous with blackmail. Scandalous paragraphs were inserted, suppressed or contradicted for fees,' the legendary British-American journalist Harold Evans observed. If the thought that there could be a public opinion to which politicians and newspapers are accountable occurred to a mind beneath a blue-gum tree, no record survived. Snobs muttered that Howe had two faults: the news he published from England was not original and the news he wrote himself was not literature.

Though Howe wept over proofs, he also loved words, hoped to make the reader smile and published the first Irish joke — first publication, not the first joke—in Australia on 11 April 1803 (an Irish angler caught in a storm cast a line beneath a bridge, hoping to catch fish *sheltering from the rain*).

'Information only' did not mean neutral news reports. The *Gazette* ran no editorials; instead George's comments peppered news stories. He did not separate fact from comment. The men who took to the Hawkesbury bush after the Castle Hill rising on 4 March 1804, 15 shot dead, 'could not long escape the certain tread of justice', he 'reported'. That his confidence was soundly based, readers discovered in the next column: all the absconders, he was 'happy to state, are now in custody.' Nine swung from what Howe called 'the fatal tree,' hanged in public.

When he lay in Elizabeth Easton's arms from 1803 to 1810 — she bore him five children — sexual betrayal caught his eye. Two sailors on the make left their money with two lasses 'as security for their speedy return' after a merry hour in a Rocks bar, but when they returned found the money gone and the women on the floor, too drunk to talk.

The first Sydney letter to the editor, addressed to that authority and prophet of the mechanical age, The Printer, had the same theme. Women could not be trusted. While husbands were away, wives played, drank and sang; they made 'devotions to Bacchus.' It was as if 'Orpheus had been among them with his lute,' wrote A Subscriber on 2 April 1803. George published a letter from the editor thanking his correspondent, hoping for more and constructed convenient contributors' boxes at the Sydney issuing store and Parramatta Courthouse window.

The 'taylor', John Jaques, in his shop behind the Sydney Hospital, became the first advertiser on page one of the first issue. He made two promises still made every minute in the digital age: he promised cheap — an 'abatement in his charges' — and reliable: 'all orders with which he may be honoured shall be carefully and punctually executed'. Howe made what remains a standard offer, reduced rates for repeated ads, one-third off for second and third insertions, and printed one hundred copies, sale price 6d.

Early advertisements did not reflect bigotry; perhaps 'no Irish' was so commonly accepted that spelling it out was unnecessary, but the notices of the early house- and maize-sellers, and the entrepreneur Simeon Lord, are not overtly bigoted. There were standards in the prison colony. Gentlemen seeking servants required 'the most respectable references'; a farmer demanded that a shepherd's character withstand 'the most minute inspection.'

Though Howe's main theme was that punishment was a certain consequence of crime, he loved telling stories above all.

The execution of two Castle Hill men, convicted of taking seven silver spoons, a spy-glass, razor, pistol and clothes from the dwelling house of M. Declamb on 15 February 1803 dominated page four on 26 March. Howe reported: The Rev. Samuel Marsden 'administered the only consolation the unfortunate men were capable of receiving, the only balsam that could alleviate the agonies of reproaching conscience.' On Thursday 22 March at 11 am the three ascended a temporary scaffold on the end of the cart. The gallows was erected as close as practical to the crime scene.

As 'the executioner was about to drive the cart away, [Patrick] Macdermot was reprieved. As soon as he descended, [Patrick] Gannan and Francis Simpson were launched into eternity. Simpson behaved penitently during the whole of his confinement; but Gannan, as if insensible of the terrors of his situation, conducted himself with unbecoming levity until the near approach of death, when he listened with much attention to the exhortations of the [preacher] and, we feel the highest satisfaction in adding, also died a penitent.'

Under the heading 'Erroneous Statement', a double-spaced paragraph on page one read: 'In our account of the execution in the last page of this paper, we beg leave to apologise ... Patrick Gannan behaved himself with a penitence becoming his situation, but Francis Simpson died truly impenitent and hardened.' The first correction appeared at the same time as the error, but that obdurate recidivist, mistaken identity, had started his still-unfinished innings in Australian newspapers.

• • •

Howe's equivalent of today's international wire services were the ships whose English and continental newspapers he scanned for news; Governor Phillip Gidley King's death in Surrey on 7 September 1808 did not reach the Gazette till seven months later on 23 April 1809. The British declaration of war against Spain on 24 January 1805 appeared in the Gazette 15 months later on 27 April 1806.

Sometimes Howe credited the ship: 'By the Atalanta we are favoured with the following interesting particulars...' With the opportunism inherent in news reporting, he quoted on 30 July 1809 the Malaga Gazette, a provincial Spanish paper, that the French Emperor Napoleon Bonaparte was in possession of Madrid.

While news moved with the speed of sail, fear of communication was instantaneous. It was everywhere. In March 1806 Joseph Smallsalts talked with J. Pullen and others in Pullen's house in the Brickfields, and the conversation lurched into denunciations disrespectful of His Majesty's Government.

Two of the party to the conversation loyal to convention said they would turn Smallsalts in.

Pullen, an old man, cursed them.

Smallsalts was tried for uttering inflammatory and seditious words. Having said 'I will be worse than Tom Paine [the American revolutionary writer] if I am thwarted' he was sentenced to one hundred lashes and hard labour in the Newcastle coal-mines. After the flogging, on his journey from the Hawkesbury to Newcastle, mocking jailers affixed the sign 'Thomas Paine' on his back.

Pullen too was charged: with having permitted a seditious conversation in his house, and keeping it secret. He was jailed till he could find a good behaviour bond of £50 and two sureties of £25 each. Howe reported the convictions, omitting the words: reporting them would have rendered the Gazette seditious. Though the treatment left a hole at the centre, publishing a story that irked and mystified readers was better than prosecution. Howe was indignant: Smallsalts had been treated leniently 'for several years'.

Time-pressure on a one-man weekly reinforced the dominance of the chief source and subject, the government. When the police superintendent sought the public's help in apprehending 'a notorious depredator and well-known bush ranger', William Page, in 1806, Howe published the ad, including the first publication of the phrase 'bush ranger' but not the story; there might have been a day's work in it.

He sought readers like himself, honest workmen who knew their place and hoped to prosper by keeping it. Part of him was the Dewitt Wallace (Reader's Digest founder) of his time. When he published Twelve True Old Golden Rules, Howe was distilling folk convention like a Digest editor: Marriage is honourable; we ought not to have an idle hour; is it not enough to be taxed once by Government, without being taxed twice by folly, thrice by drunkenness, four times by laziness?

In the fifth issue he changed publication day from Saturday to Sunday; Saturday publication had forced him to omit 'interesting' material. Sunday publication would mean he could include all Ship News for the preceding week. Howe's faith in the Sabbath did not stop the press; news had priority. [As we will see, Melbourne legislators banned Sunday newspapers as a violation of the Sabbath from 1889 to 1969.]

• • •

The Gazette never reflected a longing for liberty or equality among convicts, emancipists or men of the New South Wales Corps. It was the voice of authority and Government, the source, subject and censor of information. The Gazette, a key to the information loop and bound by it, spoke for it, most potently with the subliminal suggestion that there was no way out, not only because the newspaper was part of government, but because an alternative would be an alternative source of authority, a challenge to the whole set-up. That was the point: it was unthinkable. In 1803 they did not allow doubt to pester them. They knew what was what. The Gazette and its editor set boundaries with this sanction: they did not know they were setting them. The boundary required the censor's invisibility.

Governor King, hypersensitive to the printed word, acted out his neurosis. He did not trust his secretary, William Chapman, to detect all nuances capable of damaging the Governor's reputation in the colony and the Home Office. When he did the censorship himself, not even extracts from the London papers, nor advertisements for respectable shepherds, escaped his eye. He took pleasure in it, laughing over the page proofs. The same man smiled so warmly at nine-year-old Robert Howe perched on a stool in the printing office in 1804 that Howe remembered it years later. When anxiety wormed its way into his interior he complained to Lord Hobart in May 1803 that New South Wales Corps officers had published not only 'seditious drawings' of him but also satirical verses. The 'Pipes'— mocking, scurrilous anonymous verses inserted in drain-pipes and walls where passers-by might find them, were written by those driven to deride authority. 'Birthday Ode', about a Sydney birthday celebration for King George the Third began:

> The levee assembled by royal command
>
> Composed of the forces by sea and by land
>
> Of surgeons, civilians and men of the law,
>
> And other descriptions, with many a flaw,
>
> The great King presided, as chief of the clan —
>
> A wicked, oppressive, notorious man …

With the hypersensitivity to public prints found in many born to authority but not eloquence, King scribbled rebuttals to Lord Hobart. His respect for monarchs meant he always 'celebrated their birthdays with every demonstration of joy my situation would admit of.'

When he came to

> I'd civilians give trust, confide in new faces
>
> Make magistrates of them and give them new places

King thought there could be no better proof that the 'assassinating author of this anonymous libel' was a military man.

When Governor William Bligh succeeded King on 6 August 1806, Robert Howe said, 'there was not much need of a censorship' because Bligh 'supplied the Gazette with nothing but official notifications.' Though Bligh was arbitrary and censorious, putting three merchants in jail for three months for a letter he deemed offensive, George was more worried about paper supply. Having survived on Spanish paper, he complained on 7 June 1807 that the rising price forced him to vary the size, shape, even the colour, of the newspaper. The Gazette was becoming a chameleon: 'All our eccentricities have been imposed by insurmountable necessity.'

The Gazette suspended publication from 30 August 1807 to 15 May 1808 because Howe had no paper. He missed a big story: the Rum Corps deposed Bligh on 26 January 1808. For eight months Howe sought income as a tutor in grammar and stationary retailer; when he resumed on the newspaper he kept his head down. He took the opportunity to raise the price from 2/- to 3/- for four issues and hinted that prompt payment might cancel the increase. Letters, orders and advertisements would be received at the Shakespeare Hotel; journalism gave a man a thirst.

Howe the entrepreneur was expanding, publishing an annual Almanac from 1806 — his sentence ended on 4 June — and working as employment and real-estate agent, lost-property and post-office. But subscribers maintained their form and on 18 December 1808 he again begged them to clear their debts; payment in wheat would be acceptable. But readers remained long of pocket and short of arm. On Christmas Eve Lieutenant Governor William Paterson directed that Government stores always be open to receive grain to settle Howe's accounts.

A heavy iron Stanhope press accompanied Governor Lachlan Macquarie, sworn in on 1 January 1810, from England. Levers allowed pressmen to work it with the same facility as the lighter old wooden press; the Gazette shifted from Government House to George Street, the heart of commerce. In his heart and in business he coupled with women able to make their own way. On 5 October 1812 the Reverend William Cowper joined him in holy matrimony to Sarah Wills, a widow merchant and ship-owner with five children in the church of St Philip. He branched into sandalwood speculation with Mary Reiby, an entrepreneurial widow with seven children who was dressed as a boy when arrested for horse stealing in Lancashire. As a measure of his standing, Howe and thirteen prospering gentlemen established the Bank of New South Wales. John Thomas Campbell, who had worked overtly at the Bank of Ireland and secretly as the Gazette censor was elected chairman. On the surface it was a step toward prosperity, autonomy and better beer but they all feared a letter in the Gazette might undo more than the bank. It might undo authority.

By Thursday 2 January 1817, the censorship, about to be revealed but not lifted, has been a state secret for 14 years. But one man is determined to expose religious abuse in the first piece of investigative journalism published in New South Wales. The reporter is John Campbell, Governor Lachlan Macquarie's secretary. Campbell also has an undercover job: newspaper censor. Not every conspiracy theory muttered in the sly-grog shanties multiplying around the finest harbour in the world is a fantasy.

Howe is chatting in the printing office before dinner with compositor George Williams. Sneering at the 'government paper' is a cliché on the prison frontier, common as galahs on ghost gums. Philosophers in the Blue Lion bar, searchers for reason in rum from Parramatta to the Rocks know the Gazette is leg-ironed. Suddenly Campbell bursts through the door, a letter-to-the-editor in his hand.

Campbell tells Howe: 'Set the letter immediately. Let no-one see it.' No record survives of Howe or Williams' surprise at the order that a letter intended for every pair of eyes in New South Wales as far as beautiful Van Diemen's Land, should be kept covert.

As Campbell ducks out, Williams, puzzled at the signature Philo Free, a settler at Bradley's Head, starts setting the 1220-word letter. (It is Howe's longest story.)

Campbell, Governor Macquarie's close friend and secretary wants to expose abuse by missionaries in New South Wales and the Pacific islands. But he also knows to be careful, he knows his voice is not his own. When his clerk, Michael Robinson, saw him writing the expose a few days ago, Campbell quickly dissembled. He was not writing it, he told Robinson, he was just transcribing a reader's letter.

Campbell believes the Reverend Samuel Marsden, the colony's most influential preacher and magistrate is two-faced, a lyre-bird trying to worm his way into Macquarie's confidence while surreptitiously seeking to undermine the Governor's authority.

There is no love lost between Campbell, a man-of-honour who wounded an officer in a duel after a racetrack row, and Marsden the 'flogging parson'. For his part, Marsden believes that Campbell, an ex-Irish banker, though son of a vicar, would 'lose no chance' to wound Jesus' servants: 'a greater enemy … never existed to the Gospel of our blessed Lord.'

After setting the first lines of Philo Free's vitriol, Williams, unhurried by Campbell's urgency, broke for dinner. He will not be rushed. Williams' work and voice is his own. (In 1816 when he signed a petition to the House of Commons complaining that Macquarie had flogged and imprisoned three free men, Macquarie told him to his face he was 'a seditious and rebellious scoundrel.'

Whether the work, the physical and intellectual exercise of printing and delivering the newspaper, helped him out of depression, or whether he longed for a bed of rose petals — Thus, we hope to prosper — Howe mixed viscous ink from shark oil, charcoal and gum and worked the press to capacity, 50 sheets an hour.

By the time George Williams finished hand-setting — finding every metal letter and comma individually from his stack of types and placing them one-by-one in the page — it was Friday morning.

Philo Free said:

> The South Sea Islands philanthropists in 1813 cheerfully subscribed their money under the assurance that they [would render] humane services to the Natives of the South Sea Islands. To this day we have never been favoured with a single report of the application of the funds and we are not likely to be. ...
>
> A missionary spirit has pervaded the islands, introducing the art of distillation. An ardent thirst for the influence of this spirit pervades the inhabitants of all the islands with which we have any intercourse. The exertions of the worthy head of these sectarian visionaries in propagating the Gospel by such means, and the transmission of muskets and cutlasses will no doubt redound to the honour of the Christian Mahomet and the church so planted, whilst the pecuniary advantage of the chosen few will not be altogether overlooked. Those who bolt the pork and profits, should in my opinion un-bolt their coffers, and bear all the expenses of their gospel venders and bacon curers.
>
> I am one who wishes to introduce civilisation and the doctrines of Christianity among the [Aborigines]. In a conversation with members of the New South Wales Bubble [most supported the] establishment of schools for the children of the poor and the spread of Christian knowledge among heathen natives.

He had, he said, the vanity to hope this would encourage charity toward the natives of their adopted country.

Even among cynics who mocked the printed word and visionaries whose eyes glazed over reading authorised eight-point Roman, Philo Free elevated blood pressure. To say preachers used rum to entice islanders to the ways of Jesus was blasphemous enough but in frontier Sydney the letter also poisoned the reputation of the leading preacher, landholder, magistrate and farmer, Samuel Marsden. The letter does not name Marsden but no-one doubts that by the wounding phrases the 'Christian Mahomet' the 'pecuniary advantage of the chosen few' and 'those who bolt the pork and profits', Philo Free means the flogging Parson.

Because it controlled the newspaper, Government was itself degraded by every attempt to publicly scorn the principal clergyman and magistrate in 'the only Vehicle which here exists of Public intelligence,' according to Marsden's solicitor William Moore.

Philo Free was undermining the authority of church and state on a frontier where convict philosophers mocked authority beside the golden wattle, the didgeridoo reminded them that blacks' songs and sounds were as alien to the British as their custom, law and tradition while the scorching sun, shrieking cockatoos and incessant mosquitoes tormented their ears, skin and psyches.

Marsden, who had been sponsored by the Clapham Sect of wealthy evangelical Anglicans, abandoned study at Magdalene College, Cambridge, on 1 January 1793, when he accepted appointment as assistant to the Chaplain of New South Wales, recommended by the legendary missionary leader William Wilberforce. Strong as an ox, Marsden in New South Wales, working the work ethic, bred sheep that farmers mentioned in the same breath as John Macarthur's merinos. He believed work achieved salvation and wealth measured not just financial but also spiritual worth.

In the year that troubled Philo Free, 1813, Marsden, looking beyond established boundaries, started a society with two visions: to protect South Sea Islands natives against outrages by Europeans and spread civilisation by proselytising Christianity. But when Governor Macquarie proposed a more elevated ambition, to civilise the natives, Marsden the pragmatist doubted any scheme could do that. 'The natives have no Reflection — they have no attachments and they have no wants.' Macquarie, a liberal koori sympathiser, was offended.

For his part, Marsden found Macquarie indifferent to his status, authority and dreams. Though a believer in the noose and lash, Marsden was also, to his enemies' bewilderment, capable of compassion. He chose this moment to put his authority at stake in a fight over words and told the Governor the day after Philo Free published that the Gazette was 'a vehicle of abuse and scandal' to his name and character. It was not the first time.

Macquarie said coolly that he regretted anything appearing in the newspaper to Marsden's prejudice.

Marsden said he would never rest till he exposed the author, walked away and asked Judge Advocate John Wylde, to prosecute Howe for criminal libel.

Wylde, who enjoyed a thriving practice in London, wore three wigs as the government's legal advisor, independent prosecutor and judge of the Criminal Court. When he met Macquarie in Parramatta, Macquarie again expressed his regret. Wylde told the Governor it would be helpful if Macquarie said publicly that Philo Free did not have his support. That might be enough for

Marsden. Wylde hoped to calm a notorious public scandal that travelled like the wind from Bondi to the Blue Mountains, quickly and privately.

Macquarie too hoped that would work. When Wylde returned to Sydney he tried to manipulate Marsden into a civil suit. Because the criminal law said *the greater the truth the greater the libel*, even if Howe were convicted the controversy would continue. Readers might think and say the editor had gone down because Philo Free spoke the truth about the missionaries, rum and muskets. Wylde offered to mediate.

If he listened, Marsden did not hear; if he heard, he did not understand. He asked Wylde in a letter on 7 January to charge, or allow Marsden to charge, Howe with criminal libel. Then began a dance of words and meaning to keep quiet the question every politically conscious colonist wanted to know: who is Philo Free?

Wylde went as far as to ask Campbell: Was Philo Free's letter authorised?

Campbell said the objectionable passages had escaped his eye: pressure of business. He regretted the letter had induced Mr Marsden to start criminal proceedings, but because he had approved publication he would pay Howe's costs.

The Gazette published Governor Macquarie's disapproval on 18 January 'in Justice to his (Macquarie's) own Feelings' and fairness to the benevolent missionaries.

How had the letter been published? Macquarie and Wylde stuck to Campbell's *too busy* line. It had 'inadvertently, from the great Pressure of Government Business in the Secretary's office, got admission into the Gazette.' (No record exists of anyone asking Campbell *Did you write it?*) His Excellency withdrew 'all Government Sanction, Authority or Concurrence [which] its Insertion might perhaps otherwise be considered to have bestowed.'

The statement was also a strategic and psychological mistake that increased the temperature of the debate and the likelihood of litigation. Marsden said he looked forward to proving it 'an official falsehood'.

In a heated conversation at Wylde's dinner table in April Wylde again pushed Marsden toward civil action, saying Marsden did not understand the difficulties of proof in criminal libel. Truth was irrelevant. In a civil suit, on the other hand, the Court would judge what was true. Could not two gentlemen negotiate a settlement?

This argument only reinforced in Marsden the rigid principle and self-belief that made him who he was. He rose from his chair, strode to a corner (perhaps the symbolism was unconscious) and told Wylde: 'I have been driven into a corner by the Government; I have now thrown away the scabbard and I will never give in till I have gained redress.' Whatever it cost.

Wylde: 'I cannot blame you.' (Wylde's advice to Marsden did not stop him adjudicating at trial through conflict of interest. There were not enough lawyers in New South Wales.)

Nine months after publication, Marsden's lawyer William Moore told a Criminal Court of Judge Wylde and a jury of six officers on 21 October that if the censor existed, he must have slept as he read Philo Free.

Was the censor satisfied with 'merely reading the few first and the few last lines before giving what he calls his official imprimatur? ... I trust, gentlemen ... that the present and all future censors of the press will be taught that they are not with impunity to make the columns of a Government newspaper a vehicle for the assassination of character,' Moore said.

'How will it be considered in the mother country when such an attack ... is found to have been made in the only public journal of this Colony, and that too under the sanction and censorship and avowed official imprimatur of the Secretary to the Government?'

Mother London originated the fear of print now being played out in convict Sydney. After English philosopher Jeremy Bentham wrote in an 1809 treatise on libel that the liberty of the English press 'has all along maintained a rickety, and maintains a momentary half-existence', the treatise was suppressed for violation of that very law. In 1812 Lord Chief Justice Edward Ellenborough, told the jury in the libel trial of John and Leigh Hunt, proprietors of The Examiner, an influential radical paper then with a circulation greater than the London Times, that the question for them was 'whether we are to live under the dominion of libellers or under the control and government of the law.' Men in high office must have immunity from criticism, or government would be impossible. If journalists could ridicule great men, disorder would rule the world.

Marsden's attorney reflected that reasoning. 'It was [the Secretary's] duty, not only as censor of the press, if such he is, but also as a member of the Christian Church, to have prohibited the insertion of so indecent an allusion to the sacred pages of our faith [as 'gospel vendors and bacon curers'] said William Moore

Marsden was feeling the strain. 'Fightings without and fears within attend me,' he told an English confidante. 'The struggle is very painful.'

After a three-day trial Judge Wylde said the evidence did not even establish that Campbell had written the letter. George Williams' testimony that the letter was in Campbell's handwriting was, Wylde said, the 'uncorroborated' evidence of an 'urger'. When four officers of the jury of six nonetheless voted to convict Campbell of criminal libel, Wylde drafted a verdict that Campbell was 'guilty of having permitted a letter to be printed in the Sydney Gazette which tends to vilify the public conduct of [Samuel Marsden] as the agent for propagating the Gospel to the South Seas.' No such offence was known to English law, or to that specially modified English law applying in the convict colony. Wylde had two priorities, hushing it up and protecting Campbell, a hidden agenda that prevailed when it came to words no matter what the law said.

Moore could not believe his ears. He told Marsden: 'It is no verdict at all.' Campbell's solicitor Frederick Garling too was incredulous. No punishment could be awarded on such a verdict, he said. Wylde, with the elasticity that still marks judges' administration of Australian newspaper law, turned around and said no sentence would follow it.

On Tuesday 28 October Moore told the Court Marsden intended to bring a civil action for libel, which would permit Campbell to prove the truth of the letter. Moore wanted a result known in London. A ship was about to sail. He agreed to admit at trial that

> The Missionary Societies for promoting Christian Knowledge and Religion had been the means (of course unintentionally) of introducing in the islands of the South Seas, the art of distillation, and the use of musquets and cutlasses; and that pigs, pine trees and New Zealand flax, had been articles of barter between the natives of the said islands and the missionaries at those places.

A week later Howe, emphasising Campbell's 'hasty review' of the letter, continued to pretend that Campbell was not Philo Free. In a Respectful Address from the Printer to a liberal Public on 1 November, Howe said it was unfair for him to be called as a witness for Marsden, when he was also indicted as printer and publisher and anything he said might jeopardise his defence. He uttered what was to become editorial orthodoxy: 'I trust I have not transgressed the limits of fair discussion. I have avoided any expression of personal feeling and confined myself to a statement of facts ...' When he regretted 'the necessity of appealing to public opinion' Howe meant by the phrase a tribunal, arbitrary, capricious and untestable, through which witnesses to public hangings agreed on the guilt of those they had seen launched into eternity, and by which any public official could support conformity. Wylde considered whether to prosecute Howe for contempt, but did not do so, he told the Bigge Commission, because 'the statement formed what is termed the leader of the paper and did not purport to be a formal report of the trial.' (Editorials are subject to the law of contempt in the same way as the rest of the newspaper. What he said has never been the law. The politician in Wylde once again overruled the lawyer, who had thrived in a London practice for ten years, later became Chief Justice in the Cape of Good Hope, South Africa, and was knighted.)

For nine months between 2 January and 25 October Campbell was not required to answer: *Are you Philo Free?* When Marsden began a civil suit for libel, why did Campbell not say that the letter was true? His solicitor, Frederick

Garling said that at the time he did not know Mr Campbell was Philo Free and had he known 'I should have advised him to avow it.' George-street knew, as four officers of the jury did, but the author could not tell his attorney in confidence.

At the civil trial Judge Barron Field did not allow Moore's admission of the truth of the libel to be admitted in evidence. On 1 December he awarded Marsden £200, with £110 for the Provost Marshall's costs and £46/3/9 for Howe's costs; Campbell paid Howe's costs; Garling's charges, Garling said, were at least £120. (The judge resented Howe as editor. He always provided the *Gazette* with his own reports on proceedings, he told the Bigge Commission on 15 June 1820. Without them Howe would publish drunken bombast disgracing the court.)

Campbell finally admitted writing the 'hasty and inconsiderate' letter 'in the midst of much hurry and with little previous reflection' in a letter to Governor Macquarie on 31 March 1819, two years and three months after publication. He had been indignant at the disrespect Marsden showed when he failed to attend a Parramatta meeting of Aborigines Macquarie convened a few days before the letter appeared; Marsden had been in a house a few yards from the meeting. The two libel trials cost Campbell 'not less than £500,' Macquarie told Earl Bathurst. 'Mr Campbell is sincerely sorry.'

Not that sorry. When Macquarie granted Campbell a tract of land for a horse- and cattle-stud farm on 17 October 1819 Campbell named it *Philo Mount*. Some, including Commissioner Bigge, thought the sexual joke another attempt to irritate Marsden and disgrace the Government.' (Philo Free wrote occasional letters to editors in Sydney and Launceston till 1829.)

The censor responsible for the main public voice in New South Wales sought to tell a big story anonymously, inflame religious controversy in secret and slip responsibility to the printer, who accepted the burden and kept it hidden while he faced prison and crippling costs. The first great trial of press freedom in Australia had been a shadow play. While bush ants, bees and cicadas shared information to capacity as they had for a million years, the most intelligent animal tied a knot in his tongue.

• • •

Happy George established the first Australian newspaper dynasty of two generations, and began a tradition of news in leg-irons. While free settlers, merchants, visionaries and men of the land trickled into Sydney and Hobart in the 1820s and 1830s, eight editors struggling for press freedom served between them six years' and three months' jail for words they published. In *Freedom on the Fatal Shore*, professor John Hirst dealt with the difficulty of the first freedom not being there by a technique not available in journalism: he ignored it.

Military Governors, reflecting the culture that pervaded the Colonial Office, tried to keep editors on a leash, seeing authority itself and themselves in particular as far above vulgar public debate and noisy nosey journalism. In England in 1817–30 'The Government believed that the press had a protean quality; something that eluded all control, saturated the country, and monopolised the public imagination with impunity,' British historian Ben Wilson wrote in *The Laughter of Triumph* (2005). 'This sense of ubiquity and invisible, almost organic, diffusion played on the deepest fears of ministers, who were frightened of something which defied their control.' The dangers they cited were based on fear more than evidence. In England, servants with murder in mind, Jacobin conspirators; in Australia, convicts, blacks and radicals. But once they asserted control, Governors stopped the pretence. When the versatile ideologue Edward Smith Hall went to jail in 1829 for criminal libel published in *The Monitor,* he continued publishing, and publishing libel, while in jail. Governor Ralph Darling released him with two years still to serve.

No-one was *responsible* for censorship. The language the British brought to the island continent girt by the Indian and Pacific oceans implied boundaries on action, and also on thought. *Don't go too far* it admonished men and women who had sailed 10,000 miles in 90 days. *Moderation in all things.* The thought that a free press, while the key to accountability at Home, could not fit without catastrophe in convict New South Wales and Van Dieman's Land, caused the learned counsel to the Colonial Office, James Stephen — who felt like 'a man without skin' in public — to draft laws to license and tax newspapers which Office lawyers themselves later found unlawful. Governors wanted the House of Commons to curb the Sydney Press; the Colonial Office sought to impose censorship without responsibility. Men on the spot would do it, no London fingerprints.

Chapter 3

News in Leg-irons

1821–1829 *Robert Howe*, The Sydney Gazette, New South Wales Advertiser *and* The Australian Magazine, Dr William Redfern's horsewhip, Samuel Terry and the Bank of New South Wales; W.C. Wentworth and the Court of Quarter Sessions.

As he put the *Gazette* of 12 May 1821 to bed, George Howe had fulfilled his hopes of prospering. Recovering from the years of penury from 1803 to 1810 when he believed he needed miracles to survive, he had a small fortune, £4000. After he locked away the notices — prisoners missing, servants sought, Jamaica rum and hearth brooms for sale — Howe died at his home-office in George Street.

Robert, 25, quickly wrote an obituary for the *Gazette* and his father's stone: 'In memory of George Howe, a Creole of Saint Kitts; born 1769, died May 11th 1821, Aged 52. He introduced into Australia the Art of Printing; Instituted the Sydney Gazette; and was the First Government Printer. Besides which, His Charity Knew No Bounds.' The certificate recorded a cost: the death was alcohol-related.

Howe, ironed to authority, made a newspaper chain, believing that accepting a manacle to conformity was his main chance. His conversation with readers was an emphatic monologue: the readers' task was to listen, understand and subscribe. He knew their only other option was dropping into the void of anxiety where there was no reliable information on what authority was up to.

Robert Howe humbly hoped to earn the trust of the new generation pushing the colony's 'rising prosperity' among the 21,554 Europeans in New South Wales. When he was optimistic Robert relished the power of the word. 'Thank

God the press is in my hands and therefore fear not,' he wrote in a diary for his friend the Methodist missionary the Rev. Walter Lawry. 'Let our enemies write, my brother — I will print. Let them pen all their Satanic heart can dictate. I will print upon every occasion the truth...' But when he was down he found journalism 'a slippery path' he wished he never strayed on; it was 'a horrid life to be ever trafficking with the wicked...'

Howe published *The Australian Magazine, or Compendium of Religious, Literary, and Miscellaneous Intelligence* — pious, devout and spiritual, the month his father died. Howe's lawyer friend George Allen, a Methodist, thought the Wesleyan editor Ralph Mansfield deserved great praise. Only the 'few illiberal and un-Christian persons' who found too much religion in the magazine disliked it. 'Will such persons think there is too much religion in Heaven?' Though many hoped with Allen that good news would enrich readers as well as advertisers, reality said otherwise and the second issue, 16 months later in September 1822, was the last.

The young Robert had found comfort and enlargement in the body. In 1819 his fellow-philanderer, Elizabeth Lees, made him father to a son. But in 1820 he was 'wonderfully and mercifully visited by God and snatched from infamy in this world and Hell in the next.' Methodism had become his light in the world and the *Gazette*. Believing religion was the one path to progress, the only escape from depravity, he had married a currency lass, Anne Bird, the year George died. 'Tell me not what I *was,* but what I *am*,' he begged worshippers in the Wesleyan Chapel.

Part of him had longed to record not just the public, but also the inner struggles, the twists and turns, newspaper work required. 'Had I to pen the detail of the sinuosities [dishonesties] of my office, it would more than fill this book,' he wrote for Mr Lawry, his soul-mate, an energetic Wesleyan proselytiser then seeking converts in Tonga.

The twists and turns of journalism remained inside his head. Part of him had wanted to keep it secret. After he was convicted of criminal libel and fined £50 in July 1824 he said he felt obliged to insert any correspondence that came through the Censor. Had the libellous letter been sent to him, not the censor, it would 'never have graced out columns'. Though Robert acknowledged he had been 'justly found guilty of libel', the politics of publishing was changing and the censor becoming accountable. Robert was his father's son and kept his head down, but while George collaborated in secret censorship, Robert believed censorship imposed responsibility on Government though accountability was still an idea too extraordinary to be uttered.

• • •

Walking home along the Prince Street pathway from the Mission House at 9.15pm on 15 June 1822, Howe saw stars bright and hard above the red-gums. After he said 'goodnight' to Ewin Forbes near the Reverend Ralph Mansfield's gate he saw a man approaching and moved toward the road to let him pass. Sensing danger his hand tightened on his stick. The man rushed at him; he felt 'something like the blow of an open hand very violently' on his left breast. The man grunted something, perhaps 'there!'

Howe, blood spurting from his chest, screamed 'murder!' a cry Ewin Forbes heard as he entered Mansfield's study. People rushed into the street. As Mansfield bent over him Howe, fearing death, begged his dear brother to be father to his unborn child.

A rusty bayonet had penetrated his chest for an inch or so. James Mitchell, the surgeon of the 48th Regiment, examining him within 45 minutes said cellular membranes around the wound were filled with air; Howe had 'great difficulty breathing.' The bayonet had punctured his lung. James Bowman, principal surgeon, said Howe's life was in danger.

The Gazettes published at 2pm the day before the attack, and the previous Friday, 7 June, advertised a Mr John Davidson, 'Supercargo of the Medway, leaving the Colony in the said vessel, requests all Claims to be presented.' Davidson believed the suggestion that he was a cargo supervisor ridiculed him. Everyone knew he was a convict; convicts could not supervise; convicts could not sail away. Howe was 'sporting with his feelings'.

Davidson's acquaintance Henry Durban testified that Davidson, talking with convicts, had fondled a dagger and said 'this would be of service to Mr Howe,' or 'three inches of this would serve Mr Howe'. Another witness insisted Davidson had been joking, he was *laughing* when he fingered the dirk. Howe could not identify the attacker, gave two names of men worth checking, both cleared, and testified that he 'never imagined' Davidson was the one.

He had spoken to Davidson perhaps three times. Three or four weeks before the attack, he had seen a man with a stick looking in at a window of the Macquarie Street Chapel. He walked around and found Davidson though he 'took no notice of it at the time.'

John Campbell said Davidson was quiet and orderly, the opposite of malicious; he had never heard his character questioned. 'It appears from many sources,' the *Gazette* reported 'that the unhappy man is occasionally, if not always, deranged'. A sentence of transportation would preserve a life and restore confidence in authority.

Judge-Advocate John Wylde, sitting in the criminal court on 30 September 1822, said the evidence was wholly circumstantial and the case of 'peculiar complexion which demanded the most jealous attention'; then he retired for five minutes, returned with a verdict of guilty of attempted murder and sentenced him to death. Colonial Office lawyers commuted the sentence to 'transportation for life' — to Norfolk Island — on 22 December 1823. Howe began to refer in his diary to events 'since my death' and make mordant remarks about assassination.

When Ann Bird gave birth to their first son, Robert Mansfield Howe on 11 November 1822, he was ecstatic: 'I am now legitimately Father Howe.' To one sombre intimate, Robert seemed frivolous. After a supper with Robert and other Methodist Sunday-school teachers, the tormented solicitor George Allen thought his and Robert's innocent mirth degenerated into levity. Next morning Mr Allen noted his 'great sorrow and regret. Religious persons should not encourage levity. It grows upon them. We cannot be too serious and we should always be so.'

Sometimes a boastful tone suggested insecurity. In the last few years, the *Gazette* said on 7 April 1825, Australia had grown mainly 'from the efforts of the Colonial Press.' In Hobart Town Mr Evan Henry Thomas was expecting 'two improved presses, and a large font of type, with paper and all other materials necessary to produce a journal (it is said) equal in magnitude to *The Times*.' (*The Times*, the world's first paper to use a reel-fed Koenig Press, printed 1000 copies an hour; on the *Gazette*'s hand-operated flat-bed machines a good operator could print 20 hand-folded copies an hour.) A week later Howe 'reported' that the cane fields of Port Macquarie would equal the sugar and rum output of the West Indies; its tobacco crops already 'exceeded everything … hitherto known in the West Indies, or in America.' Heaven and earth would 'conspire to Advance Australia', a slogan which Howe, its chief promoter, thought 'ancient' by May 1829. Whether he spoke for commerce or the cloister, Robert Howe's excess was becoming part of the Australian language.

Riding a horse in George Street on 23 November 1827, as he neared his house, Howe saw the surgeon Dr William Redfern behind him in a gig. That morning's *Gazette* contained a needling reference to Redfern's role in a complex schism among directors of the Bank of New South Wales. Some, Howe reported, would insist on Samuel Terry, the Rothschild of Botany Bay, taking his seat as a director with his friend Dr Redfern; this would provide '*a balance in trade.*' Should that happen he said, a second group would wind up the bank up and establish a new one. Dr Redfern, a gifted emancipist, sentenced to death for mutiny aboard the *Standard* in the British Navy in 1797, was incensed. (Redfern who fell out with Terry, his ally on the board, married Sarah Howe, Robert's step-sister, on 4 April 1811.)

Howe, seeing a horsewhip in the doctor's hand, found it 'prudent' to ride to his yard; Redfern followed in the gig. As Howe was about to dismount to the printing office steps, he said to Redfern at the gate 'Have you any business with me? If so, come in.' Robert thought icy politeness would be enough.

The story had put Redfern in a different mood. He stepped from the gig: 'How came you to mix me up with Mr Terry?'

Howe: 'I think Mr Terry as fit to be [on the bank board] as you.'

Redfern hissed 'Do you?' and leaped at Howe, whipping him.

Howe struck back with a 'sword cane' about the thickness of an index finger; it snapped just short of the handle. At Redfern's trial Howe said had the sword not broken he would 'certainly have run it through [Redfern's] bowels.'

Homicide was not required. Howe, pursued by Redfern, threw the handle to the ground and ran into his kitchen. There — defensively, he said — he grabbed an iron pot. Howe's cook grabbed Redfern and his wife struck the surgeon several times with a parlour broomstick. Howe wrestled the whip from Redfern and 'whipt him out of the yard'; Redfern's head was covered in blood — Howe said he 'bled like a pig.' The editor's back had twenty welts; an eyewitness noticed both were 'winded'.

Fifteen minutes later, Howe, on his way to the Police Office, passed W. C. Wentworth's chambers and saw Redfern preparing legal payback. The surgeon shook his fist saying: 'I have another whip yet in store for you.'

At Redfern's trial two months later Wentworth the advocate who could look into the eyes of a juryman and persuade him to doubt the evidence of those eyes, pitched the argument that the whipping had been provoked, Redfern had been repeatedly libelled in Robert Howe's *Gazette*, criminally libelled, and this publication was itself a constructive breach of the peace. Howe was therefore the initial aggressor. The Chairman of the Court of Quarter Sessions, William Foster, ruled against him. He could not admit issues of the *Gazette* into evidence to prove the libels. If they were libels, it would not justify the assault. If they were libels, Redfern could sue. The issue was 'totally immaterial.'

This ruling had as much effect on Wentworth as a kookaburra's laugh. There were two questions for the Jury, he said: first whether Redfern had struck the first blow and second, if he did whether Howe had constructively breached the peace, making him the actual aggressor. He did not believe Robert Howe on oath; Howe was a public nuisance.

The Chairman said *a clear case of assault* had been made against Dr Redfern.

After a half-hour retirement the jury foreman announced a verdict: 'Guilty — but we recommend mercy on account of the aggravated assault.'

Spectators roared.

The disbelieving magistrate asked the foreman their reasons.

Foreman: 'We can't tell who struck the first blow. It's that which puzzles us. We can't come at that.'

There was more laughter; Wentworth had found the pulse of another jury.

Magistrate Foster: 'Then, gentlemen, you are not agreed.'

Foreman: 'We are all agreed that the defendant is guilty of the assault. We are only at a loss to know who struck first.'

There was more laughter and a babble of voices till a juror was heard clearly saying they all agreed Redfern was guilty of assault, but had been provoked.

When Mr Foster asked Wentworth if he had anything to say in mitigation, the barrister made a speech so long it had many dreaming of a cold Coopers' draft, insisting Robert Howe knew Samuel Terry was not a friend of Dr Redfern, he knew the report was false, he had published it to hold Redfern up to contempt. After a reply by Howe's counsel, Mr Foster said that having considered the jury's recommendation and 'other circumstances within the knowledge of the Bench,' he fined Redfern £50.

When Howe's 'dear brother' Ralph Mansfield, a Methodist missionary ardent for temperance, became joint editor on 1 January 1827 Mansfield said his political principles would be Howe's and the Government's. Howe put his politics clearly on 9 December 1826. He had 'devoted the very best years of his life to the Government of these colonies'. Whomever he pleased or offended, he would never use his pen 'to the prejudice of His Majesty's Government'.

Fishing near Pinchgut Island in Sydney Harbour on 29 January 1829 with his three-year-old son Alfred Australia and a groom, as Howe reached for a drink a sudden squall capsized the newly-purchased boat; he struggled for ten minutes to save Alfred, pulling him away from the groom in panic then entangling his own arms in the fishing lines. A passing boat rescued the groom and the boy; after 'many hours' dragging by government and private boats they found Howe's body 'though a long time in the water was not at all disfigured'. He was 33.

Mansfield, with Howe's executor, Richard Jones, a conservative pastoralist, winemaker and Anglican lacked Howe's drive and were on the verge of a fire sale to the Sydney Herald when Ann, with Jones' reluctant support, intervened and appointed William Watt, an emancipist with a sharp eye and sharper pen, as editor. Australia's first woman press mogul supported Governor Burke's liberal pro-emancipist administration and in 1836 sought Bourke's permission to marry Watt; the couple wed at Port Macquarie on 9 February 1836. Jones, fiercely opposed to ticket-of-leave men, triggered a foreclosure that transferred ownership to Robert Howe's eldest son, Robert. After Watt drowned at Port Macquarie in 1837, Ann remarried and lived in Sydney till her death on 17 November 1842.

Chapter 4

The Vagabond Free Press

1824–1827 *Robert Wardell, The Australian*; Governor Thomas Brisbane, Chief Justice Francis Forbes, Earl Bathurst, John and Hannibal Macarthur, Governor Ralph Darling, Attorney General Saxe Bannister, Archdeacon Thomas Scott, Henry Dumaresq.

You will propose that no Newspaper be published without a License, [and] that every such license be forfeited upon the conviction of the Publisher, Printer or Proprietor for blasphemous or seditious libel.

Earl Bathurst to Ralph Darling, 12 July 1825.

The first free editor, Robert Wardell, a barrister-visionary, believed that without newspapers people might believe in witchcraft. When bread was scarce they might blame the baker, not the drought. Newspapers were civilizers. 'A free press is the most legitimate and powerful weapon that can be employed to annihilate individual influence, frustrate the designs of tyranny and restrain the arm of oppression,' Wardell wrote in his first editorial in *The Australian* 14 October 1824: *The Australian* would be 'equally unmoved' by favour or fear.

He saw a profound parallel between Government and press. Newspapers, 'a modern machine' adapted to society's changes by changing 'as the British constitution has done', gradually. Like the British constitution, the Australian press would not hurry and stumble; it would evolve. Only the pace of evolution was in issue. Wardell was thinking in months, the Government in decades.

Born in Yorkshire in 1793, Wardell owned and edited *The Statesman*, a progressive London afternoon daily, where he met his publishing partner, William Charles Wentworth. Both applied unsuccessfully to be New South

Wales Attorney General. Lord Liverpool's Tory Government preferred a conventional land-law scholar, Saxe Bannister.

Like Robert Howe, Wardell was hungry for economic and political progress to enhance the colony, *The Australian* and himself. With the European population already 27,357, towns — in Wardell's words — were springing up in trackless deserts. The plains were in high cultivation and the arts encouraged. Only 'an illiberal policy on the part of the government, impolitic public measures, or the ignorance and folly of public men' could hinder progress.

On the day *The Australian* first published, the Chief Justice, Francis Forbes, required free settlers instead of military officers to sit on juries in the Courts of Quarter Sessions, a step toward liberty Wardell thought the people would long remember; the coincidence was 'auspicious'.

Would the new journalism catch the reader's eye? Would Wardell's advertisers of colonial cheese, Brazil tobacco, English soap, Derwent potatoes and Jamaica Rum enhance their sales? Daniel Cooper begged to inform the public he had established the Australian Brewery in George Street. The best English and colonial hops produced a 'strong sound and most wholesome beverage.' He would take payment in wool, leather, shoes, soap, candles, wattle-bark, fish oil, grain, sawn timber and salt kangaroo skins; from the exceptionally thirsty he would take land or houses 'at the market price of the day'.

Wardell promised accuracy. 'We shall on no occasion insert any article of news that is not fully authenticated … It is measures, not men that we assail … It is the errors of a system — the vices of office that we condemn.' There would be *no personal attacks*.

News was breaking fast and late. As compositors and pressmen put the issue to bed, Wardell got wind of a big story: ex-convicts had been `carefully weeded' from lists of potential jurors. This reflected the views of the Attorney General, Saxe Bannister. Wardell thought trial by jury would be but `half complete' with emancipists excluded.

When a letter-writer dubbed *A No-Party Man* wrote that excluding former convicts was `agreeable to established law and usage' from which deviation would be 'pernicious' Wardell said: `We readily insert the letter. It forms part of our duty and part of our system to admit observations on both sides of any question.' For a generation there had been but one side — the government's — to any question. Now Wardell was proposing a radical change: balance! An Aussie doctrine of objectivity started with common-law ideas of balance expressed by a barrister-editor pushing for independence against Governor Ralph Darling who thought the press as dangerous as a brown snake.

In England Wardell had survived a prosecution for criminal libel at *The Statesman* by the arch-Tory Constitutional Association and was acutely aware that a newspaper suffused with fully authenticated fact would go under if readers turned away readers turned away. He would try to 'amuse readers of all classes and all tastes' and spare neither labor nor expense in making *The Australian* as complete as possible. The first issue reported that ten bushrangers had made their appearance between North Harbour and Broken Bay; 'it is said they are well-armed'. Wardell cited a 'prevalent report' as the source. 'Fully authenticated' had a special, a *newspaper*, meaning, something like 'common in conversation'.

Given Wardell's optimism that newspapers could educate, entertain inform and civilise, why did he think so many looked down their noses at the press? 'Every man finds they are not written for him alone.' (He meant, but did not say, every woman too.) He quoted (without naming the great satirist) Alexander Pope:

> Hard task to hit the palate of such guests
>
> When Oldfield loves what Dartineuf detests.

Wardell's printer was George Williams, the agitator George Howe sacked.

• • •

London. When he thinks of the Press, James Stephen, Counsel to the Colonial Office, speaks as if cocaine-snuff has undone his rational mind. He tells his friend, Van Diemen's Land Governor George Arthur, on 24 August 1824:

> You never should have been subjected to the monstrous absurdity of living under the dominion of any low-minded vagabond who can turn a paragraph and get possession of paper and type.

Stephen, a high-minded intellectual who says he feels raw in public, like 'a man without skin', tells Arthur that in a Colony to reform the dregs of English jails 'the evils of what is called a free press would soon be so overwhelming that I know not how General Darling has managed, or you will manage, to grapple with them.'

Influential in the Church Missionary Society, Stephen is wrenched between temptation and denial. His first cigar is so good he never smokes another. After a sniff of cocaine-snuff, he pours it out the window. Stephen does not spell out the evils of the free press because they are as obvious as the need for authority: too obvious to mention. He thought Governor Brisbane's free-press experiment 'imbecile' and he now shapes Colonial Office policy on Australian newspapers and has the ear of Earl Bathurst, Secretary of State for the Colonies.

When Wardell and Wentworth planned *The Australian* the gifted barristers with matchless self-esteem believed they could make a new world on the new frontier. Wardell despised landowners who, whatever they said in public, in private opposed trial by jury, muttering that the colony was 'not ripe' for it.

Some of His Majesty's ministers fell for that reasoning. Wardell spoke with the political tone colouring conversation in George Street and the Blue Lion.

The paper identified with Sydney-born currency lads and lasses, chief among them its co-proprietor William Charles Wentworth, whose urge to break boundaries led him across the Blue Mountains with Gregory Blaxland and William Lawson in 1813, but Wardell the dreamer understood the readers were pragmatists and change would come step-by-step. With his help readers could understand everything 'from the overturning of a coach to the overturning of an empire'. Accurate reports protected everyone against the 'detestable calumnies' and 'invented facts' that were the currency of conversation.

• • •

Francis Forbes, the New South Wales Chief Justice, was a prodigy who studied with 16-year-olds when he was 12. When he read law a few years later he pondered not only legal reasoning and precedent but also a more fundamental question: whether law made by imperfect men could render justice. Born in Bermuda in 1784 and provisionally appointed Attorney General of Bermuda two years before he was admitted to the bar, praised by peers for insight, diligence and attention to detail, he was appointed Chief Justice of Newfoundland, Canada, on 24 August 1816. After the Governor issued widely-detested regulations for salmon-fishing in Sandwich Bay Forbes declared the system invalid. At 32 he had an eye for the limits of the law.

Unwell (stomach trouble) and believing he would find sub-tropical Sydney more congenial than icy Newfoundland, he drafted the Act establishing the New South Wales Supreme Court and heard in August 1822 that Lord Bathurst had great pleasure recommending his appointment as Chief Justice.

Many looked up to Forbes not just as a lawyer but also as a subtle, insightful humanist. Dr William Redfern, surgeon, thought Forbes 'clever and sensible'; he understood the difference between law and justice and would be popular. John Macarthur junior wrote his father on 8 December predicting problems for those very reasons. Forbes was 'a man of great talent and estimable character. Judging from his conversation, he has theoretical views respecting public liberty, and, I am afraid, he will be occasionally inclined to question local regulations which, although of manifest utility, are not strictly sanctioned by law.' Tests of Forbes' character, talent and liberalism were coming.

Thomas Brisbane, New South Wales Governor from 1821, detected no trouble in early issues of *The Australian* in early 1824. Since Dr Wardell and Mr Wentworth had not asked his permission and he agreed with the Colonial Office that he could not stop the paper without Executive Council approval, he thought it 'expedient to try the experiment of the full latitude of the freedom of the Press.' To enable Lord Bathurst, the Tory Secretary of State for the Colonies, to 'judge how far this newspaper is conducted with moderation,' he despatched copies.

Noting *The Australian*'s freedom, *Gazette* editor Robert Howe asked Brisbane, a liberal already persuaded that execution did not deter crime, to abolish censorship on 14 October 1824. Grumbling that he would now have to pay Howe for Government printing, Brisbane complied immediately. Reporting to Bathurst three months later, he declined 'for the present' to predict the consequences of *The Australian*.

Brisbane's media problem was less the Sydney press than landowners' conversations and letters which conveyed fact, rumour and Tory gossip from sources such as John and Hannibal Macarthur and Archdeacon Scott to the Colonial Office, the House of Commons and Bathurst's sympathetic ear. Brisbane complained on 21 May 1825 that 'private channels of information' were carrying stories to London 'to the dishonor of the Government.'

One such story was that Brisbane had sent convict women to Emu Plains for 'impure purposes'. When news of this scandal reached England, Brisbane complained to Bathurst that he now had, once again, to rebut 'false statements'.

Brisbane relied on a Wardell editorial about that pain of the dominant male in New South Wales, the want of women. Three years ago, Wardell wrote, there were fifteen men to every woman. Nothing had been done. When thirty-two women convicts volunteered to labour beside men at Emu Plains, Priests cried the Church would be overturned and the mandates of Heaven violated. When Brisbane agreed to the scheme, hypocrites were eloquent in their reproaches. What had happened? Eight women had been rejected as not strong enough for field labour. Of the other twenty-four Wardell said '*nineteen* are married! Have been made *honest women*!' Only two had been returned to the Parramatta Factory for misconduct. Despite this, Wardell said sardonically, the good taste of the followers of Christ had prevailed and the violations of divine law that produced nineteen steady families had been stopped.

When he read the 'moderate' *Australian*, Earl Bathurst responded in panic. 'From a cursory reading, it was obvious that to exempt Publishers from all restraint [by the Governor] must be highly dangerous in a Society of so peculiar a description,' the humane reactionary said in special instructions to Brisbane's replacement, General Ralph Darling on 12 July 1825.

He did not say that in truth editors, publishers, printers and proprietors could be jailed, fined and bankrupted for criminal libel for accurately reporting government wrongdoing or that the principle governing such trials was *the greater the truth the greater the libel*. That editors are jailed for journalism shedding light on Government wrongdoing is as hard to find acknowledged in English official thinking as a midnight needle in a haystack.

'Even in England no person enjoys that absolute discretion with regard to the publication of Newspapers which, as I collect from Sir Thomas Brisbane's dispatch, is claimed by the Editors of the Journals which he has transmitted,' Bathurst said.

Restraints on the liberty of the press had been imposed [in England]. The names of printers, publishers and proprietors had to be delivered on oath at the Stamp Office and printed in every issue. Publishers had to enter a bond to the Crown to secure payment of any fine for blasphemous or seditious libel, but these Acts did not apply in New South Wales.

> I am not aware of any reason why you should not, with the advice of the [New South Wales] Legislative Council promulgate a law to the same effect, and extending somewhat further the principles [of] these Acts.
>
> You will therefore avail yourself of the earliest opportunity of proposing the enactment of a law founded, in general, upon [these Statutes].
>
> You will further propose that no Newspaper be published without a License to be applied for to the Governor; such license in no case to continue for more than one year [but the Governor could extend it with the advice of the Legislative Council]. You will further propose that every such license should be, ipso facto, forfeited upon the conviction of the Publisher, Printer or Proprietor for any blasphemous or seditious libel. The Licence ought, as in England, to bear a stamp; but as it is resumable, with a Duty not exceeding one pound.

The state of mind induced by thinking of the evil and tyranny of the printing press permitted Earl Bathurst to dream there was still newspaper licensing in England: licensing had effectively been abolished in 1695. He did not stop there: each issue ought to be subjected to a Stamp Duty.

When Darling arrived in Hobart on his way to Sydney on 24 November 1825, giving Arthur the instructions, George Howe's son Terry published in *The Hobart Town Gazette* a fantasy that pleased Arthur, Darling and Bathurst: 'The immediate presence of a Commander is attended with the happiest effects. It gives life and vigor to the community generally — inspires confidence and promotes loyalty, unanimity and social order'.

The press menace required uniform legislation in New South Wales and Van Diemen's Land, Darling told Arthur, because 'It is obvious that any restraint upon the editors [in Van Diemen's Land] would be a very imperfect, in fact inoperative unless a corresponding step was adopted in New South Wales, inasmuch as a free circulation [in Tasmania] would still be open to the journals of the Sydney editors,' he said. (*The Australian* could no more survive on its Tasmanian circulation than it could print on a possum.)

Darling, born in 1775, brought zeal, ambition and single-mindedness to the prison Colony. He served in the British Army for thirty-one years and was military ruler of Mauritius for four. Though the governing principle of life was obedience, the inner man debated the value of conversation. On one hand, speech was dangerous. It was better to shut up. That way, hair-splitting lawyers would not trip him up. But another Ralph whose hand ached writing despatches home at night longed to be heard. Robert Howe made the *Gazette* the Governor's loyal voice, but it was not enough. The inner Darling heard a single voice of parental authority, not the sound of the human condition, competing voices. But he was in a different state of mind when he arrived. He told Arthur on 21 March 1826: 'We are so quiet here' he had not thought of Bathurst's instructions.

• • •

One of the obstacles to free conversation and a free press in New South Wales was Saxe Bannister, preferred over Wardell and Wentworth as first Attorney General. Born in Sussex in 1790 Bannister owed his appointment not to his legal skills — he was a land-law scholar — but the favour of the Tory Colonial Office to which his tight conservatism, in his own view and that of the Colonial Office, entitled him. In October 1823 when Bannister was appointed Attorney General John Macarthur junior wrote: 'You know, my dear mother that in fact, he owes his appointment to me.'

He arrived in Sydney in April 1824 with a salary of £1200 and the right to practice as a barrister, bringing with him the new Charter of Justice that separated the Supreme Court of New South Wales from that of Van Diemen's Land.

The Chief Justice, Francis Forbes, thought Bannister brought 'false' and 'foolish' expectations, 'a great over-estimate of his own talents and the revenues of the [NSW] bar.' Bannister's draft Bills for the infant Legislative Council became 'the jest of the Chamber'. An energetic advocate with a puffed view of his legal skills had to try to contain the advocacy and energy of Robert Wardell and William Wentworth.

That Bannister broke bread with the exclusives John and Hannibal Macarthur and Archdeacon Thomas Scott and whinged incessantly of the inadequacy of his huge salary, ate away at his status in emancipist New South Wales. When more democratic institutions — trial by jury, the Supreme Court, the Legislative Council — were established and noisy disrespectful editors were agitating for the rights of the people, an accident of history and Tory partisanship made the first Attorney General a clown of jurisprudence. Bannister approved Governor Brisbane's experiment in press freedom, but was the last man to help freedom or the Governor.

• • •

Gentry, magistrates, merchants, landholders, farmers, traders and other free residents assembled on 19 January 1826, at a meeting presided over by the popular sheriff, John Mackaness and begged to inform Governor Darling that while they could boast of the loyalty to the Crown of those born and educated in the United Kingdom, there were also men scattered in the silent woods of Australia, who `had been neglected... and deeply feel this neglect.' Only a popular elected legislature, as in the American and West Indian Colonies, could `make us a happy and contented People.'

The danger increased every day. 'The safest way to render a country fit for the full enjoyment of civil liberty is, after the manner of the American colonies, to use the people to it early.' Darling replied as if he had not heard a word. He had not formed an opinion on what they said; he must therefore say nothing. A 'just confidence in the government' would attain their objects.

Reporting the meeting, Robert Wardell focused on conflict and personality. In Wardell's eyes the critical meeting offended Archdeacon Thomas Scott, an ex-officio member of the Legislative Council and snob who disdained to have a newspaper in his house. Scott thought himself a giant among pygmies. The meeting had given him sore offence. With the boldness of free men, the people dared to proclaim their wishes to the Governor. And the Sheriff, Wardell wrote sarcastically, had dared sanction disloyalty and sedition. Scott, one of the exclusives making what Wardell called 'behind-the-curtain representations' to Darling called on Sir Francis Forbes and asked the Chief Justice to tell sheriff Mackaness that Scott was withdrawing his friendship. Scott had cut the Sheriff, Wardell said sarcastically. But since the Governor received the address courteously, he had accordingly countenanced sedition. Scott 'must, to be consistent, cut Him [Darling] next.'

Early in February gentlemen enjoying an excellent dinner at the Sydney Hotel resolved that sheriff Mackaness' portrait be painted and hung in a public hall. Wardell said satirically on 16 February that if Scott's view prevailed. 'First ... the sheriff is cut, then...the Governor must be cut ... then the grand jury must be cut and we shall run the risk of seeing the Colony cut altogether.'

When he read these peremptory satires Bannister told Darling it was not his duty to scour newspapers with a prosecutor's eye. He would not trawl for libel unless he must. Any libel of the Archdeacon was trivial.

Though Darling thought Wardell's mockery `no doubt extremely impertinent and irritating ... to the Archdeacon' nothing reflected on Scott's public character or conduct as a member of the Government. It was not the Government's job to defend officials for acts unconnected with their public positions. If the Government did this, it would, if burdened with a 'captious' official soon find 'party squabbles would supersede matters of real importance.'

• • •

John Macarthur, born in Plymouth Dock, England on 13 August 1766, was with his wife Elizabeth the first volunteer immigrant to Sydney, a founder of the wool industry and that most dangerous of gentleman, a man of honour. He fought three duels, supported the rum coup against Governor Bligh in 1808, and hoped to impose his will on men in New South Wales as he imposed it on merinos.

Wardell's view of the Act to establish John Macarthur's Australian Agricultural Company, was emphatic. The statute created a monopoly that would augment neither capital nor population; it would prevent immigration; it was a vice. UK Ministers had been hoodwinked. 'The whole of the business is a mere bubble,' *The Australian* said. A week later Wardell's leader said if the Agricultural Company's first blossoms were any indication it would bear disastrous fruit.

Again and again the handsome, articulate Wardell filled his columns with the threats Macarthur's company posed to the colony and its people. But when Macarthur called on Darling on 29 April 1826 bristling with irritation the Bindi-eye under his blanket was Robert Howe, not Wardell. Howe had been libelling him for the past six months, Macarthur told Darling, voice rising, and Darling was bound to defend all members of the Government.

Darling replied that Macarthur, an appointed Legislative Councillor, had told him not three weeks ago that he had an agreement with Howe to write in the *Gazette* against *The Australian*. If Howe had in fact libelled Macarthur, the law was open to Macarthur as it was to anyone. The entrepreneur was boasting publicly that he would destroy Howe and saying in private that he never failed to ruin a man he found obnoxious. In a 'Most private and confidential' letter to Under Secretary Hay, Darling said Macarthur was a man of strong passions: winning mattered more to him than accomplishment. When he spoke of 'destroying' people, he did not exclude even *Governors.*

As for turbulence in New South Wales, the people 'to a Man' appeared *devoted to the Government.* The exclusives led by Macarthur were a party of but five members — Macarthur, the Archdeacon, Thomas Hobbes Scott, the Attorney General, Saxe Bannister, the Surveyor General and the surgeon, Mr Bowman, Macarthur's son-in-law.

Maurice Margarot, a Scottish martyr transported for sedition in 1794, dubbed Macarthur 'the Perturbator'. Typically, Macarthur thought journalists villains and dozens of character-readings depended on the thought: men the press applauded were 'almost certainly utterly abandoned.' Journalists were dealers in malignant falsehood, infamous hounds. When Robert Howe was treated to the wool-man's disdain he responded that Macarthur owed his social eminence to 'the petty retailing of three-watered grog.' Insult was becoming a form of greeting.

When he heard Macarthur was returning to England, Wardell suggested in *The Australian* of 13 May 1826 that he might buy a seat in the House of Commons for between £2000 and £5000. If wealth bought influence, Macarthur would have it; instead men derided him. With large tracts of land covered with merinos, cattle and horses he employed numerous shepherds labourers and maids. His wealth should cause rains of praise, but this was far from the case.

Wardell, insisting that 'we look at facts only — we record facts only' — told readers, among them members of the Commons and the Home Government that if they listened to John Macarthur they would become acquainted with Macarthur's opinions but 'nothing else.' Opinion had the substance of smoke.

Darling told Under Secretary Hay he was sure the intent of Bathurst's instructions on the press was to repress licentiousness. There was no licentiousness. There was no need for an 'obnoxious' stamp tax. The editors would resent it; the yield would be paltry. If he was wrong, Darling said, he would be told — but he would be satisfied to find he had not misread his superior's 'liberal intentions'.

• • •

Robert Wardell said Robert Howe had stolen news from *The Australian*. A single copy of the Hobart paper of 24 February 1827 arrived at Sydney Cove by ship late on Friday 9 March; Wardell set a Hobart story from it for the next issue on Thursday. When he read the Tuesday *Gazette*'s Hobart Town News, his blood pressure climbed: it contained a paragraph of *The Australian*'s Hobart story. He immediately questioned his compositors and pressmen; all denied leaking to 'the religious man'.

Wardell's ear heard lies in the denials. On Wednesday an anonymous letter named one pressmen and suggested Wardell ask him how many of Howe's men went to *The Australian* at 10pm on Tuesday, how much gin they brought and who gave them a folded piece of paper as they left?

Wardell discovered two of Howe's men had visited. He did not know the quantity of gin, but one of them, a 'fat chubby Scotchman', very drunk, had folded a piece of paper, pretended to vomit and left the office.

Wardell's revenge, an editorial on Saturday 17 March headlined HOW...e TO LIVE BY PLUNDER was cutting. 'We forgive "the pious man" for his literary larceny. We pardon the piracy because it is proof of good taste.' After shovelling trashy nonsense and coarse invective, Howe could take 'good rich stuff' from *The Australian* and fill his pages through gin and bribery. But 'he must [not] sink to "EXCLUSIVE INFORMATION"; he may talk of "important intelligence" and "latest news" whenever he can secure a copy of *The Australian* overnight, but nothing about *exclusive*; our pardon will not extend to that.' The incident might be remembered at evening prayers; 'Thou shalt not covet thy neighbour's news' might be a text at the next gathering under the Canopy of Heaven.'

When his satirical imagination turned to Colonel Henry Dumaresq, Darling's brother-in-law and clerk of the Legislative Council, Wardell became the Alexander Pope of Sydney Cove. Dumaresq, a distinguished soldier wounded at Waterloo, loathed vulgar speech and Australian familiarity and pressed on Darling the view that a licentious press could no more thrive in a convict colony than virtue prevail in hell.

When short of news, Wardell wrote, Robert Howe would think:

> My friend Colonel Dumaresq will lend me anything. … if ever we should desire to live by plunder, we'll think … we'll think … of what? … of 'my friend the Colonel' … and his paper … and the FAT CHUBBY SCOTCHMAN!!!

Dumaresq required satisfaction for the insult. After Wardell and Dumaresq both fired three times and missed — the musket balls tore clothing — Wentworth, Wardell's second, finally persuaded Wardell to apologise and Dumaresq to accept.

He had the aggression to provoke a duel and the cojones to risk his life on the field of honour, but manners governed Wardell's standards for corrections. 'When we are in error, which we are proud to say seldom happens [there are] none more prompt than we are to offer manly reparation.' Again, 'when we are justified in what we say, let folks assail us according to their stomachs when we are not justified it is our duty to submit; it is becoming in us to apologise.' Robert Wardell apologising? You could hear the kookaburras cackling.

Chapter 5

Duelling with Authority

1826–1827: *Edward Smith Hall, The Monitor*; *Robert Howe, The Sydney Gazette and New South Wales Advertiser*; *Robert Wardell, The Australian*; *Lawrence Hynes Halloran, The Gleaner*; Governor Ralph Darling, Chief Justice Francis Forbes, Attorneys General Saxe Bannister, William Moore and Alexander Baxter; Under Secretaries Richard Hay and Robert Wilmot Horton.

A free press tends to counteract that eternal propensity of our social natures to make slaves or dupes of one another. The tendency of the press is to equalize mankind; and the policy of our little state is only an enlarged prison-discipline; the Press tends to set all free, the State to hold one half in servitude.

Francis Forbes, New South Wales Chief Justice, 6 February 1827.

The Press, formidable everywhere, is from the peculiar composition of this Community, extremely dangerous here. In the present state of the Press, the tranquillity of the Colony cannot be preserved.

Governor Ralph Darling, 9 February 1827

With eminent connections including the famous anti-slavery campaigner William Wilberforce and the sheriff of London, Edward Smith Hall and his wife Charlotte landed in Sydney on 10 October 1811. A Government grant of 700 acres, seven cows and five convict servants opened the farm gate, but after struggling on the soil — his biographer, Erin Ihde, suggests a romantic attachment to land conflicted with the hard reality of living off it — Hall turned to his first passion, proselytising, in 1813 starting the NSW Society for Promoting Christian Knowledge and Benevolence.[1]

As first cashier of the Bank of New South Wales in 1817 he slept as required overnight with the money in a colony swarming with convicts. But Hall also believed transparency enhanced humanity and he thought a frontier where labour was crooked and employers were slave-drivers needed Press sunlight as it needed air. The Governor should publish the rations and wages available for assigned convicts; when his were ill, he fed them broth.

As he sought stories to win readers and advertisers from Robert Howe's 23-year-old *Gazette* and Robert Wardell's 16-month-old *Australian*, the novice editor deployed modesty in the first *The Monitor* on 19 May 1826. He would not dwell on rivals' flaws. He mused that in London where 50,000 to 100,000 read a newspaper, a parvenu editor might promise prodigious progress. In Sydney where 30,000-odd European souls were the outer limit of his reach, his first promise, 'more English and foreign information', was already tired. While Governor Darling was capable of error, and 'may do wrong, which the King cannot do' Hall would 'loyally attribute errors to his 'councils rather than to himself and we consider his person too sacred … to become liable to the rude and familiar attacks of a Newspaper.'

Hall also believed an Englishman in New South Wales had the rights of an Englishman at home. Settlers might risk their lives on the perilous voyage but they did not shed English rights anywhere on the planet, not even in New South Wales. In a colony where the five-member Legislative Council (quorum: two) met in secret with no record of debate, no settlers had a vote and no official was elected, this made him a radical and on top of that his faith reinforced his politics. 'If ever we see the holy wrath of our Clergy falling chiefly on the wicked poor, while rich sinners form their chief society' this would not 'promote Christian discipline,' reformation or morals.

Governor Ralph Darling was torn. Uneasy about independent scribes, Darling also wanted his superiors to see him (as he wanted to see himself) as relaxed as a goanna on a rock in the sun about that mechanical marvel, the printing press. On 19 May he thought that Hall, then worrying about the disappearance of three of the first five newspaper parcels sent by his London agent might if anything try to curry Government favour.

'[*The Monitor*] professes to be independent and I am sure it is though it speaks of the Government in very favourable terms,' he told Under Secretary Richard Hay a few days later. Earl Bathurst's instructions had been to repress licentiousness. Neither *The Australian* nor the *Gazette* was licentious; neither had attacked the Government in the five months since he arrived. A stamp tax — imposed in England from 1712 to confine the reach of newspapers —

would be a step backwards. It would cost more politically in editors' resentment than it would grow the struggling colony's revenues.

With Darling tranquil about the press menace, Hall prepared to defend himself in court against a rival editor who also believed in print and the Lord but was temperamentally Hall's opposite. The Reverend Doctor Laurence Hynes Halloran, a passionate Anglican teacher torn between ideals and lust, could not restrain his hand from writing ribaldry and libel, but while his subconscious always found an obscene or wounding phrase, he had magic in the classroom: the boys could hear a pin drop.

Halloran was born in Ireland on 29 December 1765, orphaned as a baby and cared for by an uncle, started a grammar school at 21, married, and enrolled as a naval chaplain. Posted to South Africa, he resigned from the navy after a conviction for libel and returned to England at 46, ruined financially, separated from his wife and children. Reuniting with them at 52, he won passage to Sydney by counterfeiting a note for accreditation as a curator.

Governor Lachlan Macquarie gave him a ticket-of-leave in 1819. Supported by the wool entrepreneur John Macarthur, he established Sydney Grammar School in 1820. After his wife died in October 1823 at the birth of their twelfth child, in August 1824 when he was 59, he married Elizabeth Turnbull, 17. Imprisoned for debt, the lecturer with libido advertised talks on ethics, astronomy, history and theology.

Edward Hall was Halloran's polar opposite. Hall combined a puritan loathing of ribaldry and sexual display, with a desire to see the news clearly and report it with 'sense and moderation'. From *The Monitor* masthead, a Cyclops eye stared out on Sydney, Parramatta, the Hawkesbury and the Blue Mountains, above words from William Shakespeare's tormented Moor, Othello: *Nothing Extenuate nor Set Down Aught in Malice*. As Wardell and Hall stretched funding and energy to keep asking questions, the Governor who had to answer them developed deep anxiety. All he knew of labourers, fishermen, blacksmiths, drunks and attorneys, what they said and what they did — especially attorneys — he could not trust. Any parchment might conceal treachery between the lines as any blood-gum a bushranger.

Among the editors, competition for readers and advertisers obliterated their core common interest in independence. When the prolix Hall, writing as 'Fidelitas' criticised Dr Halloran in the *Gazette*, Halloran sued for libel, winning the hollow victory of one shilling's damages 'without costs'.

Conservatives resented that the elite had no newspaper. The most conservative paper, the *Gazette,* supported Darling, but angered the Exclusives led by John Macarthur. When his wife Elizabeth told him emancipists had dined at Government House, Macarthur cried that God knew where this would end. Exclusives believed in their right to land, convicts and influence as in their right to breathe the air beneath the blue gums. Macarthur proposed a Tory paper; nothing came of it.

Though his natural tone was overstatement, Hall worried about boundaries. 'Freedom of discussion, while the public good is promoted, is lawful — but freedom to stab your neighbour's character is unlawful,' he wrote in *The Monitor* of 23 June 1826.

When Hall wrote that he did not believe any magistrates in the world were as ignorant of the law as those in New South Wales, street-wise Robert Howe wondered publicly who would trust a journalist 'scarcely seen in a Justice room.' Howe's implausible innuendo suggested Hall's indolence: while Hall sat sipping tea by the fire his newspaper published falsehoods to angry anarchists in the Blue Lion bar, Sussex Street.

Charlotte, delivered of a stillborn baby in August, died leaving Hall alone with eight young children. He began to doubt progress. The British Government was flooding New South Wales with sycophants, military and clergy who had never smelt the air of freedom. He told readers, some who thought as he did and some who thought of going home as giving up, that he wished he could retire to a thatched cottage in old England and look no more on the mildew rotting the roots of the kingdom of New South Wales.

• • •

While the overworked Chief Justice Francis Forbes, recovered from cholera in Bathurst from February to May 1826, John Macarthur and Archdeacon Scott pressured Darling toward press prosecution. When Darling invited law officers and barristers to a Government House dinner in June to welcome back the Chief Justice, Saxe Bannister at first accepted but next day, when he heard Dr Wardell was also invited, asked to be excused.

Darling said this rudeness was 'not to be misunderstood'. All lawyers had been invited. Whatever Bannister's problems with Wardell, they should not prevent him from attending a formal Government House dinner.

Bannister retorted that it was the Governor's duty to publicly rebut newspaper libels because if he did not the public would think he approved them.

When Darling requested more detail, Bannister said *The Australian* had unjustly attacked the Macarthurs, the Australian Agricultural Company, the clergy, the Archdeacon and the magistrates since the beginning of the year. People should not be left in doubt that the Governor found defaming public men unacceptable. Under a free press the Governor's responsibility to 'counteract the evils which its ... licentiousness must produce on a depraved Population' became stronger still.

Bannister suggested Darling start another Government newspaper. Darling talked to Robert Howe, who at first liked the title *The Pure Merino* but later mocked the idea: perhaps *The Aristocrat* or *The Exclusionists* would work, with an image of Governor Bligh rising from a feather bed. A confidential committee of gentlemen considered it, but while the idea was beautiful, paying for it was less so and once again nothing came of it.

Irritated to the point of sarcasm, Darling told Bannister on 21 June that since the King of England and his Ministers would not tell the Governor whether or not to dine with Dr Wardell, without any personal affront to Mr Bannister, the Attorney General could not have 'such authority.' When he required advice on any *legal* matter, he would ask Bannister for it. On all other matters he had 'no desire to place you in so unpleasant a predicament as that of giving opinions on subjects with which you have no right to interfere.'

Bannister submitted his resignation next day; Darling pushed the Home Government to accept it while he pressured Bannister to prosecute Hall for a paragraph in *The Monitor* of 14 July 1826: 'The moment Governor Macquarie left, Major Goulburn set open the doors of the convict barracks, and whoever wanted a servant took one.' The Government had defaulted on agreements to provide ten convicts for every thousand acres of land.

Though he had no doubt the report was criminal, Bannister, still waiting for his resignation to be accepted, thought prosecution would be inept because *The Australian* had been just as troublesome as *The Monitor* and unprejudiced men thought Darling could not stand up to Dr Wardell. 'If such be the public opinion, the effect of prosecuting [Hall] a new and needy Editor, and of passing by [*The Australian*] will be attributed to motives likely to defeat the purposes of the prosecution.'

An attorney whose craving for better pay settlers mocked in streets and drawing rooms from Bondi to the Blue Mountains interpreted public opinion to the ultimate authority at Home.

Hall wrote in *The Monitor* of 28 July 1826 he would never be a sneak who smiled at great men in Sydney while 'raising a powerful party against them in Downing Street.' *The Monitor* would report the Governor with 'honest severity'. This would protect the Governor against 'secret cabals which like a concealed mine explode in London.' Darling could answer the open criticisms of *The Monitor* and *The Australian,* whereas secret correspondence could poison Downing Street against him without Darling knowing anything of it. *The Monitor* did not work like that. It was a free perpetual public commission of inquiry.

Darling responded to Bannister on 19 August:

> When The Australian attacked the Government, the Attorney General was the companion and friend of the Editors, Dr Wardell and Mr Wentworth, and lived on terms, I am assured, of unusual

intimacy with them! The same Clerk was employed in common with them!

Darling said Bannister had not at that time urged the government to prosecute *The Australian*.

> The Attorney General would not invade the liberty of the press. [In time] he and the editors quarrelled. The Australian attacked him and continues to write against a Party [the Exclusives] of which the poor man was unconsciously the humble instrument. Now when The Australian supports the Government 'it is to be prosecuted: it has written against Mr Bannister's friends!!' Mr B. says unprejudiced persons believe the Government is afraid of The Australian. This will prove that he has no claim to be included among them.

As insults multiplied between the Governor and Attorney General the Press began to embody the other's faults in the other's eyes. Bannister said the unworthy paper's 'vulgar scurrilities and irreligious tendency' had not deprived it of Government attention. Darling replied:

> As to 'vulgar scurrilities', the Press has never, since my arrival, been more fruitful in this respect than when assisted by Mr Bannister's friends. The 'irreligious tendency' of the Paper can only apply to the insertion of the Police Cases. Why is it to be expected that the Papers here should be more particular than elsewhere? When the Attorney General sets the example of acting professionally without pay, the Editors will perhaps become indifferent as to the sale of their Papers.

Bannister replied as if Madeira loosened his tongue. Officials defamed by *The Monitor* could have an order setting out the Governor's regard for them, together with a *'suitable reward in land or money'.*
Darling quickly responded:

> 'If constables and others whose conduct is animadverted upon in the newspapers are to be rewarded in this manner, the candidates for censure would, I fear, be very numerous. There is something so singularly extravagant and eccentric in the idea that the soundness of mind which produced it must be at least doubtful.'

Darling hoped prosecution might strengthen the Government with the people but also feared Wentworth and Wardell could dominate in the Supreme Court, undermining Government authority.

The Monitor on 8 September 1826 wrote that a £1 government levy for the temporary occupation of 100 acres, and a royalty of a 1/2d-per-square-foot for cedar cut on government land were taxes, tolerable only if imposed by an elected House of Assembly. Darling thought this seditious. But when *The Australian* attacked the measures on 13 September, Darling dismissed it as hot air, Wardell was posturing as independent. A month later Wardell had a Government grant of 560 acres in a choice section of a Bathurst valley. (Darling's brother-in-law Henry Dumaresq courted and cultivated Wardell believing *The Australian* might be helpful.)

Darling put the 'injurious tendency' of several *Monitor* articles to the Executive Council on 6 October 1826. Persuaded that 'the tone of the Newspaper would be changed' and the editor cease his 'intemperate style of writing' Councillors decided against it 'for the present'. Darling submitted Bathurst's instructions; the Council would not be pushed and let them 'lay over for further consideration'. (The 'reasoned tone' Hall aspired to eluded him. NSW Chief Justice, Jim Spigelman, wrote in 2002 that Hall never paused 'at the border between zeal and self-righteousness.')

• • •

Two privates of the 57th Regiment, Joseph Sudds and Patrick Thompson, asked a York-street shopkeeper, Michael Napthali, to see material for shirts between 8 and 9 pm on 20 September 1826. For a few minutes the pair examined samples, bartered over price and chose calico. Napthali measured out 12 yards; Sudds picked up the cloth and walked into the street saying over his shoulder to Thompson 'I'll leave you to pay.'

Thompson chatted with Napthali for a few minutes till the shopkeeper remarked on the obvious: he was waiting for his money. Thompson told him to collect it as best he could and followed his mate out the door. Napthali did not pursue him: a private in uniform might be armed. A few minutes later he found a constable, who arrested the pair.

The crime was a stunt: Sudds and Thompson hoped to be cashiered and returned to England after serving a brief transportation for the offence on Norfolk Island.

They had not been paying attention. Five months earlier, two men from the 57th, John Jones and John Dougherty, shot themselves in an arm believing that self-maiming which rendered them incapable of military work would mean they could go home. General Darling feared that self-shooting might prove contagious as an escape route and ordered the two to work as scavengers at the Norfolk Island barracks, saying 'Let no man deceive himself. Whoever shall commit a like base and disgraceful act may be assured of a similar fate.'

The Court of Quarter Sessions on 8 November sentenced Sudds and Thompson to seven years' transportation to Norfolk Island. Darling commuted the sentence to seven years work in irons on the public roads. Then he personally designed heavy collars with six-inch spikes chained to ankle irons so the men could not straighten their backs. These were then specially fashioned at the lumberyard. On 22 November, stripped of their uniforms, dressed in yellow felon's clothes, they were drummed out at Wynyard Square — a public humiliation to symbolise their disgrace.

Sudds was admitted to the jail hospital the next day. Wardell wrote in *The Australian* that the collars and chains were 'carrying severity to extremes … The men cannot lay their heads down to rest.'

He argued that the Governor had not commuted the sentence (commutation meant mitigation) but had clearly increased it And increasing a sentence was beyond his power. The King could not do it. Did the Governor really have greater power in New South Wales than the King in England? By what magic influence? What was more, since Sudds and Thompson had intended 'not to steal, but to pretend to steal' they were therefore not guilty. The ink had barely dried on Wardell's remarks when news that Sudds had died on 27 November, after telling the surgeon 'I will never work in irons', reached the editor.

Saxe Bannister's last Supreme Court appearance on 20 October 1826, prosecuting Robert Howe for criminal libel after the British Government accepted Bannister's resignation, put the mocking Wardell in mind of an over-driven ox. 'Had you but seen him, reader, how he carried the Jury from politics to law, from law to the press, from the press back again to law, how he shed a tear of sorrow over the crimes of the press exulting with delight in the errors of the press ' Chief Justice Forbes told the seven-officer jury the speech was 'painful'. Later Forbes said: 'If I had entertained doubts of Mr Bannister's sanity before, they were confirmed by his conduct on [this] occasion.' (Despite the suggestions of the Governor and Chief Justice, there is no evidence Bannister suffered mental disease, as conceived of then, or now. But he had a taste for melodrama. After he dropped the remark that Wardell was 'the scum of London' Wardell required satisfaction on the field of honour. They fought at Pyrmont. After a shot apiece, the seconds cried 'enough'.))

After retiring five minutes the jury found Howe not guilty. Forbes thought Bannister, having neglected to pull the press into line, deliberately chose a weak case to demonstrate that prosecution would not succeed.

Alexander McLeay, Colonial Secretary, invited Wardell to inspect the chains in the Secretary's office. The editor could see they would not stop a man lying down to sleep.

> Your informant states that at the time the chains were put on him "he was so ill as to be scarcely able to stand." You add that the surgeon ordered the instruments, which tortured him, to be removed." Both these statements are incorrect.

The point was semantic. The chains were not the problem: it was the collar with inner studs and external spikes. 'As the object of every honest Journal is to inform and not to mislead the Public, you will, I have no doubt, in justice to the government insert this letter in your next Paper,' McLeay said.

Wardell published the letter, saying he respected the Government's well-meaning humanity. Only for a moment had he been shaken.

> The fair and candid letter constrains us to make this admission. We hate evasions. The letter does not descend to evasions, or seek to conceal one fact. We certainly do regret that in the minute points of the information which we communicated to our readers on Wednesday, we were not strictly accurate. We have seen the chains, and though they have not those horrifying appendants annexed to them, which would prevent the wearer from taking rest, still they are not fit for use under English law. Their construction, however, is exceedingly light and not calculated to inflict torture.

Dr MacIntyre told Darling and McLeay at Government House on 29 November that a dissection of Sudds' body revealed inflammation from the chest to the throat and acute bronchitis. His legs were swollen. The Governor and Colonial Secretary instructed MacIntyre to be precise — they used the word 'particular' — in his written report, yet to be delivered. MacIntyre said he had been very particular, 'knowing the rascally newspapers will report the case.' He found Sudds' abdomen liver and brain were healthy and though the throat contained slimy, frothy mucus and the windpipe was a 'reddish colour', 'no apparent disease was found.' *No apparent disease.* MacIntyre, probably Wardell's source, left open the possibility that Sudds had been, in Wardell's phrase, tortured to death. As Wardell demanded an independent coronial inquest, the acting Attorney General, W.H.Moore, called on W.C.Wentworth on 6 December to demand 'for God's sake' that *The Australian* stop saying Sudds had been tortured. Wentworth told Moore the best advice he could give the Governor was that which had already appeared in the paper. He 'perfectly approved' *The Australian*'s comments and thought Darling's treatment of Sudds and Thompson 'a flagrant violation of all law and humanity.'

The rates of suicide, self-maiming and theft in the 57th Regiment were higher than those of any other regiment in the garrison, and also 'any other regiment ever stationed here before.' An inquiry into these facts should have been conducted many months before Sudds' death. The coronial inquest demanded by *The Australian* and *The Monitor* was the only means of establishing how Sudds' had died. Why had it not been conducted?

A special Executive Council meeting on Saturday 9 December put Sudds' chains and irons on Jesse Geer, a foot soldier of Sudds' size in the 57th Regiment.

'It was proved by actual experiment,' Darling reported to Earl Bathurst, 'that Sudds could not have sustained any injury from them.' Neither Darling nor his brother-in-law, Henry Dumaresq, who wrote the Council minute, detailed the precise experimental suffering inflicted on Geer.

Wardell and Hall's reporting of the sensational story was unfair and inaccurate in Darling's eyes. To show how seriously he viewed it he added another word: *absurd*. They had a political agenda, he told Earl Bathurst on 15 December:

> I need not appeal to Your Lordship whether, in a Colony with a Press endeavouring to incite the Soldiers to Mutiny and the convicts to insurrection, some measure, calculated to make an impression on the Troops, was not indispensable. The News Papers, to answer the purposes of the moment, would fain make it appear that Cruelty and Torture have been practised. But I need not defend myself against such absurd imputations. That same day, Darling read Hall's character to Parliamentary Under Secretary Robert Wilmot-Horton. He was a man without principle. Though he was poor, supported eight children and knew prosecution meant jail, he was also a newspaper missionary. Only force would divert him. He associated with [William] Walker, an expelled Wesleyan missionary and Father [John Joseph] Therry, a Roman Catholic Priest. 'These people are dangerous from their connections with the convicts, whose cause The Monitor warmly espouses.'

He had not ordered Hall prosecuted for sedition because he did not wish to embarrass Wilmot-Horton, steering the new New South Wales Bill through the House of Commons. If he prosecuted Hall, petitions would be sent home.

As it was now too late for petitions he intended to order prosecution if Hall kept provoking mutiny and insurrection.

Darling said he had not heard of Sudds' illness until after he died. In an impassioned defence to his superior, the Governor voiced the politicians' perpetual theme: editors might speak of justice, they might report Government unfairness, but where was newspaper fairness when it came to Governors?

> With equal justice might I be charged with the death of William Watts, who was removed from the jail to the hospital at the same time as Sudds and died a few hours after Sudds.'

Watts had not been drummed out. He had no extra chains.

> This man's case is not considered by the Editors of The Australian and The Monitor to be important to the proceedings of the moment and these Papers are therefore indifferent to his fate. A death which cannot be rendered instrumental to [their] objects excites no interest in their minds.

Governor Darling's failure to understand the nature of news was comprehensive. Wardell and Hall, he said, were campaigning for a 'petition to [the United Kingdom] Parliament [to grant] trial by jury, a Legislative Assembly and other institutions recognised by the British Constitution.' They had seized on the case of Sudds and Thompson to 'induce the People to politics'.

• • •

The duel was a hole in the news.

Confined to officers and gentlemen, duelling was drama with a philosophical ingredient, the distance between what judges said the law was, and what it really was. If a gentleman posted a notice in a club that another was a coward and blackguard, not only the principals were guilty of wilful murder after death in a duel: so were the seconds. So was the notice printer. That, said Chief Justice Forbes, was the law.

After a third mate killed a chief mate in a duel, the jury quickly returned a verdict of manslaughter; Forbes, with Justice James Dowling, sentenced the officer to three months' gaol. Hanging was the standard penalty for heifer stealing. When Robert Wardell in *The Australian* of 17 March 1827 said readers wanting to live off plunder should think of Colonel Henry Dumaresq, Eliza Darling's brother, the Colonel required satisfaction. Both remained standing after three shots; W.C.Wentworth, Wardell's second, persuaded Wardell to apologise and Dumaresq to accept. No newspaper reported it; conversation filled the news-void.

As Robert Howe in the wake of the Sudds and Thomson furore contemplated publishing the *Gazette* daily after fourteen months of Wednesday and Saturday with the slogan *The Wicked Flee-eth Where No Man Pursueth, But the Just Are As Bold As A Lion*, a group of gentlemen planned a paper factory to cut imports valued at £5000 to £7000 a year. Howe, Hall and Wardell exchanged insults over whose circulation was biggest and the tension between Bannister and Wardell coloured Robert Howe's editorials through October. Howe thought it scurrilous of Wardell to say Bannister resigned to escape dismissal: Bannister was a more profound lawyer than Wardell.

Wardell had been in Sydney for two years, Howe wrote, without venturing beyond Parramatta. He was in his study writing leaders and law on the Sabbath and his leisure hours were spent '*we will not say where* — certainly not in the company of statesmen and politicians, nor yet in churches or chapels.' Howe did not pursue the innuendo as to where the bachelor-editor's libido might take him.

When he had sought Darling's support for a new newspaper *The Gleaner* in early 1827, Lawrence Halloran ran into the Governor's resentment. 'I have no wish for his assistance,' Darling told Hay. He thought Halloran wrote 'well though intemperately' and 'may *possibly* feel that he is likely to gain more by writing on the opposite [government] side than by uniting with them [Wardell and Hall].' 'I shall not enlist him or engage anyone in defence of the Government.' That Halloran was an erotic poet and compulsive libeller was not the problem. Darling said even a pro-Government newspaper 'gives importance to the Opposition Papers and increases discussions, which otherwise would not have existed.' In the Governor's subconscious silence was golden. Then there was the content. 'With such men as Dr Wardell, Dr Halloran and Mr Hall, more than ordinary circumspection will be required. I have only to hope they may not render extraordinary measures necessary.'

Halloran published the first *Gleaner* on Thursday 5 April 1827. He tried to believe the safety of the people was the supreme law, but the 'unfortunate proneness of the multitude to look with a suspicious eye at every act of their Rulers' troubled him. The passions of carpenters, blacksmiths, jockeys, cooks, labourers, shepherds, sailors, sealers, whalers, gentlemen and convicts then numbering 32,000 in New South Wales, were readily aroused. In *The Australian* he read 'artful misrepresentations'. Freedom of the Press could degenerate; Dr Wardell could make it a public wound.

To stamp-tax and licence the newspapers as Earl Bathurst proposed, Darling required Forbes' certificate that the tax and licence were consistent with English law. Forbes told Darling on 1 December 1826 that he doubted this. He cited Lord Ellenborough: 'The law of England is a law of liberty; and consistently with this liberty, we have not what is called an imprimatur; there is no such preliminary licence necessary.'

Part of Forbes was conservative. He told Horton six months later 'governments are founded in opinion and formed by events. Whoever abruptly attempts to make violent alterations, merely because they are better in the abstract, is a traitor or maniac.'

Part of him was a liberal optimist. Where was it written that an Englishman in New South Wales gave away his rights because convicts cultivated the soil on which he trod? He had never read such words as a lawyer.

The optimist prevailed when Forbes on 2 April 1827 advised Darling that he would certify any press law 'so far as I am authorised by Law'. How far was that? The Chief Justice left Darling adrift on a sea of doubt. Two weeks later Forbes told Darling the NSW Legislative Council lacked authority to restrain the constitutional right of a British subject, 'the right of freely discussing all matters in which his private or public interests are concerned.' Only the UK Parliament could abolish that right.

Halloran's subconscious evoked a military fantasy for journalism:

Troops of the British and French armies advanced within musket-shot at the battle of Fontenoy. An officer of the British Foot Guards removed his hat and exclaimed: 'Gentlemen of the French Guard, fire!' To which an officer of the French Household Guard replied: "No gentlemen, we never fire first, do you begin!" The Gleaner would conduct itself politically in that spirit, 'generous, gallant enemies ... not savage Mohawks.

Why had he started *The Gleaner?* 'I am compelled to write for bread.' He had endured losses and disappointments; his young family depended on him. Poverty was no dishonour 'especially when resulting from unavoidable contingencies, not personal demerits.' He thought Press influence 'powerful and extensive' and

> I pin my faith on no man's sleeve
>
> Nor write save what I know of, or believe.

Halloran published *The Gleaner* for nine pence for seven Thursdays, then switched to Saturday. By September he was satisfied that in his brief editorial career his writings had been 'the faithful transcripts of his genuine sentiments.' He had never sacrificed principle at the shrines of power or popularity. Which left him where he now was: destitute. *Gleaner* subscriptions barely covered printing costs. On 17 September tobacconist Thomas Jones — counsel Robert Wardell — sued before Judge Stephen in the Supreme Court for libel in Halloran's satire '*A pipe for a tobacconist*' which said a tobacconist had written an essay to check the crime of smuggling

> 'And then to prove infallible the thought,
>
> Himself offended and himself was caught.'

Assessors awarded Jones £25 damages and costs; the first Sydney editor to fail by overestimating the number who thought as he did, said 'we will never pay a farthing, much less the amount the Assessors (most miserable appraisers of character) have awarded the tobacconist' and published the last *Gleaner* on 29 September. Darling appointed him coroner in 1828 then dismissed him when he threatened to defame Archdeacon Scott. He died in Sydney on 8 March 1831.

• • •

Edward Hall, Robert Wardell and Robert Howe had to wear themselves out reporting the news. As proprietor, they had to look at themselves as a reporter with an eye for costs and efficiency and as an editor, check facts, tidy grammar, apply the dictionary in their head and layout pages to make a thousand facts attractive to the casual reader's eye. Then, on foot, horse, mule, carriage donkey or pontoon, distribute to subscribers.

Each edited his newspaper not only for the readers, subscribers, advertisers and government officials in Sydney but also for the Colonial Office and House of Commons in London. Should Hall Howe and Wardell exposed Darling's administration, they would bring down the weight of the law of libel on *The Monitor, The Australian, The Gazette* and themselves. If they offended the Colonial Office, Earl Bathurst could silence them with the authority of the mother of parliaments. If they made the newspapers a chorus of approval, they would lose readers and advertisers among the emancipists, risking circulation and survival.

• • •

A woman prisoner charged with having received Irish linen stolen from Government House appeared on 17 January 1827 before the Chairman of the Court of Quarter Sessions, William Carter. Magistrate Carter told the jury: 'The prisoner is indicted for receiving property stolen by *some person or persons unknown* — whereas it appears in evidence that a man is now in custody on suspicion of being the principal in committing the robbery — you are therefore bound to acquit her.' They quickly did so.

Wardell found this farcical. In Mr Carter's mind, mere arrest of the suspected linen-stealer was equivalent to conviction. 'For the first time it has been discovered, and the discoverer is the learned Chairman of the Court of Quarter Sessions, that apprehension on a charge is equivalent to a conviction, that suspicion of crime amounts to legal proof of guilt,' he wrote in *The Australian* of 20 January 1827.

When he was in this mood, the fact that the woman had been acquitted and the charge was defective meant nothing to Wardell, whose prose bore the energy of the Pacific as it boiled onto Manly beach. 'The farce of assembling Juries may now be dispensed with, for the Chairman can determine all cases by intuition — for a man is KNOWN to be a thief as soon as he gets into the fangs of the police.'

Darling's anxiety now exposed him to the Chief Justice. He told Forbes: 'The papers have now had a sufficient run: the Government cannot with propriety any longer abstain from endeavouring to check the evil. Mr Carter is a faithful adherent of the Government, and entitled to its protection and support.' He instructed the acting Attorney General, William Moore, to prosecute Wardell for criminal libel.

As Moore prepared to prosecute, Carter started a civil suit and criminal prosecuution. Forbes told Carter he was obliged to choose one or the other. When he elected prosecution, Wardell challenged the proceedings on technical grounds and Forbes dismissed the application. Darling told under-secretary Hay that Forbes was guilty of 'permitting the libellers of the Government to escape Justice through the chicanery of the law.' Community support for Wardell was too strong; prosecution would be in vain.

'Nothing was easier than to irritate people against authority. That was the object of the Papers at present', Darling wrote to Under Secretary Horton on 6 February 1827. Colonel Arthur had sent him drafts of two newspaper Bills so the Governments of New South Wales and Van Diemen's Land could unite to restrain the Press.

He showed Forbes the Bills, who said if anything were to be done he should recommend enactment [in N.S.W] of the Law as it stood in England. Darling said that with *The Monitor* and *The Australian* 'No means, however infamous, are neglected which may be likely to shake the Government, or rouse the prisoners and the people (I might add the Military) into opposition and hostility.' Darling drew Horton's attention to Hall's article on the Press. Hall had the gall to say as if he were Thomas Jefferson that any excess of words could be redressed by an answer in words. 'Licentiousness in New South Wales would always draw that censure sufficient to prevent it gaining ground. No license or censorship would ever be necessary to prevent intemperance in the public press.'

Darling said in a confidential despatch to Under Secretary Hay on 9 February 1827:

> The Press, formidable everywhere, is from the peculiar composition of this Community, extremely dangerous here.' When settlers' dreams were not realised instantly the newspapers blamed 'harsh and unnecessary' Government restrictions.
>
> It is impossible not to perceive that, in the present state of the Press, the tranquillity of the Colony cannot be preserved. The Community is of a very peculiar description. The respectable are supine, while the Press is busily employed sowing the seeds of discord and dissension'
>
> The people are taught by the Papers to talk about the rights of Englishmen and the free institutions of the Mother Country, many of them forgetting their actual condition.' New South Wales was in its infancy. Not three settlers could give up their time to a Legislative Assembly. People were indifferent. 'The evil of this place is the passion that New South Wales should be the Counterpart of England.

Forbes was torn. He told Horton on 6 February 1827:

> A free press is excellent, indispensable in a free state because of its tendency to counteract that eternal propensity of our social natures to make slaves or dupes of one another; but for that reason perhaps it is not suited to a state of society where one half of the community are worked in chains by the other; the direct tendency of the press is, in short, to equalize mankind; and the direct policy of our little state is only an enlarged prison-discipline; the first is to set all free; the last to hold one half in servitude. An unrestrained press is not politic or perhaps safe in a land where one half of the people are convicts, who have been free men. Yet I must not leave out of the account that the other half of the people are free and that, as an abstract right, they are consequently entitled, as of birthright, to the laws and institutes of the parent state.
>
> It is a mixed question, and requires to be carefully examined. If you take away the freedom of public opinion upon matters of government, you take away a legal right.

If Forbes declared licensing and stamp tax to be beyond the power of the New South Wales Government, Darling's accusation that the Chief Justice was usurping Government and exposing settlers to convicts, bushrangers and blacks would be the focus in the Blue Lion, the Shakespeare, back-street bars and dining rooms throughout Sydney.

When Saxe Bannister had sued Wardell by proxy for libel, Robert Howe was dismayed; he thought that 'after an affair of honour, every feud should have ceased.' While Howe disliked Wardell's politics 'his growling and all the rest of it' the suit 'really disappointed' him. Freedom of discussion should be more valued than that. But when Justice John Stephen dismissed the suit on the technicality that Bannister's attorney failed to prove what everyone knew, that Wardell published *The Australian*, Darling was alarmed. He told Forbes on 2 April 1827 that 'the trial has furnished ample proof that there are individuals here who do not pay much regard to the sacred nature of an oath.' Restraining the Press could no longer be safely delayed. It would be difficult, if not impossible, to identify editors with their papers. (In the real world, calling on the editor and asking him if he were indeed editor would be the end of the argument.) Would the Chief Justice again consider Lord Bathurst's proposal?

Forbes said if the newspapers were licentious, why had there been no prosecutions? He knew of no 'sensation caused by the papers among the prisoners of the Crown.' Newspaper licensing was repugnant to English law; he would not certify it.

The treatment of the stamp tax might have been a song for a street satirist. On 27 April the Act, closing the ownership loophole Wardell exploited, passed the Council. On 2 May, with Forbes absent at a Supreme Court sitting, five Legislative Councillors, Lieutenant-Governor William Stewart, Colonial Secretary Alexander McLeay, John Macarthur, Charles Throsby and Archdeacon Thomas Scott, approved a stamp-tax of four pence. Colonel Dumaresq, the Council clerk, walked to the court where Forbes was trying a capital offence to check whether Forbes approved the amount. According to Dumaresq, Forbes said he saw no objection.

When he read the tax published in the *Gazette*, Forbes said that if he had told Dumaresq he approved it, he did not remember. But there was a more fundamental problem. The purpose of a tax had to be 'distinctly and particularly' stated. The real purpose was not the one in the preamble, to 'defray the charges of printing public Acts, Proclamations and Orders'. That cost about £120 a year. The 4d. duty would yield £1800 a year. The real purpose was not to cover printing costs. *It was not even to impose a tax. It was to ruin opposition newspapers.*

As Forbes parsed, dissected and weighed the issues, a source leaked the secret council proceedings and disclosed that the Stamp Duty lacked the Chief Justice's certificate. The 'law is not worth the paper it blackens' Wardell wrote on 25 May 1827.

Never inclined to lower the temperature of a conversation, Robert Wardell chose this day to free his most wounding inner satirist. The Stamp Duty Act would immortalise Governor Darling. Posterity would be 'dazzled by the blaze of his glory and will exclaim, what a consummate politician! What a profound legislator! Would to heaven that we knew the length of his *****, for surely so much wisdom and magnanimity must argue something superhuman.' He signed it *Vox Populi*.

Enemies of the Press had one argument, Wardell said: its influence on the prison population. And what was that influence? The free press 'has been the means of abolishing illegal floggings, transportation and even hangings, without a jury. The prison population feel they are protected and the effect is visible in the orderly habits they have acquired.'

When Bannister's replacement Alexander Baxter, an advocate comforted by brandy, arrived in July 1827, Darling remained pessimistic. If Baxter failed — 'and how can he succeed — the field will remain in possession of Mr Wentworth and Dr Wardell and the Government will be worsted in every Contest.'

While he looked forward to the theatre of the Vox Populi prosecution, Wardell on 3 August 1827 derided a Government Notice in the *Gazette* which said the Bench of Magistrates had jurisdiction over convicts assigned to settlers and could remove prisoners from settlers who failed to feed or clothe them properly. Forbes told Darling the issue was 'a pure point of law' which only courts could determine. The Notice had no effect. Wardell lamented its ignorance and asked rhetorically what they should all do should an 'IGNORANT AND OBSTINATE MAN' occupy the Governor's office.

Prosecuting Wardell for seditious libel on 29 September, Baxter sought to make censorship invisible. 'It is far from my intention to call into question the right of free discussion on a public measure.' But free discussion running wild was a pest worse than Pandora's box.

Wardell told the jury of seven military men he had often defended others successfully and hoped to do as well for himself as a client. He represented the whole colony, resisting 'those who by crushing me, would crush the liberty of the Press and put out the light that shines on evil deeds.' Chief Justice Forbes said Wardell had been writing on a great public issue on which everyone had the right to express an opinion 'but this must be done within proper bounds.' The jury retired at 3 pm. At 4 pm the foreman returned to tell the Chief Justice and Justice John Stephen they could not agree and believed agreement was not possible. (Five voted for conviction, two for acquittal.)

Forbes discharged them. Wardell said the jury performed their duty nobly. 'They acted like Britons! Like men!' Robert Howe thought the non-verdict 'unfortunate'. Baxter tried again, prosecuting Wardell for Vox Populi on 22 December before Forbes and Stephen. After six-and-a-half hours the jury officers found Wardell not guilty on the first two counts and could not agree on the third; Baxter agreed that was the end of the matter. Robert Wardell could vulgarly mock the Governor in a newspaper sold throughout New South Wales and Van Diemen's Land and get off before a military jury under the Governor's command. Darling complained that Baxter lacked legal knowledge and experience and would not move without direction. Wardell and Wentworth kept bar and bench 'equally in subjection through their effrontery and talent.' The British Government thought New South Wales an asylum for fools and madmen.

Chapter 6

The Hobart Press Musket

1816–1888 *Andrew Bent, Henry Emmett* and *Evan Thomas*, The Hobart Town Gazette, Southern Reporter and Van Diemen's Land Advertiser; Governors Thomas Davey, William Sorrell and George Arthur; *Terry Howe*, The Tasmanian and Port Dalrymple Advertiser; *Robert Lathrop Murray, James Ross*, The Colonial Times; *Gilbert Robertson*, The Colonist and The True Colonist; Chief Justice John Lewes Pedder; Attorney General Joseph Gellibrand; *John Charles* and *George Davies* and The Mercury.

No matter what its principles, it is still a Newspaper and as such a public good.
Andrew Bent, editor, *The Colonial Times* 6 November 1827

If the Lieutenant Governor is to be called a tyrant with impunity, there is an end of our liberties.
Attorney General Joseph Gellibrand 26 July 1825

'The cause of outlawry and violence is to be found in the factious principles disseminated in the colony through the medium of a licentious Press.'
Lieutenant Governor George Arthur, November 1825

Andrew Bent's love of words on paper was a love of shapes more than meaning. His pleasure in creating the letters of the Roman alphabet approached Eros. Born in London in 1790, he was charged with a 16-year-old friend in October 1810, after starting as a printing apprentice, with having stolen 'a coat valued at 2/-, a tippet [cape] valued at 6d, two pairs of boots valued at 15/- and two shoes valued at 5/-.' Arrested trying to sell them, they said they bought the goods in Drury Lane and pleaded not guilty. After he was sentenced to death and the sentence cut to transportation for life, he arrived in Hobart on 2 February 1812.

An optimist to the core, he arranged with Governor Thomas Davey, who turned a blind eye to the dangers of journalism (and much else) to publish *The Hobart Town Gazette and Southern Reporter*. The first issue — day unknown as copies disappeared in the void — appeared in May 1816. The newspaper necessarily depended on revenue from Government Notices and Davey persuaded himself the notice 'Published by Authority' on page one increased circulation, but he admired Bent's drive and energy, thought the paper 'a deserving little work' and was happy that Bent published it at his own expense. Bent required no editorial direction; even better, he required no subsidy.

Davey's successor, easy-going William Sorrell, appointed Henry Emmett editor in 1824. Since Bent owned the type, Sorrell thought — he had bought it from the Government — the right of property entitled him to print the newspaper. But in his mind the question of control was finely balanced. If the Government owned the metal type 'it would be quite legal to stop his press as *surely no press can be allowed in these colonies without a licence.*'

Emmett, a prosperous sheep-and-cattle farmer with six children and conservatism to match his fortune and family, who was Bent's opposite in temperament and values, stretched Bent's flexibility and capacity. Emmett had a second job: chief clerk in the colonial secretary's office, topping up the £100 salary he drew as editor to sustain the champagne style he knew he deserved. Emmett was later sacked as registrar of the Court of Requests for lifting wine-license money to pay for an expensive house. (In 1833 Bent offered him the editorship of his third newspaper, *The Colonist*; when Governor Arthur told Emmett privately it was not wise for a man with four sons, employed by the Government, to join the hostile press, Emmett turned Bent down.)

Bent thrived on printing; pressure converted him into a publisher as indifferent as the blood gums to threats and promises. An energetic improviser, he made his own ink. Short of type, when he ran out of lower case a's, he made do with cApitAls. Short of capitals, he rendered government house hobart town saturday in rude breach of grammatical orthodoxy. Forced to use quarto Chinese paper when his press required foolscap, he hand-glued sheets together.

The obsessed typographer pressed on, driven by the energy of black letters on white pages, paid in English shillings, Spanish dollars, rupees, rum, tobacco, tea, wheat and traders' notes — and the traders, used to buying tobacco and rum on three years' credit, squeezed his cash flow to a trickle. In inner conversation he wondered if his mind was really sound.

Could a paper flourish? Not likely. That was the objective reality. A more subjective threat was on the way.

• • •

George Arthur, born in Plymouth, England, in 1784, was a short but not small soldier, intense, ambitious, a devout Calvinist and rigorous administrator to whom words of criticism crawled from a despatch page like red-back spiders. He sailed into Hobart as Lieutenant Governor on 11 May 1824 to a prospering Colony.

Arthur doubted Van Diemen's Land was ready for the responsibility the UK Government was foisting on it. He told a welcoming group of landholders, clergy, magistrates and respectables on 28 May he trusted their example would reform the morals of that very large class, the convicts, this being essential for domestic peace.

Arthur's huge dark eyes were lit with a glint of goodness and his thin lips rarely elongated to smile. Some thought him the saint of Hobart Town; others heard even in his thanks a tone so cold it chilled the blood. Politically, he believed there was 'nothing to fear except truckling to radicals.'

His severe exterior hid an inner man who longed to communicate and laboured at his desk for twelve, sometimes eighteen, hours a day, on despatches that revealed his craving to be understood. 'It will seem strange, I fear, to my Lord Bathurst that my predecessor conducted matters apparently so smoothly, whilst there has been so much commotion during my administration. But I will venture to say no man can do his duty to the Crown in this colony and be popular ...'

He based his hopes on men of substance, men he could trust, editors not among them. Within two years he tormented himself with the thought that the 'licentious Press [is] an instrument calculated, beyond all others, to do injury.' *Men who felt free to speak would also feel free to act.* In striving to alienate the community from the Government, the press strove to destroy the unity on which survival depended. In Arthur's mind the press was the enemy. Andrew Bent personified the press in Hobart Town.

In the primal rivalry between sons and fathers, sons elect to fight the old man on his own ground or claim new ground where the father has not set foot; perhaps, the subconscious whispers, because he could not. After the first Sydney editor, George Howe, went to his grave his oldest son Robert published *Gazette* supplements saying *'see that?'* to the old man.

George's second son Terry went to Hobart in 1824, then to Launceston where he published the first *Tasmanian and Port Dalrymple Advertiser* on 5 January 1825. Again he cut new ground: George had never seen the Tasmanian bush. The brothers supplied each other interstate news.

Journalism did not require reporters to identify sources; a 960-word story on the Matthew Brady gang in the *Gazette* 26 November 1825 contains no direct or indirect quote from Brady, his gang of fifteen or the sixteen men they kidnapped in six days. 'They [the gang] are continually expressing disgust at their mode of life and the certainty of being apprehended,' the reporter ends, without quoting a word of that disgust and certainty. The editorial technique is: *Tell, don't show*.

Governor Arthur offered a 25-guinea reward, increased to 100 guineas or 300 acres, for Brady's capture. Matthew Brady, a gentleman bushranger who spoke politely to men and treated women gently, posted on a Kempton hotel door: 'It has caused Matthew Brady much concern that such a person known as George Arthur is at large. Twenty gallons of rum will be given to any person that will deliver his person to me.' The *Gazette* reporter omitted this swagger: what worried the Governor most and interested readers most was what the newspaper was least likely to report.

With five children depending on him — his wife Mary helped manage the paper — Bent worried incessantly about them; provider-anxiety tormented him at noon as at 3am. When Attorney General Joseph Gellibrand estimated annual *Gazette* income in 1825 at between £1000 and £2000 on a circulation of 400 to 500 copies a week he omitted costs.

Proud of printing, Bent valued independence more than income and dreamed of a Big Tasmania. Arthur thought the *Gazette* spread ex-convict principles; to Bent it spread 'instruction into dark and remote corners'. To the Governor and the publisher the newspaper and the facts it reported never looked the same.

Fifty liberals headed by Anthony F. Kemp on 25 January 1825 asked Governor Arthur to remember that justice delayed might inflame bushranging. Suspects, their friends and associates, angered by men and women the law presumed innocent spending months in jail awaiting trial would sympathise with wild men dangerous to settlers, their daughters and the law.

Arthur responded that the Press was to blame. The licentious Press would influence the convicts, who were predisposed to evil and could not distinguish liberty of writing from liberty of acting. Seeing the Government insulted with impunity, its policies called weak and imbecile, fed the illusion that 'resistance to the constituted Authorities might prove successful'. Misled by the words of lawless journalists, convicts threatened respectable settlers' property and safety. From Arthur's perspective, the power of journalism was vast; it was itself accountable for laggard prosecutors and dilatory justice. Arthur organised vigilantes to hunt convicts like kangaroos; a satirist mocked them in *The Van Diemen's Land Warriors,* published by Andrew Bent in 1827.

Arthur told Bent the printing press and *Gazette* belonged to the Government. Though Bent left most editorial work to his editors — snobs, reactionaries and Governor Arthur whispered he was illiterate — he would not bow to Arthur's anxiety or authority. The stand-off was about politics more than money; if Bent valued money more than independence, he could take dictation and stroll around Battery Point as Arthur's prosperous companion. At the core of island politics and Arthur's sense of self was the question who would control the voice of Van Diemen's Land.

Arthur's mind was fixed: a free press in a convict colony would be the 'height of imprudence'. With land-owners whispering anxiety into his ear, he persuaded himself settlers would gladly forfeit a small part of their rights in return for keeping newspaper agitation away from convicts. A musket ball in a horse or rider regularly showed where that agitation might lead. In the Governor's eye, Bent, who had reported 'loyalty pervading every breast' at King George III's 69th birthday celebration on 4 June 1817 was a menace. In dark moods Arthur persuaded himself that even popular Sorrell had 'dreaded' a free press. A month after Arthur landed Bent, stepping into the unknown, testing his independence from Government, sacked Emmett and appointed Evan Thomas, who believed a free press could set readers free, as editor. Thomas was an Irish teacher who tried his hand in Hobart as property-dealer, pastry and biscuit-maker, innkeeper, poet and playwright.

Though both Bent and Thomas believed in the free press, that was not enough to make them brothers. 'Sometimes when articles have been printed, [after Bent's editing] I have not known my own offspring,' Thomas said. Still he hoped to make the newspaper a 'beacon placed by divine graciousness on the awfully perilous coast of human frailty.'

Who would guide the light? In Arthur's eyes 'this absolute unrestrained freedom [of the press] in a small community, composed of such inflammable materials, is incompatible with the well-being of society and the safety of the colony.' That editors who published under threat of imprisonment for criminal libel in trials applying the principle 'the greater the truth, the greater the libel,' enjoyed 'absolute freedom' was a fantasy of law-and-order men.

With Arthur in that frame of mind, Bent sent Thomas to Sydney on the Phoenix to put the case to the Governor-in-Chief, Thomas Brisbane, that Bent owned the *Gazette* and the newspaper was independent. Brisbane, who had just lifted censorship from Robert Wardell's *The Australian* in Sydney, agreed immediately. Thomas had an unspoken argument: Bent was resourceful, skilled and energetic. He was not a drain on the purse. He was a gentleman and above all, a known quantity. Brisbane got his drift. If Arthur did not like Bent's paper, Brisbane told Thomas, 'he can establish a new one.'

Returning to Hobart 'big with triumph,' in Attorney General Gellibrand's eyes, Thomas borrowed from the King James Bible, writing the first draft for the *Gazette* of 8 October 1824 to Bent's instructions. At times inspired, then careful and exact, then full of creative tension, they rewrote for four hours. An inspired time produced words that stung Arthur like a yellow wasp. Brisbane's decision showed *'even the sling of an outraged "weak one", when brandished against the Gideonite of tyranny, must be irresistible.'*

Gideonite was a warrior who liberated Israel from the Midianites. Then again, the Gideonites had hanged their enemies on the hill before the Lord. In backstreet bars and wharf taverns, the drinkers who read the passage with a shout of laughter and lager thought — the ones who thought again after the first rush that that mournful bastard Arthur at last had a poke in the eye — it meant a particularly hateful tyranny. That the little *Gazette* had got away with it was for months the talk of drawing rooms in Sandy Bay and the bars in Stodart's Hotel, the Union Tavern and the Bricklayer's Arms.

But what on earth — this was this was the core of conversation and the key for a libel prosecution — did it mean? Thomas' rhetorical flourish turned on an obscure, ambiguous Biblical phrase. In the next issue Thomas said the piece was 'penned in a spirit of gratitude completely unblended with rancour.' That was legal strategy talking: revealing malice would be fatal for the defence. Readers unfamiliar with authority and law creating a secret language for those in the know struggled to read between the lines. A magistrate, Mr T.G.Gregson, thought they would be lost in the fog. The rhetoric was 'the brainless drivelling of a poetical imagination. A person of ordinary education could understand nothing from beginning to end.'

In Thomas's mind, though the *Gazette* was a sacred sentinel, there were fences around the green grass of press freedom. After inviting letters-to-the-editor on 14 January 1825 he cautioned a reader who wrote about corruption in high places: 'The Supreme Court is the place to reveal the facts, not a newspaper.' Next week he said 'The Angler would fish in troubled waters but we will not let him.' Yet he also argued for a free press as if he agreed with Thomas Jefferson that 'the press is impotent when it abandons itself to falsehood.'

No-one need worry about 'unjust vituperation' with a free press, for 'no sooner does the poison spread than an antidote overtakes it.' For every abuse of free speech, the remedy was more speech. Truth would prevail in the free market of ideas; under censorship lies would flourish.

Gellibrand detected another Bent libel in the *Gazette* of 11 February 1825; Thomas wrote about a lawsuit in London against Arthur by his subordinate in Honduras, Lieutenant Colonel Bradley. (Arthur sacked and imprisoned

Bradley for siding with slave-owners; Bradley sued for false imprisonment and won £100 damages.) Thomas made a reference to how the Hobart officers should conduct themselves 'if they wish to escape, as Colonel Bradley did not, extra-martial incarceration and ... expulsion from the army.'

Under the pressure of litigation, self-doubt he did not commit to paper and probably inner torments he hid from himself, Bent thought again and yet again of the Gideonite piece he had co-authored with Thomas and came to see the text as 'the silly drivellings of a slop editor perfectly unintelligible.' He sacked Thomas (or accepted his resignation: Bent said he sacked Thomas; Thomas said he resigned after Bent mutilated a leader-proof till it resembled a dissected wombat; perhaps it was a dead-heat) and replaced him with Robert Lathrop Murray on 8 July 1825. In doing so, he gave a voice to an editor and writer whose style, opinions and life all affronted Governor Arthur.

Murray, born in London in 1777, educated at Cambridge University and commissioned as an army officer, married Alicia Marshall in 1797 and Catherine Clark in 1801. Convicted of bigamy in 1815, he argued that the first marriage was legally flawed. While Catherine petitioned the Prince Regent, Murray published an *Appeal to the British Nation* and petitioned the House of Commons against his sentence of seven years' transportation. All failed, but in Sydney he was pardoned soon after he arrived and rose from Police Office clerk to assistant to the police superintendent. He sailed to Hobart in 1821 when he was 44.

Murray, writing as A Colonist, showed he was another crank who believed in free discussion. He rebuked Thomas for telling readers to go to the Supreme Court: 'There is a tribunal to which everyone has, or ought to have, access. It is yours. Yes Sir, yours ... the Press.'

Arthur had the wowser's anxiety: he was shocked to discover Murray living in a state of 'open concubinage'. In Arthur's eyes Murray's years with the police did not redeem him. A sickening example of the wickedness of the human heart, he violated the morality restraining sexual passion.

Arthur tried to persuade himself that Murray was held 'in universal contempt'. But when he thought again of what Murray was writing — scurrilous attacks, gross paragraphs, the 'official *Gazette* of the island converted into a powerful engine against the Government ... libels in every shape' — and especially when he thought of Murray's friendship with the Attorney-General, Joseph Gellibrand, he knew the man was dangerous.

On the afternoon Bent published the Gideonite leader, 8 October 1824, Gellibrand told Arthur it was a gross criminal libel. It tended to bring Arthur and the Government into 'hatred and contempt'. Bent should be prosecuted. Arthur responded: 'My character is not the least likely to suffer, or my Government to fall into contempt. Besides, the poor man has a large family and is

I think likely to suffer from the measures to which I must resort. Therefore pray do not disturb him.' Three days later he asked Gellibrand for particulars about press and type for a Government newspaper.

Gellibrand asked again for permission to prosecute. But Arthur was wary of settlers perceiving him as driven by personal revenge. Doing nothing would injure no-one.

Contemplation can make a word-wound fester, especially when new offences suggest the guilty publisher is not aware of his crime, let alone remorseful. Five months later, on 18 March 1825 Arthur said Bent continued to 'publish gross falsehoods' and was trying to degrade officials and scandalize the Government. He asked Gellibrand to prosecute Bent 'forthwith' for all the libels on and since the day of the Gideonite.

When Bent heard, he buckled, offering to identify the author. The self-made man convinced himself a printer could escape liability by appointing a competent editor and identifying offending editors or correspondents. The printer could wash his hands of liability; that would be common-law justice for a craftsman. Bent also thought he would do better arguing his own case than hiring an expensive attorney.

• • •

Andrew Bent, Evan Thomas and Robert Murray joined seventy at dinner at Stodart's Hotel on 7 April 1825 to celebrate the anniversary of Sorell's arrival in Hobart; the progressives at the banquet tables roared when, after the toast to Lieutenant Governor Arthur, the band struck up 'There's na Luck About the House.'

Evan Thomas, responding to the toast to 'the liberty of the press', said he hoped intellectual growth would 'never again be arrested by a censorship.' Another said liberty of discussion would never be offensive, because it would be 'controlled by public opinion.' As they bantered, Robert Murray acknowledged what everyone with an ear to the ground knew — he was A Colonist.

After this effrontery, Arthur told Gellibrand he was astonished that Gellibrand, a husband, a father and Attorney General of Van Diemen's Land could associate with so immoral a character as Robert Murray. It was not just that Murray was immoral. What was worse was that he was famous for it; his decadence was *notorious.*

Arthur acted on the strategy he had pondered since the day of the Gideonite. He talked with Dr James Ross and after Ross had a word with Terry Howe offered them the joint job of Government Printer and editor of a new Government *Hobart Town Gazette,* with Howe's salary £300. In politics and publishing, Terry was his father's son. He found partnership between

Government and newspaper natural, congenial and profitable. The status quo was safe and sound.

Ross, a doctor of law born in Scotland tutored Arthur's children from early 1825. A letter to a friend suggests his acquaintance with fiction: *'I teach my own children, nine in all, at the same time that I write paragraphs [for the Gazette]'*. When Ross walked into the *Gazette* office in mid-May 1825 seeking type and a press, Bent offered him equipment to print a Journal the size of the *Gazette*. Ross said James Neil, a young Arthur favourite whose father had run a printing house in Edinburgh, could be the printer. Terry Howe had turned down the chance. Despite the £300 the offer in Bent's eyes was temporary because it depended on Arthur staying in power. Then Howe changed his mind, he and Ross accepted the offer and the *Gazette* editor, Evan Thomas, said in a remark that both the journalist and the reader knew was false, and also true: 'we announce the fact [of the new newspaper] with considerable pleasure.'

Police Superintendent A.W.H. Humphrey gave Terry Howe 'Runaway Notices' offering rewards for men and women gone bush; he published names and descriptions in single-page supplements. For apprehending *Matthew Brady, dark brown hair, blue eyes, 26*, convicts were offered free pardon and passage to England. The directors of the Bank of Van Diemen's Land put the price on Brady's head at $70.

In Arthur's mind the affinity between journalism and bushranging was natural. Bent was up to his ears in it. In 1818 he published the book *Michael Howe, the Last and Worst of the Bushrangers of Van Diemen's Land*, by Thomas E.Wells. Every gentleman knew a journalist after a story was a burglar. And the biggest story in Van Diemen's Land in 1825 — bigger than the settlers urging trial by jury, bigger than blacks' vicious attacks on settlers and whites' murderous responses, bigger than taxation without representation — was Matthew Brady, bushranger.

The question whether a man could call his tongue his own in Van Diemen's Land came before the Chief Justice, John Lewes Pedder. Some who saw the Court as political theatre found Pedder a Tory and strict constructionist to whom metaphor was alien. Arthur found him 'so tedious and minute that life is too short to wait for his opinions.'

• • •

For eight weeks from 25 June 1825 Hobart readers had dual-identity journalism, two identically named and numbered *Hobart Town Gazettes*. The first impostor carried a letter from A Colonist, mocking Robert Murray's column with every stab at the Governor reversed to praise.

Bent's trial began on Tuesday 26 July before a packed public gallery. Attorney-General Gellibrand uttered the prosecutors' aphorism: he was 'a friend rather than an enemy to the true liberty of the press', a glorious liberty to which they owed all other liberties.

The case turned on the question that fascinated, irritated then bored citizens for nine months: what did 'Gideonite of tyranny' mean? A witness for Bent said: 'I think it is absolute nonsense. I cannot understand it to mean anything. If it said "Caligula of tyranny" I would know what it meant.' So a man who loved the printed word was driven to calling testimony that what he published was absolute nonsense.

Gellibrand thought the meaning clear:

> It is obvious that it was intended to describe Lieutenant Governor Arthur as a tyrant. A tyrant he would have been if he had ordered a body of soldiers to take away the defendant and his press! ... But how does he act? He does not even put a stop to this paper ... He allows it to continue.

Gellibrand said '*If the Lieutenant Governor is to be called a tyrant with impunity, there is an end of our liberties.*' If Bent could publish that Arthur was a tyrant it would not automatically convince people Arthur was Napoleon, but it would imply that Bent, being free to speak was also free to act. There was the trouble. Freedom would be a contagion.

Pedder told the jury fair and temperate discussion of public issues was permissible, but if a person imputed wicked or tyrannical motives to 'an officer of such high rank as His Honour the Lieutenant Governor', it became a libel. The Chief Justice did not trouble to pose as independent. The prosecutor had so ably made the case that by saying more 'I really fear I am weakening the strengths of [his] arguments.'

The Clerk of the Court read Bent's written defence.

> In defending myself, I shall occupy but little time.
>
> I am a plain man, accustomed only to the active duties of my business. The articles were printed and published by me, and nothing more. I believed that I could [rely on] the discretion of the gentleman [Thomas] whom I employed. I addressed a letter to the Attorney General, in which I undertook to give up the authors. I never had the remotest intention of printing a libel and if I had even understood that any part of the matter charged was libellous I never would have printed it.

The military jury convicted him.

Murray was outraged. The Attorney-General would make a beautiful speech about freedom of discussion and end with 'that dreadful but—that terrible word which precedes a position both undefined and undefinable'. It was impossible for an independent printer to keep clear of the incomprehensible vortex of the law of libel.

When Bent appealed on the grounds that he had been convicted of composing, printing and publishing the libel but there was no evidence at all that he had composed it, the Chief Justice accepted the argument and upheld the appeal. The law made the editor a fake and the judge a lackey.

Six days later Bent appeared before Pedder on eleven charges of criminal libel. Truth was irrelevant. The first, an editorial of 18 February, said that though power not allied with virtue 'may strut and fret its hour upon the stage' it would surely be followed by 'abasement and remorse'. The second was nearly identical, with a difference only in the innuendos (the meanings the prosecution attributed to the words). The third and fourth were struck out because of defects written by the Solicitor General, Alfred Stephen. The fifth, by *A Colonist* on 25 February, scorned sinecures:

> Why, Sir, more places have been created since the departure of our true friend, the late Lieutenant Governor Sorell, with larger Salaries tacked to them, than are considered necessary in New South Wales, where the population of Sydney alone is nearly equal to that of our whole island! And the best joke is, that these places are all comfortable sinecures! Nothing for the worthy Gentlemen to do.

The sixth, seventh, eighth and ninth counts were abandoned. The tenth was for an editorial on 20 May:

> It is much better that a few supine, ignorant and extravagantly hired Public Officers should be galled for their misconduct, than that a whole community should be crushed, enslaved and subjugated. The truth is that the Colonel [Sorrell] well governed this island with a fixed and amiable view to its elevation — that he reasoned before he presumed to act. Have the merchants been insulted? Have public judgments been set at naught, and public feelings been violated? Has proper intercourse between the governed and the Government been rudely curtailed or unwisely interfered with? These and numerous other truly caustic questions might be now advanced. Nevertheless, as our Monarch's delegate may yet become more popular, if he will condescend to learn wisdom from experience we shall at present abstain from saying much which, though deserved, might convey offence

Thomas, saying 'our pen is loyal and shall ever remain so' asked if the *Gazette* should show loyalty as the *Sydney Gazette* did, by offering editorial 'sugar-candy' to abject functionaries and criminals. The editorial, properly attended to, would erect 'a shrine of respect for Lieutenant Governor Arthur' in the heart of every honest colonist.

> In The King v Bent on 1 August 1825 Attorney General Gellibrand addressed the seven-officer jury for two hours. I admit most distinctly, that the Editor of a Newspaper has a right to discuss public measures of every sort. But in so doing he must limit himself strictly to policy. For if it goes further, and attributes corrupt motives, it is a Libel. It is impossible that the Government of any country can be charged with acting tyrannically and oppressively, without such charge being a Libel.

He found the debate on sinecures disturbing.

> There was a warm controversy in this newspaper between writers signing themselves 'Q', 'A Colonist' and 'Common Sense'. The grand theme was sinecurists. I wish to know where these sinecurists are. I suppose I am called one of them.'

The jury found Bent guilty. Murray was not prosecuted.

Bent, awaiting sentence, stopped the charade of the two *Gazettes* and started *The Colonial Times,* edited by Robert Murray. Arthur was riding high: in two months he had had Bent twice convicted of seditious libel and Thomas sacked as editor. The Government *Gazette* was in the Tory hands of Terry Howe and Robert Ross.

It was far from enough.

In mid-September Arthur complained he was 'entirely at the mercy of the printer'. Robert Murray was writing vile untruths that the Governor was 'helpless to contradict'. 'I am beset with difficulties and quite at my wits end,' he wrote to Under Secretary Robert Wilmot-Horton on 14 September 1825.

The core of his troubles, he said, was Attorney-General Gellibrand, still intimate with Robert Murray, who visited Murray at his house, talked with him about his column and even allowed Murray to sit next to him in court.

> Although I still think that every vicious character in this Colony should not at his own pleasure be allowed to establish a Paper and become the Organ of Public Morals and independent principles, yet I am now more at my ease, and advert to the subject only in explanation of the absurdities which have appeared seemingly 'under authority' during a period of eight or ten months in the Hobart Town

> Gazette. But now comes the acme of my troubles. Will you believe it possible that the Attorney General, an officer whose constant aim it should have been to aid the Government and suggest improvement, if he saw aught that was wrong was in close union and daily communication with [Robert Lathrop] Murray. There is nothing so difficult to prove as a fact that is notorious. And even if it could have been proved, what was to be done?

After the conservative Alfred Stephen resigned as Solicitor General, saying it was impossible to work with Gellibrand 'whose political relations and private practice I consider inconsistent with the honor and dignity of his office', Arthur asked Pedder and two JPs to investigate eight charges against Gellibrand, the first being his open association with Murray (the rest concerned professional conflicts of interest). Arthur told Gellibrand on 11 September 1825:

> 'The question [for] the Government is not whether your conduct has been strictly professional or legal, but whether it has been honourable and upright. The impression has long gone abroad of your connexion with an Individual who has been the known systemic opposer and calumniator of the Government.'

A conservative Governor and Solicitor General were aligning against the liberal Attorney General whose criminal offence was friendship with a liberal editor. On September 20 Gellibrand told Pedder he declined his invitation to attend tomorrow's Commission hearing as it was 'neither legal nor constitutional'. The Attorney General did not 'consider his private conduct open to the investigation of *any man*;' as for public conduct, 'he courts any public inquiry'. The Commission met in a room in Pedder's house, public and press excluded; Murray thought it a Star Chamber.

When Gellibrand said he would submit to the Commission if Pedder could show it was grounded on a particle of law, the Chief Justice responded: 'It is not our duty to do so.' Arbitrary power remained in reach.

By November 28 Arthur saw in the Press the roots of bushranging. 'The cause of outlawry and violence is to be found in the factious principles disseminated in the colony through the medium of a licentious Press.' Convicts, predisposed to evil, were 'unable to draw the line between liberty of writing and liberty of acting'. Seeing the Government insulted with impunity led them to the delusion 'that resistance to the constitutional authorities might prove successful.'

Pedder and the JPs reported in December that Gellibrand continued to associate with Murray not only after he knew him to be A Colonist, but also after he knew that fact was so widely known it was notorious. This encouraged Murray and Government critics who would 'naturally conclude that they may safely vilify the Government when they see the Attorney-General thus publicly countenance the notorious author of such writings'.

When he reported to Arthur on the Church Establishment and Schools in Van Diemen's Land on 13 February 1826 Archdeacon Scott thought it his duty to remind the Governor of the fundamentals, vile abuse of freedom of the press, itself among the greatest of God's blessings on mankind, among them.

> How far the promulgation of blasphemy, resistance to the Government and countenancing all the lowest vices of mankind, even to the justification of adultery, with a ridicule upon our religion and its Ministers, can be construed into the benefits of a free press, I confess with all my veneration for freedom of discussion and expression of opinions, I am unable to understand.

A cleric who would not allow a newspaper in his house said he revered free speech, regretted its abuse and only after detecting a defence of adultery in the press (he did not say where) asked authority to put on the bit and bridle.

Conservative ideology made Gellibrand's friendship with Murray itself seditious. The Pedder committee found him guilty of conduct not befitting his high office; he was suspended as Attorney General in February 1826, then removed. The noisy wine-lovers at Stodart's Hotel welcomed his return to private practice. One of his first clients was Andrew Bent, who appeared for sentencing for his second conviction on 29 March, after waiting seven months.

Gellibrand was less effective as Bent's defender than he had been as his prosecutor. Chief Justice Pedder, saying it did not matter that Bent was not the author, for there was little difference between the person who made the poison and the one who disseminated it, sentenced him to three months' jail and a fine of £200.

When Bent was tried again for the Gideonite and Honduras libels two weeks later on 15 April, Gellibrand argued that had he been prosecuted on publication in October 1824, Bent would have sacked Thomas immediately, then published cautiously; he was a victim of delay. Acting Attorney General Joseph Hone implied Arthur was responsible. The delay had various causes: 'It would be unjust to some of the first persons in this island if I were to say more.'

After deliberating an hour, the jury found Bent guilty of the Gideonite libel, not guilty of the Honduras libel. On 22 May he was sentenced to another three months' jail, to start when his current sentence expired, and fined £100. Pedder said 'I trust the sentence will teach the defendant not to be the tool of a faction of the very worst description.' Fines and fees totalled £518. Friends of the Liberty of the Press raised £250.

Journalists in London were outraged. The paper read most carefully by Lords and gentlemen, *The Times,* said: 'A judgment so long delayed could answer to no useful end.' The sentence was 'so tardy as to amount to torture', and so irregular it was an 'outrage'. Arthur continued to believe that in a colony alive with bushrangers, where the Aborigines remained indifferent to the gift of the white man's civilisation and the government had been 'shaken by the licentious attacks of a radical paper', independent journalism would be dangerous. The men who argued for trial by jury, representative government and a press restrained only by law were common criminals.

Terry Howe and James Ross ended their partnership on the *Gazette* in February 1827; Ross became sole Government Printer and *Gazette* publisher and expanded the boundaries of self-contradiction. He approved newspaper licensing. Newspapers 'accused, judged and condemned honest citizens.' They were biased in favour of the one citizen in five hundred who would write and publish, and against the four hundred and ninety-nine who could not. His fundamental problem was that a newspaper not commissioned by the Supreme Executive Council and not hereditary lacked authority and therefore authenticity. A newspaper driven by printing, editorial and advertising skill was not legitimate. No trace of journalism spoiled Ross' newspaper: Government advertisements, tenders for jail repairs, the date and time of departure of the next mail ship to England were as near to news as he approached. Those who thought George Howe a stenographer had not considered the manacles a doctor of law could accept.

Governor Arthur's mistrust of public opinion fed his fear of the Press. 'I shall suspect myself, and you may therefore well suspect me also, if my administration be ever a more popular one,' he told Under Secretary Hay in January 1829. He struggled to overcome the fear, part of him believing God's plan included even journalists. 'There are weaknesses to every character. If we have not enemies to watch over and expose them, they would soon gain an injurious tendency.'

While editors, merchants, farmers, drinkers and optimists talked of representative government, trial by jury and freedom of the press, Arthur continued to see the island as a jail and his function one of spreading terror of transportation throughout England Scotland Ireland and Wales. Bent, with Thomas Gregson and George Meredith moved on. Gregson, popular, gregarious, a farmer who loved horse-racing and hunting with hounds, agitated for trial by jury and when Arthur revoked *The Colonial Times* licence organised protests and petitioned the secretary of state. Meredith had an inner need to walk to the edge. Serving in the marines in 1805 he climbed the 55-metre Pompey's Pillar in Alexandria to fasten a Union Jack in place of a Napoleonic liberty-cap. Lady luck smiled on him. He was away from home in Oyster Bay in

October 1825 when the Brady gang ransacked the house and kidnapped and killed a servant. With Bent and Gregson he hoped to make *The Colonist* 'unsuspiciously' advocate the cause of the people. The three believers in the people appointed Gilbert Robertson editor. Though the Friday weekly would be The Journal of the People, its slogan implied a well-understood limit: *England expects every man to do his Duty*. Robert Howe sneered in the Sydney *Gazette* when the Brady gang was captured that it would greatly diminish the *Colonial Times* subscription list.

Bent, hoping *The Colonist* would be zealously independent and patriotic, promised letter-writers to keep them safe from Crown Officers checking for libel and acknowledged that for editorial policy mere statements were 'valueless unless redeemed by practice.' The paper would be the 'only effective check on misrule and the only safe antidote to misrepresentation.' He sold it to Robertson who changed the title to *The True Colonist* For Truth, the King and the People from 5 August 1834 and, from 2 January 1835, Tasmania's first daily newspaper.

Robertson, born in Trinidad in 1794, embraced life. While muttering about Arthur's autocracy grew louder, he published four criminal libels, the first that Arthur, correcting a clerical error in a land allotment, made it a forgery, the second that Arthur stole government hay for his private use, the third a libel of a Hobart lawyer, W.T.Rowlands, the fourth that Arthur supplied his nephew, Captain John Montagu, with building materials on a back-dated letter of licence; Montagu had used them to build a splendid mansion.

Robertson, convicted of the first three libels, sentenced to thirteen months' jail and fined £200, then came before Mr Justice Algernon Montagu on the charge of having libelled the judge's nephew and secretary, John Montagu. By that time he was imprisoned in a cell above the guardroom at Hobart Jail, where he found two iron-barred windows his only comfort.

Justice Montagu took a whip to words. 'The licentious and degraded state of the Press is one of the worst features in this colony. It is impossible even to conceive any publication more infamous — more monstrous — more atrocious — than the libel which you have published upon Captain Montagu.' As for Robertson: 'I believe all you have said to be as false as hell and I believe you knew it to be so when you published it.' He personally cared nothing if the Press vilified him, for he knew his duty. But he was aware that other men bayed like dogs because of the newspapers. 'This colony is too much Press ridden and I wish all good men — I wish the clergy — I wish all Christians — would come forward and oppose it.'

So a judge sick with rage at newspapers said he cared nothing for the Press and asked all who believed in the Holy Trinity to oppose it. He told Gilbert Robertson: 'I consider you are a tool of a miserable party of agitated disturbers, by whose directions you have been acting … I once knew you to be a respectable member of our society, but now your writings are a pest even to Botany Bay.' Saying 'I perfectly forgive you,' the judge sentenced the editor to twelve months' jail and a £50 fine; this leniency was 'the last spark of kindness I have left for you.' Should he publish further libels 'I will imprison you for three or four years.'

The sentence finished *The True Colonist* as a daily. From 20 March, the paper reverted to twice-weekly, sometimes weekly, publication. Reformers met in the Argyle Rooms in September to form a Political Association. Henry Melville was secretary till the general meeting in October.

Melville sought in occult philosophy and astronomy the answer to the mystery at the heart of things. In 1830 he published *Quintus Servinton,* the first Australian novel, written by Henry Savery, whose character sketches of men who ran the colony enlivened *The Colonial Times* in 1828. Melville bought *The Colonial Times* in 1830 and *The Tasmanian* in 1831. Later that year, he and Robert Murray published the *Tasmanian and Southern Literary and Political Journal.* In May 1833 he published the *Hobart Town Magazine.* In 1834 he and Murray published the *Tasmanian and Austral Asiatic Review.* By October he was publishing the *Trumpeter,* an advertising paper, and writing histories of Van Diemen's Land and freemasonry.

Progressives who thought history was on their side formed the Political Association on 5 October to campaign for government representing the people. Within a month, the shadow of the law fell over Henry Melville. On 23 October Chief Justice Pedder sentenced Robert Bryan and James Stewart to death for stealing a heifer. In *The Colonial Times* of 3 November, Melville said Arthur had driven Pedder in Arthur's coach to Launceston for the trial; the Chief Justice and the chief executive were of one mind. The trial was a violation of British justice and a collusion between the executive and the judiciary. He believed Bryan was innocent and most colonists believed it too. Robertson, writing white-hot from Hobart Jail, called it a Got Up Case. When Melville came before him, Pedder, acting he said, 'as judge and jury in his own cause' sentenced Melville to twelve months' jail and a fine of £200.

Jail did not slow Melville's pen. In mid-December he finished an essay on prison discipline and a *History of Van Diemen's Land,* where he lamented Arthur's administration, hoping the next historian would tell a more agreeable story. Arthur released Melville at Christmas, saying his sentence was 'undoubtedly open to objection', and released Robertson a few days later when he heard his wife could no more abstain from alcohol than she could care for their children.

When news of Arthur's recall reached Hobart in May 1836, Robertson said it was 'welcome intelligence … [Arthur was] the patron of falsehood, hypocrisy and deceit—the protector of perjury and rewarder of perjurers.' About to board the boat home, Arthur was tempted to try the law again. Joseph Gellibrand was walking the streets of Hobart in June with a libellous placard saying there were still crawlers collecting money to buy a plate for the Governor who abused convicts and land distribution and authorised felons to break into settlers' houses. Some at the Executive Council on 13 June urged him to put the knot of libel in Gellibrand's tongue — but Arthur, fuming, refrained.

Robertson urged the colonists to give Arthur something symbolic of his administration, like 'a shivered fragment of crockery'. In *The Hobart Town Gazette*, Dr Ross remained an echo: 'Governor Arthur has made the colony.'

• • •

Born in London in 1813, John Davies drew his ticket to Van Diemen's Land by a conviction for fraud on 6 December 1830, arriving in Hobart in August 1831 when he was 18. A prison report said he was 'a bad character, audacious and impudent'. Released in October 1837, he joined the police in Sydney. As chief constable at Penrith in 1840, he married Elizabeth Ellis on 16 December, resigning three months later when his foster-brother Edward was hanged for bushranging, moved to Melbourne, reported for *The Port Phillip Gazette*, acted at the Pavilion theatre and drummed up support for another actor on the public stage, Judge Willis. After a spell as chief constable at Portland and Government clerk in Sydney he attacked William Kerr's wife in *The Port Phillip Patriot*. Publisher John Fawkner apologised for him; he was fined £15 for criminal libel.

The law as deterrent was ineffectual. In 1852 Davies took Elizabeth and sons George and Charles to Hobart, where he ran the Waterloo Hotel and started the *Hobarton Guardian* in 1847 which he incorporated in the *Hobarton Mercury* he started on 5 July 1854. In court or the street, he had to prevail. Hospitalised in 1852 after a brawl with another editor, he demanded compensation. A solicitor sued for assault. John Davies served a month in prison in 1860 for assaulting Samuel Hill, a *Mercury* political writer and brawled with two other journalists.

The tradition continued when he appointed John Donnellan Balfe *Mercury* editor in 1868. Davies required Balfe, an Irish-born state MP who had been Queen Victoria's bodyguard, to abstain from alcohol and vote according to his editorials. Mockers wondered which was harder, but he was dismissed after four months for drinking and in 1869 a select committee declared that tying an editor-member to consistency with editorials was a breach of privilege.

He ate competitors: the *Mercury* went daily in 1858 and by 1860 had swallowed four papers, *The Colonial Times*, *Tasmanian Daily News*, *Daily Courier* and *Hobart Town Courier*. Elected member for Hobart in 1861 he resigned because of a petition that he was ineligible because of his Government printing contracts. Next year he was elected member for Devon, a seat outside Hobart. His son George started at *The Mercury* as office-boy, worked as a journalist and rose with the buoyancy of the proprietor's son to general manager; Charles worked as an engineer in the Victorian railways and joined *The Mercury* as trainee manager in 1869. The brothers took over *The Mercury* in November 1871. John Davies died of a heart attack in Hobart on 11 June 1872.

• • •

Born in London in 1830, Henry Richard Nicholls migrated to Melbourne in 1853, went to Ballarat, joined the *Diggers' Advocate*, enrolled at the Eureka stockade and hoped to keep the red flag flying. Dismayed by the digger's want of discipline, he left before the revolt, organising a petition of amnesty for the rebels. Having seen a poetic possibility of a 'blaze around the earth', universal revolution, in *The Coming Hour*, he hoped the world title fight capital v labour could be settled, a win for both sides, by cooperative enterprises. He started the People's League, campaigning for the right to mine on private property but foundered on the diggers' indifference.

He feared ignorance in action, detested demagoguery, preached co-operation and believed in salvation by education. Free libraries could be classrooms. He joined the Ballarat *Times* in 1858 and edited the *Ballarat Star* as sole proprietor from 1875 to 1880.

Charles Davies appointed Nicholls, 53, editor of *The Mercury* in 1883 . 'The interests of society are less carefully guarded than those of the individual', he said, urging men to work in a 'lofty spirit' for Federation. Great things could not be done without great ideas.

On 7 April 1911, when he was 81, he published a leader *A Modest Judge* saying the President of the Commonwealth Court of Conciliation and Arbitration, Justice Henry Bournes Higgins, was 'what is called a political Judge, that is, he was appointed because he had well served a political party. He, moreover, seems to know his position, and does not mean to allow any reflections on those to whom he may be said to be indebted for his judgeship.' When Counsel in the Arbitration Court said Broken Hill labour organizations were 'the most tyrannical that he had known,' and added, 'moreover, they are encouraged by their Union and the Government of this country,' Mr Justice Higgins said: 'You are not entitled to speak disrespectfully of those above us.' Whether he meant that the Union or the Government 'is above us' is said to be some what uncertain, because as the Unions are supposed to rule the Government, it is held that they must be regarded as the supreme power, and must not be lightly spoken of, no matter what kind of language they may use themselves, *The Mercury* said.

Nicholls was charged with contempt. On 7 June 1911 the High Court decided there was no contempt. The Chief Justice, Sir Samuel Griffith, said: 'The only question for us to determine here is whether these words are calculated to obstruct or interfere with the course of justice or the due administration of the law in this Court.' It was impossible to answer *yes* to that question. No order would be made.

Mr Nicholls had properly expressed his regret for having used language said to be capable of being construed as disrespectful comment which he did not intend. He had properly withdrawn any such imputation. 'But that, of course, does not render him guilty of an offence which he has not committed.' In Hobart a reception at the Town Hall celebrated Mr Nicholls' acquittal and 28 years' service at *The Mercury*. Editors in Adelaide, Brisbane, Perth, Melbourne and Sydney telegraphed congratulations. Mr W. Gunn, of Duncarron, wrote that he had been on the staff of the first daily paper in Scotland 61 years ago; age prevented his attendance.

Mr Nicholls said to applause he had no doubt that 'the action of the Commonwealth Attorney-General, who thought fit to launch a thunderbolt at me, has something to do with this occasion. That thunderbolt has proved to be a kicking gun, which knocks the owner down and not the game.' The High Court had established a principle that would operate all through the Commonwealth. 'I am told by a very good legal authority that I am to be handed down to a sort of dusty immortality in the law-books, as the defendant in what will be regarded as a leading case, in which the King was evoked to crush an editor.' Judges on the Bench should be as open to criticism as any other person.

He died of pneumonia at his home in Battery Point on 13 August 1912, an unfinished leader on his desk. At *The Mercury's* 70th anniversary on 5 July 1924 the paper said it had been a 'news purveyor and guide, philosopher and friend to Tasmania.' In 1822 in London *The Times* reported that fifty British editors had been fined £10 as rogues and vagabonds for advertising foreign state lotteries. Only two years ago the United States Government ruled journalism a 'learned profession'. The world had moved. 'The journalist is coming into his own.' The editors hoped *The Mercury* was 'an organ of practical common-sense.' It had been in Tasmanian hands for 158 years when Rupert Murdoch bought it on 28 March 1988.

Chapter 7

Sedition in a Prison

1828–1831 **Edward Hall**, *The Monitor* and *The Sydney Monitor,* Archdeacon Thomas Scott, **Atwell Hayes** and *The Australian,* the **Rev. Ralph Mansfield** and *The Sydney Gazette*; Governor Ralph Darling, Chief Justice Francis Forbes, Justice James Dowling, Attorney General Alexander Baxter.

The most valuable of all liberties, that of the public press, does exist: the press is as free as air! Those who have made this concession have however the power of withdrawing it, and may declare that even this mighty advantage is unsuited to Australia.

Justice James Dowling, 8 June 1829 as he jailed *The Australian* editor Atwell Hayes for six months for seditious libel.

Audacious scribes! To such a height
Your factious frenzy's risen
I fear 'mongst convicts you'll excite
SEDITION in a PRISON.

Atwell Hayes, verse from Sydney jail, *The Australian* 30 June 1829.

Governor Ralph Darling feared newspapers would provoke mutiny in the Hyde Park Barracks, insurrection in the Essex-street jail. When he shared his anxiety with Lieutenant-Governor George Arthur, Arthur offered the thought that where editors spoke freely, archdeacons, brewers, constables, workers down to yardmen and zoologists, would act as if British liberty flowed in the Derwent. *Men who felt free to speak would feel free to act.*

Darling wanted to avert this catastrophe by shutting editors up, but tried to fob responsibility onto the government at Home. Then he proposed a Stamp Tax that would bankrupt *The Gleaner*, *The Monitor* and *The Australian* in a month or two. That it would incline the government to ignorance was irrelevant in Governor Darling's mind.

Edward Hall had moments of optimism when he rejected the Botany Bay grovel. 'Gaming houses and little hells and brothels are licensed in England,' he said in *The Monitor* of 5 July 1828, 'but what have we to do with the vices, follies, bigotries and old moral ulcers of England?' The same day he published of Archdeacon Scott that the character of a minister was as delicate as that of a woman. The first step from the path of virtue could seldom be traced.

The angered Archdeacon sought out Attorney General Alexander Baxter, who prosecuted Hall for seditious libel. At the trial on 29 September Hall told Justice Dowling and the seven-officer jury that bringing him before a Court for writing of the public actions of public men made a mockery of freedom of the Press. If what he wrote of the Archdeacon really was libellous, he must put his pen away. When a man accepted public office he knew animadversion would follow. Hall recommended that Scott be honest, magnanimous and humble. Let him say: 'I will put up with it.'

He might have been speaking in a void. The jury returned with *guilty* in less than an hour. Baxter told Hall he would ask for no punishment. Because of this Wentworth said in January 1829 when they returned for sentencing that it would be pointless, churlish, to try to arrest judgment. Then the judge astonished them, fining Hall £1 and imposing a £500 12-month good-behaviour bond. Another offence would ruin him. The editor said he would sooner leave his pen on the shelf than write as a sycophant. He advertised to sell the paper in January, February, March and April, but no buyer emerged: there was only one Edward Smith Hall.

Robert Wardell sold *The Australian* to Atwell Edwin Hayes with two staff, reporter Edward Ledsham and compositor Joseph Monks, both on tickets-of-leave, on 1 July 1828. Nine months later as Ledsham took notes in the Supreme Court before Chief Justice Forbes, a constable Lackey dug a truncheon into Ledsham's ribs. The reporter at first affected to be so professionally focused that he did not notice. Then, as the truncheon turned his ribs blue, he said he was too busy, he could not leave. Eventually forced to go, he asked two men to come with him as witnesses. One said he saw Lackey take the reporter to the Hyde Park Barracks.

Constable Lackey's boss, F. A. Hely, Principal Superintendent of Convicts, told Hayes if he did not surrender the compositor Joseph Monks he would be prosecuted for harbouring a prisoner illegally at large. Hayes ignored the threat. Chief Justice Forbes had ruled in the Convict Assignment Opinion of

3 October 1827 that a settler assigned a convict 'has a legal right of property in the services' of the convict. (Forbes did not say so, but the right was essential to slavery.) Accordingly, the right could only be withdrawn by legal process.

Between eight and nine at night on 17 March constable Lackey broke into Hayes' house, seized Joseph Monks and, said attorney W.C.Wentworth, over Hayes' protests and 'without warrant or any legal authority' forced Monks to the Barracks. When Hayes sued for damages, the jury awarded him £50.

Governor Darling revoked the assignment of Peter Tyler, *The Monitor* foreman printer, the same month hoping to inhibit Hall's capacity to 'disseminate poison.' When Tyler returned to the office to pick up clothes, Hall persuaded him to return to work. He was gazetted as illegally at large; the magistrates court fined Hall £3 for harbouring a runaway. In June the Supreme Court quashed the fine and awarded Hall £25 damages.

These illegal exertions cost the Government nearly £600. Sir George Murray, head of the Colonial Office, told Darling it was wrong to withdraw convict servants from newspaper proprietors merely because they criticised the government. The power was not to be used for political purposes; it was designed to protect convicts from vicious masters. Darling must refer such cases to the Executive Council.

Hayes was not inclined to self-censorship. He wrote in *The Australian* on 27 January 1829 of Sudds and Thompson that the House of Commons would decide whether *will* was to be substituted for *law* and whether an iron collar was fit for the neck of an Englishman. 'We can never believe that the author of Sudds' punishment ... is a fit person to rule over a British Colony.'

William Wentworth argued at Hayes' trial in the Supreme Court on 8 June 1829 that since each officer-juror was paid an extra 15s. a day, it was a gift the Governor had it in his power to *withhold*, or to *bestow*, a pretty addition to an officer's pay, equivalent to the full pay of a Major. Since the Governor was (formally) prosecutor, such inducement might interfere with the Jury, it was perfectly possible that it might; ergo the law and the Judges were bound to provide, as far as human foresight and wisdom could, against possibilities. Justice Dowling:

> [The U.K.] Parliament has assumed that the peculiar state of Society here renders it as yet unwise to impart to it trial by Jury and representative legislation. It is conceded however, that the most valuable of all liberties, that of the public press, does exist, that the press is as free as air! Those who have made this concession have however the power of withdrawing it, and upon just grounds, may declare that even this mighty advantage is unsuited to the atmosphere of Australia. This can only proceed upon a supposition that the laws now in force, have not the power of restraining the

> excesses of this popular right, or that its possessors know not how duly to appreciate its importance.

Justice Dowling declared the passage seditious and jailed Hayes for six months with a £100 fine, his surety of £500 and two others of £250 to be of good behaviour for two years. What *The Australian* published till 20 June 1831 would be the key to the good behaviour and the fate of the £1000. Supporters including Justice Stephen's son Francis, a barrister, paid the fine.

Hall's tone after Darling revoked Tyler's assignment was that of an editor who experienced pressure as summer rain. On 22 November 1828 he published an editorial saying Darling crossed the names of officers he considered too liberal or soft-hearted off the jury lists. People in Britain would think with 'favour and pity' of those convicted of libel by such juries. Chief Justice Forbes declared the sentiment seditious.

While Hall believed it was his duty to write the truth, they all said that. Hall went two steps further: he acted on it, and acted on it as he awaited trial for having done so. On 9 March 1829 *The Sydney Monitor* (Hall changed the title on 16 August 1828) reported that after Dennis McCue, an old Irish convict, had been discharged from prison under Supreme Court order, Frederick Hely, Superintendent of Convicts, held McCue in 'the putrid air of the barrack dungeon for six long tedious weeks.' (Hely was the main witness against Hall for harbouring Peter Tyler.) On 30 May 1829 he reported a convict saying Captain F.C.Crotty, the Commandant at Port Macquarie Prison, bought sows for £7 from a convict but failed to pay. Afraid of the lash, the convict did not demand his money and the sows grew fat on the King's corn. At trial Hall said he offered Crotty right-of-reply in the same issue; his only motive was the public good.

For the first time the judges divided on a major question of law. Trial by jury was also the main political issue in George-street, the Hyde Park Barracks and the Blue Lion. Forbes, Dowling and Stephen debated the issue late into the night in Forbes' chambers on Saturday 6 June and again on Friday 19 June; though they were warm with each other, their minds could not meet. Justice Stephen found it a violation of common sense and the soundest principles of British justice that a commander-in-chief could appoint junior officers as jurors in a case he prosecuted. And the UK Parliament had provided that naval and half-pay officers, outside the Governor's command, could sit as jurors. It could have been done in this case.

Forbes agreed with much of Stephen's reasoning. A jury of officers, he said in the nights in chambers, did not have a community of interest and feelings with the accused, that reciprocity of rights and obligations which was 'essential to the notion of peers or equals'. Officers were a small body, governed by laws peculiar to themselves and nominated by their commanding officer. They lacked essential qualities of a jury and could not give a proper 'verdict of the country.'

There he and Stephen parted company. In practice, Forbes said, he had tried many criminal cases with officer jurors and 'I can truly affirm that their verdicts have always been considerate and just.' Stephen voted for a new trial, Forbes and Dowling to uphold the conviction. In the court filled with those drawn to the theatre of life, including some who heard voices and some who hoped to find dignity in all those accused of offences in New South Wales, on 20 June 1829 with Dowling and Stephen beside him Chief Justice Forbes sentenced Hall to 12 months' jail for the Darling sedition, three months for his criminal defamation of Captain Crotty.

The raw sandstone, the iron bars, the mosquitoes which ate him alive, the grated window which cut his view of the sky into tiny squares, even the loss of liberty, undermined him less than the tedium. He relieved it by writing.

On 20 June, the day his sentence started, he published a long report on skullduggery by James Laidley, the Chief Commissary, in the Irish salt-pork tender.

The Australian published Hayes' verse from his sandstone cell on 30 June:

> Audacious scribes! To such a height
> Your factious frenzy's risen
> I fear 'mongst convicts you'll excite
> SEDITION in a PRISON!

Having convinced himself that Darling was guilty of at least a high misdemeanour, if not murder, in his treatment of Joseph Sudds, William Wentworth despatched a notice of impeachment to Sir George Murray, secretary of state for the colonies, on 1 March 1829. Truth had not been characteristic either of Darling's conduct as a man 'or of that system of misrule which comprises his public administration.' Sudds and Thompson, who had been convicted of petty larceny, were guilty only of trespass. Had Darling inquired into the suicides, maimings and thefts in the 57th Regiment he might have found them caused by discipline harsher than in other regiments. One ground of Wentworth's impeachment was that Sudds and Thompson had endured torture at Darling's order. Another was the use of irons unknown to law. A third was the drumming-out ceremony, a high misdemeanour.

In response ninety-five landed proprietors and merchants sympathetic to the Governor made an address in July. They had long observed the Governor 'grossly vituperated by licentious public writers in a manner calculated to inflame the minds of the lower orders and to produce discontent and insubordination among the prisoners of the Crown, for no other purpose than to promote the interested views of such writers.' They hoped the Home Government would appreciate the Governor's sacrifice of his health and comfort in discharging his arduous obligations. The political opinions of the opposition newspapers were 'not those of the more intelligent classes of the community.' Darling responded:

> The press has undoubtedly indulged itself to a most licentious and criminal extent in its endeavours to degrade the Government and excite public discontent. None but the ignorant, however, the slaves of popular clamour, have been deceived by the specious garb 'the freedom of discussion' which these writers have assumed. They are now making atonement to the injured laws of their country and justice is satisfied.

He was most gratified to hear them say that the politics of *The Australian* and *The Sydney Monitor* were not those of the more intelligent classes.

> These journals have laboured incessantly to propagate a belief that they are the voice of the public, well knowing that they are not tolerated by any man of character.

As long as His Majesty was pleased to consider his services desirable, he would be happy to devote them to the welfare of the Colony.

Hall reported from jail that the Colonial Secretary, Alexander McLeay, placed a fake document before the Supreme Court in the Jane New case involving the Governor's power to withdraw convict servants from their masters. Justice Dowling found this was true — McLeay wrongfully altered a date — but irrelevant. The jury took 'a few minutes' to find Hall guilty. On 21 November 1829 he published a letter saying slave-irons had been imposed on Joseph Sudds 'contrary to the eternal principles of justice and the law of England.' Had there not been a substitution of *will* for *law*? On 19 December the Supreme Court ordered forfeiture of Hall's £500 recognisance in Archdeacon Scott's case.

Neither Darling nor Arthur suggested that extreme measures against the Press might *unite* editors against a menace to the first freedom. Though editors faced the same problems in digging out and publishing news, and their work in writing, editing, publishing and distributing was as alike as blue gums to blood gums, they could not work together to defend the press. On Christmas Eve 1829 Hall complained that he had been in jail for nine months with six still to come. The Chief Justice sentenced him to another nine months, for the *will* for *law* letter to start when the current sentence expired, and six months for the McLeay libel, to start 'at the expiration of the former sentence.'

Mr Hall asked 'Might I ask in which jail I am to be confined?' Chief Justice Forbesreplied: 'In Sydney jail.' Hall walked back to the jail whence he had walked to court that morning; a man of principle did not require irons.

The Rev. Mansfield published the landowners and merchants' 4 July address to the Governor and Darling's reply on 7 July. William Wentworth, for Hall, sued for damages for libel. Mansfield's report of 'gross vituperation' and licentious writing was 'a cowardly attempt to deprive a fallen man of his daily bread.' Fellow-feeling for a brother-editor would have stopped him publishing so venomous a libel. The only question was the extent of damages for a dastardly attempt to injure a man 'already immured in jail'.

James Bradley, a school-teacher who visited Hall in jail, said the libel applied equally to the editors of *The Sydney Monitor* and *The Australian*: 'I think they have suffered equally for the public cause.' It was too much for them to endure both the punishment of the law and the lash of the press at the same time.

Mansfield's report included his deep regret that Darling had been:

> grossly vituperated by licentious public writers, in a manner calculated to inflame the minds of the lower orders of the community' against his administration, and to 'produce discontent and insubordination among the prisoners of the Crown.'
>
> The press has undoubtedly indulged itself to a most licentious and criminal extent in its endeavours to degrade the Government, and excite the public discontent. None but the ignorant, however, the slaves of popular clamour, have been deceived by the specious garb — 'the freedom of discussion' — which these writers have assumed.

Robert Wardell for Mansfield told the jury they all knew this was the land of novelties, but these proceedings were the greatest novelty the colony had yet witnessed. He could scarcely believe his learned friend on the other side (Mr Wentworth) when he said this was a libel of Monitor Hall. Was it not an advertisement [for the *Monitor*]?

> Gentlemen, instead of imputing very serious offences to the plaintiff, this publication was calculated to increase the circulation of his paper.
>
> I call upon you not to tie up the press altogether by countenancing actions of this nature. If they were suffered to prevail, no editor could put forth any article of news, however necessary it might be to publish it, without subjecting himself to the chance of a prosecution. At 6pm on 1 April 1830 Justice Dowling directed a special bailiff to lock up the jury and allow them nothing but candles till they reached

> their verdict, to be delivered to him at his house. At 10pm they found for Hall, 40s damages.

Robert Wardell on behalf of Wentworth asked the Supreme Court to compel Mansfield to show why an information for criminal libel should be filed against him. Darling said, and Mansfield published, that Wentworth's letter of impeachment was 'a gross and absurd compound of base and incredible calumnies' which provided 'ample means of judging the character and motives of its author.' Roger Therry, for Mansfield, on 3 June 1830 asked Forbes to admit the letter of impeachment, then circulating as a pamphlet in Sydney, in evidence. Forbes did not allow it, saying it would make the Supreme Court the medium of 'publishing criminal charges against the Governor who is not before the Court.'

The jury found Mansfield guilty. The Government editor who had accurately reported the address of the Governor's main supporters and Darling's response was guilty of criminal libel. He was fined £10 with costs of £69. When Darling told the Executive Council he had been acting as Government publisher and 'should be relieved of the whole of these expenses,' the council agreed.

With Hall as plaintiff and accused wearing a track between the jail and the courthouse, publishing from a sandstone cell with the freedom of the wind, Darling on 27 January 1830 reached again for the gag of legislation and submitted to the Legislative Council a Bill imposing banishment to Norfolk Island for between two and seven years for a second conviction for sedition. The Council approved it two days later. Hall published the image of a coffin on 20 February 1830 saying liberty of the press, born under Sir Thomas Brisbane, had been strangled under Ralph Darling. 'I shall rise again.' He petitioned the House of Commons, saying Sydney editors would be more degraded than those in Rome or Petersburg, jurisdictions which did not pretend that the press was free and the censorship was open and unashamed.

When James Stephen saw the legislation in the Colonial Office in London he said: 'So long as General Darling is Governor of New South Wales it would be idle to hope for any moderation in the writers for the newspapers.' Darling had 'incurred very great unpopularity' and needlessly embittered colonists by a severe temper and ungracious manners. 'The practical effect of this law must be to silence every journalist who is not an avowed supporter of the Government.' He could not say whether so extreme a measure was inevitable. But unless the Governor could show such necessity, 'the Bill is indefensible as being in its whole frame and spirit, repugnant to the law of England.' The Colonial Office disallowed it.

On 17 May 1830 Darling wondered if he could silence the pestilential *Monitor* by seizing the press; Attorney General Alexander Baxter and Crown

Solicitor William Moore told him there was no legal power to do it. When Darling sought a second opinion from the judges; Forbes, Dowling and Stephen said the law officers were correct. When Moore prosecuted Hall on 27 September for publishing without providing sureties the jury quickly acquitted Hall because Moore neglected to prove Hall published the *Monitor*, Darling thought if this was not treachery it was evidence of Baxter and Moore's 'gross ignorance or neglect'.

Displaying a tenderness for Hall the man stronger than his anxiety about Hall the editor, Darling on 6 November released him from jail. Then the anxiety resurfaced. 'His sense of this act of grace, nearly two years of his several sentences being unexpired, is exemplified by his continuing his calumnies …,' he told Viscount Goderich on 17 February 1831.

When his letter of recall arrived on the Camden Darling gave the howl of a man wounded by events beyond his comprehension. There was no dissension in New South Wales, he told Goderich. No place could be more tranquil. All men and women appeared happy and contented. If he had made errors, surely allowances could be made. While he exerted himself to maintain His Majesty's authority, he had to cope with 'habitual drunkards filling the most important offices, speculators, bankrupts and radicals.'

Viscount Goderich had stamped the authority of his name on the 'gross calumnies which Mr Hall published against me.' With the fear of the printed word that distorted his Governorship, Darling marked its end. The endeavour to conciliate Mr Hall would not only mean 'the ruin of this Colony' but also 'ultimately lead to the destruction of every colonial Government in the British Dominions.'

23 October 1831. Glass lamps at *The Sydney Monitor* office spelled out: He's Off. At night the sky over the harbour was bright with fireworks; house bonfires lit blue gums and the Blue Lion. In the *Gazette* Ralph Mansfield thought the party at William Wentworth's estate, rowdy with men and women feasting at the famous advocate's groaning tables, was an orgy of the lowest rabble of Botany Bay. Not a gentleman would have been there. Common people could not resist a free swig at the bung-hole of a gin-cask. Atwell Hayes' *The Australian* reported free-thinking people burned and hanged the Governor's effigy in divers parts of Sydney. Darling, briefly dressed in authority, had been the 'tool of a junta of rapacious and despicable men'.

Freedom Lost: A history of newspapers, journalism, and press censorship in Australia.

Chapter 8

'I shot the doctor for your benefit'

1834: *Robert Wardell* is murdered.

The boys met by chance. When he first saw John Jenkins in the bush south of Cooks River, Emmanuel Brace turned to run, thinking Jenkins was a constable, but Jenkins told him he too was 'in the bush' and gave Brace a musket, they teamed up. Brace had gone bush when he discovered his master at Cooks River planned to charge him with insolence and disobedience. Jenkins told his new mate that he had escaped from the Georges River iron gang.

Three days later Jenkins cocked a musket at an old man and the pair stole fowling piece, sugar and clothes. They left the ancient bound hand and foot, made a raft and crossed the Cooks River into Dr Wardell's property at Petersham, where they built a bark gunyah and lived in it two weeks till a man with dogs and a gun disturbed them. Venturing into Sydney, they met Thomas Tattersdale, former chimney sweep, a life-prisoner known to the constables, near Cooper's distillery. The three entered a quarryman's house; Jenkins told him to lie down or he would knock his brains out. He handed over the key to his box and they took twenty shillings in silver, a towel, pair of scissors and three pounds of gunpowder.

Next morning, Sunday 7 September 1834, back at the Wardell property, the trio made a ring on a gum tree with a mark in the centre and shot at the target; Jenkins came closest. After breakfast they dozed in the gunyah. As they snoozed, Robert Wardell left his house, the Sarah Dell Cottage at Petersham, on a white stallion just after 12.45 pm; he was wearing a coarse cotton-linen jacket, blue breeches and a black hat, joking, good-humoured and pleased with himself; the groom noticed he had difficulty holding the snorting horse.

At mid-afternoon, Emmanuel awoke to see 'a gentleman on a white horse.' Dr Wardell asked Brace who he was, meaning was he a convict illegally at large, or was he entitled to be there?

Brace was silent.

The editor turned to Jenkins: 'Who are you?' Jenkins told him: 'I'm a man.' Wardell did not sense trouble: 'Who are the other two?' Jenkins: 'They are men also.'

Brace testified that Wardell bent, grabbed a stick leaning against a gum tree and gestured above his hat with it, as if signalling to others; the horse was restless, prancing about. Wardell said: 'You are only three poor runaways — you had better come along with me.'

Jenkins, a black silk handkerchief at his neck, picked up a rock and told Wardell to go away. Wardell said: 'Don't you do anything with that.' Jenkins whispered to Tattersdale: *get the piece*. Tattersdale hesitated, fumbled in the grass for the musket and stalled, thinking: so far it's fifty lashes. If Jenkins shoots him it's death.

Still Wardell did not react.

Tattersdale picked up the musket and stood hesitating. Jenkins shouted 'If you don't give me the gun I'll knock your bloody brains out' and snatched it. He strode towards Wardell, levelling the gun.

Wardell: 'What — are you going to shoot me? For God's sake don't do that!' 'By God I will' said Jenkins, and fired from beside the stallion's shoulder. The muzzle, Brace said, was 'not more than one yard' from Wardell.

Wardell cried 'Oh dear, oh dear, I'm killed'; his hat fell to the ground. The horse retreated a step or two then galloped over rocks into the bush, where Wardell slipped from the saddle, staggered a few steps and slumped over a fallen gum tree. Hunter Street surgeon John Neilson testified that the shot severed the left subclavian artery. A person would not live more than a minute after such a wound. *The Australian* reported the body was 'crimsoned over with his own heart's blood.'

By evening Wardell's neighbours and servants were alarmed. The groom thought he saw the white horse in one of the paddocks but the night was too dark and the bush too dense to tell; they stopped searching when the moon went down. Half an hour before sunrise next morning, a search party set out, found Wardell's hat at the bushrangers' hut and a few minutes later, his body. Blood saturated his clothes.

The Australian and *The Sydney Gazette* quickly despatched reporters to Petersham; both had on-the-spot accounts in their Tuesday issues. Both emphasized robbery was not the motive. *The Australian* reported 'eight and sixpence in silver and gold coin were found upon his person'; the *Gazette's* man said 'the deceased's watch and money were found on his person … Either plunder was not the object of the murderers, or fancying that they had missed their aim and that a pursuit would be instantly commenced, they fled with the utmost haste.'

The Gazette reporter's speculation was more accurate than many an eyewitness account. As Dr Wardell disappeared into the gums Jenkins said urgently they must go 'as quick as we can'. As they swam Cooks River, Tattersdale nearly drowned; Jenkins saved him. On Sunday and Monday nights they slept in the bush. On Tuesday morning Jenkins and Brace went into Sydney and ate a breakfast of chops, a loaf of bread and beer at the *Sailor's Return* at the Rocks. Gazing out the tap-room window Emmanuel saw images of home and freedom, ships in the Harbour; the name Black Warrior stuck in his memory. As he read of the crime in *The Australian,* under the headline *Dreadful Murder of Dr Wardell of Petersham*, he learned for the first time whom they had killed.

They rejoined Tattersdale, who was too notorious to show himself, in a paddock outside town, lit a fire and slept. Three days later, on Friday 12 September, *The Australian*, reporting Wardell's funeral, said that while everyone earnestly desired the speedy detection and punishment of his murderers 'as yet, however, there are no accounts of any clue by which they may be discovered.'

Troops from the 17th Regiment were posted along Cooks River; the Custom House boat at Botany was ordered to Georges River to help move troops and police for the manhunt. Governor Darling ordered special military parties at Liverpool and Sydney to help.

The boys knew their danger-point. On Friday evening John Chessney, a private in the Mounted Police, spotted Tattersdale in the bush near Cooks River and asked him who he was. Tattersdale said he was 'in the bush.' Chessney asked who was with him. Tattersdale at first denied there was anyone with him 'but afterwards,' Chessney said, 'admitted that there were two men lying in the scrub near [Judge Alfred Stephen's] house.' With a corporal, Chessney, guided by the reluctant Tattersdale and one of Judge Stephen's servants, found Jenkins and Brace lying in the scrub near Liverpool Road. 'We presented our carbines at them and told them to surrender,' Chessney told the committal hearing on Saturday 13 September. 'They got up and held up their hands and we took them in custody.' The police found a musket, a fowling piece and a canvas bag full of ammunition.

Jenkins fascinated newspaperman Edward Hall. He reminded the crusading editor of another boy in the bush, twenty-three-year-old Jack Donohue who had been shot dead at Bringelly four years before and whose spirit was caught in a song with an Irish melody, a song banned singing in any public house, on pain of loss of license.

Hall the portraitist in eight-point Roman, saw Jenkins as 'bluff, jolly, square-faced [and] rather *good* looking.' The jury, after a retirement of perhaps two minutes — the door barely closed, *The Australian* said — found Jenkins and Tattersdale guilty. They were asked if they had anything to say, why sentence of death should not be passed upon them.

Jenkins had rivers of meaning to spill. He had not had a fair trial. A bloody old woman had been palmed upon him for Counsel. He did not care a bugger for dying, or a damn for anyone in court; he would as soon shoot every bloody bugger in court. *The Australian,* edited by Wardell's radical successor, A.E.Hayes, thought 'b—-y b—-r' and 'd—-n' went quite far enough in print; at the *Monitor* Edward Hall printed one 'b—-y' and a 'd—-n'.

Chief Justice Forbes donned the black hat saying he had no clemency to exercise, he had only to pronounce sentence according to law that they be taken to the gaol and thence to the place of execution on Monday morning, there to be hung by the neck until they were dead. Their bodies were to be delivered to the surgeons for dissection.

Jenkins said he wished to confess to several robberies to save innocent persons from punishment.

The Chief Justice told Jenkins to apply to the clergyman of his religion for anything he might have to communicate of that kind.

Suddenly Jenkins struck Tattersdale two 'tremendous blows' to the face, knocking him down, then struggled violently with the guards. Forbes watched as if struck dumb. *The Australian* said it took a dozen constables to handcuff him; he was dragged into the street ranting against the judge, the jury and all humanity.

Next day, Jenkins asked to see the gaol Governor. He drew a plan of the courtroom and said 'just before me there were four military officers sitting, and a sword of one lay upon the table in front of where I stood; I measured my chances, made up my mind to the attempt, but did not like losing an opportunity of being avenged on Tattersdale, or else I would have jumped on that table fought my way up to the bloody judge and served him out; then you would have had some fun.'

A big crowd gathered at the scaffold on Monday morning to see him launched into eternity. Jenkins, arms tied, attempted to run up the ladder, affecting nonchalance. Hands untied, he tugged one of the three nooses. (The third was for a wife-killer). As Edward Hall watched he thought Jenkins not only hoped to show no fear: he felt none.

On the gallows Jenkins said: 'Good morning my lads — as I have not much time to spare I shall only tell you that I shot the doctor for your benefit; he was a tyrant and if any of you should ever take to the bush, I hope you kill every bloody tyrant you come across.' [*The Sydney Gazette* of 21 September 1827 called Wardell a 'tyrant, monster and scoundrel' meriting exemplary punishment.] He asked them to pray for him.

He declined to forgive Tattersdale, but after entreaties by a clergyman, shook his sobbing accomplice's hand. Hall heard him utter a shocking blasphemy: 'Don't cry lad, don't cry, we shall be happy enough in ten minutes.' The hangman pulled the hoods down and adjusted the nooses; the platform fell. They died, Hall said, with 'the usual muscular agitation.'

With all Wardell's convict servants in custody after the murder, the Solicitor General said an unnamed political party [the Exclusives] having a 'favourite theme that insubordination raged among the prison population … stupidly insinuated that the unfortunate deceased gentleman was shot by his own servants.' On the facts he was to submit, the jury would find they had 'no foundation whatever in truth'.

Nowhere was life as insecure as in New South Wales, the *Sydney Herald* said on 15 September. The vicious and disgusting system of convict labour was to blame. The *Herald* pointed the finger of suspicion at Wardell's servants, all held in custody. Atrocious murders of their masters by convict servants were threatening to destroy the colony. *Let Britain be her own gaoler, and no longer destroy our lives our liberty and our property by the annual importation of her bands of assassins.* Australians, like their American brothers, must annihilate the system. Dr Wardell's assassination had caused a great sensation in the public mind.

Freedom Lost: A history of newspapers, journalism, and press censorship in Australia.

Chapter 9

Faith

1835–1851: **John Dunmore Lang**, *The Colonist, The Colonial Observer* and *The Press*; **Edward O'Shaunessy**, and **William Watt,** *The Sydney Gazette*; **Henry Parkes**, *The Empire*. 1931–2009: **Frank Devine**, *The Weekend News* and *The Australian*.

The Colonist will not be sacrificed for the paltry consideration of gain.

The Rev. Dr John Dunmore Lang, The Colonist 5 March 1835

The power of newspapers is the power of song, the power of the ballad, which can be more powerful than the law. What is it that stays in men's minds, the Statute of Limitations or the Song of Solomon?

Henry Parkes, The Empire 3 May 1851

[Editing a newspaper] is itself sufficient and satisfactory evidence that an emancipated convict is not a really reformed character and cannot therefore be trusted [with] so dangerous an engine as the public press.

J.D.Lang, The Colonist 18 June 1835

The editor and preacher, Reverend Dr John Dunmore Lang, a flinty Calvinist of the Church of Scotland, wanted *The Colonist* to be more than a weekly journal of news reports, more than a secular pulpit. The press, he thought in April 1835, was the most powerful engine Almighty God ever enabled man to use. The French and American revolutions creating the new world gave the mechanical press inquisitorial power over public men, from monarchs to the meanest constable. There was no escaping it: the press was the Fourth Estate.

Born in Greenock on the River Clyde in Western Scotland on 25 August 1799 to William Lang, wood-merchant, and Mary Dunmore, as a toddler Lang dreamed of preaching. At five he said 'I am going to be a minister.' What would he say? 'I will say "... Sinners, be good and do good and ye shall be happy".' On the Clyde, in the Church of Scotland, at the University of Glasgow he attended from his twelfth year, Lang absorbed the principles of the one true faith.

On New Year's Eve 1835 he wrote a first-issue policy for *The Colonist; or Weekly Journal of Politics, Commerce, Agriculture, Literature, Science and Religion, for the Colony of New South Wales*. Newspaper policies show editors thinking of the core of our art and craft, catching and holding the reader's attention. Practised in puffing the public self, the editor creates a balanced journalist, judicious and unhurried — an impossibility: journalism is always in a hurry. The essence of Lang's editorial was to allow readers to believe Lang was on their side, or at least not hostile to what any reader held dear.

On that last evening of 1834 taking the first steps on his long journalism journey, he used the phrases 'useful knowledge', 'right principles', 'moral welfare', and 'the general advancement of the colony', inviting readers to fill the words, wineglasses of meaning, to their own taste. Aussie sceptics would raise a glass to useful knowledge, right principles, moral welfare and general advancement, then demand to know what Lang meant by them.

As editor and most-prolific contributor, Lang implied high-mindedness. He would not scour police reports to gratify prurience; those with tastes for boxing and horseracing would have to look elsewhere. He would not, he said, pollute *The Colonist's* columns with news contravening pure Christian morality.

In his thirty-sixth year, Lang the liberal editor burned with the energy and ideals of one just baptised in the craft. He was 'satisfied ... that the Press was the only proper instrument for its own purification.' In particular he strove to '*put down the Convict Press.*'

Driven by the perpetual hope that the next sentence might contain a spark of salvation, Lang wrote compulsively for *The Colonist* and the audience at Home. In a four-month voyage to England in 1833 he wrote by hand more than 800 pages for his two-volume *An Historical and Statistical Account of New South Wales*, later extensively reviewed, excerpted and used as a reference in *The Colonist*.

His news-sense made some wonder whether Lang was a journalist or *The Colonist* a newspaper. The front page on 12 March 1835, section headline

Colonial Politics, story headline *The Bible a Safe Book for Persons of All Ages and of Every Standing,* began with the news of Ahab, the King of Israel's campaign to take the Syrian city of Ramoth-Gilead. On 9 April 1835 a story lifted nearly 3,000 words from the Encyclopaedia Britannica. 'The word *newspaper* is properly speaking a misnomer' when applied to *The Colonist* he told readers on 2 April 1835. Its purpose was to 'elevate the intellectual, the moral and the religious character of this colony.' In this sense, Dr Lang pioneered the Australian impossible.

In his eyes *The Sydney Monitor, The Australian, The Sydney Herald* and the *Gazette* published 'worthless and pernicious trash', the 'disreputable and disgraceful', content of 'a prostituted press'. Lang's image of himself dealing with his four brother-editors was that of an upright shopkeeper thrashing street-fighting dogs, sending them yelping back to their kennels. That the dogs' interests were his escaped his rhetorical attention.

The Colonist of 7 May 1835 regretted 'ludicrous' typographical mistakes in the *Gazette* and suggested that the cause of still worse flaws in *The Australian* was that its printing office was flanked by hotels and its compositors and proof-readers were always 'half-seas over'. The *Herald* had fewer typos but that was only because the *Herald* largely comprised 'extracts from old newspapers and older periodicals' and compositors made fewer errors setting type from printed text than from original, hand-written, journalism.

When he came to their treatment of the Joseph Sudds and Patrick Thompson scandal, the *Gazette, Australian* and *Monitor*, the three divisions of the emancipist press, had stationed themselves on the highways of the colony for five years like a trio of blind organists, grinding away at the everlasting tune of 'Sudds and Thompson':

The Sydney Monitor editor was the 'master of the band' and many a delightful 'solo' did he play to his favourite tune; for

> Every scribe had his note, and I heard not a sound
>
> But Sudds, Sudds and Thompson, from morning to night.

Edward Smith Hall had written about nothing but Sudds and Thompson for years in a colony as interesting as New South Wales in the 1820s: he was unfit to be editor. Hall called himself a patriot, but 'the libellous representations in his worthless paper of our climate soil and society' had been published throughout Europe 'for the purpose of deterring reputable families from emigrating.' Hall called himself Protestant, yet the *Monitor* was the vehicle of 'the grossest libels on the Reformation that have ever seen the light in this colony.' The William Cobbett of Australia called the Campbelltown hills small mountains; he babbled of green fields like Falstaff in his last moments; he was in his dotage.

Lang believed barristers who took fees with both hands, preachers who became mere wool-growers, and journalists who conducted the press on mercenary — he meant commercial — lines degraded the community. *The Colonist*, published on Thursday, would be different. It would 'not be sacrificed for the paltry consideration of gain.'

If religious certainty made him despise currency, it also gave him a clear eye for a threat to independence. *'Pay me and I will puff you,* are the terms of the agreement between the high contracting parties, the advertisers and the press,' he wrote on 9 April 1835. 'Pity that justice should not be done to the public, or that useful and important information should be withheld from the community, for the sake of somebody ... who sells train oil and colonial tobacco ...'

Lang would break the unhealthy nexus between journalism and advertising by 'excluding advertisements ... entirely, and [printing] an additional sheet, containing nothing but advertisements, for extensive and gratuitous distribution.' He urged the reform on all newspapers; all ignored him; Lang cleverly ignored it himself. The advertising supplement would separate editorial and advertising content, but it would not stop tobacco merchants pressuring journalists to overlook smokers' cough. Nor was Lang's disdain for greed rigid enough to stop him publishing advertisements for Black Rappee Snuff, American Fig Tobacco and 'genuine Havannah, Manila Cuba, Chin surah and Sandoway Cigars.' He faithfully reported meetings of the Temperance Society, deplored the bullock-drivers' swearing and felt grief and disgust at the sexual promiscuity all around him. But he was not excessively Calvinistic toward liquor merchants; the first issue promised at 'very low prices' wines in 18-gallon wooden casks — Port, Sherry, Teneriffe, Marsala, Muscatelle and Cape Madeira. The Royal Hotel advertised brandy, gin, whisky and rum-shrub and sought two honest sober and capable waiters.

After six months *The Colonist* had 700 subscribers but Lang's desire to exclude ads was still frustrated. There had been staffing problems. Of three literary men he hoped would write for him he discovered just before the launch one had died, one had another job and the third was going bush. The ads helped fill the space left vacant by the missing literary men; besides, they helped meet the 'large expenses'.

Lang wrote signed and unsigned letters to the editor and paid close attention to that great news source, Dr J. D. Lang. Sometimes he hoped to make the reader smile. When *The Sydney Herald* asked him to pay advertising rates to reply to an attack, he said readers would appreciate the *Herald* editors' 'desire to do good, if they are paid for it'. He mocked 'comma and semi-colon criticism' and 'English on stilts'.

When others used the language of excess Lang used excess in reply. Disgusting expressions were heard on the lips of men, women and *children*. All except clergy were addicted to the evil and pernicious habit of swearing. Profane oaths and ribald jests made his blood creep. It was unmanly and degrading. The law should punish it 'equally with robbery or drunkenness'. Nowhere was the commandment not to take the name of the Lord in vain more profaned than in New South Wales, not even in America. Framing public conversation in black-and-white pushed Lang to purple prose, but it is hard to detect where the verbal certainty papers over doubt.

He applied the discipline of fact flexibly. He had been told, he said in the issue of 15 January 1835, no fewer than fifteen unmarried female convicts were confined to the Lunatic Asylum because of their disappointment at low wages. *He had been told*. The phrase signalled Lang's awareness that what he had been told might not be true. Still, he had been told it, and while he could not prove it to be true, on the other hand no-one could prove *the fact of the telling* was untrue.

Seven years earlier Robert Wardell considered the obligations to the reader arising from 'it is thought' 'it is said' when applied to Robert Howe on the *Gazette*. Howe published a rumour that Wardell had apologised to the chairman of the court of quarter sessions. There was not a word of truth in it, Wardell said. Were the learned chairman to solicit an apology 'we would sneer in his face'. Howe 'received on the wings of rumour' what he published. Wardell offered a character-reading: Howe was wayward, silly, violent and rude, untutored by experience, unrefined by reading. His low and vulgar journal was the product of a low and vulgar mind.

Lang had 'circumstantial accounts' of the ruin of 'several well-educated and highly reputable females' who had been 'unable to withstand the arts of accomplished villainy with which they were assailed on their arrival.' Hearing stories of a magistrate who boarded a female emigrant ship to 'select a concubine or two' he was sick at heart. He thought female immigration a moral and a spiritual danger to New South Wales, since the notorious preponderance of males, 56,000 to 22,000 females in 1836 mostly comprised convicts prohibited from marrying.

Lang's image of the emancipist editor was of a man with ankles still blue from double-iron fetters. Having 'no character of his own' he would, according to 'well-known principles of human nature', reduce all to his own level, make virtue vice, become a literary dictator and distort the characters of reputable men. He feared emancipist-editors would be more influential than pulpit or court, scatter firebrands, arrows and death and diffuse moral pestilence.

When it came to the man who personified this pestilence, Edward O'Shaughnessy, then editing *The Sydney Gazette* for Ann Howe, Robert's widow, Lang disposed of O'Shaughnessy by a definition. It was true, he said, that a convicted felon could serve out his sentence and become reformed. This was not the case with O'Shaughnessy. Why not? *Because he was an editor.* 'The voluntary assumption of the management of the press by an emancipated convict … is itself sufficient and satisfactory that such emancipated convict is not a really reformed character and cannot therefore be trusted … with the management of so dangerous an engine as the public press.' There was no hope for reform until the press itself was 'in the hands of men in whom the public could place confidence …'

Lang denounced O'Shaughnessey in passionate essays on *The Literary Profession, Or The Colonial Press* on 2 April and 21 May 1835. The Doctor thought the *Gazette* a low, villainous paper, though it was not the only one, publishing trash. The brazen O'Shaughnessey, 'just as bad at heart as he was when he was legged in Dublin' was one of those literary convicts whom Sir Robert Peel 'rightly considered far more dangerous to the reputable portion of this community than the poor Irish white-boy or English machine-breaker.' Where else in the Empire could a man who only yesterday was a transported felon edit a newspaper? The words pulled up a curtain on a Supreme Court drama: did the words defame the Irish poet?

O'Shaughnessey, for whom the juice of the barley was inspiration and trouble, had been assigned to Robert Howe, who gave him a job as *Gazette* general reporter and a home at the *Gazette* office in Charlotte Street. After Howe drowned in January 1829 he worked as reporter and sub-editor till Ann Howe appointed him editor in June 1833.

Whether O'Shaughnessey, who had a satirist's ear for the wounding phrase and a natural storyteller's way with words could edit a newspaper was one of the big political questions of his years as editor from 1833 to 1835.

The courthouse was crowded on 13 June 1835. Lang, believing the case involved 'a pure question of morals rather than of law' also believed he could not trust any lawyer to defend him on such a question. He represented himself. He knew the emancipist class was bent on his ruin, with money no object. In defamation, one of the most wearying, time-wasting, money- and emotion-draining suits known to common law, he took on the giant of the New South Wales bar, William Charles Wentworth, briefed for O'Shaughnessey.

For two hours Lang repeated his certainties. He had often been obliged to sit silent, his character traduced, his motives misrepresented in the press, 'without being permitted to say a single word for myself.' Why the preacher, editor, reporter, editorial writer, lecturer and author could not say a word was a detail to which he did not address himself. (In a typical aside in *The Colonist* of 26 February 1835, after saying he would not utter a syllable, he wrote two thousand words.)

Chapter 9 — Faith

In Sydney conversation a word occurred so often he found it disturbing. People spoke not of emancipists' *crimes*, but of their *misfortunes*. The euphemism appalled him. The Press was to blame. This was the natural result of *The Sydney Gazette,* the oldest paper in the colony, the only one published three times a week, coming under the control of an individual transported for his crimes — he meant Edward O'Shaughnessey — and another convict 'holding a mere ticket-of-leave.' He meant William Watt.

This showed New South Wales was the moral, as well as the geographical, antipodes of Great Britain. The *Gazette* had been the 'prime source of pollution and the chief cause of the degradation of the press in this colony.' Never subdued by self-contradiction, Dr Lang noted that after Robert Howe drowned, the Reverend Ralph Mansfield edited the *Gazette*, followed by the Reverend H.Carmichael, then classical professor at Lang's Australian College.

It was unnecessary for him to detail the *Gazette*'s moral degradation, and he did not do so. Nor could he. He made it a rule not to read articles he found personally wounding 'nor even to look at the *Gazette* at all.'

As his address entered its second hour, Dr Lang satirically imagined a speech to the House of Commons suggesting that when New South Wales had a House of Assembly, the 'thrice-convicted felons of Norfolk Island and Moreton Bay' and the inmates of His Majesty's prison at Newgate, be represented.

> 'In an age like the present, in which the press claims for itself a species of absolute domination over all interests, over all classes of society, over all men' did not the public interest demand that editorships of newspapers be protected from emancipists?
>
> 'If a judge acts corruptly, he … may be impeached. If a barrister or attorney acts corruptly, [the Court may] strike him off the rolls.
>
> 'But if the Editor of a newspaper acts corruptly—if the director of the public press disseminates opinions that are subversive of the peace, and ruinous to the morals of society—by what law shall we bring him to justice? At what bar shall we impeach him of his moral incompetency?'

Lang's answer:

> 'It becomes the duty of every honest man … to impeach that [editor] … at the bar of public opinion, as I have done the plaintiff in the article for which I am called to answer this day.'

Lang believed in exposure. In his eyes, his libel was itself an exposure of the enormities of the emancipists. He detested the law of libel, believing that a man's reputation was not a matter for lawyers. An honest man hearing the cry 'ruffian' as he walked the highway would walk on, knowing the epithet did not apply to him. But Sydney editors who heard 'ruffian' would stand with ears pricked like horses. He believed in democracy. There was the trouble. He also believed in authority. As he cited in fluent Latin lines from Cato's advice to the Roman Senate, it was not given to the Reverend Lang to see that the law which called an editor to account was the very law which demanded his answer that day, the law of criminal libel.

Lang ended by comparing his scourging of O'Shaughnessey with Christ's purging the temple of thieves. Christ had not politely requested the unworthy to leave the temple. He had made a whip. Lang believed he had been following Jesus' example. In the last year of his life, he remembered the speech as 'the death-blow' to the 'convict Press'. It had caused a 'great moral revolution'. Reporting the effects of his work, the editor-preacher was as authentic as a lyrebird.

Lang was committed for trial for criminal libel, but O'Shaughnessey dropped the case and left the *Gazette* to work for the *Sydney Herald*. William Watt, entwined in Ann Howe's affections, was left in his place. When Lang heard Watt had asked the Attorney General to prosecute *The Colonist* for describing him as dangerous, unprincipled and subversive, and reprinting a report of Watt's trial for embezzlement, on the grounds that this would impede Watt's reformation, again Lang's view was black-and-white. Watt's ticket should be cancelled. Moreton Bay or Norfolk Island was where he should be. (Instead he lived in Port Macquarie, where he married Ann Howe, drowning in the harbour on 30 January 1837 when his boat capsized on the trip back to his farm.)

Lang's weekly *The Press* (January-August 1851) expressed sincere regret on 19 February 1851 for having wronged Thomas Icely, a wealthy landowner, stockbreeder and conservative whom the *Press* accused of fraud in selling the *Midas* in which Lang and Icely sailed to England in 1824. The story was false: Lang, published a 'well-known' rumour without checking. Why was he such a stranger to doubt? Doubt, the journalist's friend, counsels reporters and editors; doubt says *check*. Lang had so many truths to reveal he sometimes lacked time to listen.

The Chief Justice, Sir Alfred Stephen, jailed Lang for four months on 24 April for criminal libel with a fine of £100. More than two thousand supporters paid 1/- each to cover the fine and lawyers' fees. Lang said the wrong he had done Mr Icely, an appointed Legislative Councillor who never opened his mouth but was 'always ready' to do the Government's 'dirtiest work' sat lightly on his conscience. Serving the sentence sat just as lightly. The Parramatta prison Governor gave Lang his best apartment, with a garden; Lang found it 'spacious and comfortable'. The four months' enforced leisure allowed him to research and write a new edition of his history of New South Wales. An artist painted a portrait; ladies said he must be a handsome man.

In the apartment, proprietor Lang scribbled furiously to *The Press,* published by John Joseph Clayton, printed by William Nation, about *The Recent Trial for Libel*. While it was occasionally the misfortune of writers for the Public Press to fall into mistakes, it was also their misfortune when they did so to be judged not on liberal, humane and Christian principles, but on 'cruelty worthy of the dark ages.' In London *The Times* editor had been imprisoned for two months in Newgate prison, for what benefit he could not conceive. When he came to his own prosecution, Lang, writing anonymously from Parramatta prison, filling page one, said he, Lang, 'had made himself obnoxious in certain quarters as a friend and advocate of the rights of the people. The political character of the prosecution was notorious.' It was obvious from the 'extreme petulance and acerbity' of the Chief Justice. It was also evident in 'the want of anything like common courtesy' Sir Alfred evinced to Lang.

Stephen, who had been Governor Arthur's Attorney General, thought the press, like the people, required guidance. He brought an unprecedented prosecution for criminal libel, a libel of himself, against Nation and Clayton, who served one month's jail. Governor Charles Fitzroy thought the prosecution, 'scarcely compatible with the dignity and character of the Chief Justice'.

The law and the Chief Justice could no more discourage Lang than they could silence a kookaburra. On 23 July he wrote from Parramatta that if there was an Augean stable in the colony, it was in the Supreme Court, where functionaries could 'make what they like law.' When friends suggested asking Governor Fitzroy to shorten his prison term he refused. 'I would much rather [serve out the term] than be obliged to the unprincipled people who are in brief authority,' he wrote to his wife on 26 June. Their time, like the devil's, is but short'.

He was projecting. *The Press* last issue on 6 August acknowledged donations of £99/13/6 to Dr Lang's legal expenses and invited further contributions, the costs having 'considerably exceeded' expectations. After his release on Sunday morning 24 August he travelled to Sydney by carriage, preaching in the evening to a packed Scots church. He told Henry Parkes on 10 November no newspaper run by negligent drunkards could succeed.

Reading Lang today is tiring, partly because he was never one to give the reader a break and because of his self-absorption (a London reviewer of his *An Historical and Statistical Account of New South Wales,* published in 1834, suggested a new title: *The History of Doctor Lang, to which is added the History of New South Wales*. He was the editor and principal writer for *The Colonist* (1 January 1835-31 December 1840), *The Colonial Observer* (7 October 1841 – 30 September 1843) and *The Press* (1 January 1851 – 6 August 1851). He established the Australian College, won the Port Phillip seat in the Legislative Council in June 1843 and campaigned for Port Phillip's separation from New South Wales, denouncing taxation without representation and suggesting freeborn Australians might follow the American revolutionaries. He campaigned for Federation and an Australian republic, founding with Henry Parkes the Australian League to nourish and engender support for 'those great goals'.

The republic that Lang wanted, D.W.A.Baker notes in his biography *Days of Wrath*, 'could only be established by a revolution.' He was a Red Republican. In an age when no-one could be optimistic about their children's survival and everyone had buried a baby or knew someone who had, Lang and his wife Wilhelmina Mackie, suffered more than most. They had ten children; five died. They bowed their heads and accepted the loss of the little ones.

He ironed himself to Calvinism. When he published his 1828 pamphlet *Narrative of the Settlement of the Scots Church,* Lang described a Presbyterian missionary, James Elder, as a 'renegade missionary'. Elder sued for libel. Lang called another missionary, John Eyre, as his witness. Eyre testified that Elder had beaten a native in Tahiti with a stick; the jury awarded damages of one farthing. For Lang there was no going half way.

• • •

Twelve multiple-offenders working as lumpers aboard the *Governor Phillip* seized the brig several miles off Norfolk Island in 1842. A guard was thrown overboard and drowned. Another was badly beaten about the head with a piece of firewood. Soldiers and crew were driven below and convicts controlled the deck for half an hour. The master shot the ringleader, the rebels lost heart and the military retook control. During the affray or *after the vessel was retaken*, the *Colonial Observer* reported, the soldiers shot five convicts. The six survivors were brought to Sydney to face charges of piracy and murder. Against one, the Attorney General did not proceed. Another, who had helped save a soldier, had his sentence reduced to transportation for life. The other four were convicted and hanged.

Lang was angry. While it was true a guard had died, no-one had been charged with the murder. What of the piracy? In Lang's view, convicts sentenced to life imprisonment had been offered a chance to escape 'through the gross and culpable mismanagement and neglect of their keepers', which they had seized 'against fearful odds at the peril of their lives.' It was not piracy. It was not a crime. 'It was the mere attempt of desperate men to break out of their prison; and as self-preservation is the first instinct of nature, such an attempt can never be regarded as criminal, in reason or in law.'

This was not rhetorical excess: he repeated it. 'In short, we regard it as no crime whatever for a criminal to escape from prison if he can.' The fault lay with those who afforded the men their chance to escape. The executions were vindictive. They were judicial murder. Lang mocked the Governor, Sir George Gipps, for employing convicts aboard the *Governor Phillip* when free mariners were available: Gipps sought glory in penny-pinching.

J. Moore Dillon, the Criminal Crown Solicitor, wrote to Edward Alcock, the *Observer* printer and publisher: *The Late Executions for Piracy* was a gross and unwarrantable libel on the administration of justice; proceedings for criminal libel would be filed in the Supreme Court. Alcock replied on Friday that the writer was prepared to accept the consequences, 'provided the criminal information shall be filed against [Dr Lang] and not against me, my only connection with the article having been that of printer and publisher.'

Lang published both letters in the Saturday *Observer* as part of an editorial *The Rights of Men*, which repeated the libel and denied there was a syllable in it to bring the administration of justice into contempt. Lang was going to the limit. But it was not just hubris and faith, it was also that before libel juries, Lang was in form. He prevailed against O'Shaughnessy. As defendant-editor, he lost against the Reverend James Elder in 1829 and against the Reverend Lancelot Threlkeld in 1836 when Lang spoke for five hours in his own defence, but both juries, having delivered judgment for the missionaries according to law, allowed their feelings to speak in the amounts they awarded: one farthing damages. When supporters passed the hat around to help Dr Lang pay the Rev. Threlkeld's costs of £100, the money materialised as if milked from a cash-cow: throughout his life there was a great pulse of public support for Lang.

Too much support, in the estimation of the Attorney General, Roger Therry. He found it too politically difficult to proceed against Lang. On 13 January 1843 the Attorney General was 'unavoidably absent' from *R v Alcock* because of his 'engagements in another case' the Solicitor General explained. The only excuse the printer could make was that the writer was 'out of his senses'. 'He cared not for his printer, not he, what he wanted was to discuss his new code of political ethics,' the Solicitor General said. Lang had asked what the electors of Camden would think of this attack on the liberty of the press. In this slip into bitterness, the Solicitor said, Dr Lang had exposed himself. 'The jury were of course aware that the Attorney General intended to contest the representation of the County of Camden, and this was an attempt to injure him with the electors.' He knew not whether any of the jury had a vote in Camden, but was not a man who conscientiously did his duty, notwithstanding any odium, worthy of their support?

Alcock's counsel said 'the article had been termed malicious and seditious and wicked and criminal', but nowhere was it said to be wrong. The Attorney General prosecuted the printer 'rather than condescend to enter into a moral controversy with the writer'. Were Lang in the dock he 'might perhaps have come off somewhat better.' There was a time, he said, when the British criminal code was called the bloodiest in Europe. It had been liberalized — but how? 'By the unceasing efforts of moralists, of philosophers, of writers such as the writer of this article.'

On 18 April 1843 Mr Justice Burton fined Edward Alcock £200. In the next *Observer*, 22 April 1843, in *The Late Conviction for Libel: To The Friends of Humanity in New South Wales*, Lang published the libel again, saying the Attorney General prosecuted Alcock the printer, not Lang the author because he 'despaired of getting a verdict' against Lang. The Attorney would not look the real author in the face. 'General Darling's Gagging Acts were nothing [compared] to this.' That it was done by a liberal was passing strange.

He wrote a torrent. In the *Colonial Observer* 17 May 1843 Lang excerpted from the *Sydney Weekly Messenger* five columns of Lang the newspaper historian saying New South Wales newspapers depended 'on the whims of a few extensive advertisers' and accordingly independence 'could hardly be looked for'. But with 'free representative institutions', public opinion that could not be suppressed would be created.

• • •

Newspapers taught political duties as well as rights. Through newspapers people acquired sound political knowledge and the risk of convulsion diminished. In the United States there were 37 newspapers before the revolution of 1775; in 1810, when the population was 7 million, there were 358 newspapers, one to every 22,000 people; in 1830 there were more than 800 newspapers, one to every 15,000 people. In Sydney and Port Phillip in May 1843 there were 18 newspapers in 'a population of a little more than 140,000 souls. This beats America hollow.'

At three public meetings crammed with applauding supporters in April 1850 Lang raved that an Australian republic was inevitable, it was the only natural form for a nation innocent of tradition — and the British would love it. A young intellectual ivory-turner and toyshop proprietor, Henry Parkes, wrote to Lang next day that no time should be lost, men were ready for the struggle; they should use the hammer while the iron was hot.

That was the Henry Parkes with the 'great man' view of history and the idea that preceded it: that Henry and Dr Lang were among the great. But there was another Henry Parkes, skilled, ambitious and practical, for whom the republic was rooted in the here-and-now. It would be voted in. It could be put to the people. Like Federation, it was a question of steps to be taken, one foot after the other.

Lang, a 'charlatan' to *The Sydney Morning Herald*, travelled to Melbourne in mid-May; *The Argus* thought his audience 'very numerous'; the *Melbourne Herald* dubbed him a 'disappointed demagogue and red republican'. Briefly imprisoned for debt in Melbourne, he returned to Sydney, stood for a vacancy on the Legislative Council and was elected on what *The Sydney Morning Herald* thought a day of 'public calamity'.

When he started *The Empire* on 28 December 1850 Henry Parkes, a poet who began his career in journalism as Sydney correspondent for the *Launceston Examiner,* hoped to make the paper liberal propaganda. He knew nothing of printing, composing, proof-reading, hot-metal setting or libel and next to nothing of advertising, selling and distribution, but found advocating a wide franchise and comprehensive education 'intoxicating'. He had failed in business as a Hunter-street fancy goods importer through what he thought of as 'precipitate zeal': if there was a chance of falling headlong in an enterprise he would be ready to have a go. He dreamed *The Empire* would be 'an independent power to vivify, elevate and direct the political life of the country.'

Rude energy drove everything he did. When ships from England brought the latest papers, *The Empire* had a whaleboat with a reporter and four fast oarsmen to beat *The Sydney Morning Herald*, sometimes reaching the ship miles outside the Heads. Hundreds waited outside *The Empire* office. Parkes worked through the night, went home with the sun in the sky and returned after three or four hours' sleep. '*The Empire* is carrying away all obstacles, it will soon be worth £10,000 a year,' he wrote his sister in 1853. The power of the press, *The Empire* said, was 'universally admitted in this age of newspapers. Indeed, it is impossible either to evade or deny it … The influence wielded by the Press, though silent and invisible at times, is all-pervading. It penetrates into every recess of public or private, official or social life. … It realises the old myth of the hundred-eyed Argus, with this difference—that the modern Argus is never caught napping.' The newspaper was 'the embodied force which moves this progressive age.' It combined 'the momentum of the steam-engine with the velocity of the electric telegraph.' Men who affected to despise the press, judges in particular, in fact dreaded it.

Gold was the big story. Servants were stealing blankets and shovels and taking to the road. They came from California, Melbourne, China, Gippsland, and Moreton Bay. Some saw it as a lottery, a chance that could put them on easy street. The realists played percentage: doubling the price of flour and rice, they made sure of their money. They would not get rich beyond the dreams of avarice—but they would turn a tidy profit without turning a stone.

Henry Parkes believed Edward Hargraves would change the course of the river of life in Australia. Gold would populate the country, build railways, plant cotton, keep sheep-walks safe and make a nation. Hargraves prompted Parkes to think of other great Australians and find them wanting. In Parkes' mind, the lion of Vaucluse, William Charles Wentworth was a passing storm compared to Hargraves; Dr Lang was deepening the waters of democracy—but Hargreaves was a revolutionary: he was changing everything.

As he reported the rush to the Ophir diggings on Summerhill creek near Bathurst — he estimated there were 2000 diggers by late May 1851 — Parkes was cautious of the power of the press. How would *The Empire* influence the biggest Australian story since the hanging tree? Friends said *The Empire* reports from the Ophir, largely reprints from the *Bathurst Free Press*, were 'inflaming the gold-fever.' Parkes sent Angus Mackay, later Bendigo newspaper proprietor and Victorian Minister for Mines, as special correspondent to Ophir. 'Bathurst is mad again,' said the *Free Press* on 16 July in a report reprinted in *The Sydney Morning Herald* on 18 July and *The Press* five days later. Men were quitting their jobs and running to hunt gold; chaos might come. 'Men meet together, stare stupidly at each other, talk incoherent nonsense and wonder what will happen next.' *The Empire* told the diggers the soil at Summerhill creek was 'pregnant with gold.' Parkes said that from British India, America, from China and the South Sea Isles, from Tasmania, New Zealand and continental Europe, adventurers would pour into Bathurst. Australia would become the theme of the writers of the world; capitalists would study it; it would be 'respected and honoured among the Great of the Earth.'

Though his prose was sometimes purple, Parkes' eye was steady. The gold panic would be brief. There was no need to urge caution on the banks. Friends told him greed and gold would lead to blood in the snow at Summerhill Creek. There would be murder. Wives and kiddies would starve in George Street while their frantic men pressed shovels into the Ophir. Winter was close: would he accept responsibility?

His friends did not suggest what he should do. Not to report the finds was impossible. He accepted what 'everybody knew', that news from Bathurst would mean people quitting jobs and rushing to the diggings. If Henry Parkes, editor, wagged his finger and warned the diggers that gold was a curse, the root of all evil and would ruin them, he knew what would happen: 'the diggers would laugh.'

While Dr Lang believed the press could change the world, Henry Parkes, faced with the pressing pragmatic particulars of the rush to Ophir, was realistic. 'We can neither foretell the future nor stop the torrent of events. It hurries us along, as well as others.' He would faithfully chronicle events. 'And we hope that we shall not be held responsible for future evils, because we did not indulge in homilies to which no-one would listen, and perpetuate platitudes at which everyone would laugh.' He quickly imposed rules. He would not allow contributors to 'use the paper for their own purposes'. He would not allow personal bias to colour reports of speeches. He insisted on facts as the basis for criticism; he respected private life. Soon he loved even the atmosphere in the editor's room.

Compositors were short; seventeen who stayed demanded extra money in January 1856, saying the Monday paper would not come out unless Parkes paid the extra. Parkes, thinking he faced 'absolute ruin' brought it out, half-size, with reporters who had started as comps and apprentices willing to scab. After this success, on the Monday he prosecuted conspiracy charges against the seventeen. Tried before the Chief Justice, Sir Alfred Stephen and Mr Justice Therry, all were convicted and sentenced to prison for up to six weeks. When he stood for Sydney in the first Legislative Assembly election in March the city walls were plastered with his infamous conduct in 'imprisoning the printers'; his liberal ticket won all four Sydney seats.

What drove *The Empire*'s coverage was that gold news had an urgency that pressed for inclusion even when Parkes could not authenticate it. He published rumour. 'A report was current last evening that a horseman had arrived in town with two shot-belts full of gold, but we could not trace it to any authentic source,' *The Empire* reported on 21 May 1851. Shepherds abandoned 30,000 sheep in the wild bush. The rush started as farmers were sowing: 'we will have no wheat' an alarmed Bathurst friend of a Sydney jeweller wrote on 18 May 1851. Bushrangers robbed two drays of provisions. Parkes' devil joined the rush on 20 May; *The Bathurst Free Press* reported that while Mr Hargreaves accompanied the Government geologist to the diggings and washed 21 grains of fine gold from a pan of earth with his own hands before the geologist's eyes, magistrates labouring with picks and cradles had no success.

When he read the Port Phillip press, Henry Parkes detected troubadours. The power of newspapers was the power of song, the power of the ballad, which could be more powerful than the law. What was it that stayed in men's minds, the Statute of Limitations or the Song of Solomon? Parkes doubted whether Melbourne could support four daily newspapers: in London, which had the world for an audience, there were only six morning and three evening papers. The Melbourne *Argus*, the *Daily News*, the *Morning Herald*, and the *Times*, formerly the *Port Phillip Gazette*, all looked to the establishment of a Legislative Assembly; each hoped its leaders would take the lead.

Parkes' *The Empire* and Lang's *The Press* sought advertisers among the rare radicals who were also men of substance, but the cooperation — some thought the word was socialism — they both espoused did not lead to a joint-venture newspaper. The liberal giants' fatal error was valuing purity of voice above survival. By 1857 Parkes was in debt for more than £53,000. He wrote his foreman 'I have no means of meeting the wages tonight; my reserves are exhausted to the last shilling' and suspended *The Empire*. He could not speak of it for more than thirty years. Among family and friends he banned the phrase *The Empire* from conversation. Seven years in journalism left the statesman wounded.

• • •

When he edited *The New York Post*, the struggling tabloid famed for *Headless Body in Topless Bar*, Frank Devine, a Kiwi-Australian, was attacked on television for publishing photographs of a mother whose daughter had been murdered. He replied that the *Post* was doing God's work. How? 'The pictures might attract strangers' prayers.'

Describing the incident in August 1995 in his tiny cluttered office in *The Australian*, Devine labelled his own argument 'unctuous and hypocritical'. Part of him believed it. He could switch quickly from talking as himself to talking of himself. Frank Devine, *Post* editor, says the paper does God's work. Frank Devine, looking at himself with the journalist's detachment, finds what Devine said unctuous. Then again …

> 'Even the fact of a nosey journalist caring may be helpful. When I was on television in New York and I was being assailed about publishing pictures of the bereaved, I had an inspiration and said it might help by attracting the prayers of compassionate strangers. And it does that. You've assumed some of the burden of sympathy and message delivery. That's probably doing God's work.'

Born on 17 December 1931 in Marlborough, New Zealand, to a 'hard-up' Catholic family and christened Frances, Devine thought the name effeminate and changed it to Frank, after his carpenter father. When he was fourteen his English teacher at Marlborough College read aloud an essay he had written and the class convulsed. Fifty years later he found the laughter 'gratifying'. He crafted his capacity to evoke laughter into a shining career in journalism — sequentially editor of the Perth *Weekend News,* the Australian *Reader's Digest,* Chicago *Sun-Times, The New York Post* and *The Australian,* Rupert Murdoch and Kerry Packer courted him.

He experienced no crisis of faith, no 'lapse or deviation'. Had he never found faith conflicted with what he had to do as a journalist? He laughed, a booming belly laugh. 'The requirements of my faith conflict with everything I do as a human being. There is nothing at all that has been loaded on by my being a journalist.'

Chapter 9 — Faith

Towards the end of two hour-long interviews when he is writing a column about words and two opinion pieces a week, he says 'if you don't have the audience of your weekly pulpit, journalism is a very good substitute. I really mean that. Journalism to me I suppose is a Mickey-Mouse priesthood.'

What of the real priesthood? Nuns 'and others' pushed him toward the cloth when he was a child, but he believed he would have been 'dreadful' as a priest. Chastity would have been too much; 'going beyond the self is the path of the saint'. He thought John Dunmore Lang's desire to improve moral fibre in New South Wales in 1835 was still 'a strong leitmotif in journalists serious about their work. We do a little bit and at least we've done our best. You never know ultimate truth and you never achieve ultimate perfection and so you take lots of good cheer from little bits. Or even the imagination of little bits.'

As editor he said he 'toed the Vatican line'. How? In Chicago, New York and Sydney the editorials he supervised reflected Catholic policy and 'less-than-blatant display was often my attitude to pro-abortion [news stories].' ... 'It is not ever an unpopular position to believe in something that transcends human reality. As a journalist or editor or columnist, you don't arouse much hate by sticking up for religion. If you are faking it of course that becomes obvious in a flash. But if you are on the level you are probably courting popularity rather than risking hatred ridicule and contempt.'

Before he finished high school, *The Marlborough Express* editor, Selwyn Vercoe, offered him a cadetship. He won admission to the University of New Zealand but at 17 found money more exciting. There was no local radio station; television was years away. In Marlborough the medium was *The Express*. It was *The Paper*, 'a big presence'.

Vercoe, a literary man, gave him reading lists, including the complete works of Richard Brinsley Sheridan; in carefully orchestrated conversations he would probe the young reporter's understanding and was 'huffy' when Frank neglected the reading. Each month the District Court came to Marlborough for two-day hearings and at 19 Frank was sent to cover it. He discovered he could memorise up to ten minutes of cross-examination and write it word-perfect in longhand in his notebook. He had to start writing within a half-minute and if he talked to anyone the recall would disintegrate: he saw his memory in flames. He wrote more than 3,000 words a day, a broadsheet page, without shorthand and did not remember a mistake.

He headed for England with a friend, ran out of money in Perth, applied for a reporter's job on the weekly *Western Mail,* and after five years on the *Mail* and *The West Australian* his talent marked him as one of those freaks of journalism whose work makes the reader smile. He married a reporter on the women's page, Jacqueline Magee, worked as foreign correspondent in New York, London and Tokyo for nearly ten years for the Herald & Weekly Times group and returned to Perth as editor of the Saturday afternoon *Weekend News*. Then the board sacked the man who hired him, the brilliant *West Australian Newspapers* managing director Jim Macartney and the light went out. He edited *The Reader's Digest* in Sydney, suffered a heart attack then accepted Rupert Murdoch's offer to edit the *Chicago Sun-Times*, then *The New York Post* in 1986. He loved being a 'prince of the city' in Manhattan but it drained him. On Sunday, his day off, he saw five movies to clear his mind of the newspaper detail that filled his consciousness to the point of collapse from Monday to Saturday. He returned to Sydney to edit *The Australian* in 1988. Murdoch, who had been impressed as much by his warmth as his editorial skills sacked him after fifteen months. Characteristically, neither said why. He wrote columns for 17 years and died on 3 July 2009, of prostate cancer his daughter Miranda said. At the funeral the priest said there would be a pack of cigarettes in heaven for him.

Chapter 10

Port Phillip Press Partisans

1829–1840 **John Pascoe Fawkner,** The Melbourne Advertiser and The Port Phillip Patriot and Melbourne Advertiser; **Thomas Strode** and **Phillip Arden,** The Port Phillip Gazette; **George Cavenagh,** Port Phillip Herald.

The light of learning will be carried into the remotest regions of the earth by the mechanical press and lead the savage of Australia, the heathen of every nation, to drink of the everlasting waters of salvation.

George Arden, editor, Port Phillip Gazette 29 May 1840.

The day is fast approaching when the press by inciting discussion will expose warfare as one of the almost incredible absurdities of a past age.

George Arden, 29 May 1840.

He lacked readers, printers, advertisers and doubt. With a tyro's chutzpah, John Pascoe Fawkner shipped a plough, horses and apple trees aboard the *Enterprize,* creaking through flat-calm Bass Strait on 6 August 1835, without type, a press or printer's devil. Fawkner dreamed under a leaden sky. He had started the *Launceston Advertiser* on 9 February 1829 and talked with Andrew Bent about a Port Phillip newspaper. At forty-two he was skilled, experienced, hungry and knew what he thought of as the 'mystic' art of printing; he knew deadlines, defamation and dropped fonts.

No adventurer hitching camels in search of an inland sea knew less about the way ahead. After the *Enterprize* left George Town on 27 July a gale forced it back. Wretched with seasickness, under pressure from creditors, he returned to Launceston — 'road very lonely and tiresome' — then bounced back to the ship a week later. Those with an eye for the inner man wondered if the turn-back or the bounce-back was the key.

Fawkner, small and wiry, had the energy of a volcano and optimism verging on insanity. Born in London on 20 October 1792 to Hannah Pascoe and John Fawkner, a metal refiner and fence sentenced in 1801 to fourteen years' transportation, he travelled with his parents and sister Elizabeth in David Collins' 1803 Port Phillip expedition of 300 which settled at Sullivan's Bay from October to March, pioneering marked by rancour, theft, mass protest, and brutal retribution. Two marines court-martialled for protesting took 700 and 500 lashes as the high-minded liberal Collins watched.

Chaplain Robert Knopwood, an Anglican aphorist with an eye for pretty women who found comfort in the bottle as much as the Gospels, tended their spiritual needs and a patch of cucumbers, melons and onions. The family, having heard the song of rainbow lorikeets as well as the 'death-like silence' of the Port Phillip bush, sailed for the Derwent River, Van Diemen's Land.

As a goat-shepherd alone for weeks in a sod hut on his father's farm at Glenorchy and as he worked an adjoining 50 acres Fawkner began to ask the question 'why?' of the way things were, the answers shaping his psyche as journalist, entrepreneur, politician and rebel. Then the ideas encountered authority.

Fawkner sailed his whaleboat on 15 April 1814, with eight English, Irish and South American convicts he hoped to liberate from slavery to Recherche Bay, 150 miles from Hobart. They felled blue-gums, sawed planks and twined stringybark rope, building a ship for escape to South America, sailed back to Hobart in early June and put to sea in the new lugger dubbed *Liberty*. Flaws in carpentry subverted their daring: in two days the blue-gum casks were leaking. Nearly out of drinking water, they anchored near the mouth of the Derwent River and six put ashore to liberate sound casks.

Officers aboard the government schooner *Estramina*, struck by the 'singular appearance' of the raw-eucalypt *Liberty* boarded and arrested the fugitives. Three magistrates including the Rev. Knopwood, sentenced Fawkner on 23 August 1814 to 500 lashes and three years' hard labour for having aided and abetted the attempt.

Fawkner, a 5-feet-2-inch rebel with long fair hair habitually topped with a floppy felt hat, provoked authority to the extremes with which it responds to reformers possessed of certainty. He thought flogging a punishment 'worse than death', which tormented the sufferer in mind as well as body. It should be 'blotted from the face of the earth.' After a reduced two-years in the cedar sawpits at Coal River, Newcastle, he returned to Hobart in 1816 to sell liquor unlicensed, cart firewood and timber and bake bread. In one deal the law caught him: a magistrate fined him for selling short-weight bread. In another, a peer defrauded him of £160 in a supply contract. Fawkner's response to a failed deal was to find the flaw, adjust the strategy and make another; the deal drove him.

With his 'guardian angel' Eliza Cobb he travelled from Hobart to Launceston in December 1819, sleeping under a cart with clothes, goods and Fawkner's means of survival, 'saleable commodities'. He could not tell the truth about Eliza. She was transported in 1818 for having stolen a baby. Fawkner would say for years he had chosen her from an immigrant ship. A man most thought honest but many found unreliable invented a story about his wife; he hid his core.

Fawkner supervised construction of the Cornwall Hotel — two stories, thirteen rooms, with accommodation for ten and a seven-stall stable — for £2500 in 1824. He thrived as publican, managed a horticultural nursery, ran a coach service between Launceston and Longford and taught himself the bush-lawyer's art, appearing as advocate in magistrates' courts for six shillings. No learned sneer or barbed insult troubled him. He grew tall in argument; angry words nourished him.

Seeing barbarism in the noose and cat-of-nine-tails, he attacked hanging and flogging, biased to the rights of man. In his eyes he was a partial journalist — partial to truth. 'It is the public duty of a Journalist to dispel delusion,' he said atop the editorial on 20 April 1829. Reaching this goal — one editor and reporter wrote the paper — meant, he acknowledged, journalists would make powerful enemies. But he sang the song of harmony in eight-point Roman. The *Advertiser* would never be 'prostituted' to 'scurrility, calumny or sycophancy'. The journalist's duty was to promote goodwill, not fan the flame of animosity. The main story on that first *Advertiser* day was the 'Exorbitant Price of Bread'. Though the price of wheat had fallen there was no corresponding drop in bread-price; the man who had sold short-weight applied the experience.

He reported four bushrangers, a sheep-stealer, highway robber, arsonist, bullock-stealer, dwelling-house thief, and two who had broken into their employer's store, sentenced to death. After seven hangings on 16 February and six next day, Fawkner thought it 'most melancholy, nay most appalling' that thirteen had been launched into eternity in 24 hours, all in 'sound health and most of them able young men.' None had killed.

His questions of the criminal justice system inclined to Socratic. What was the point of flogging? Who were best served — the believers in the whip, or those who never called the scourger? Who had the most runaways? Did men who behaved as brutes expect their servants to defend them against convicts driven to the bush by floggings?

Urging Governor George Arthur to record use of the scourge accurately, Fawkner had no doubt the tally would show three times more floggings perpetrated by 'a few great men' than all the rest. Gentlemen Van Diemonians despised cruelty to dogs while they laughed at cruelty to servants. He made the *Advertiser* a voice of emancipists and human rights. He sought transparency. 'We have to contradict the statement in last week's paper respecting the blacks being seen near the Cataract Hills,' the *Advertiser* reported on 23 February 1829. The original report was 'wholly without foundation'. The source was 'a drunken servant on the opposite side of the river.' The paper diagnosed the error. The servant had sought 'to evade punishment for leaving his master's farm without permission' and invented the kooris. Assigned convicts were outside the congregation of civilised discourse.

Press influence brought Alexander Pope's *Epilogue to the Satires* (1738) to his mind:

> Yes, I am proud, I must be proud to see,
> Men not afraid of God, afraid of me:
> Safe from the bar, the pulpit and the throne,
> Yet touch'd and sham'd by ridicule alone.

Those who thought the poor were immoral reflected the cant of the day. They should look at Lords and Archbishops. Satire was the strongest weapon against vice: those who dreaded no punishment still feared contempt. A satirist could be considered a 'supplement to the Legislative Council.' In frontier Launceston, 'that radical Fawkner' shook the branches.

Detained for debt by the Launceston sheriff after the *Enterprize* returned, Fawkner finally landed in Port Phillip on 16 October 1835. After attending the first Port Phillip settler funeral on 1 July next year he wondered 'how many more would be committed to the dark house within the next five years, how many will strong drink hurry there prematurely? I fear a great many.' The doleful thought triggered another: 'I hate the grave, let my mortal remains be placed on a pile of timber and reduced to ashes; this will prevent the loathsome worms from preying upon me.' Manic Johnny Fawkner was acquainted with melancholy.

Even sons of Britain would be feeble without 'that mighty engine, the Press,' Fawkner wrote in pen, in the first *Melbourne Advertiser* on New Year's Day 1838. Not only would the newspaper's intelligence enrich readers, he said poetically: the 'resplendent light' of publicity would shine on 'roads to wealth' for adventurers. He did not detail how the spotlight would cause coin to multiply in a speculator's purse; already Port Phillip's giant strides astonished neighbouring states.

Sydney journalists declined to be astonished. At year's end a reporter travelling from the capital said there was easy work for burglars in Port Phillip; break-and-enter in a town with four constables and seven hotels would be as easy as chewing roast potato. Old Sydney scribes looked down on frontier Melbourne. As Fawkner started to shape Yarra psychology, settler civilisation was too feeble to penetrate the bush let alone cross the Murray River.

A 'very small degree' of support would establish a newspaper, Fawkner the optimist said. Till then the handwritten paper would be an advertising sheet, given away. (A shadow fell between word and action: he sold up to 32 weekly handwritten copies — anonymous unacknowledged scribes helped — for a shilling.) In his diary, Fawkner characterised a regular at the Cornwall Hotel, the warm-hearted, abandoned Melbourne founder John Batman, as a cheat, illiterate and drunkard, 'King John the First of Port Phillip'. Fawkner, ever a stranger to objectivity, saw Batman in Bearbrass as a bore with a short pipe, drunk when he could get liquor and when sober 'a specious hypocrite'.

Fawkner was not deterred by the task of writing thirty copies of a four-page foolscap newspaper; he had energy to make bees look indolent and kept a free copy for reading in the taproom of Fawkner's Hotel in William-street (the first licensed premises in Melbourne) on a shelf in a window where the light was good. He advertised for cattle, cedar, windowsills and palings and turned a room of the weatherboard two-storey hotel into a library with English and colonial newspapers, books of history, theology, novels, poetry and a modern encyclopedia.

When the bone-weary explorer Edward John Eyre arrived overland from Sydney on 15 July 1837, he found the hotel clean and comfortable. A young historian, James Bonwick, wondered if any publican in the wide world associated the spirits of poets and philosophers with spirits in the bottle as habitually as the frustrated teacher Johnny Fawkner.

Amusing some, he angered others quaffing in the back bar by denouncing them drinking rum he sold them minutes earlier. After shipping 25 gallons of gin from Launceston he remarked prissily: 'if drunkenness is to be abolished, sports should be more frequently encouraged.' Those with an eye for the inner man saw the father in the son: booze had disintegrated Johnny's father. Fawkner contradicted himself; he contained multitudes; he had much to say. On those rare occasions he stopped talking, a contemporary said, he felt compelled to write. A cockatoo could no more stay away from a green gumtree than Fawkner stop scribbling.

Atop editorials, the first Melbourne newspapers printed principles that moved reporters to laughter over a pot of beer. After he bought a second-hand wooden two-pull press and waste type from a Launceston printer, Fawkner's *Port Phillip Patriot and Melbourne Advertiser,* first published in print on 26 February 1838, followed the misogynist Scottish Calvinist John Knox: 'I am demanded of conscience to speak the truth, and therefore the truth I speak impugn it whoso list.' (The impenetrable slogan had a long life and adorned *The Argus* in the 1950s.)

Authority was not ready to hear. 'Before Mr Fawkner can publish a newspaper, it will be necessary for the editor, printer, publisher and proprietor to make an affidavit before me in the form prescribed,' the Colonial Secretary told Port Phillip Superintendent, Captain William Lonsdale. The drama of press freedom in Sydney and Hobart became a bureaucratic quibble in Melbourne.

Londsdale suppressed the *Patriot* at the end of March because it had not the licence required by the Licensing (Printing) Act 1827 (UK). To acquire the licence, Fawkner had to swear affidavits before the Colonial Secretary in Sydney. The eloquent defender of the free press left his paper unpublished because a two-week trip was too much. For Yarra gentlemen who wondered how far the entrepreneur would go to fight for principle there was one answer: not to Sydney.

Fawkner's potential audience, among them carpenters, house-servants, bullock-drivers, stable-hands, parsons and impersonators rose from 224 in November 1836 to 3,511 two years later. Thomas Strode, an ambitious printer from *The Sydney Morning Herald*, saw the gum-stumps in Collins Street, said 'it is useless to establish a newspaper for black-fellows and kangaroos,' and prepared to return. But when William Rucker, agent for the Derwent Bank, and a merchant, John Hodgson, heard of the remark they sought out Strode and told him he was mistaken: there were many whites in Port Phillip and many more were 'certain to come'. They would provide job-printing — now contracted to Launceston — and advertising.

Strode, quiet and flexible, had migrated from England to Adelaide in 1836, then to New South Wales where he published the *Hunter River Gazette*. He would have a go.

George Arden, an articulate teenager, took stock overland on speculation from Sydney to Port Phillip and saw his opportunity. He returned to Sydney, head teeming with ideas for a newspaper to report 'the glorious tidings of such a splendid country to all the inhabitants of earth'. Arden loved Port Phillip and loved its prospects still more. An acquaintance introduced him to Thomas Strode, his ideological twin. Strode had prepared for the Sydney government a budget for a Government Printing Office in Port Phillip. Arden, an eloquent defender of the status quo, started the weekly *Port Phillip Gazette* on 27 October 1838 believing merchants were the heart of Australia Felix and survival was a business venture. Arden hoped to put before capitalists visions of riches 'unparalleled in the world.' His reticence as a gentleman and his instinct that it was prudent for an editor, especially a Tory, to keep his head down, brought him to one of the pillars of objective journalism. He would 'never thrust our private matters on the attention of the public.'

In inner conversation he wondered whether language was a human invention or divine gift; the scholar-believer saw God in the printed word. Printing 'appears to be the perfection of the human intellect, and by some has been referred rather to a divine than a human origin,' he told an audience at the Mechanics Institute on 29 May 1840. Every branch of science was 'increased and multiplied by the mechanical agency of the Press' which saved the light of knowledge to let it shine on ignorance.

He was also troubled. The press that spread the Gospels could also transmit atheism. It could serve lawlessness. While good and evil competed on the page, the day was fast approaching when the press 'by inciting discussion' would expose warfare as 'one of the almost incredible absurdities of a past age.' The savages of Australia would 'drink the everlasting waters of salvation.' The newspaper, a 'daily epitome of men and manners', imparted information alike to Queen Victoria's palace and the bushman's hut.

He did not allow his elevated views to distract him from what readers wanted. On 29 May 1839 he reported (no source) that in Boston a Siamese twin, Mr Chang, struck a gentleman. When the gentleman had Chang arrested for assault and battery, his identical twin, Mr Eng, threatened to sue for false imprisonment. The law could not be enforced. Arden thought it 'a singular and most difficult case.'

Characteristically, his reason for choosing *Port Phillip Gazette* as masthead reached into English history. When Queen Elizabeth opposed the Spanish Armada in 1588, he said, she caused to be published a newspaper to feed curiosity and allay alarm. This was the origin of the Government Gazette, which had ever since had the most 'salutary and constitutional' effects. Arden's boundaries kept his public persona from realising that 'government gazette' had become a sneer in the public houses of New South Wales.

Strode was a craftsman who made cheap type-cleaning fluid from she-oak ash, cut type fonts from kauri pine and invented an India-rubber press; he knew his place but also believed printing could be a step to transcendence.

After seven months with no newspapers — Fawkner supervised builders erecting his hotel and carted goods for immigrants and shopkeepers — Arden, owner-editor and Strode, printer and publisher, announced they would publish *The Port Phillip Gazette* at 8am on 27 October 1838. As they pulled the first proof, Strode saw the press-bed and part of the type had worn and sunk, leaving no print in the centre of the sheet. As he struggled to even the type Strode, beset with deadline tension — 'the newspaper business, unlike any other, has to be conducted against time ' — saw eager readers gathering at the

Queen Street office. 'White people appeared to ooze out of the gum trees in all directions.'

They were tired of waiting. Their eagerness, far from pleasing the printer, increased his anxiety. Fearing they would force entry, Strode barricaded the doors and windows. Finally he placed a blanket beneath the press-bed and saw to his 'intense delight' that this raised the type enough to produce a 'tolerable impression'. At noon they started printing. They did not step outside the office to sell the first copies: when they took down the barricades readers rushed them with shillings; subscribers pressed pounds on them. They had brought a list of 80 subscribers from Sydney and quickly expanded it to 300. They aspired 'To assist the enquiring, animate the struggling and sympathise with all.' Two weeks later Arden joined the Melbourne Club. His heart was with the squatters, 'educated, gentlemanly, intelligent' men, drovers and shepherds on a great scale, who were prepared to endure 'mere animal existence' to build a future.

Walking down Collins Street, Strode heard a shout to stop. Turning, he saw a man running after him, 'long hair in wild disorder'. Chest heaving he told Strode: 'This day six months, neither you nor your wife nor your children shall have a crust of bread to eat. Mind what I say.' Strode replied: 'Who are you? You must be mad or drunk.'

'I'll let you know who I am,' was the reply. Then, said Strode, 'he turned on his heel, hurried up the hill and vanished into a taproom at the top.' Startled storekeepers watching from their doors called Strode over and told him the madman was Johnny Fawkner. Surprised and stung, Strode could not decide whether pity or contempt was strongest in his heart.

He arrived at a popular hypothesis: Fawkner must have been 'possessed of the Devil' to use such words of an honest tradesman, his innocent wife and children. What caused the lapse? Fawkner sought to 'monopolise' Port Phillip newspaper publishing. To those who found this view rabid, Strode made a parallel reply: history depicting all character favourably would be 'a picture without shadows.'

• • •

The *Port Phillip Herald*, first published on 3 January 1840, editor George Cavenagh, another former *Sydney Gazette* man, hoped to be 'Impartial, not neutral.' The gulf between what proprietors said they would do and what they did made journalists laugh and readers reach for their whips. Cavenagh took the vow of chastity: he would not permit personal detail, private life, to be splayed in the columns of *The Herald*. He would notice 'measures, not men.' He would not dirty his paper or besmirch readers with tosspot gossip.

As he penned these delicate standards he was perhaps thinking of the fiery liberal Fawkner who later swerved and screeched like a sulphur-crested cockatoo, denouncing the 'ultra-democrats and stump orators' he feared could ruin the colony.

The alliance backing the *Gazette* was short-lived. By 11 April 1839 the banker William Rucker who had persuaded Strode to start the *Gazette*, charged his partner Arden with having published a vile and scandalous libel. The magistrate imposed a bond of £100 with two sureties of £50 for Arden to appear for trial when it pleased the Attorney General and dismissed Arden's counter-charge that Rucker had threatened to assault him.

By June the *Gazette* reported Melbourne thriving as Rucker had predicted: it was a sea-port rich in natural resources, commerce, population — 5,832 — houses, residents, property and wealth, second only to Sydney. Next month Arden the snob was sneering at his banker backer. He bitterly regretted having met Rucker. As himself 'a gentleman by birth, education, rank and character', he should not have stooped to meet a 'dealer in slops and spirits.'

When Arden moved back to Sydney in September 1843 he wrote 'nearly the whole' of *Arden's Sydney Magazine of Politics and General Literature* because he would rather trust his own talent than 'inflate the conceit of scribblers whose abilities are below mediocrity.' Who did he mean? 'Youthful, but especially native [Australian] writers.' The 64-page journal included biographical sketches of members of the Legislative Council, a weighty review of the new New South Wales constitution for elective self-government, an account of a steam-driven aerial machine and a list of names of insolvents. In the editor's address, Arden apologised for the magazine's 'frequent faults' and asked for readers' generosity; in 'little more than a fortnight' he had written, arranged, compiled and had it printed. He hoped Mr J.S.Prout's illustration, an ink drawing of the tank stream, would not damage his fame.

Covering the first sittings of the Melbourne Courts of Quarter Sessions, in May 1839, the *Patriot* was embarrassed. It quoted the fundamental principles of newspapers' court coverage citing an English judge: 'We administer the laws in the presence of the country through means of the newspapers.' Fawkner: 'The press is faithful to its trust — the Judges are faithful — and the people see through the press that they are so, and have implicit confidence in their integrity.' But in Melbourne there was a break in the circle of trust and confidence. Fawkner apologised for the 'scantiness' of the report on Arden's trial on Thursday 16 May for libelling Rucker (Arden was fined £50 and imprisoned for 24 hours.) The difficulty, Fawkner said, was 'our reporter got drunk and was very properly put into the watch-house.' He was consequently unable to report the Chairman's lucid and dispassionate remarks. The decision was 'very so-so.' John Wood, convicted of common assault on Dr Barry Cotter, the first

Melbourne surgeon and druggist had been sentenced to one month's imprisonment and a £100 fine, whereas for Arden's 'malignant and malicious' libel the penalty was much lighter — an injustice in Fawkner's eyes. A liberal newspaperman, believing in the free press, wanted the law to come down on a conservative competitor. Competition engendered by the primal impulse to be first with the news was winning against public interest in the full story.

Arden fought a duel with Dr Cotter, the surgeon who referred patients to himself as the town druggist, on the racetrack on 27 May 1839. At sixteen paces Cotter, trembling, fired at Arden, the shot coming as close as 'the palsied state of (Cotter's) nerves would allow'. Arden then fired away from the 'tottering' surgeon, an act of mercy the *Patriot* dismissed: 'We and the public generally blame Mr A. for condescending to stake his life against such an article,' the paper said, attributing the information to a 'confident' informant and heading the paragraph 'Wars of the week (weak)'.

Finding type hard to procure from the Sydney newspapers, Strode convinced himself the proprietors believed the prospects for a Port Phillip newspaper were 'chimerical' and Strode's attempts to buy cast-off type were a ruse to start another Sydney paper. Paranoid second-guessing was part of the business.

When he contracted a compositor from Sydney for 12 months in 1839, Strode at first found the craftsman 'exemplary', but later regressing to the bottle became 'insolent and disobedient'. At 6pm, hours before the paper could be put to bed, the man told Strode to 'get the paper out yourself the best way you can' and walked away. Next morning Strode issued a summons. 'Such contumacious conduct on the part of a workman could not be tolerated.' But the compositor was not ready to give way in the first Melbourne press industrial dispute. He hired an attorney to argue that because his duties required 'mental ability' he was an artist, not a workman, so the Masters and Servants Act did not apply. Strode could not charge him.

Strode called George Cavenagh, *Port Phillip Herald* editor, as expert witness. Cavenagh's evidence made the management position clear. 'A man might acquire the knowledge of composing without being able to read or understand the sound of a single letter.' The magistrates decided compositors were subject to the Act and liable to imprisonment with loss of wages for neglect of duty. They imprisoned the compositor for one month. When the craftsman returned to work Strode found jail had been as useful as usual: 'still perverse', the compositor was sentenced to another six weeks.

The *Patriot* published an open letter to Cavenagh from Melbourne compositors saying his testimony detracted from compositors and damaged the dignity of the printing profession. That praise as well as a pay-rise might enhance productivity was beyond Cavenagh's understanding but he worked like a navvy, bringing out 12 issues single-handed, setting every syllable, sleeping (he said) two hours a night for six weeks, picking up so many lines of type he abscessed his forefinger. It was, Bonwick said, a 'miracle of labour'; he did it 'without dummies and without delay.' A frustrated writer, Strode envied Arden's literary flair and believed his own capacity with the pen was stunted, but in journalism he was ahead of his time. The lightning speed of the telegraph in transmitting information was not its only merit, he said in 1869. He quoted a London report that the telegraph taught the 'much neglected art of *word pruning*.' If journalists had to pay for each superfluous word at telegraph rates it would be a blessing for readers and save 'reams of paper and gallons of ink.'

Rivalry quickly triggered verbal excess. When Strode offered one of Fawkner's pressmen a 10/- a week rise to shift to the *Gazette*, Fawkner 'reported' that two of Strode's compositors had been imprisoned, a warrant had been issued for a third and two had been threatened with gaol in the last five months. (He gave no names or offences.) Under the heading 'To the Printers of Great Britain and the Colonies' Fawkner said Strode had for so long 'domineered the White Slave population of the [Sydney] Herald office, Sydney, that he is oblivious of the rights and feelings of Freemen.' That Strode was an insensitive slave-driver was not his worst flaw in Fawkner's eyes: he was from Sydney.

The three editors promised well-mannered journalism, but found so little good in themselves and each other that courtesy eluded them. When Cavenagh, in *The Herald*, decried the 'deplorable personality and scurrility' displayed in the Melbourne press,' John Fawkner, *Patriot* proprietor, said Cavenagh had been editor of the 'most intolerant, bigoted and lyingly censorious journal in the colonies,' and was now 'the greatest disgrace to the Melbourne press.' *The Herald* was a 'truly despicable journal'. Cavenagh responded by publishing an extract of 'this elegant specimen of the polite literature of Australia Felix.'

The Herald, the businessman in Cavenagh said, would cost subscribers and advertisers the same as the other papers, one shilling per issue or 10/- a quarter, advertisements 3/- for six lines, 3d. for each extra line. The editors split the six days of the week available for publication, understanding that Sunday was the day for Christian virtue, not for buying, selling or reading newspapers. The *Gazette* published Wednesday and Saturday, the *Patriot* on Wednesday till 24 July 1840, then Monday and Thursday, *The Herald* Tuesday and Friday. *The Herald* and *Patriot* used the first all-iron hand Stanhope press, the *Gazette* the Columbian invented in America in 1813.

Cavenagh expressed his hopes for *The Herald* as visionary principle manacled to practical reality. He would not be partial. His 'sole aim' was a trifecta: 'Our country's our God's and truth's'. A trope guided his journalism. What did it mean? *The Herald* would be 'strictly Protestant in principle.' Editorially, Cavenagh was an anti-Catholic bigot: *The Herald* would 'nip in the hand every symptom of sectarian tolerance or priestly ambition.' He was also a pragmatist, survivor and Melbourne journalist. After hiring from Sydney William Kerr, a Scot with gout in his left arm and acid in his pen, Cavenagh lost Kerr to the *Patriot*, a loss he regretted loudly and often. Early in 1845 he hired a short, short-sighted, well-educated, energetic young man from Tipperary, Ireland, as reporter.

Edmund Finn, born on 13 January 1819, went to school in a 'broken-down two-room thatched tenement' with John O'Shanassy, later Premier of Victoria. Finn trained for the priesthood without taking orders, arriving in Melbourne on 17 July 1841. After he ran into O'Shanassy in Collins Street, Finn advertised in the *Herald* for employment as a private tutor in Greek and Latin classics, geography, English grammar and arithmetic, 'salary no particular object.' (As a favour to Finn O'Shannassy paid 10/- for three insertions.) He caught Cavenagh's eye with sharp paragraphs and poetry and took to reporting, he said, 'as a fish to water', quickly developing sources all over Melbourne. He knew every inhabitant, said a contemporary, and 'everything that was going on.'

He married Anne Riedy on 21 April 1849. After she delivered the first of their five children something happened and Anne became what Edmund Finn junior described as 'hopelessly and incurably insane.' Finn switched immediately and apparently completely from tavern carouser to teetotaler. His son said that in thirty years he 'never once flinched' from giving up drink. The genial, compulsive reporter, sometimes writing 'the entire paper from title to imprint,' stayed with *The Herald* from 1845 to 1858.

When a would-be politician with 'more bank-notes than brains' asked Finn in 1855 to write him a speech and teach him 'how to speak it properly' Finn told him not to make a fool of himself. The politician said his mind was made up. Finn set his price: £15/15/0 for the speech and £5/5/0 for the elocution lessons. Cash on delivery. The dyslexic, semi-literate politician accepted, paid the £21 and lost the election. Finn's account gives no hint of whether he thought well of himself for making the deal, but he was clear on one point: he was selling a speech only. There would be no *Herald* puffery.

In private a politician could seek a reporter's help. Superintendent Charles La Trobe put the public position in a letter to Governor Sir George Gipps in October 1839. His welcome had been 'as the papers would say *enthusiastic*'. Grave folk made grave addresses; the gay made bonfires and fired off fowling pieces. The lower class got drunk, prosecuted and fined—'all in my honour.' Then the second scene: 'The newspapers (I understand for I have not had time to read them) begin to give me a great deal of excellent advice.

It was beneath La Trobe, a poet-administrator who had written non-fiction books on Switzerland and North America, to read vulgar Melbourne journalism. A colonial leader who admitted noticing the same newspaper as a common man — even the *Patriot*, which called La Trobe 'our good genius' — would lower himself.

When George Arden published an elliptical reference to John Fawkner Senior's conviction for receiving stolen goods, John Junior gave a howl of pain. Describing Arden as 'the abortion who professes to conduct this degraded print [the *Gazette*]' Fawkner said 'if he [Arden] were a man he would step forward and prefer his charges against his nameless foe. He dare not.' Arden had been a guest in Fawkner's house for 'social evening refreshments'. He had used the library. Fawkner had loaned him English journals and allowed him to copy from his private journal. In return, what did this 'mean, reckless wretch' do? — 'Why, attempt to stab us in the back.'

When Arden said he conducted the only journal in Australia Felix Fawkner responded: 'We beg leave to tell him that he, George Arden, is the *only* journalist in the Colonies who has had the disgrace of being publicly expelled from a Club — the Melbourne Club.' Two weeks later Fawkner sneered that the 'pert boy editor of the *Gazette*' invaded privacy, trifled with the feelings of a wife and mother, violently attacked an auctioneer 'and even a poor baker'. Mr boy Editor, a 'self-dubbed gentleman' lacked the brain to compose these attacks; he had plagiarised them. The six-shilling advocate skewered Arden with the spite of insecurity.

Cavenagh, who gave him the opportunity of his life, did not impress Finn, who thought his editor 'utterly insincere', as hollow as a drum, lacking tact, budgetary discipline and managerial skill. In really dark moods Finn thought Cavenagh lacked backbone. Finn and Fawkner, the 'Neddy and Johnny' of Melbourne journalism, were given to insult as greeting. When he saw Finn approaching on Elizabeth-street Fawkner would say 'hello Papist pigmy'. The friendly Finn passed over 'Papist': religious tension rarely disturbed him, but he resented the diminution: Finn was five-feet-two; so was Fawkner.

On the street and in the newspapers, spoken and written Australian was becoming the language of insult. Gentleman George Arden sneered that the *Herald* was the product of a 'vulgar mind', edited by the venal George Cavenagh — who had once been a Sydney milkman. A *Herald* editorial was 'demented', the *Patriot* 'contemptible'. As an old man, Finn was still staggered at the venom of early Melbourne insults. The *Gazette* called the *Patriot*'s editorials 'tirades of a blathering old b—h'. The *Patriot* called *The Herald* a 'dung-hill cock' and *The Herald* called the *Gazette* a 'consummate ass'. They were, the old reporter thought, 'up to the ears in muck'. Competition was yielding the standards of the dung-heap.

When Finn reconnected with his school-friend John O'Shanassy who was not only Irish but also tall, Fawkner coined a new epithet: Finn was 'big Jack's jackal.' Finn thought the *Herald* 'a quasi-Irish organ'. Cavenagh distributed free copies of the first issue, Friday 3 January 1840, written and edited in a one-story, one-room tenement in Elizabeth-street, printed in a weatherboard Little Collins Street printery, to 'every respectable inhabitant of Melbourne and the adjacent country.' No doubt there would be mistakes [in distribution] till the news-runners became acquainted with the town; he craved readers' indulgence.

Fawkner stepped aside as *Patriot* editor in April 1840, appointing attorney J.P.Smith to the chair; Fawkner remained proprietor and frequent contributor. His father, now living in Melbourne, contributed what to Eddy Finn's eye were 'wild, incoherent' pieces under the by-line 'Bob Short'. A year later Smith became a police court lawyer and William Kerr editor.

Businessmen called a public meeting at the Lamb Inn, Collins Street, now draining drinkers from Fawkner's Hotel, for 4 June 1840 to urge the appointment of a resident judge. Cavenagh, reporting the merchants' consensus in the merchants' paper, *The Herald*, said Port Phillip was 'all but shut out from the protections of law.' But the editor and his trader-readers were less afraid of the winds that might howl down Flinders-street without the shelter of law than they were resentful of authority imposed from Sydney. A judge who imposed the law on quarterly visits from Sydney was an insult, Cavenagh said. Justice could not be confined by Sydney's purse-strings; the law was not a rabbit-trap for sale.

Writing for the people in the *Patriot*, Fawkner thought equality before the law was the issue. Because the Crown did not pay for defence witnesses to go to Sydney 'the rich guilty man may escape but the innocent poor man has no chance to disprove' accusations. If justice eluded men accused of robbery, it also eluded victims. A merchant robbed by a highwayman would do better to forget about it than 'neglect his affairs, absent himself for weeks from home and peril his life by two sea voyages' to testify for the prosecution in Sydney.

By that time the consensus in Port Phillip for a resident judge — they saw it as a step to separation — included all but those outside the law. Swindling debtors plagued honest trader-advertisers. Troubled by cheats, *The Herald* warned subscribers who had failed to pay 'times out of number' would have their names published; Cavenagh would see if shame caused gentlemen to settle.

When Alfred Arden, charged with supplying firearms to Aborigines, pleaded guilty and was fined £5, Arden, seeking acquittal in the court of public opinion, wrote to Cavenagh asking him to correct the story, for which there was not 'the shadow of a foundation.' Cavenagh published the letter — and with it one from the reporter, William Corp, who quoted the police office record: *'Appeared Alfred Arden, charged with giving firearms to certain aboriginal natives. Defendant pleaded guilty. — Fine £5.'* Corp, who turned out copy 'like a writing-mill' before the bottle turned his career to the wallaby track, said 'I should observe Mr Arden did not appear in person, but that a gentleman entered the plea for him.' Cavenagh was pleased to trip a bully.

• • •

The crow of bankruptcy never flapped away to the bloodgums. Subscribers paid late, advertisers resentfully. As agents, auctioneers and importers complained early in 1841 that advertising rates in Melbourne were extortion even by Sydney standards, rumours spread of a free advertising sheet to be got up by merchants associated with the Auction Company. Should this happen, Cavenagh said in a *Herald* editorial, 'The Press knows its power, *and how to exercise it too*, if called upon to act in self-defence.' Even *The Sydney Herald*, with circulation and advertising 'beyond all precedent', had increased rates. He was prepared to prove Melbourne rates were no higher.

Irritated by Arden's claims that the *Gazette* was 'the leading journal' in Port Phillip and Fawkner's boasts that the *Patriot*'s circulation was 'nearly three times' that of its competitors, Cavenagh on 1 June 1841 published circulation figures 'known to every compositor' showing the *Herald* with 666 subscribers, the *Gazette* 600 and the *Patriot* 420 (all published twice a week); Melbourne had 4,479 people, the Port Phillip district — what was to become Victoria — 11,758. The *Patriot* and *Gazette* each sold 50 casual copies, *The Herald* eight. 'Thus it appears that *The Herald's bona fide* circulation is 132 copies weekly more than the *Gazette*'s and 492 more than the *Patriot*'s.' Edmund Finn said 'in 1841 the three Melbourne newspapers were not far apart, as *The Herald* circulated about 700 copies, the *Gazette* 650 and the *Patriot* 600.' These tiny circulations, were, Finn said, keeping the three papers financially afloat. Wages were low, employees few.

Editorial staff comprised the editor-manager and one reporter, paid about £3 a week. Compositors too earned £3 a week. Thomas Strode advertised on 20 July 1839 for a compositor 'if a good hand and can work at Press' 50/- a week and 1/- an hour overtime. The *Patriot* would pay steerage from Van Diemen's Land or Sydney. By 25 September he was offering 60/- a week to two SOBER compositors. Those 'in the habit of working one week and DRUNK the next need not apply.' He offered free passage from London as well as Sydney, Hobart and Launceston.

When the papers had no money — reporters said they were 'in Queer Street' — reporters and compositors sometimes waited weeks for their wages. Cavenagh's *Herald* was the exception, Finn said: George always paid 'every farthing' of wages on Saturday. 'The rhino was there.' The auctioneers who dominated spending on newspaper advertisements were 'on the whole liberal and impartial' between the three papers. Cavenagh, with the astigmatism afflicting editors scrutinising their own sales figures, invited readers to reflect on how the 'personal abuse and low scurrility' of the *Patriot* and *Gazette* had helped the *Herald* to circulation 'unprecedented in the history of the newspaper press'.

He published *The Herald* on Tuesday and Friday mornings; after noon on Monday and Thursday no advertisement could be withdrawn, but 'fresh ones will be received until six o'clock'. No verbal communication could be attended to. He would not receive letters with postage owing.

After a year Cavenagh believed the Melbourne Press would bear comparison with that of any British colony. He had volunteered his services as a journalist in the cause of Australia Felix and spared neither trouble nor expense in reporting 'the latest, most interesting and important information'. Sometimes the yield was sparse. On 6 May 1840 *The Herald*'s Launceston correspondent said: 'I have nothing of importance to communicate this week.' Cavenagh published it.

George Say, a retailer short of cash, threatened a libel suit when Cavenagh reported the shortage on Friday 14 May 1840. On Saturday Mr Say at a public meeting accused the editor of blackest malevolence. The report was 'false and unfounded'. Mr Say went over the top. His language, *The Herald* reported, 'would have disgraced an iron-gang man'. The cool Cavenagh said Mr Say was squandering money on libel lawyers that he should have used to pay his debts. He was attempting extortion. His dishonoured bills were flying about Collins Street. Cavenagh cared not three farthings whether or not Mr Say proceeded with his action. 'No jury that ever entered a jury-box would give a verdict against us.'

Say's Cheap Emporiums was a substantial *Patriot* advertiser; double-column display ads offered cayenne pepper, ginger wine in three-dozen cases, black silk Norwich shawls and other imported goods 'much cheaper' than hitherto possible.

When Fawkner reduced advertising rates on 13 May 1839 from 3/- for six lines to 2/- and for 3d per line to 2d, Say was among the first to take advantage of the one-third reduction, offering 'The only good CHEESE to be had in Melbourne.' The substantial wholesaler and retailer also advertised in the *Gazette* bonnets from Scotland, gloves, collars, braces and a 'good assortment of Colonial Timber.'

Cavenagh's big story was Sydney, its parsimony, its authority, its distance. The transplanted New South Welshman knew what he wanted as an editor beside the Yarra River—'relief from the intolerable burden of the laws and regulations of a penal colony.' The law was a menace. Reporting that drays in Collins and Elizabeth streets were often so deep in mud that eight bullocks could not pull them out, Cavenagh ran a lyrical leader *Our Wants* on 26 June 1840. Melbourne's first want was a Supreme Court and a resident judge 'with all the paraphernalia of a Supreme Court …. so that there may be no occasion whatever to refer to Sydney.

> We want a lighthouse at the entrance to the harbour …. We want pilots and a pilot establishment …. We want signal stations …. We want Post Office communications with shipping …. We want a public wharf …. We want a jail …. We want a hospital …. We want a Court House …. We want a Coroner …. We want a Powder Magazine …. We want roads to the interior …. What has been done for Port Phillip?'

Sydney was as far from understanding as it was from Melbourne. There was not a man in Melbourne who did not favour immediate independence. While it was fashionable in living rooms around Sydney Harbour to scoff at Melbourne mania, it was 'rather singular that all who come here' should be infected. Fawkner wanted Melbourne's 'streets free of tree-stumps'.

Ghosts haunted the newspapers. A pale Irish banshee who fancied George Arden appeared on nights when the *Gazette* in Collins Street was deserted. She sat in the editor's chair reading his letters. Jupiter Brown, a veteran compositor, saw her when he dropped by the office in the evening. Brown told Finn he approached the ghost but when he got within talking distance his tongue twisted and his brain froze. Finn thought this was from Brown's trips to the Imperial Tavern.

The *Patriot* ghost was of a compositor Fawkner bullied then fired; he went on a bender, and drowned in the Yarra. His ghost returned to the empty Collins Street office, scattering metal type around the floor. Fawkner responded with 'terrible tantrums' when he saw the pied lines around the linotype. He swore, Finn said, yet another vengeance on the dead man, should he ever get hold of him. After Finn joined *The Herald* in 1845, when its offices comprised two detached cottages by the Little Collins Street entrance to Royal Arcade, he was proof-reading in the editor's crib when compositor Jem Mullins came in for corrected proofs. Finn looked up and said: 'Well Jem, have you seen the devil tonight?' Mullins, shaking, pointed to the blazing wood fire in the corner. 'Look, Sir, there he is! Look—look how he thrusts out his tongue and grins like a cat!' Mullins, not for the first time, had seen the ghost of Charlie, a street Arab boy George Cavenagh hired as printer's devil. (He was an apprentice; metaphorically the printer's devil was responsible for omissions, spelling and all other printing — and editorial — errors. When something went wrong, the devil did it.) Charlie, smart, precocious and useful, died after he hitched a lift atop a city baker's cart and fell to the street, fracturing his skull. All Charlies' confreres regretted his death. But Finn again thought the ghost grog-induced; once Mullins left *The Herald* Charlie was seen no more.

When he was young his peers at the London bar thought John Walpole Willis shone. Lanky and sharp-tongued, at twenty-three he published a book on interrogation. But as the young scholar fed his memory the molecular pedantries of equity-law — his obsession as a lawyer — his troubled psyche inflamed his abrasive personality.

Appointed to the equity court in Upper Canada in 1827, he found that the governor and his brother-lawyers reacted more to his tart tongue than his scholarship, but his democratic instincts touched a chord: when the governor removed him from office the House of Assembly prayed for his reinstatement. Willis returned to London to pursue the argument before the Privy Council, which first affirmed, then reversed his dismissal. He was appointed vice-president of the Court of Civil and Criminal Justice in British Guiana in 1831, then to the Supreme Court of New South Wales.

The Chief Justice, Sir James Dowling, entertained Willis as his houseguest when he arrived on 3 November 1837 but they abruptly discovered they would never see eye-to-eye. Gossip about their estrangement quickly segued from quiet asides in chambers to raucous exchanges between tosspots in public bars. Dowling went as far as asking the Governor, Sir George Gipps, to mediate in March 1840 after Willis made remarks about Dowling in the judges' robing room.

Mr Justice Willis had a cheek. He could not open his mouth without a pun falling from it, and believed he understood the mysteries of jurisprudence in a way Chief Justice Dowling never would. Politically, Willis was red-hot. He thought using convicts for servants was slavery. Judges should not have slaves— he never had and never would. He went out of his way to disapprove of the Chief Justice's convict-servants, in a manner Sir James found 'vexatious'. But by then Sydney litigants in equity queued for years. Justice, said the *Sydney Gazette,* which normally found much to say for the way things were, had become 'fraud, folly and villainy'.

Willis was not a folly-fixer. He proposed to Governor Gipps an equity court, separate from the Supreme Court; Justice Willis would preside, with the title Chief Baron. While his thinking was fixed, his tact was negligible. As Sir James delivered a judgment Willis said, voice rising: 'Why does he not get his facts straight?' Dowling said Willis was a fellow 'whom some people think cracked.'

At Willis' suggestion, Dowling removed the thorn in his side by appointing Willis first resident judge in Melbourne in April 1840. When he heard the news, John Fawkner was not too shy to say it was an editors' victory. The appointment had been 'chiefly wrought' by the Melbourne Press, that 'all powerful organ.' He congratulated the colonists of Australia Felix on a 'consummation so devoutly to be wished.'

Two weeks later the *Patriot*, with Fawkner's journalism becoming self-satire, attributed prosperity to a resident judge and predicted Willis would not be 'influenced by local interests or associations.' Another reporter thought the judge a court comedian. With no theatre in town, Edmund Finn said, Judge Willis was 'as good as a play'. No-one could tell what he would say next. When Willis abruptly ordered the dandy solicitor Edward Sewell to shave his moustache, roaring that the Court was no place for a 'whiskered pandour or a fierce hussar' the flustered Sewell fled to a nearby barbershop, returning clean-shaven minutes later.

Men with barristers' bounce found Willis got under their skin. Redmond Barry, a promising young barrister, later Supreme Court judge, whose last legal act would be to don the black cap for Ned Kelly, complained that Willis's attitude was 'so contemptuous towards me' that he found it difficult to continue. Willis replied he would not 'suffer any man at the bar to address me in such terms'.

Some thought him deranged. Fawkner thought him a pillar. Judge Willis had told a Sydney jury only last May that justice was affected by the 'certainty rather than severity,' of punishment. Attorneys gossiping in chambers and the Lamb Inn about the 'three pee's' exchanged clues and conjecture about the *Port Phillip Patriot*'s partiality to Justice Willis. What was making Johnny Fawkner, of all people, a crawler?

Freedom Lost: A history of newspapers, journalism, and press censorship in Australia.

Chapter 11

Port Phillip Patriot Partiality

1838–1845 *William Kerr, John Duerdin, John Curtis, Edward Wilson* and *The Melbourne Argus*; *Edmund Finn, George Cavenagh,* Magistrate Edward St John and *The Port Phillip Herald*; Superintendent Charles Joseph La Trobe; *The Port Phillip Patriot*; *Melbourne Daily News.*

As editors, George Arden, George Cavenagh and William Kerr competed for stories, sales and advertisers. As businessmen, they were clones. Some advertisers were saying they could get printing done at lower rates than those agreed by the three, said a notice in the *Patriot* on 2 January 1843. The rates were fair, reasonable and 'similar' [they meant 'identical'] in every respect. *In no instance whatever will the present prices be departed from,* the *Gazette*, *Herald* and *Patriot* declared in italics. As journalists the three competed in denunciations, particularly of each other. As businessmen, they coalesced into conspiracy against the public interest. They set uniform wages for compositors, the men who set lines of type and composed them into pages designed by the sub-editors.

Reporting servants' struggles for fairness and masters' for prosperity, editors sympathised with masters. A *Patriot* report of £441/10/5 employers owed to various servants in March 1843 included an attack on the 'working part of the population' whose wages demands were bankrupting employers. Employers who failed to pay were not identified. Newspapers spoke for employers. 'The high rate of [pay for] labor will ruin or prevent the advance of this colony … Facts speak for themselves and cannot be contradicted,' said the *Gazette* in May 1843. Employers were reduced to 'sneaking about the Police Office like so many thieves and vagabonds … simply because they are unable to meet the demands of their labourers.

There were limits to editors' solidarity with employers. In the 1842–44 depression, squatters on remote stations charged staff 5d a pound for flour — which meant men with families paid their employers most of their wages for essentials. *The Herald* found the rates 'extravagantly high' and the squatters 'obstinate'.

George Cavenagh was puzzled in the spring of 1847. Why was magistrate Frederick St John, a blusterer widely suspected of corruption, on such good terms with his star reporter, Eddy Finn? Why did St John, who had never shown a gift for public relations, not only talk to Finn, whom no-one thought for sale, with courtesy bordering on tenderness but also offer news tips, sometimes hand-delivering notes to *The Herald* office? What on earth — Cavenagh asked Finn — was going on?

Eddy deflected him. There was no story, the reporter said. There was nothing in it.

During a lull after lunch in the District Court, in July 1847 Finn, in court to report for *The Herald*, laughed at a passage in a novel he was reading during a lull. Mr St John, on the bench with the coroner, Dr William Wilmot, turned on him. 'Do you think you are in a bear-garden?'

Finn would not be bullied. Perhaps 'others in court' would be at home in a bear-garden.

St John: 'This is *my* court and I'll make you behave yourself in it.'

Finn tried comedy. 'It was the book I was reading that laughed, not myself …'

The magistrate threatened to 'make very short work' of Finn should he interrupt 'the proceedings of my Court again.'

Finn: 'Major St John, even at the risk of being prosecuted for contempt, I must respectfully submit that your oft-asserted theory [of] this Court being *yours* is based, to put it mildly, on misapprehension…

St John: 'Confound you, will you stop that jawing of yours? … Look here Brodie [Charles Brodie, Chief Constable] if that fellow says another word, lock him up for six hours in the watch-house.'

Finn stood, bowed to the bench and walked from the court as Brodie sniggered.

At 7pm Finn knocked on St John's door in Brunswick Street.

St John ushered him into a backroom where a log-fire crackled. He gestured for Finn to sit at the table, walked out and returned with a bottle of whisky. It would give Finn a taste he hadn't had 'since you left the land famous for potatoes and poteen.' He stirred it with hot water and sugar.

'How do you like it?'

Finn could not resist. 'It's the best unpaid-for whisky I ever drank.'

St John, then licensing court magistrate: 'What do you mean?'

Finn: 'No doubt it's part of your present from Mr.——— [a spirit merchant] who is interested in a licence for a tenant.'

Shouting about Finn's 'audacity' in coming to his own home to insult him, St John stood up, seized a metal poker and, poking the fire, said the two were alone in the house. According to Finn, he threatened to break Finn's head.

Finn, in his memory, played Mr Cool. He took another sip and suggested St John put his bluster in his pocket and his poker aside. There was no Chief Constable to lock him up. St John's 'outrageous' treatment of him forced him to his present position.

St John had taken enough bribes to ruin fifty men. Finn, whose confidential sources included the Chief Constable, had a list of a few. Pulling a sheet from his jacket, he said 'have a little patience while I recapitulate them.'

As Finn read the list — St John receiving a case of whisky, a hamper of wine, a load of hay, a bag of potatoes, a wheelbarrow of bottled beer, a fat goose, a load of wood, a basket of butter — the magistrate squirmed in his chair 'like a cat on a hot griddle.' Finn had names, dates of delivery, even the quality of wine. He asked St John: 'Is it to be peace or war between us?'

St John said list was a sham. He did not believe there was anything on it.

Finn handed it over; St John threw it on the fire and poked the logs. 'You confounded little thief, there goes your pack of lies, and a brass pin would make me shove you up the chimney after them.'

Finn laughed. 'Major, you must suppose me a born idiot if you fancy I would be fool enough to hand you that paper if I had not the original at home. Why man, it's only a copy, and surely as a magistrate of no small experience you must know that an original is the real thing.' (He polished the paragraph for history; the real Eddy Finn did not speak like a pompous git.)

St John mixed another whisky, changed tack.

He believed the Irish were good-hearted. His wife was Irish. 'Give me your hand and promise solemnly that what has passed tonight [between us] shall never be revealed as long as I am in the colony, or alive. From your years, you will in all likelihood outlive me, and when I am dead I care not who knows. Promise me this, and you and I, so far as I can prevent it, shall never quarrel more.'

Finn agreed.

The magistrate asked that none of the conversation be reported. 'This was easily managed,' Finn said, 'as only the one reporter was present.'

On the bench, St John expressed horror at bribery. He had 'no mercy' for a policeman who drank a free glass of beer.

On 3 July 1848 Fawkner spoke at an open-air meeting in the public space behind the library and hospital campaigning for Superintendant La Trobe's recall. 'Gentlemen, the enemies of the people impute to us bad motives and worse language; let us this day contradict them. I come forward to rid the colony of a nuisance in the person of our ruler. His private character I leave unassailed; his public conduct has been mean, base and contemptible.'

La Trobe had spent £450 on a private road to a friend's house. He had delayed the erection of lighthouses at Cape Schanck and King's Island and was responsible for the loss of the hundreds in the wreck of the immigrant ship *Cataraqui*. He had ineptly promised 'to play second fiddle' to Governor Sir George Gipps when Sir George visited Melbourne in October 1841. He had publicly licked dirt. What did 'second fiddle' mean, Fawkner asked? It meant that whatever dirt the Governor required La Trobe to eat, or inflict on the people, he was the man to do it and had done so 'to the fullest extent of his limited capacity.'

Then there was La Trobe's condoning corruption.

> 'Does he not openly patronize a man notorious for receiving bribes? Aye, bribes from all conditions of men — from the half-dozen eggs or the pound of butter, up to a cow, or a calf, horses, grog, wines, champagne, brandy and gin. Yes. There is a man present who gave this official a cheque lately for a portion of rum which he did not get. Yet the cheque was never returned. ... Yet this official is sustained by La Trobe; and though informed of such facts, has he cut the venal receiver of such bribes? No! Has he not refused to have this affair investigated? ...The Superintendent supports the man who, it is said, lives upon bribes. It is misrule, a deep hatred of the people, an insult to all classes.'

The crowd understood he meant Major St John, then Commissioner for Crown Lands. The speech 'fell like a shell', said Eddy Finn.

Eighteen department heads and senior officials including St John, met on 7 July, drafting a letter urging La Trobe to investigate the slanderous and false assertions and assuring him on their honour as gentlemen that none had taken a bribe. As the allegations dominated conversation from bank parlours to the lowest tap-room *The Herald* and *The Daily News* at last caught up with Collins Street and reported that St John was the man.

Fawkner wrote to La Trobe on 13 July saying he was prepared to substantiate the accusations before any impartial court. La Trobe replied that 'any specific charge or charges of misconduct ... which may be transmitted in the proper form' would have the Government's 'full and immediate attention.'

Fawkner took the case to the people, writing to the newspapers setting out St John's corruption. That gave the magistrate his opportunity: the letters to the papers, unlike the one to the Superintendent, were not privileged.

St John sued Fawkner for libel. Now what citizens had whispered behind their hands was the subject of a public lawsuit involving the best-known citizen of Melbourne. Fawkner did not step back. What he had published, he said in the pleadings, was true. He sought out Eddy Finn. Could Finn provide evidence — names, transactions — of St John taking bribes? Finn would not help. He knew if he produced the dossier the chances were 'five hundred to one' the jury would find for Fawkner. Fawkner approached him again; again he remained silent.

Why? Part of Finn was a show-off who liked parading insider's knowledge. He drew the line against vulgar defamation. When proprietor Samuel Goode and editor William Kerr started the bi-weekly *Courier* on 6 January 1845, Finn said it was the 'most libellous publication ever issued in the colony', never out of the trouble it deserved. It survived little more than a year. Goode's second newspaper *The Albion*, a 'filthy weekly rag' written by Kerr and John Curtis, the hard-drinking sketcher, once a candidate for Melbourne Treasurer, was killed by a criminal libel prosecution for a defamation of Sidney Stephen, a barrister, for which Goode was jailed for two months. That was just, in Finn's eyes. There were roaches among his peers.

After eight witnesses gave evidence of bribes to St John, Mr Justice aBeckett told the jury in his opinion Mr Fawkner's charges against Mr St John had not been substantiated. Some were 'presents and could not be called bribery.' If they agreed with him, they should find for St John 'not in vindictive damages, but such an amount as would fairly meet the justice of the case.' The jury was locked up for the night. In the morning the foreman reported there was no possibility of a verdict. (Five favoured Fawkner, seven St John.)

Each had to pay costs. Supporters covered part of Fawkner's. St John resigned as Commissioner, took the *Stag* to England and never returned.

Finn, old and nearly blind, told the full story of *St John v Fawkner* and the glass of hot whisky for the first time in the 1880s. He excused himself saying he was 'no private detective'. There were other witnesses. He had not profited from, nor contributed to, St John's corruption. Fawkner and his followers could have continued the fight. The best reporter in Melbourne sided with silence.

• • •

When he started the Melbourne Argus on 2 June 1846, William Kerr's career in journalism had a pattern common for ambitious reporters: seeking a paper whose values reflected his own he jumped early and often. Kerr learned reporting at Henry Parkes' The Colonist in Sydney in 1837 after migrating from Scotland, switched to the Gazette, moved to Melbourne in 1839 where he worked as reporter with George Cavenagh on the Herald. In 1841 Fawkner hired him as editor of the *Port Phillip Patriot and Melbourne Advertiser*. There was a gulf wide as Carpentaria between the public Kerr and the private man.

The public Kerr stung like a bee. When he made his signature remark 'I'll not be put down' in the city Council, councillors blanched. Eddy Finn thought Kerr's journalism about John O'Shannassy comprised ruthless libel. He was an 'impudent, bullying braggart'. One of Finn's unidentified sources found the private Kerr harmless, obliging, good-natured, as generous as the day was long though he made more enemies than any man in Port Phillip. Soft and fat, with a big head, he had gout in his left arm and his right hand carried a cudgel. After he became Town Clerk in 1853 he grew 'as docile as a well-trained hound.' He would speak 'not only civilly, but submissively', twisting his spectacles.

With the *Patriot* insolvent early in 1845, Fawkner's father bought it to avert bankruptcy and sacked Kerr, who sailed for Sydney as friends with deep pockets spread rumours he was looking for big money to establish a Melbourne daily. When he hired William Corp on 1 April 1845 to report the Supreme Court, Insolvent Court and domestic intelligence excluding shipping news, police intelligence and the municipal council, Fawkner Senior agreed to pay the reporter £2 a week. But the proprietor withheld £1 a week, payable 14 days after the end of each quarter. He agreed not to write for another newspaper and 'to pay for all time and loss occasioned by his own neglect in proportion to the time or matter neglected.' Corp, fast, accurate, prolific and a drinker, was under Fawkner's thumb. Should the old fence find Corp guilty of neglect, he could cut his wage in half.

Fawkner — Eddy Finn said old colonists now thought him a spoiled child — inflicted 'illiterate vaporings' and 'ungrammatical jargon' on the paper as editor till he hired a powerful writer, James M'Eachern, from Sydney.

Rumours about Kerr's daily so unnerved the Fawkners that they turned the *Patriot* into 'the first daily newspaper in Melbourne on 15 May 1845.' Samuel Goode started the bi-weekly *Courier* on 6 January 1845; Kerr became editor in June. Men who felt their reputations unjustly tarnished by Kerr's energetic journalism litigated it into insolvency early in 1846.

Kerr convinced himself that fellow freemason Henry Moor, an Episcopalian solicitor with a lucrative practice, failed to resist pleasures of the flesh. When Bishop Perry appointed Moor diocesan registrar, Kerr said in the Melbourne *Argus* he was 'a little surprised'. Moor had been Mayor of Melbourne in 1844–5 and Eddy Finn, who saw a 'merry twinkle in his eye' thought in those years that the Henry Moor with deep pockets was also the best-liked man in Melbourne.

In Kerr's eyes Moor was another character, better suited as 'father confessor for the *Eagle*, or *Mother Scott's* establishment than to hold office in a Christian Church.' (The Eagle Inn and the Scottish Hotel in Bourke-street had been reported to the licensing magistrates as houses of ill-fame.) Mr Moor's attorney put the case to Judge aBeckett (a *Herald* contributor) and a jury of twelve in the Supreme Court: the words, he said, defamed him. (*Herald* editor George Cavenagh, called as a juror and challenged by Kerr's attorney, said he had 'certainly formed a very decided opinion as to who ought to succeed' and was excused.)

After a long retirement, the jury foreman said they could not agree. Bailiffs took them to the Prince of Wales Hotel in Little Flinders Street, where they remained till midnight, when they were escorted to the judge's home in East Collins-street. The foreman told judge aBeckett they were unanimous in finding for Moor but could not agree on damages. Ten thought £250; two would not agree. The judge recorded a three-quarters verdict for £250 and discharged them.

At sheriff's sale to pay the £250 and the lawyers on 8 May 1848, an old attorney, John Duerdin, bought the paper for £350. Kerr's wealthy friends stuck by him, but he would not pull his head in. After the first verdict an *Argus* leader said: 'every street, lane and alley in the city' resounded with the nauseous details of Mr Moor's brothel exploits. Moor had obtained money 'or rather an order for money'. Kerr would not exchange positions with him for 'ten thousand times' the amount. Poetry became a weapon. On 24 March 1848 Kerr published 'The Rake's Decision' by Erato:

> The 'Scottish' and the 'Eagle' my patronage shall share
> My office makes it legal, to go and visit there;
> I'll frolic with the lasses, and feast my carnal sight,
> On the shameless work that passes in a bawdy house at night.

Kerr had the tactical sense of a galah. Erato wrote:

> If vice in virtue flourish, don't you presume to check it;
> Virtue be yours to nourish, and vice leave to a B——tt.

When the second *Moor v Kerr* libel hearing started on 12 August 1848, *Argus* reporter John Curtis swore he did not know who his editor was. He gave his copy to the [printer's] 'devil'. For all he knew, the 'devil' might be the editor. He might infer something of the editorship, but absolute knowledge of it he had not. He was scarcely an hour a day in *The Argus* office. He corrected his own proofs.

Captain G.W.Cole swore the libels pointed to the plaintiff. As he read them shouts of laughter interrupted him.

Redmond Barry, counsel for Kerr, argued that Moor's character 'stood so high that a libel could not affect him.' Judge aBeckett: 'It might as well be said that a person stands so high that every shaft might be let fly at him ⃝'

The jury retired. It returned and the foreman announced there was no prospect of a unanimous verdict. He asked the judge to allow them to retire to a hotel for six hours; there was not so much as a chair in the jury-room.

Mr Barry objected; the judge agreed.

When Mr Barry suggested they retire 'to the Scottish, or the Eagle' there was a shout of laughter.

They retired till 8.50pm when the foreman announced a verdict for Moor of £500 on the first count and 1/- on the second and third counts.

At a second sheriff's sale on 2 November 1848 the auctioneer knocked *The Melbourne Argus* press and types down to Edward Wilson, an English gentleman who to the regret of his family had radical political views. Born at Covent Garden, London on 3 November 1813, Wilson sailed to Sydney depressed after a business failure. (His partners failed to tell him their capital was borrowed; he lost his inheritance and savings.) He leased a cattle-run near Dandenong with a Melbourne innkeeper, James Stewart Johnston, in 1842. Though farming wasn't for them and they sold the lease four years later, Wilson attracted attention at public meetings as a sharp speaker and in *The Argus*, under the name Iota, as a writer with a clever pen. After a visit to South Australia in 1848 — he thought the Wakefield experiment yielded 'freedom from antiquated abuses, with more liberal institutions, with a happier people [than England]' — he borrowed to buy *The Argus* with Johnston from Kerr for £300.

Wilson became *The Argus'* principal writer; Kerr continued for six weeks. Eddy Finn thought Wilson more cautious than Kerr about libel. But on 4 April 1849 the police court committed Wilson for trial for publishing a criminal libel of Judge aBeckett contained in a speech by alderman Johnston in the City Council on 1 December 1848.

Judge aBeckett would decide whether Judge aBeckett had been libelled.

The trial did not continue for reasons not recorded.

The Argus went daily from 18 June 1849 and took over the *Melbourne Daily News* (re-named from the *Patriot* on 9 October 1848) from 1 January 1852. Wilson shipped forty compositors from England, doubled its size from mid-1852 and reduced the price from 3d to 2d. His drive, eye for what readers wanted and skilful pen brought increases in circulation from 5000 in May 1852 to nearly 20,000 by the end of 1853. He also increased the paper's influence and revenue. He nearly ruined it. With a staff of 140, costs per copy were 5½d, the sale price 2d and advertising did not cover the gap. Lauchlan Mackinnon persuaded Wilson that every new subscription brought bankruptcy closer. He bought Johnston's share of the business, increased the price to 4d and advertising charges by 25 per cent.

The Argus campaigned against squatters' 'ruinous monopoly' of Victorian farming under Wilson's slogan 'Unlock the Lands'. He believed in journalism. He believed in controversy. Tall, dark and sombre, he thought apathy the main enemy of the people. To Henry Parkes he was 'a Radical of the Radicals'; Wilson looked forward to working with Parkes and 'hunting sycophancy, and corruption … and unpatriotic selfishness to their kennels.' When Charles Gavan Duffy arrived in 1856 and Wilson promised him a list of fifty reforms, the first was 'Justice to the Aborigines.'

George Higinbotham succeeded Wilson in 1856. Born in Dublin on 19 April 1826 he reported for the *Morning Chronicle* where he sometimes drowned in the speech, forgot to take notes and had to seek help from colleagues. Admitted to the bar in London, he arrived in Victoria on 10 March 1854, contributed to *The Melbourne Morning Herald* and *The Argus*; Wilson appointed him editor in August 1856. James Smith, a staff writer, thought he 'addressed himself to an ideal public' comprised of multiples of himself, intelligent, disinterested, incorruptible. That was the problem: there was a fair proportion of stupidity, ignorance and selfishness everywhere. If everyone were Higinbotham it would be easy to have Plato's republic on the Yarra. George lacked the daily editor's capacity to reach a conclusion in seconds: he always sought more, more detail, more fact, more argument. Sometimes he was pedantry bottled. He resigned in April 1859, won Brighton in 1861, argued for votes for women in 1873 and after serving as Attorney General was appointed to the Supreme Court in 1880 and Chief Justice in 1886, declining a knighthood as a 'base, contemptible distinction'. He died on 31 December 1892.

Henry Moor's third libel suit was for the assertion in *The Argus* of 18 December 1850 that Moor was a 'double-faced, unprincipled schemer'. Mr Barry argued for *The Argus* that the words were mere comment on the public career of a Legislative Councillor. When *The Times* of London called Sir Robert Peel a 'dissembling traitor' no one dreamed of a lawsuit.

After an hour the jury foreman said they could not agree. When a sick juryman asked for a biscuit and glass of water, the judge allowed the biscuit but would not allow dinner till the verdict. At 7.20 they found unanimously for Mr Moor. Damages: one farthing. Mr Moor resigned from the Council.

Some thought him a fake. The man who couldn't stop talking had become a clown. 'I know the people — I do. I mix among 'em, I do, for I am one of the people myself and worked for eighteen years in a sawpit,' a *Melbourne Punch* satirist had Fawkner say on 2 August 1855. *The Argus* used to be a people's paper but 'now runs down the people's friends. Why, it said something against me the other day — against me — against ME.' *Punch* was just what the country wanted. He didn't mean it was always right, 'but in most respects it is — for in most respects it agrees with me.' A year later *Punch* mocked him as a plastic poseur.

• • •

In March 1847 a shepherd asked Joseph Forrester, a Collins-street jeweller, to test an apple-sized ore he had found in the roots of a tree that had blown down about sixty miles from Melbourne. He declined to say where. The shepherd said he would return. Mr Forrester found the specimen was 65 per cent gold. He told his friend Captain Clinch, master of the Flying Fish, trading between Melbourne and Hobart. Clinch, a natural storyteller, more sensitive to the needs of the public than Mr Forrester, told the golden apple yarn to the *Hobart Town Courier*, which published it on 19 May 1847. When the Flying Fish returned to Port Phillip with the *Courier*'s scoop on the most important story they would ever have, Melbourne journalists knew how to react. They did not take it seriously. It was a hoax.

Eddy Finn later saw a man who lit his pipe with a £5 note reduced to begging and another who used champagne bottles for ninepins ending his days as a pauper in the Melbourne Benevolent Asylum. In Geelong a 'madman' shod his horse with gold horseshoes; a thirsty digger at the Imperial Hotel in Collins-street ordered golden stirrups. *The Argus* said men foamed at the mouth and women fainted.

Cabs being 'few and dear' reporters walked to report coroner's inquests, police courts, the Town Council and special meetings. On those rare occasions when news in Brighton or Williamstown had to be reported, they rode on horseback. In the 1840s the highest-paid reporters drew £3 a week. No papers paid expenses. On the other hand, no reporters paid for drinks in hotel bars. 'They could order what they liked and drink it free,' said Eddy Finn. No constable would lock a reporter up 'be he as drunk as Bacchus and as uproarious as a lunatic.' Even scurrilous paragraphs rarely yielded a shaking or black eye. Knocking down a reporter was 'unknown'. Some public figures including Justice Willis gave reporters copies of speeches. No early reporters were stenographers, but by abbreviating longhand and writing quickly those with retentive memories could report several columns 'which read much better than they were delivered.' Speakers who had been reported and rewritten like this were not just satisfied — they were thankful.

Finn met the *Melbourne Morning Herald* shipping reporter, back from the Lysander, just arrived from Adelaide early in the afternoon of 11 November 1850. Quickly flipping through the South Australian papers, he found English news included a separation bill splitting Port Phillip from New South Wales and had passed both English houses of parliament.

Unable to find his editor, George Cavenagh, Finn quickly briefed the printers for a special edition and rushed to write copy without sparing exclamation marks. Beneath the headlines Glorious News! Separation at Last!! Finn combined the modern news-report, editorial and column for the big occasion: 'We lose not a single moment in communicating to the public the soul-stirring intelligence that Separation has come at last!!! The Australian Colonies' Bill, with the amendments made in the Lords on the 5th July, was agreed to in the Commons on the 1st August, and only awaits the Queen's signature to become the law of the land. The long-oppressed, long-buffeted Port Phillip is an Independent Colony, gifted with the Royal name of Victoria, and endowed with a flourishing revenue and almost inexhaustible resources; let all colonists not lose a moment in their hour of triumph in celebrating the important epoch in a suitable manner. The 'Public Rejoicings' committee would assemble without delay. 'Now is the day and now is the hour!' For this act of justice to Port Phillip, and every other good gift, may God bless the Queen.'

As typesetters, compositors, proof-readers, pressmen and printers did their work, Finn tracked down his editor and 'gave him a memo. of the intelligence'. Cavenagh's buggy distributed the special edition. When *The Argus* suggested suspending newspaper publication for a day to allow newspaper employees to enjoy the Separation carnival, Cavenagh said each paper should drop one day's publication. The typesetters adjourned to Clark's Waterman's Arms in Little Collins-street where they resolved to have three days off. If the newspapers could publish without them, 'well and good'. Newspapers suspended publication on Friday 15 November, Saturday 16 and Monday 18; each biweekly missed a day.

A gaudy procession from the Government Offices in Lonsdale Street to the Prince's Bridge opening on Friday 15 November included a *Herald* printing press on a wagon drawn by eight horses, beside it stood Johnny Fawkner flanked by William Clarke and Samuel Goode. As the wagon moved slowly through the raucous crowd the press printed leaflets Fawkner had written. 'The PRESS is omnipotent! Its diffusion is not only wide, but universal; its voice penetrates the deepest recesses of the forest; crosses the widest plains, the highest mountains … Not a hut in the wilderness but feels the powerful influence of that Lever of Freedom — THE PRESS.' Fawkner, waving copies above his head, handing them out as the Press printed still more, was becoming a performance proprietor. Next day, on a steamer trip to Corio Bay, the printers ran into rough weather; Fawkner, seasick, recovered to organise a dance on the quarterdeck as they docked at Geelong.

Talleyrand's aphorism that 'the principle object of language was to conceal thought' had never been better exemplified than in the Melbourne press, a Yarra River scholar given the space of a monthly the *Illustrated Australian Magazine* thought in January 1851. The fournewspapers were pervaded by a 'gossipping, chattering, prying,' spirit with an air of intrusive Yankeeism and purse-proud effrontery. 'Everybody's business is discussed by everybody. Hardly a day passes in which the newspaper, pandering to the appetite it has fostered … fails to serve a dish of the kind for which it is the approved caterer.' Merchants and tradesmen found it necessary as an advertising medium. Agitators flew to it. Some subscribed from fear, others from curiosity; all wished it would mend its manners. Most were conducted single-handed. Of 30,000 citizens, four have *elected themselves* to be supreme arbiters of the destinies, moral, social and political, of the remaining 29,996. In the leading journals of England one man wrote on politics, another on literature, another on theatre, another on music, another on law and yet another on science. Then there were foreign correspondents and contributions from well-known men high in rank and talent. This was a powerful engine, the 'fourth estate'. But while the great English newspapers were rarely dogmatic or egotistical, editorial dogmatism was standard in Port Phillip papers. Certainty begat silence, it vetoed discussion. The tone implied: I am, Sir, absolute. And when I open my mouth let no dog bark.

Dogmatism and complacent assumptions were commonplace on subjects which even a statesman such as [William] Pitt or a philosopher such as [Edmund] Burke would treat with hesitation and reserve. The Melbourne editors seem 'to have forgotten … that the office they have assumed requires an experience, industry and information which are neither to be had gratis, nor to be picked up by a mere purchase of type.'

Insulting epithets and spiteful innuendoes riddled Melbourne journalism. It was time not only to cry shame! Shame! 'but to spurn from our doors the journals where such foul and impertinent malignancies find a space.' The spirit of the pen should be that of the gospels; the reader should be in no doubt that the editor was a Christian and a gentleman. In a Christian's hand, the pen was responsible to God as well as man.

Readers from blacksmiths to barristers to brewery sweeps said of the *Herald*, *Patriot*, *Gazette* and *Argus*, separately and together, 'there is nothing in them'. That was natural, a man with an international eye who tried to get below the surface said in the *Australasian* in July 1851. Men who perused *The Times* of London on their breakfast table reporting every corner of the globe could scarcely expect the same in a community of 25,000.

Pitiless Yarra readers demanded a leading article every morning, even when there was no news. How could editors fill the void? In the quest for 'racy and piquant' stories, the flaws, faults and failings of their brothers of the quill were always a possibility but they were also too well-covered, 'a thrice-told tale'. Public functionaries, being most conspicuous, were next in line for the glare of the spotlight. Even private individuals emerging from obscurity were selected as victims by one paper or another. 'The great vice of the colonial [Melbourne] press is scurrility and vindictive personality.' Even in England readers preferred the venom of Grub-street to the majesty of Milton. 'Violent personality' was a characteristic of every colonial press; editors in the rural U.S. were famous for it.

Even so, the thinker was surprised by the quantity and quality of the Melbourne newspapers. The press was evidence of 'extraordinary vitality' in the body politic; it showed the 'life-blood of the social organism beats strong and vigorous.' Constant property sales, the influx of capital and labour and the absence of established trading connections 'all necessitating frequent advertisements are doubtless the chief causes of this newspaper phenomenon.' Editors and reporters were invisible.

He thought of the Patriot as a *Scorpion*, egotistical and ferocious. It should replace John Knox's phrase about conscience demanding truth with 'a homelier phrase, "MANGLING DONE HERE." *The Herald*, the *Chameleon*, was in favour at the Club. It loved authority. The *Gazette*, the *Firefly*, was edited by a handsome young knave who would sacrifice any virtuous citizen for a telling article, but was more anxious — the thinker meant this as a compliment — to please his readers and make the paper pay than to save the state or glorify itself. *The Argus* had yet to win its place among the 'invisible infallibles.'

For all its faults the press was openly discussing public questions and preparing the people for free institutions. By diffusing market information it tended to equalise prices in neighbouring colonies and maintain the balance between supply and demand. It digested huge piles of English papers, offered intellectual food and counteracted the inertia induced by solitude in the bush.

Premier John O'Shannassy appointed Finn, now earning £8 a week, Legislative Council Clerk of Papers on £400 a year in June 1858. When *The Age* jibed at this, the *Herald* laughed it off: 'though we have lost a Finn we are going on swimmingly'. When Finn ran into Fawkner in a Parliament House corridor in August 1869 Finn, bantering with his old mate, refused to shake Fawkner's hand. He'd just seen Fawkner shake hands with the Irish giant O'Shannassy: 'and you ought to be ashamed of yourself.' Fawkner didn't get Finn's lame joke. 'Have you had a shindy with big Jack? I thought you were thick friends.' Finn laughed and said in Latin: Johnny Pascoe, I absolve you.'

Fawkner said: 'don't bother me with your dog-Latin.'

Finn translated.

Fawkner said he understood all now; he must be off.

It was their last conversation. Fawkner died a few days later on 4 September 1869. After writing stream-of-consciousness biography and history dense with novelistic detail, following random memory-triggers into structural chaos, Finn died, blind, in a North Fitzroy bluestone cottage on 4 April 1898.

Chapter 12

King David's Duty

1827–1908: **Ebenezer** and **David Syme**, *The Age*; **G.F.H.Schuler, Alfred Deakin**, special correspondent for the *London Morning Post*; *The Herald, The Morning Herald*, **George Dill** and **Hugh George**, *The Argus*; Speight v Syme.

The Age enjoys the profitable distinction of the largest circulation of any journal on this side of the planet. … It is not only a mine of gold for its owner; it is a great political force.

Rev. W.H.Fitchett, Australian editor, The Review of Reviews November 1892

The freedom of the people and, of course, the freedom of the press leave nothing wanting. There is nothing too high, nothing too secret, nothing too sacred which might not be called to answer to this powerful forum. In Germany one cannot imagine such a situation.'

German immigrant Hermann Beckler in an 1857 letter from Melbourne to his brother Carl.

In his memory David Syme's childhood was void of feeling. Born in North Berwick, Scotland, on 2 October 1827 to Jean and George, a Calvinist who never smiled or encouraged him, he was the youngest of seven in a family which attended church twice daily, allowed no games, no cricket, football, hopscotch or cards and no days without study. After his older brothers Ebenezer and George left for college, David, hungry for experience, asked his mother if she would ask his father if he could go to sea. She returned with the answer: no. David would have run away but knew his mother would grieve. Alone, he taught himself navigation and smoking: he thought smoking important for a sailor.

George required David 'to do as he was told and ask no questions.' If he did anything well, he was not to feel pleased. To laugh was wrong, to love a duty. As he grew older his father's contradictions puzzled David. George was kind, helped anyone who asked and with adults he liked, dinner conversation was rarely quieter than uproar. Why did this genial gregarious man ask for obedience but not love from his children? In a lifetime of asking David found no answer.

He remembered one conversation. In the 1842 election fishermen, tenant farmers and labourers leaned to the Whigs. There was no secret ballot. George called the family together and told them solemnly he intended voting Tory but this might affect their interests. Should he abstain? David was flattered by the consultation.

The Tory won by one vote and the Symes cautiously stayed indoors for a week; when David opened the back gate a brick whacked the fence next to his head. George died three years later when David was seventeen. His promising brother Ebenezer worked briefly with a Baptist congregation then moved to London as assistant to John Chapman who owned the *Westminster Review*.

Ebenezer studied theology and Mandarin to become a missionary and practised preaching on street-corners in Manchester and Liverpool. *Westminster Review* contributors included philosopher John Stuart Mill, the leading liberal voice of the age, Horace Greeley, founder of the *New York Herald Tribune*, the *Tribune's* European correspondent, Karl Marx, the transcendent poets Lord Byron and Alfred Tennyson. Ebenezer was influenced by the novelist, George Eliot, then assistant editor, who thought while Ebenezer's passion for reform was pure, he could do better as a writer, there was too much 'slash and scoff.'

David too developed a satirist's tongue. A North Berwick minister he said, prayed 'with an unction all his own'; a nearby Free Kirk man preached 'one long tearful appeal to the Almighty for mercy.' The more he thought of the dogmas of Calvinism, the less he thought of them. Original sin, predestination, arbitrary salvation, offended his sense of justice: he thought God's children were not required to grovel.

He learned Greek, Hebrew and Latin, studied Arabic and hoped to be an Oriental linguist but lacked the ear and 'rubbed along somehow by sheer hard labour.' As he stretched reason for the meaning of the Holy Bible he lost faith. Working to the point of collapse triggered clinical depression. 'I could take no interest in my work nor indeed, in anything else.' He took the fashionable 'water-cure' at Grafenberg, stayed in Berlin, Vienna and Heidelberg, discovered Hegel fascinated him more than theology, and returned to Scotland after a year acquainted with German and philosophy and with 'restored health.'

Three months after he was hired as proof-reader on a Glasgow newspaper a friendly manager hinted he need not be so severe on the leading articles. He thought his prospects miserable. The despatches of a special *New York Tribune* California correspondent sparked the thought that San Francisco had room for everyone, perhaps even a man with no training, influence or capital.

He sailed from London at the end of 1851 taking a 'small library' of books and papers on geology and gold mining. When he reached San Francisco the city was in flames. He caught a steamer to Sacramento next morning with a blanket, underwear and gun, leaving the rest of his gear at a store in a trunk.

On the American River he camped next to an Irish couple, their son, an African American and two British men. The Irishman, hearing a story about his wife and the African, loaded his gun walked to his tent, and shot the black. Not a word had been spoken. They threw the body in a hole. Syme, hands blistered, back strained, prospected for months, retaining his eye for irony. Alone in Indian country near the wild Tuolumne River in the Sierra Nevada mountains in California, he rested on a boulder, thinking he was where no white man had ever been when his eye fell on an empty sardine can.

Hearing of the 1851 gold discovery in a place the Aborigines called Ballaarat in Australia he booked passage for Melbourne on the *Europe*. Close-calls and near-misses filled his subconscious. Within a week the passengers, strangers to Yankee enterprise, found themselves on short rations. The captain lacked a certificate and missed Hawaii; after they had run out of water they landed on Tutuila island in Samoa. Handsome friendly men and beautiful women gave them pigs and coconuts. He resisted the lure. In the New Hebrides, half-starved, armed, they procured coconuts and yams from islanders wielding spears. They ate the last coconut two days from Sydney and when they docked he took a steamer to Melbourne, landed short of money, slept on a tabletop in a Bourke Street hotel and next day walked with an acquaintance to Castlemaine.

They took only half an ounce of gold a day. Bendigo was no better. He heard of a strike at Korong but found it was just a rumour. Sleeping with his face to the opening in a slab hut on the way back, he suffered tonsillitis, could not speak or swallow and thought he might die. But he recovered quickly, and riding with a mate to a new Beechworth strike, lunched at a hotel near Wangaratta, recently visited by bushrangers. Syme and his mate, each with a revolver, 'thought we were capable of taking care of ourselves.'

As they approached roadside ghost gum saplings three miles from the hotel they suddenly saw three horsemen emerge ten paces ahead, blocking the road.

Syme sidled his horse toward the trees, Colt in hand.

'Do you take us for bushrangers?' the leader asked Syme.

'I do,' said Syme. His ear heard banter.

'Is that a revolver you hold in your hand?'

'It is.'

The bushranger played curious. 'I have never seen one like that before. Will you let me see it?'

Syme: 'I never let it pass out of my hand.'

The man laughed. 'Good-day to you.' The three put spurs to their horses. Syme said he had learned 'never to be cocksure of anything.' He was twenty-six and been 'perfectly certain' no-one could take him by surprise on the gravel beneath the ghost gums.

Francis Cooke and Co, merchants and stockowners of Elizabeth Street Melbourne, published the first issue of *The Age* on 17 October 1854, promising 'comprehensive, accurate and impartial' news-reporting and support for 'popular movements.' Three months later, with daily circulation at 6000, liberals and radicals attended a public support meeting at the Athenaeum Hall in Collins Street. They promised to raise money and resolved to expand paid-up capital and issue shares.

When *The Age*, *The Argus* and the *Morning Herald* reduced piece-rates from 2/6 per thousand en's (the letter 'n' was the average width of all typeset letters of the alphabet) to 2/- in December 1854, compositors struck *The Argus* and Henry Cooke told *The Age* comps he could not afford 2/6. Francis and Henry announced they would publish the last issue on 30 December and when they offered it for sale for £3000 on 28 December there were no takers.

Twenty-three compositors formed a cooperative, each paying £25 a share and leaving their wages, except for hand-to-mouth expenses, as the working capital. They elected two Athenaeum radicals, David Blair and T.L.Bright, co-editors.

Blair, born in Ireland to Scottish parents, joined Dr J.D.Lang's Presbyterians in Sydney in March 1850, worked on Henry Parkes' *The Empire*, then, hungry and ambitious, moved to Melbourne where he was *The Sydney Morning Herald* correspondent, *Argus* sub-editor and secretary of the Anti-Transportation league. At 34 he teemed with energy and opinion.

Confident of immortality, he attacked free-thought 'hanky-panky' and believed the New Testament was literally true, no metaphor about it. When he joined Bright, another ex-*Empire* man who kept a profile so low a blank remains, on *The Age* his dogmatism embraced free-selection, representative government and separation of church and state. His biographer, J.I.Roe, thought him too dogmatic a scholar, too unimaginative a writer and too principled a politician.

Ebenezer Syme stepped from the *Abdalla* to the Melbourne dock in July 1853. He quickly became a regular *Argus* contributor, helped start and edit the *Digger's Advocate*, a short-lived radical journal, and drafted resolutions for the Eureka rebels at a 6 December 1854 Melbourne protest meeting. Ebenezer who enjoyed the compositors' faith and commercial staff's confidence, joined Blair as *The Age* editor in late December 1854 in the compositors' cooperative. When the cooperative, short of cash and cooperation, failed, Ebenezer, funded by progressive merchants, bought *The Age* for £2000 in June 1856. As editor he sought an eight-hour day, votes without property qualification, equal electorates, and education free of religion and fees. David joined as his partner on 27 September 1856 as Ebenezer won election to the Legislative Assembly. He died of tuberculosis on 13 March 1860 aged 34.

One of the congregation in David Syme's head was a mystic; he was on the committee of the Victorian Association of Spiritual Progressives whose influential membership included Alfred Deakin, Mrs Syme and their five daughters. The VASP experimented with hypnotism and medical clairvoyance and the resonance of past lives. One speaker read the meaning of events through vibrations retained in objects.

On July 1861 *The Age* circulation was 16,000; by December 1873 it was 20,000, which *The Age* said was 'more than double the circulation of any other daily journal south of the equator.' In the early 1880s it was selling 38,000 copies a day, 'unprecedented in Australian journalism and equal to nearly three times the combined circulation of the other two Melbourne morning newspapers.' *The Age* circulation was four times that of *The Argus,* eight times that of the *Telegraph*. The *Bulletin* of 4 April 1891 reported 'the daily circulation of *The Age* averages over 100,000 copies, probably a few thousand more than the total circulation of any four Sydney dailies.' By 1899 it sold 120,000 a day. (All circulation figures are unreliable but might approximate reality exaggerated.)

Talent was hard to find in the 1860s. Around midnight Syme ground his teeth reading the editorials, striking out a phrase, rewriting a sentence, sometimes the whole piece. He was annoyed as the printer's boy knocked on his door that what he had clearly laid down in the editorial conference as editorial policy had been misunderstood. The great communicator sometimes failed to get across to men he had hired, men on his side. When the paper went to press at 2am an employee brought his horse to the door; he rode home five miles to Booroondara and was 'rarely' asleep before 3am.

The Age had two reporters from Ireland, one Catholic, one Protestant, both disabled. Gerald Supple, near-blind, Syme said, could not read and 'knew nothing of what was going on.' (Supple had his demons. A barrister-journalist, he shot and wounded fellow advocate George Paton Smith, later Attorney General, in La Trobe-street on 17 May 1870, killing a bystander.) J.W.O'Hea suffered a social disability: having written special articles for *The Times,* London, he thought it unnecessary to notice events in Melbourne. Syme, writing to a friend, said he had to feed both men subjects from year's end to year's end and there was hardly a decent writer to be had for love or money.

He mocked the self-interest school of economics which taught that self-interest would deliver such wealth as the world had never seen, 'like rain from heaven' falling on just and unjust alike. The school made the self God. Syme argued that the fair go governed buyer and seller, master and servant, man and wife, parent and child. Fair play even ruled the race-track. What would become of racing if jockeys were got at, false weights declared, horses doctored and owners paid to lose? Such practices, Syme said, were not unknown. What if they became the rule?

From 1 January 1849 *The Herald* was *The Morning Herald*. After peaking as the highest-circulation Melbourne daily, it shrivelled its appeal to readers and advertisers. The proprietor, Robert Collins Levy, advertised surplus printing machinery. David Syme, planning the experiment of an evening paper, bought it in December 1868. Two weeks later *The Morning Herald* was *The Herald*, published at 5pm, delivered by office carts 'to the various suburban agents as soon thereafter as possible.' On 8 February 1869 a group of journalists and compositors launched a new morning paper, *The Daily Telegraph*, managed as a cooperative by the ex-*Morning Herald* foreman printer, C.F.Somerton, edited by Howard Willoughby.

The *Telegraph* folded, insolvent, on 30 April 1892, having fallen into the hands of proprietors whose desire to protect Sabbath observance over-rode both the imperative of profit and the compositors' convenience. None of the mechanical work of producing Monday's paper could be done on Sunday; there was a midnight-to-midnight shutdown. Of course, a friendly parliamentarian conceded, not even the proprietors of *The Daily Telegraph* could stop news such as fires or accidents happening on Sunday or journalists attending to report them. Reporters took notes of sermons on Sunday. There was nothing wrong with that.

Syme owned *The Herald* for two years. He changed its motto from 'Impartial, not Neutral' to 'Give me the liberty to know, to utter and to argue freely according to conscience above all liberties.' He appointed Graham Berry, owner-editor of the struggling Geelong *Register*, an up-and-coming reformer, as the first evening editor. Berry had read *The Decline and Fall of the Roman Empire* on the counter as a young shop assistant. He believed in manhood suffrage. He believed in breaking the power of the squatters and the Legislative Council. He was David Syme's brother.

Yet after he accepted Syme's invitation, he thought it 'one of the worst things I ever did.' He took his eye off *The Register;* it never recovered. After three months, Berry said, 'I had made *The Herald* talked of, got it a circulation of 5000 and good advertising business.' Syme executive William Poole, a former *Herald* editor, sacked him with a month's notice. Berry met Syme and Poole in the counting house. In a 'stormy' meeting, Berry told Syme and Poole what he thought of them.

Next day Syme wrote as Mr Ice Cold.

> Dear Sir — I have carefully considered the question that formed the subject of our interview yesterday and have, I am sorry to say, not been able to alter my decision. Mr Poole's notice of Saturday last may therefore be considered final.
>
> We discussed the matter so thoroughly yesterday that it is not necessary for me to do more than state the conclusion I have arrived at, or to add one word to what I then said regarding the zeal and industry displayed by you in the interests of the paper.
>
> I am, dear Sir, Yours truly, David Syme.

In 1865 a leading free-trader and former Attorney General, John Dennison Wood, sought a jail term for criminal libel for David Syme amid a constitutional crisis. The core of the crisis, marked by monster meetings at the Exhibition Building, the Wood Market in Elizabeth-street, the Geelong Town Hall and other venues was whether the free-trade, squatter-dominated Legislative Council could reject the tariff legislation of the reformist government elected in 1864 which was dominated by the Attorney General, former *Argus* editor George Higinbotham. The free-trade *Argus* on 27 January said Higinbotham was a cornered rat. He attached the tariff to the appropriation bill. Rejection would mean the Government lacked money to govern. The Council said its right to veto individual money bills could not be abolished by tacking them onto appropriation and on 25 July blocked supply. *The Age* on 13 and 15 September published a story of a conspiracy to overthrow the constitution involving Wood.

Syme was committed for trial for criminal libel on 20 September 1865. The cool Syme who had told an enraged reader shouting 'what would happen if I threw you out that [*Age* office] window?' "Why man, you'd break it", was now white hot. Wood, a clever, honest, spiteful lawyer, a leading free trader born in Tasmania, educated in Edinburgh, sought jail for the leading protectionist.

Said Syme in *The Age* 21 September:

> The foiled clique, bent on suppressing free discussion of public affairs now vent their spleen against the only metropolitan newspaper which is neither to be bribed nor coerced.
>
> Let Mr Wood go on and do his worst
>
> We know who are at the bottom of this business and they will be dragged into open day. We desire nothing better than that they go

> on, in order that the public may learn the perils which attend the path of any journalist who has the courage fearlessly to discharge his duty and protect the constitutional rights of the people
>
> We shall not discuss the influences which have been used to bribe or intimidate this journal. The usual revenge of the meanly mercantile mind has been resorted to. Advertisements have been withdrawn and subscriptions stopped, the old game played so successfully while Mr O'Shanassy was in office has again been resorted to. And since all other means have failed, it is thought to overwhelm the paper with the cost of vexatious proceedings
>
> On the mere production of the papers containing the offending paragraphs, Mr Syme is committed for trial.
>
> Had Mr Wood possessed a manly spirit he would have facilitated a hearing [a civil libel trial] to determine whether the statements were true or false. He would have laid bare his political character and professional conduct and allowed the public and magistrates to judge whether the comments were warranted or not.
>
> But that is not Mr Wood's mode of vindicating himself. He sends his counsel to defend him, and he remains outside.
>
> This journal will be ready to meet Mr Wood at the next Criminal Sessions and we promise him that we shall not imitate his example and take shelter under any plea which will prevent the whole case coming out.

He did not make the objection that truth was irrelevant in a trial for criminal libel. In Melbourne in 1865 as readers enclosed half-crowns, pounds and guineas 'a tradesman' sent 10s saying putting down the people's press would end 'all true progress' in law truth had the weight of the air over the Yarra.

Syme mocked Wood in a tone suggesting he could not be touched. 'Like other men of his stamp Mr Wood dreads nothing so much as a free press. He exhausts his vocabulary in abusing others but whines most pitifully at the slightest castigation of himself.' When his journalism was challenged Syme disdained even profitability: he might have been J.D.Lang. To flatter the rich and forget the poor, 'to caress in the leading columns those whose names appear most frequently in the advertising sheet' was journalism at once facile and profitable. He believed truthful journalism made profit possible.

He objected that forty of the jury pool were importers, merchants or connected to merchants who were likely to be free-traders prejudiced against *The Age*. The jury could not agree. On 29 November the jury at a second trial failed to agree. Wood lost his seat in the January 1866 election.

• • •

Victorian politicians, some disdaining press tone, some resenting its influence, some seeking to get square, used a weapon neglected in New South Wales — the power of parliament to declare words published in newspapers a contempt and punish editors, acting as prosecutor, judge and jury in its own cause.

When George Dill, publisher, saw William Palmer, parliamentary Sergeant-at-Arms, in *The Argus* office in Great Collins Street with an order in his hand, Dill knew what to say: nothing. He accepted the order without a word.

He also did nothing. The order required him to appear at the bar of the Assembly on Wednesday 9 April to answer for a scandalous breach of privilege. Dill was not surprised.

The Argus had laid into the chairman of the Police Committee, William Frazer, the member for Creswick, on 4 April 1862 for 'officious' and 'uncalled-for meddling' with the police. Nothing was more likely to destroy police discipline than 'the interference of such a man as the member for Creswick.'

With these words Dill crossed the psychological and political barrier separating the private man from the public official. Mr Frazer was 'some kind of privileged ruffian' chance had 'pitch-forked into the House.' The contemptuous tone made law-makers suspect Dill thought himself and *The Argus* above them and didn't know who they were.

Mr Frazer complained to his Assembly peers that the words were a scandalous breach of privilege; they quickly agreed and ordered the Sergeant's visit. When Dill failed to appear, the Assembly declared the non-appearance another contempt and the Speaker, Sir Francis Murphy, issued a warrant for his arrest.

Taken into custody on 29 April, Dill was uncooperative. When Murphy asked him in the Assembly 'have you any explanation to offer for your non-attendance?' Dill said *I decline to answer*. He had been questioned less than a minute and revealed no more than that his name was George Dill and he published *The Argus*.

Murphy told Dill to leave the chamber. When angry debate ensued the shorthand writer was ordered not to take notes.

Dill returned; the Clerk read the article.

Murphy: Are you aware that [the article] reflects upon a member of this House and upon one of its committees and the House generally? — I decline to answer.

Murphy: Have you any explanation to offer in regard to that? — I decline to answer.

A member: Do you wish to retract or apologise?

Mr Dill: Not in the slightest.

Mr Levey: Do you wish to name the author? — I was not asked.

If I ask you, will you give the name? — Ask me.

I ask the name of the author. — I refuse to give it.

After another debate with Hansard censored, the House resolved Dill to be guilty of contempt and breach of privilege and committed him to the custody of the Sergeant-at-Arms for one month, unless the parliament was sooner prorogued. (The House could not imprison for longer than it was in session.) He remained in custody for one month. Two days into the sentence, his barrister, A. Michie QC reminded the Supreme Court the House of Commons had sentenced a man to life imprisonment, whipping, branding and a fine, for offensive words.

Suffering of that order was not required in Melbourne. After *The Argus* said on 16 March 1866 that a ministerial statement 'fairly bristled with falsehood' the Assembly declared the words a scandalous breach of privilege, 39 votes to 21 and Hugh George, *The Argus* publisher, was detained in a parliamentary apartment adjoining that of the Sergeant-at-Arms for which he was charged *like a wounded bull* £5 a day. After staff visiting George removed corks from wine bottles, the Sergeant informally sought the Attorney General's advice: was partying while imprisoned for contempt permissible? On 4 April an MP complained of tyranny: it was 'improper' to dictate how much Mr George might drink with friends. The House of Commons itself recognised such indulgences. The Attorney General said the Sergeant-at-Arms was entitled to stop Mr George entertaining his friends. The £5 was for sustenance and other charges. George was released after three weeks.

• • •

The 30 March 1867 *Leader* said: 'That Mr [William Nelson] McCann and his friends having conspired at the commencement of the session to fill their own pockets from the Treasury, they generously desire that the class to whom they are indebted for their seats should share in the plunder.'

McCann responded that all members 'have been subjected to much abuse by the press of this country.' He had been a pressman himself. All he wanted from newspapers was that they 'set forth fairly and honestly the views held by public men' and subject them — the views, not the men — to 'fair and reasonable criticism.' When he moved that the article was a scandalous breach of privilege, police were investigating McCann for forgery; he was convicted in August and jailed for seven years.

When merchants and shipping agents, members of the Free Trade League, withdrew advertisements from *The Age*, David Syme said this was cutting off the nose to spite the face. 'As to how far their business purposes have been served thereby, they are the best judges. If they can afford to do without *The Age*, they must be aware that *The Age* can do without them, the paper said on 1 January 1867. That day Syme dropped the price from 3d to 2d. During 1866 circulation had 'almost doubled.' *The Age* clearly had a place — a party and interests to represent. In its own sphere it was a power, and the sphere was growing. 'Wherever population is, *The Age* and its opinions have currency. Having got circulation, advertising must follow.' As long as free-trade shop-keepers were prepared to take money from protectionist customers, they would advertise in a newspaper that kept those customers coming through the door. Five weeks later circulation had 'nearly doubled' again.

He believed in ideas. Some called him 'King David' in a tone suggesting he was a tall poppy ready for a blade. To alliterative John Norton he was 'saturnine Syme'. He rehearsed editorials in his head, talking to himself, then talking to his readers through his writers. He was a statue of liberalism, a protectionist surrounded by free-trade merchants building networks to bring King David down. They mailed calfskin notices of cancellation. Draining glasses at South Yarra dinners, they mocked the character they imagined him to be — dour, bleak, unbending. The big men of the big end of Melbourne imagined David Syme as a caricature of themselves.

He thought of press freedom as no more than that of 'the humblest individual'. The Press had no licence. A politician might slander a person in Parliament, with no redress. 'But a newspaper has no such privilege, and if it makes a charge which it fails to sustain it must pay the penalty.' He looked to history: 'At first the [British] Press was a newspaper and nothing more, simply a purveyor of news, a recorder of current events.' Later it assumed another function, of 'interpreter or commentator or propagandist.'

> The Press has also been described as the organ of public opinion. But a newspaper is something more than an organ of public opinion; it may represent public opinion, but it also helps to form public opinion. A newspaper, if it is of any account at all, has its own opinions. It does not ask the man in the street what he thinks, but it tells him what he ought to think.
>
> It presents him with the facts, shows him what these facts imply and how they affect him. It even has the temerity to tell Parliament what it ought to do under certain circumstances; what grievances it ought to remedy and even how to remedy them. Members don't like to have their attention drawn to such matters by a newspaper. They call it dictation. But if members attended to their duties there would be no occasion for the Press to interfere. But whether they like such

criticism or not they have to submit to it, so long as it is made in the public interest.

The Australasian Institute of Journalists waited on Premier James Patterson on the night of 26 July 1893 to ask that the weight of the law of libel be lifted from Victorian newspapers. They wanted journalists to be as free to report public meetings as they were to report parliament. Fat chance. Mr Joseph Henry Abbott MLC who had started the *Digger's Advocate* with Ebenezer Syme, introduced the journalists. The question was not new, he said; it had been frequently ventilated. The amendment was in the public interest. Mr H. Short, a vice-president, said liberalisation was not just in the interests of newspaper proprietors; it was in the interests of the public. Proprietors of the Bendigo *Advertiser and Independent, Ballarat Courier* and *The Herald* put the case. The Premier said his personal views were entirely with the press. A Bill to do what the deputation wanted, introduced by Mr Isaacs last session, had his cordial support. The press had great power and led public opinion. He had travelled a great deal and thought the Victorian press was of a higher standard than that of New South Wales and infinitely superior to any American paper; in a literary sense it could not be surpassed even in England. The deputation had an able advocate in Mr Isaacs. The Bill had his support. They could rely on his sympathy. 'The deputation thanked the Premier, then withdrew,' the *Age* reported. Once again Australian journalists hoping to free the press had been duchessed.

Premiers 'continually' consulted David Syme about forming Ministries. Necessarily, he thought. *The Age* made and unmade Governments. He was 'always consulted' He 'knew the ins and outs of everything'. Had he kept a diary it would have been 'a complete secret political history of Victoria.' He was aware of the interest in such a diary but he couldn't do it. 'I abstained from keeping a diary, because I regarded these matters as confidential, although there was never any such stipulation made.'

The English agricultural labourer, he wrote in 1871, 'has no ambition because he has no hope.' He had to drudge on to the end, the jail or the workhouse. Was the prevalence of crime a wonder? The English poor had been driven into large towns, living in hovels, dens and garrets, in the ignorance and want that bred crime and disease. He looked to France after the revolution. 'The law of primogeniture was abolished, and the large estates were broken up. The effect was magical.' He looked to Virginia and Maryland. When vast estates were parcelled out on the British model slavery became an economic necessity. He looked to the Swan River. The free settlers had large grants of land, but no labor: they petitioned for convicts in 1849. In America and Australia the effects of landlordism were much alike, Syme wrote in the *Westminster*

Review. In America it led to slavery, in Australia to convictism. The British should break up great estates. He had no doubt this plan would be denounced as revolutionary. It *was* revolutionary. 'It is no use attempting half-measures when whole ones answer better, and are as easily carried.'

He covered the waterfront, writing *Outlines of an Industrial Science* challenging Adam Smith's orthodoxies (1881), *On the Modification of Organisms* (1891), a critique of Charles Darwin's dangerous idea, and *The Soul: A Study and an Argument* (1903). The editor who tried to speak with the voice of the people had a part in the conversation of humanity. To his biographer, barrister Ambrose Pratt, Syme's blue-grey eyes suggested 'polished steel'. Looking at Syme's portrait at 80 Pratt's loving eye saw the old man's hair as iron-grey. His mouth was often compressed in a straight line, but to Pratt's eye the lips were 'shapely curves'. The square chin revealed his granite will; he had scarcely aged in 25 years.

The White Australia policy was written in the sandstone of consensus. The Mongol race from the 'flowery land' was inferior to the Aryans. *The Age* worried about the weight of numbers: the view from Collins Street was that 400 million Chinese were a horde that could swamp Victoria from Warrnambool to Bairnsdale. Everyone, everything south of the Murray River could go under. The leader and feature writers worried about the 6000 Chinese in the Northern Territory, who, they said, outnumbered whites six to one.

The pattern might spread. Already *The Northern Territory Times* advertisements sought guides to conduct 500 Chinese to the McDonnell Mountains ruby mines. The Mongolian was pushing to 'the very heart of Australia.' Why should Victoria be a spittoon to the Chinese Empire? *The Age* asked on 18 June 1887, when General Wong Yung Ho and Consul General U Tsing, Commissioners of the Chinese Government, visited Ballarat.

At the Town Hall General Ho opened a can of worms. Chinese in good circumstances would never leave their native land, he said. Migrants to the Victorian goldfields came from 'the poor class of the Celestial Empire.' For *The Age* every country was obliged to protect its citizens from the evils of pauperism, 'especially when the paupers are aliens in religion, in language and in race.' *The Age* hoped it would never be 'necessary for the people of Victoria to throw a cargo of Chinamen' into Port Phillip Bay as the people of Boston had thrown a cargo of tea. They all knew where that would lead.

Charles Henry Pearson had an intellectual's answer to *The Age*'s question. Born in London on 7 September 1830, the tenth son of an Anglican clergyman, he was drawn to Christian socialism at Oxford University, became professor of modern history at King's College, migrated to South Australia in 1864, bought a sheep farm near Mount Remarkable and suffered the worst drought since utopian settlers sailed to Kangaroo Island in 1836.

Returning to England, he argued in *Essays on Reform* that conservative apathy was more to be feared than revolutionary fervour. He returned to South Australia in 1872, then moved to Melbourne University as lecturer in history and political economy. On 11 February 1875 he predicted inventions like the sewing machine would unchain women from housework so they would compete with men as equals. At the university his eloquent liberalism influenced Alfred Deakin and Theodore Fink, later chairman of the Herald and Weekly Times. In eleven years contributing to *The Age* and *The Leader* he attacked blackbirding. After his speech at the National Reform and Protection League's 'monster meeting' at the Princess Theatre on 19 February 1877 the *Melbourne Punch* said the professor was aligned with the communists. To the Yarra squatters, bankers and pastoralists, the professor of democracy was a class traitor. Pearson looked beyond the mighty Murray and the redgum Gippsland cottages and the Tidal River at Wilson's Promontory. He saw the big picture. White and coloured labour could not exist side-by-side. If the Chinese worked the mines and sugar plantations in Bundaberg and Cairns, it was not just the whites in Australia, but the whole civilised world, that would be the losers. Australians were 'guarding the last part of the world in which the higher races can live and increase freely.' Pearson, who thought the ideas fermenting in Melbourne surpassed socialist experiments in Europe, believed blacks and Chinese would come into their own. 'We shall wake to find ourselves elbowed and hustled, and perhaps even thrust aside by peoples whom we looked down upon as servile'.

As the commissioners wrote their impressions for the Chinese Government, *The Age* let them know that for furniture-workers, market-gardeners, cigar-makers and candle-fashioners, the issue was survival. A Trades Hall Council meeting In Lygon Street, Carlton on 17 June 1887 applauded *The Age's* courage in covering the Chinese question. Until they read *The Age,* Mr J.W.Barrett said, they had not been aware of the extent of the evil. *The Age* article should be broadcast throughout the colony. A woman told a typographer, Mr Hancock 'I buy tea from a Chinaman because it is cheap.' That was the secret of John Chinaman's success. *The Age* had spoken nobly and deserved every tradesman's thanks. In Cheltenham on 22 August 1887 the Rev. Mr Caffyn said the authorities should be told the Chinese worked seven days a week. Steps should be taken to stop them working on the Sabbath; market gardeners put their hands together.

The Shipping Difficulty was a newspaper euphemism for the maritime strike. But numbers gave journalists their perpetual difficulty. When a crowd gathered in Latrobe Street on Tuesday morning 5 August 1890, *The Age* reporter estimated '900 to 1000' present; speakers repeatedly spoke of 2000 to 3000, 'figures,' the reporter wrote, 'which were twice or three times in excess of the truth.' Socialists spoke of a revolution that might be introduced peacefully, or more quickly were its supporters 'ready to fight'. By next Saturday shearing sheds had adopted union rules at Puckawidgee, Deepwater, Boomanoomoona, Boonoke, Quaimong, Illilawa, Toganamain, Moolpa, Dollar Vale and Toogimbie. Wool from two non-union sheds, Kooba and Croonboon, was under close surveillance. In Sydney 'the wharf labourers have resolved not to touch it.' A report from Sydney said the steamer Janet Nicholl had unloaded smoothly since the owner, Mr B.B.Nichol, 'discharged the Kanaka crew and agreed to employ union seamen.'

To *The Age* it was 'very significant that the Trades Hall Council is denounced as fiercely by the so-called Socialists as [by] any other authority in the land.' These agitators were 'the declared enemies of all authority, human and divine.' They 'repeat the ravings of the French anarchists.' A story of a police raid of brothels in Fitzroy said 'a number of Greeks, Frenchmen, Germans and Italians were living off the proceeds of immorality of Australian and English girls.'

The ship owners refused to negotiate with the maritime officers while they remained affiliated with the Trades Hall Council. *The Age* was contemptuous. The conservative press argued that the officers' affiliation with labour unions subverted discipline on board ship. This was false. The unions had no 'sympathy with disorder and neglect of work.' If ship-owners took on the combined unions 'they run the risk of being beaten'. The ship-owners were unnecessarily provoking a great struggle; they were childish. *The Age* hoped the unrest would lead to stable industrial relations satisfactory to all.

Blue-merino carriage cloth at £50 a roll was food for moths in the Newport railway store-sheds, *The Age* chief-of-reporting-staff G.F.H.Schuler reported on 3 March 1892. Schuler brought a forensic novelist's eye and an accountant's eye for numbers to waste and corruption in the railways.

From 20 March 1891 to 14 March 1892 *The Age* piled detail upon detail about what had gone wrong. Lines had been built and stations manned not because they were needed but through pressure from the local member. When the chairman of commissioners, Richard Speight, was appointed on 1 February 1884 with two 'dummy commissioners', Alfred Agg and Richard Ford, the average railways employee, of whom there were 10,000, cost £103. By 1892 there were 16,000 permanent officers and casual hands and their average cost was £143. 'Here the secret of mismanagement is laid bare,' Schuler wrote on 1 March 1892. It was notorious that private sector wages were lower than they were when the commissioners took office, and rank-and-file railways workers were also paid less. The commissioners increased the number of high-salaried inspectors and foremen well beyond the railways' requirements. Some had duties no-one could define.

Schuler said Speight had worked at the Midland Railway Company, England, 'the land where the workforce are miserably paid and the drones revel in luxurious magnificence.' On English railways officers drew salaries of thousands of pounds a year while 'the guard or porter works 15 hours a day for a pittance of 18s or 20s a week.' This policy was being introduced in Melbourne. Porters were joining at 5s a day and worked a year before an increase of 6d a day while officers paid extravagant salaries multiplied. The 'most useless' spent their time on whims dangerous to public safety. King David's optimism informed Schuler's reporting: he believed a railway could make a profit.

Schuler, born at sea of German parents on 24 February 1854 went to school in Bendigo and joined *The Advertiser* as a mining reporter. He jumped to *The Age* in 1879 and Syme appointed him chief of reporting staff in 1890. Amiable and idealistic, ruled by duty, Schuler looked as if he loved the world and everything in it. Reporters found him modest, tactful and high-minded. The facts, the story, were everything.

After the incoming Shiels Government suspended the railways Commissioners, Mr Speight (with Agg and Ford), issued his writ in June 1892 claiming £25,000 (more than $2 million in 2019) damages for eleven separate counts of libel in 1891 and 1892. Because *The Age* reported incompetence, waste, extravagance, over-manning, and recklessness in the Commissioner's management of the railway, the Commissioner had been injured in his reputation. There was a Pacific Ocean of detail: in the opening address for the plaintiff in *Speight v Syme* before Mr Justice Hodges on 1 June 1893, Frank Gavan Duffy took three hours and twenty minutes to read the particulars.

'Mr Syme, the defendant, is in fact *The Age* newspaper,' Mr Duffy said. He told the jury: 'A man who starts a newspaper does so with no other motive than a man who starts any other business.' To make money. Good businessmen tried to make money honestly; others sought it in other ways. People were more impressed when they read something in a newspaper. They tended to take it for granted.

Newspaper proprietors had a monopoly of comment: they distributed the news and their own views. If that had ever happened to the jury — Mr John Royle, a tent-maker of Flinders-street West was the foreman; members included a Collins-street jeweller, a South Richmond politician and two printers — they would recognise 'how very inaccurate the so-called facts are and 'what peculiar twists are put on those alleged facts'. People thought the facts newspapers reported were true. There must be fire where there was so much smoke. That was the position of *The Age*. That was the power Mr Syme held in his hand.

Mr J.L.Purves KC, for *The Age*: 'Most advocates have some sort of escape door, but I burn my ships and shall fight, I think, the battle of freedom and justice as an honest man. Newspapers are one of the essential factors of our modern civilisation. Without newspapers none of the great reforms of modern times could ever have beencarried out, or any abuses stamped out.

The barrister thought the railway articles 'among the most powerful ever written. We have never had such a series published in Victoria. Never.' *The Age* said the articles had not damaged Mr Speight's reputation because they were true. The comments were fair. After testimony from 108 witnesses in 92 days of trial, the stacked documents obscured the court officials who numbered them. The confused jury indicated they had not understood their task, the arguments or the evidence. They returned 'a general verdict' for Speight and damages of £100.

Justice Hodges told them the verdict was bad in law. He required their judgment on eleven separate libellous imputations. When they resumed, the jury could not agree on ten counts. On the eleventh, alleging Speight's 'ruinous incompetence', extravagance and waste, they awarded Speight £100 damages. The second trial of 88 days ended on 26 September 1894 with a verdict for Speight on one count, one farthing damages, and for Syme on the other nine. (The suits cost Syme £50,000, more than $4 million in 2019.)

Months later Syme heard Speight was in financial trouble. He asked to see Speight's friend Ephraim Zox who told him Speight had been offered a job in Western Australia and his friends were helping him with the expensive move across the Nullarbor. Syme wrote a cheque for £100 and asked Zox to present it to Mr Speight with his compliments.

Next morning Speight went to Syme's office and said on the verge of tears: 'Mr Syme, how could you do this?'

Syme held out his hand. 'It was a great fight.'

David's older brother George Alexander Syme, born in 1822, studied theology at the University of Aberdeen, was active in the Established Church of Scotland, then the Free Presbyterian Church, became minister of a Baptist church at Nottingham, England for fifteen years, resigned the ministry and in 1863 migrated to Melbourne and briefly edited *The Age* in 1866. George was David's opposite in temperament, nervous, readily agitated, incoherent under stress, but as editor of the weekly *Leader* in May 1878 he told David he had discovered 'a young genius' and introduced the embarrassed Alfred Deakin, 22. Deakin, junior counsel to J.L.Purves KC in the Speight libel cases, had already met David at a séance. Intrigued by mysteries, by what they did not know, both explored spiritualism for answers. Deakin, a newly qualified lawyer conscious of the limits of reason, trusted his imagination and sought the poet within. He was president of the Victorian Association of Spiritualists.

When George ushered Deakin into the publisher's office, Syme, who thought poetry moonshine and reasoned from fact said: 'Aha! So this is your genius.'

Deakin nervously suggested he could contribute pieces on art and literature, but not politics. Syme agree to let him try but said *The Age* offered no real market for anything but politics. After a month's try-out writing leaders on subjects of which he knew nothing Deakin moved to the *Leader* in July 1878.

He found George uncouth 'when under stress of perplexity his most frequent mood', and his editing so conscientious it was exhausting. Never had he suffered such a grilling. It was, he said, both the most severe and pettiest ordeal he had ever faced. David intervened, insisting George give Deakin a free hand. He was paid per piece, never refused an assignment and by 1879 affable Alfred had more access to the publisher than any *Age* journalist, conversed on politics and literature on walks to Syme's Albert Park house and earned more money than he needed.

Reporters and sub-editors loathed the favouritism. Deakin saw it with a reporter's detachment: 'I was distinctly the pet of the proprietor.' In their talks Syme focused on 'facts, facts, always facts'. Poetry was mere words, fiction nonsense. Deakin, writing a thesis on the philosophy, science, history and art of poetry, found the contrast deepened the friendship.

When a deputation sought Syme's advice on a Liberal candidate to run for West Bourke against Robert Harper, a conservative Melbourne merchant, a strong candidate, Syme suggested Deakin. The deputation knocked on Deakin's Temple Court chambers and the spokesman suggested without preamble that Deakin should stand for West Bourke with the support of the protectionist Premier Graham Berry. Syme promised help; Deakin agreed.

He won the seat on 18 February 1879 by 97 votes and ended his maiden speech to the Assembly on 8 July by resigning. A polling place at Newham had run out of ballot papers at 3.30pm, disenfranchising a handful of voters. He said if he represented the majority in West Bourke, he would be returned. If not 'he had no right to be there.' He was a man of principle; he was 22. Life was a stage. On the bus home, Premier Berry said without anger that Deakin might have consulted colleagues before he resigned. 'It's all very well for you. It puts you on a pinnacle. But what of the Party, if you lose them a seat at this juncture?'

Deakin lost the by-election on 22 August by 15 votes, lost in the February 1880 general election in which the Berry Government fell and was elected member for West Bourke on 14 July 1880. His biographer Walter Murdoch, Rupert's great-uncle, noted that Deakin MP 'was never again defeated in an election.' While Victorian conservatives saw revolution in Berry's proposals to limit the Council's capacity to amend money bills and overstatement was routine in public debate, Deakin *The Age* essayist made affability his aim, conciliation his core.

Journalism taught him that writing for newspapers was hard work, poorly paid. It required patient, unremitting application. 'Journalism had gratified, amused, rewarded but disgusted me,' he wrote in 1900.

Disgusted? 'Its constant concern with those transient occurrences and superficial aspects of current affairs, which constituted the mass of its subject-matter, seemed but little more honourable than the glaring selfishness of commercial life.' A protectionist convinced by David Syme found writing for the protectionist *The Age* confining. The narrow partisanship, the subordination of all views to those of 'the paper and its party threatened to suffocate one's opinions and reduce one's mind to a machine and one's pen to that of a press hack.' These considerations 'drove me into public [political] life'. As Prime Minister for three years and three months in three interrupted terms between September 1903 and April 1910 and leader of the Opposition till January 1913, he covered tumultuous Australian politics, including the personality and principles of Alfred Deakin, as the 'special' or Sydney correspondent for the London *Morning Post*. In thirteen years of secret journalism, from 3 January 1901 to 30 December 1914, his journalist persona posed as baffled by his political self.

'A short visit to Melbourne does not explain the situation or the meaning of the Prime Minister,' the special correspondent wrote for *the Post* of 29 December 1905. 'Though he [Deakin] has lived all his life in that city, and has been prominent in politics for twenty years, there is no consensus of opinion regarding him or his policy.' Some thought Deakin chose the line of least resistance. Others saw a theorist pursuing impossible dreams.

Deakin the correspondent thought Deakin the intellectual Prime Minister had a defiant attitude and a parliamentary career 'unstable from the first; even The Bulletin mocks his excessively "affable" and invariably conciliatory demeanour.' Public life was fetid with rumour; the Prime Minister wrote a million anonymous words for £6500 for a Tory newspaper in London; no-one twigged. Journalism was as transparent as the Yarra after a storm.

Victorian legislators were clear in their minds as they made Sunday newspapers unlawful in 1889. First, they were clear they that were not doing it. As the Attorney General Henry Wrixon, a novelist who thought universal suffrage inevitable but possibly fatal, who was Syme's counsel in *Wood v Syme* said: 'The law at present forbids the publication and dealing in a newspaper on Sunday as well as all other public trading and dealing.' There was no change to the status quo. Why then, several boat-rockers asked, was the Bill necessary? A 'question had been raised,' Mr Wrixon said on 31 October, whether Sunday newspapers were covered by the Police Offences Act, section 30, which required 'Sunday to be duly observed' and 'no house, shop store or other place to be open' on the Sabbath. It was only a doubt. He did not entertain it himself. But instead of subjecting a person who tried to start a Sunday newspaper to 'troublesome and costly litigation, it would be better to make the position thoroughly clear.' A statutory ban on Sunday newspapers would make life easier for a newspaper proprietor, said David Syme's counsel.

Should a new Sunday newspaper cause newsboys to make a nuisance near churches, papers publishing six days a week would be forced to publish on Sunday; their staff would have no day of rest. (In London, Sunday newspapers had violated the day of Christian prayer since 1843, selling through clubs, barber-houses and coffee shops nearly four times the combined circulation of dailies.)

Captain Taylor: 'The compositors work on Sundays now.' Mr Wrixon: 'The Bill has nothing to do with Sunday work.'

The compositors working on Monday's papers worked on Sundays inside newspaper buildings, invisible to the public. It was not violation of the Sabbath that troubled the legislators, but visible violation. Sunday papers would add yet another temptation to distract believers from the congregation. Alfred Deakin, the member for West Bourke, said nothing.

David Syme died at home at Kew on 14 February 1908. He was 81. *The Daily Telegraph* in Sydney said Shelley's *Ode to Liberty* shaped him; he had heard chartists hammering on the door of Tory privilege. *The Adelaide Register* thought he acted out the intimacy of teaching, preaching and journalism, which were one in their educational aims. *The West Australian* said that when Syme stood for the masses against gentlemen, the ostracism his own class imposed on him 'was complete. A wall was built to exclude him.' In Melbourne *The Herald* said he had used a great public journal 'in the interests of the people'. To *The Argus* he had been a 'remorseless' advocate of protection.

Chapter 13

News Under the Sun

1846–1891: James Swan, Arthur Lyon, William Wilkes, Theophilus Pugh, Thomas Stephens, Attorney General Ratcliffe Pring and *The Moreton Bay Courier;The Courier 1861–1864,The Queensland Guardian 1860–1868; The Brisbane Courier from June 1864; Gresley Lukin; George Wight* and *The Queensland Guardian.*

'I ask you whether the Legislative Council is to be allowed to be scandalised and vilified by a newspaper? I ask if power is to be given to a paper to write anything and everything? Unless this power were curtailed, society could not exist.

Ratcliffe Pring, Queensland Attorney General, 21 August 1861, prosecuting Theophilus Pugh, editor, The Courier, for seditious libel.

James Swan, 35, at first glance saw that Brisbane houses were rare and streets but names and thought his mentor Dr John Dunmore Lang's belief that the north was ripe for a newspaper must have the weight of a wisp of smoke.

Though it was acute, Swan's anxiety was short-lived. Residents with the confidence of those with nothing to lose assured him that subscriptions and advertisements would flow like summer rain. He printed the first issue of *The Moreton Bay Courier* on 20 June 1846 with Arthur Lyon, 25, as editor. The pair sagaciously sought support from both sides of the street, commerce and the church. Beneath the masthead they ran Johnny Fawkner's quote from the Calvinist preacher John Knox *I am in the place where I am demanded of conscience to speak the truth.* What did they mean? In his first leader Lyon said the tropics hungered for 'those beneficent moral influences which have their origins in the Press' but did not identify them, leaving no hint of whether he though the task too difficult or too obvious.

While some believed if newspapers could report what they wished *society could not exist*, Lyon and Swan waved a booster flag. 'Settlements have become villages; villages, towns. Our staple articles of export, wool and tallow, have strikingly increased.' They banged the local drum: 'The weight of tyranny, misrepresentation and neglect, under which the colonists have long, bitterly and unceasingly complained, is about to be removed.' Sir George Gipps, the asthmatic liberal Governor in Sydney who had become an 'arbitrary and despotic' ruler was about to sail for England. *Regretting the decay of his health, we rejoice at his departure* said the *Courier*.

The Victoria Hotel on page one made advertising promises still old and new: the daily spread was second to none, wines and spirits included the best imported brands. Patrons would be attended with civility. Three hotels, the Queen's Arms, South Brisbane and Sawyer's Arms, were for lease. Forty-three subscribers contributed £65/17/6 to a testimonial for Dr Ludwig Leichhardt, recently returned from Port Essington, now planning the cross-country trip to the Swan River which would make his death mythological and the German philosopher an Australian immortal.

Lyon cited Adam Smith's *Wealth of Nations* and Shakespeare's *Merchant of Venice* beneath the headline *We Want A Bank* in the second leader on 27 June. The bank Lyon anticipated would follow the *Courier* line, 'the handwriting on the wall: Progress.'

Reporting a Sydney mercantile house charging 20 per cent, Lyon wanted it understood the *Courier* censured neither 'usurers or the practice of usury.' Every man was entitled to use capital and industry as he chose, within the law. Lyon sought balance in his leaders and readers, who bought the paper on Saturday for 6d. There were 2,258 whites north of Tweed Heads, 829 in Brisbane, 100 subscribers and 100 casual buyers.

Loose women upset Lyon more than the *Courier*'s meagre circulation. On July 18 he 'reported' that female convicts pouring into Van Diemen's Land were 'rapidly destroying all sound public opinion and substituting a code of convict morals in its place.'

Within the conservative Lyon was a liberal visionary who thought neither dungeons nor lash curbed crime half as well as education. He conducted the *Courier* as conversation. On 25 July 1846 Lyon wrote: 'Owing to the crowded state of our columns we have been compelled to leave out the leading article to make room for subjects of great local interest.' His remarks on the Census were unavoidably postponed. By early 1848, with the paper in financial trouble, James Swan bought him out and took over as publisher, printer and editor in

July. (He later edited the squatters' *Moreton Bay Free Press,* owned by Henry Buckley, grazier, wine and spirits merchant, magistrate and insolvent.)

Swan the man was born into tabloid melodrama in Glasgow, Scotland in 1811. The second *Moreton Bay Courier* editor never knew his father, Daniel Swan, a private with the Glasgow Highland Infantry in the war against Napoleon, killed in action on the Iberian Peninsula. His mother Janet, who had been born deaf, could not talk. When James was twelve on 2 August 1823 a Scottish tart, Mary Horn, who shared a lover with his mother, rushed at her in a hairdresser's house, shrieking that Janet had been 'looking in at my door'. Janet reflexively defended herself, raking Mary's face with her nails. Mary seized a hammer from the fireplace and in front of James, struck Janet's head. The hairdresser said it sounded like stones cracking. Mary went to jail, Janet to the Royal Infirmary where she died — of pleurisy, a surgeon testified.

At Mary's murder trial the crown prosecutor pressed James: had he seen the hammer strike his mother's skull?

James said he had seen the hammer raised above his mother's head. He had seen a 'lick' [blow] aimed but it missed his mother and struck the door. He would not say what he had not seen. He would not testify to the sound the hammer made killing his mother. He did not remember it. Lord Justice Clerk Boyle said James was the best witness, man or boy, he had ever seen. He had not exaggerated 'in the slightest'. Men and women in the crowded courtroom applauded. A bewildered jury found Mary guilty of all elements of capital murder except the essential element of intent on which they brought 'by a plurality of voices', the verdict unique to Scotland 'not proven.' The High Court ruled that while she had wielded the hammer evidence of intent was insufficient and hanging unwarranted and sentenced her to transportation for life to New South Wales.

Absorbed by words on the page, fascinated by glimpses of other worlds because his mother was mute, James was apprentice printer at *The Scots Times* and after work with a carver and gilder (the skill of making things look better than they are) in 1831 married Christina Mackay.

The charismatic cleric Dr John Dunmore Lang offered Swan work in Sydney on *The Colonist*. He arrived with Lang on the *Portland* on 3 December 1837, worked as printer at *The Colonist* for three years, tried dairy farming near Wollongong, returned to *The Colonist* and joined *The Sydney Herald* after Lang's paper succumbed to the preacher's disdain for 'the paltry consideration of gain' in 1841.

Swan was not at one with Lang's lofty indifference to profit. After another try on the land he moved at Lang's suggestion to Brisbane and after the break with Arthur Lyon, appointed William Wilkes editor late in 1848. The *Courier* would continue to be 'independent and consistent'.

Wilkes was a liberal who came by his ticket to Sydney at the Old Bailey. Convicted of stealing £11/ 12s 'from a dwelling house' and sentenced to transportation for life he arrived in Sydney on 21 November 1833. Assigned to an expedition exploring the Dividing Range, after reaching Moreton Bay he received his ticket-of-leave in 1843. In *The Raid of the Aborigines*, the poet in Wilkes ridiculed squatters' dealings with the original Australians.

In his eyes the alien eucalypts and shrieking cockatoos of the tropical bush mocked the white man. Riders tied horses to trees only to find the ground 'too rotten to ride.' A jackaroo 'well skilled in brandy' flirted with a native girl whose

> eyes would have melted the heart of a stone
>
> And her nose was adorned with a kangaroo bone.

Wilkes had blacks satirically reflecting that if they speared a shepherd the jackaroos would sit smoking their pipes:

> Yet they'll turn out like madmen and boldly give battle
>
> If they think we've been spearing their sheep or their cattle.

Warm, funny and five feet three, 'the Sydney man' was a liberal humanist, one of the short people whose size magnifies heart. He wrote as James Arrowsmith and hoped his targets would laugh should their eyes chance upon a 'burlesque never intended to wound.' While he opposed convict labour, a position that cost him with advertisers, he supported separation from New South Wales as if separation were survival.

When a Yass sheep farmer experimented with shepherds from Hong Kong, Wilkes reported that after five months the Chinese seemed contented, even happy. They were honest, clean, tactful, did the same work as Europeans and were, Wilkes stressed, *equally intelligent and hardy*. When one lost his way in scrub with 800 sheep, he lit fires around the flock to keep them together and brought them home, none missing, after three nights. This Wilkes said 'cannot prove otherwise than highly acceptable to our readers.'

His passion for separation did not still the satirist. Separation would make small fish big in a little pond. Home rule would end the neglect of a government 700 miles away. But these abstractions in the mind of a Brisbane newspaperman were as dry grass in the wind compared to the economic imperative driving the squatters, cheap convict labour. The end of transportation in 1850 deprived squatters of the low-cost farmhands, shearers, labourers and sweepers many thought their entitlement. It was important to have an advocate of separation who did not require shipped-in British convicts as part of the bargain. *The Courier* knew Dr Lang was earnest in this cause.

Wilkes hoped not only for news in the colonial press but also for grace and literacy. He reported *The Sydney Morning Herald* on a perpetual theme of Australian editors, the lack of standards in their peers.

'It has been a subject of continual pain and shame to us to witness the pollution of so noble an engine as the Press'. The *Herald* did not think small colonial populations limited only newspapers' circulation, revenue, advertising and influence. There were other distortions. Small communities 'render it an extremely difficult task to avoid personalities.' How so?

> The comparatively circumscribed field of speculation or argument will sometimes drive even an ingenious writer to an undesirable course. But there are people connected with the Press who do not blush to become slanderous by habit, if not by profession and it is these persons who tend to bring the useful and honourable pursuit of the newspaper into contempt. Their conduct is the more reprehensible, that scurrility and misrepresentation, imputing false motives and detracting from personal character add nothing to the force of discussion, but rather weaken it. If the best models of newspaper literature (the daily journals of England) be examined, they will be found to be powerful and useful exactly in proportion to the choiceness of their language and the care with which they avoid insulting their readers by ruffianism of thought or of impression. The mission of the Press is a sacred mission; and he who makes a bad use of its power and influence commits high treason against society. He is a public pest and nuisance and ought to be put down.

When the *Herald*'s Brisbane correspondent reported a mass meeting for separation at the Brisbane School of Arts he included the detail of the 'uncalled for violence, most vulgarly shown in the clenching of fists etc' displaying people who would disgrace self-government, Wilkes wrote that the *Herald* was interested only in a unanimity acceptable to the *Herald*. What fitness for self-government could exist in a community united by slavish devotion to dictation? To the Brisbane editor *The Sydney Morning Herald* was a government surrogate speaking for inertia.

The *Herald* had 'no doubt that the separation [from 6 June 1859] of the Colony of Queensland from New South Wales has been premature and illegal.' The thing was altogether wrong. The Royal prerogative had been exercised unfairly. It had sacrificed private interests. But what, the writer asked, offering that fairness to his newspaper universal among leader-writers, could the *Herald* do? 'It is useless for us to attempt a resistance in which we will not have the sympathy of the world, and in which it will be easy to place ourselves in the wrong.' The power of the British Crown was undoubted. The *Herald* sought the traditional remedy, money.

Wilkes left *The Courier* in 1856, exercised his satirical muscle editing Sydney *Punch* which lasted four issues, joined *The Empire* in 1859 after Samuel Bennett and William Hanson bought it from Henry Parkes, wrote for Bennett's *Evening News,* was imprisoned in Darlinghurst Gaol in 1865 for failure to pay rent, suffered mental sickness and died in St Vincent's Hospital on 13 May 1873; he was buried in Camperdown cemetery without religious rites.

• • •

Versatile public personas inhabited the editor Theophilus Parsons Pugh. He was a police magistrate and preacher as well as a 'wicked, malicious, seditious and ill-disposed person'. Born in the British West Indies on 6 November 1831, the son of a Wesleyan minister, he was educated in London, apprenticed to a printer and migrated to Brisbane in June 1855. He started in journalism as Brisbane correspondent for Henry Parkes' *The Empire* then replaced Arthur Lyons as *Moreton Bay Free Press* editor in Ipswich. Quickly finding squatter-enforced support for rule from Sydney repugnant, he took over as publisher, printer and editor of *The Moreton Bay Courier* in 1859.

As Lyon had, Pugh sometimes treated print as if it were as transient as conversation, not a first draft of history. On 3 January 1860 he published this report of the Court of Requests: *'Lloyd v some name our reporter could not understand. Ordered to stand over.'*

Pugh was also in touch with the preacher within. What were journalists to do with the vast public interest on three continents in vulgarities such as the illegal two-hour bare-knuckle 'world title fight' between Englishman Thomas Sayers and American John Heenan on 17 April 1860?

Pugh thought *The Sydney Morning Herald* an ostrich. 'They first publish a long and graphic account of the fight, from an able report in *The Times*, which is divested of the low slang thought necessary by the sporting journals, and then they indulge in long tirades against the depraved taste which they have found it profitable to gratify.'

As editor, what would he do? The preacher had his eye fixed on a permanent truth. 'All the public interest and enthusiasm in this matter may be very mistaken and very reprehensible, but there it is, and nothing that we or anybody else could say would nullify the fact.' Minimal coverage was *Courier* policy. 'Breathe not its name, let it rest in the shade.' But the editor also saw a great story: the fight symbolised that great duel between nations, Britain v America.

When George Wight, a Congregational minister born in Scotland in 1817, started the Saturday *Queensland Guardian* in May 1860 with the state's population at 16,800, Brisbane newspapers were protestant print pulpits. Wight, fascinated by the challenge science posed to belief, published *Geology and Genesis: a reconciliation* in London in 1857 and remained a believer in the mechanical marvel of print, proselytising in the *Guardian* under the penname Willinghood and recruiting working men to Queensland in books published in Brisbane and London.

Wight and Pugh's shared faith in print and a protestant Almighty did not stop fault-finding. When the *Guardian* planned to expand to twice-weekly publication it complained that because Government advertisements appeared only in the *Courier*, the *Courier* was 'the Government organ'.

Really? Pugh said. *The Sydney Herald* stoutly opposed liberal Governments in New South Wales but those same Governments advertised in the *Herald*, for one reason only: its superior circulation. It was the same the world over: men took wares to the best market. Government advertising in *The Courier* 'no more binds us to uphold the Ministry than the appearance of a draper's advertisement binds us to puff his establishment.' Mr Wight said *The Courier* permitted ministers to revise reports of their speeches. Mr Pugh denied it. *The Courier* had twice sought help from ministers on fiscal speeches. 'The object was merely to ensure correctness and our contemporary ought to know, if experience has taught him anything, that a like course is adopted everywhere when thought necessary.'

When he bought *The Moreton Bay Courier* in May 1861, Thomas Stephens told Pugh he believed the newspaper was a potent agent for change in politics, social progress and personal morality. The *most potent* agent. Born in Rochdale, England in 1819, to a Baptist minister father, Stephens retained the faith, owned and managed woollen mills in Rochdale, migrated to Sydney in 1849 and Brisbane in 1853, where he stuck to animal hides, prospering in Cleveland, Redland Bay, as a wool-scour, fellmonger and tanner.

Business success did not seduce Stephens to the status quo. He remained a non-conformist, a believer, a primitive Baptist; kindly and forceful, he sought to make a difference. Driven by fundamental faith, he was still clear-eyed, and never believed piety could set type or break news. An administrator, not a poet, he knew what had to be done. He knew how to get men to do it. He was shrewd, practical and tender as a woman. He did not try to make a difference by making a noise and saw Theo Pugh as a man like himself: ambitious, independent, not given to bending with the breeze. He also understood what to do with Mr Pugh: leave him alone.

On Stephen's instructions, Pugh changed the title to *The Courier* on Tuesday 14 May 1861 and made the paper a daily 'without a day's notice'. In his eyes doubling publication from three to six days a week sang of progress for the paper the colony and its 30,000 people. A journal which spared no pain to 'tell how the world goes', ventilated questions of public interest, gathered and spread information and was the jealous guardian of the rights and liberties of the people, was bound to be 'an important influence on a new country'.

(A member of the Queensland legislature from 1863 to 1877, Stephens was treasurer, colonial secretary, postmaster-general and secretary for public lands. His support for the vote for all adult males alienated squatters and conservatives and when he died on 26 August 1877 left his widow with eight children.)

Freedom of thought was the privilege of every British subject, the Queensland Attorney General, Ratcliffe Pring told a jury of twelve before Mr Justice Alfred James Peter Lutwyche on 21 August 1861. The privilege must be used properly. The boundary was where publication *tended to produce improper reflections in the public's mind*. If it did, it was illegal. The ground floor of the Supreme Court was packed; officials closed the unsafe galleries. (What reflections were improper? What did 'improper' mean? How could authority know what was in the public's mind? Why was tendency, not proof, the standard? Pring was silent on these questions. He put the boundary into words, but the words did not reveal its line.)

Pring was prosecuting Theophilus Pugh, *Courier* editor, for a seditious libel of the Legislative Council, first appointed on 1 May 1860. 'I ask you whether the Legislative Council is to be allowed to be scandalised and vilified by a newspaper? I ask if power is to be given to a paper to write anything and everything? Unless this power were curtailed, *society could not exist*.'

The hearing at the Supreme Court went to the heart of authority on the Brisbane River.

Pugh turned a learned eye to the privileges of the Queensland Parliament and the shortcomings of the Attorney General. He was at home with legal reasoning. 'Men new to parliamentary life who have not received legal training may be excused for imagining that the colonial frog can dilate itself to the dimensions of the imperial ox' *The Courier* said on 17 May 1861.

As secretary of the Separation Committee for three years Theo Pugh drove the first political priority north of the Tweed and in both journalism and the law had the help of the journalist and lawyer Alfred Lutwyche.

Born in London on 26 February 1810, Lutwyche reported law for *The Times* from 1840 to 1852. Unwell in the dank city, he agreed to become *Morning Chronicle* Sydney correspondent in 1853 and sailed from Gravesend on 4 June. Hungry for news, he found his first story before the overloaded *Meridian* reached the Channel. The barque was seriously undermanned. Cutting costs on crew wages, the managing owner showed 'contemptuous indifference to the safety and comfort of the passengers.'

The captain, Richard Hernaman, had made the trip to Sydney four times. He had sailed the Indian Ocean and Bass Strait. But after running hours before a gale with navigation flawed by error in the ship's clock, the *Meridian* grounded on volcanic Amsterdam Island on 24 August. As the ship foundered Hernaman, struggling to save a hen-coop, shouted 'now, every man for himself'; a wave swept him overboard with the cook and a Swiss passenger.

Lutwyche said he lost the journalist's detachment when he heard one of 41 children aboard asking a parent whether the voyage was over and 'hoping Aunt Sarah [in Sydney] would have a good fire, as it is very wet.' After two weeks precarious camping, praying and hoping, with some taking comfort in the salvaged wine, an American whaler took the survivors to Mauritius. Lutwyche wrote the story for *The Morning Chronicle* and arrived in Sydney on 30 December 1853 after it was published.

Nominated to the NSW Legislative Council in 1856, Lutwyche turned Governor William Denison's offer down on principle. He would not take a seat in an unelected House. But he accepted Charles Cowper's nomination to the Council on 12 September and took the principle to the people, advocating manhood suffrage and equal electorates at a mass meeting in Hyde Park on 20 July 1857. A front-foot liberal whose flair collected four thousand signatures occasioned fear among conservatives, anxiety among Ipswich squatters.

Pugh's indictment reflected the assumptions in which the law originated:

> That Theophilus Parsons Pugh, being a wicked, malicious, seditious and ill-disposed person, and having no regard for the laws of this colony, or for the public peace and tranquillity of this colony, and most unlawfully, wickedly and maliciously devising, contriving and intending to asperse, scandalise and vilify the Legislative Council of Queensland in parliament assembled, and audaciously to represent their proceedings in parliament as corrupt and unjust and to raise, excite and create most groundless distrusts in the minds of all Her Majesty's subjects as to the wish and desire of the said Legislative Council to perform and discharge its public duties in an honest and impartial manner' had published a false, scandalous, wicked, seditious and mischievous libel of the Council.

On 30 July 1861 *The Courier* published this:

> The Legislative Council of Queensland has at last acquired a celebrity, though not exactly of that kind which good and wise men would desire to obtain. It never had the confidence of the public and the only sensible thing which has originated in [the Council] was the resolution that its constitution ought to be elective. Nothing could show the necessity for making Councillors directly responsible to the people better than the conduct of the nominees of the Crown from first to last in reference to the Supreme Court Bill.

The members had refused a petition from the inhabitants of Brisbane on the pretext that they were incompetent to deal with a measure affecting the Judge's [Justice Lutwyche's] position. Having insulted the people, they next insulted the crown. They condemned Mr Justice Lutwyche's conduct as 'calculated seriously to impair confidence in the administration of justice.' They listened placidly to a traducer of his moral character (Sir Charles Nicholson, who thought Lutwyche's appointment to the Supreme Court the 'political job' of an 'ultra-mobocratic' ministry.)

> 'It is now proved that men who are destitute of gentlemanly feelings, who lack common Christian charity, who have an utter disregard for truth, who have not the slightest acquaintance with the first principles of justice' and who betray crass ignorance on the history and constitution of their country may yet be included among our senators.
>
> 'The stern impartiality which Mr Justice Lutwyche exercises on the bench has often been remarked upon as perhaps the most prominent of his high judicial qualities, but the Legislative Council has had the audacity to assert that his conduct is calculated to impair confidence in the administration of justice because he has practically evidenced a political partisanship.
>
> 'Suppose he has, what then? He has a right to evince a political partisanship if he pleases. A judge does not lose his rights as a private citizen by becoming a judge. When off the bench he is as much entitled to express an opinion on public measures as any other man.'

Ratcliffe Pring, a big fish in the 'little pond' seven times the size of Great Britain, was a wobbly upholder of parliamentary rectitude. An energetic barrister, commissioner and judge born in Devon on 17 October 1825, he migrated to Sydney in 1853, practiced in Bathurst, Goulburn and Sydney and was appointed first Moreton Bay Attorney General on separation in 1859. Drunk in the Legislative Assembly on 10 January 1872, he seized a handful of another member's whiskers and pulled his collar; when the Speaker ordered the Sergeant to arrest him, Pring said 'you will have to catch me' and sprinted into the lobby. The Sergeant, reported the *Courier,* 'returned in a few 'minutes without effecting the arrest.' After the House found him guilty of contempt he resigned and went bush, later returning to the city as Supreme Court judge.

Pring told the jury that if the Legislative Council would tamely submit to language calculated to pervert the minds of the people they would deserve all they got. He cited *Howell's State Trials*: If writers editors and printers could not be called to account for possessing the people with an ill opinion of the government, no government could exist. It was necessary for all governments that the people should have a good opinion of it; nothing could be worse than to procure animosity among the people. This had always been look upon as a crime. No government could be safe without it being punished.

He quoted Dr Samuel Johnson's *Life of Milton* (1780): 'If every murmur at government may diffuse discontent, there can be no peace; and if every sceptic in theology may teach his follies, there can be no religion.' He adopted this view; it was his own. Freedom of expression would destroy church and state.

Pugh's barrister said the editor had done his duty in publishing the article. Had he not done so he would have betrayed his trust and *The Courier* would have been unworthy of support. The crowd in the body of the court applauded. Lutwytche warned he would treat any further interruptions as contempt.

The voice of the press, the barrister said, should be the honest bark of the watchdog or bold challenge of a sentinel. It should rivet citizens' attention to errors to be corrected, abuses rectified and wrongs redressed.

Brisbane Mayor John Petrie testified that he had known the editor for five or six years and took him to be a loyal subject.

Justice Lutwyche regretted his invidious position in sitting in judgment on an article which included a warm defence of himself. The duty was far from agreeable but he must perform it. The judge failed to mention a fact that he had not just supplied information. He had written much of the article himself.

Lutwyche ruled that as a matter of law a seditious libel could not be published of the Legislative Council. He doubted the House of Commons could direct a prosecution for seditious libel of itself. Not even the House of Lords could do it.

After a few minutes retirement the jury returned with a verdict of not guilty. Spectators cheered. Justice Lutwyche, silencing them with difficulty, reminded them such conduct was unseemly. As Pugh left court friends cheered, shook his hand, slapped his back and chaired him to the Sovereign Hotel. After nightfall bonfires burnt in city streets; fireworks lit a purple sky. A speaker said to deafening cheers that the Legislative Council had 'tried it on' and been ignominiously defeated. If the upper house wished to join issue with the people again, the people were ready.

Pugh the editor appeared a dangerous radical to legislators in 1861. Two years later he was member for Brisbane in the Legislative Assembly, then police magistrate at Goondiwindi, Rockhampton, Warwick and Bundaberg for twelve years between 1878 and 1892, when his sneers at labour leaders first became public and the men and women who lit firecrackers thirty years earlier wondered if the young progressive was becoming an old reactionary. Pugh died in Toowoomba on 14 March 1896 survived by his second wife Jane Montgomery and six children.

• • •

Born in Launceston on 21 November 1840, Gresley Lukin studied engineering, stepped on the stage, joined his older brother as recording clerk in the Land Office in Roma, Queensland. Quickly promoted to chief clerk in the Lands Department, then the Supreme Court, he bought shares in the Brisbane Newspaper Company and was editor of *The Brisbane Courier* and the *Queenslander* in 1873. His taste for adventure drew him to Ernest Favenc, a *Queenslander* contributor with whom he conducted dining-room explorations for a transcontinental railway, then sponsored Favenc on the real thing. When Favenc reached Darwin in February 1879 his reports widened eyes and circulation. The Australian interior 'set at naught the deductions and theories of the scientific world'; it was 'contradictory and inconsistent even with itself'. He rode two days to reach a Spinifex fire on the horizon and found a waterhole yielding a pint an hour, not enough for a man let alone a horse.

Lukin, temperamentally at home on the shifting ground between liberals and conservatives had difficulty keeping balance financially and bankrupted himself on his own petition in 1880 after losses in real-estate and mining. Charles Buzacott, a restless Englishman who learned compositing in Sydney on Henry Parkes' *The Empire* in the 1850s, covered a goldfields flood in Clermont in 1864 from a tree overlooking the main street after his office was washed away and initiated eight-hour-day bills after winning Rockhampton in 1873, resigned from parliament in 1877 and become *The Brisbane Courier* leader-writer in 1878. He bought Lukin's *Courier* interest, became managing director of the Brisbane Newspaper Company and cut the *Courier* price in 1883 from 3d to 2d. Lukin, discharged from bankruptcy, travelled to Melbourne and the bush, bought *The Boomerang* from William Lane in March 1890 and after losing both middle-class and labor support wound it up two years later.

Buzacott took over the evening *Daily Observer* in 1884, published the three papers from the *Courier* building, returned to the Legislative Council, and in May 1903 floated the *Brisbane Daily Mail*; it merged with the *Courier* to become *The Courier-Mail* on 28 August 1933.

Chapter 14

Inflammatory Justice

1841–1842: Justice John Willis, *John Fawkner* and *William Kerr,* The Port Phillip Patriot 1839–1845; *George Cavenagh, George Arden*, Port Phillip Gazette and Settlers' Journal; Police Magistrate Frederick St John; Justice John Walpole Willis.

It would be better to live under the most despotic law than submit to the unlicensed tyranny of the Press, which would spare neither private nor public character. No man, no matter how worthy, was safe should he incur the resentment of an editor such as Mr Arden.

Justice John Walpole Willis, 19 February 1842, sentencing George Arden, Port Phillip Gazette editor, to 12 months jail for criminal libel.

As resident judge in Melbourne of the New South Wales Supreme Court when separation was the first political issue, John Willis needed the patience of a saint and the judgment of Socrates. One legal historian found him 'queer and undignified'; to Alex C.Castles in An Australian Legal History, he was tempestuous, cantankerous — and a liberal visionary.

The boy editor, George Arden at 22 thought there could be but one opinion of the one judge in Australia Felix (an early name given by Thomas Mitchell to lush pasture in parts of western Victoria): he lacked the judicial essence, sound judgment. Arden wrote in the *Gazette* of Wednesday 21 July 1841 that when Willis' persuaded the crown prosecutor to charge magistrate D.C.Simson with perjury and the jury acquitted Simson, this was 'striking evidence' of Willis' 'want of judgment' His severity, untempered with mercy, had injured an honest man.

Willis convinced himself he believed in transparency and wished his conduct to be scrutinised 'as minutely as possible,' called Arden before him and said writing disrespectfully of a judge was a high contempt. Mr Arden's words implied that he, the judge, was 'guilty of wilful and corrupt partiality.' After a brief hearing in which Arden said he had opinions that he was privileged to, and would, entertain, he 'unconditionally' retracted any expression tending to improper reflection on Willis and Willis let him go.

After Arden published on 4 August that magistrates were 'degraded' when Willis presided at the Quarter Sessions and that barristers whom the judge treated disdainfully refused to appear before him, Willis threatened to 'close his paper and put him in a place he would not want to be' if he continued reporting like this. As he reached chambers these mornings Willis told the tipstaff: 'Bring me the *Gazette* and the *Herald*.' No *Patriot*.

When *The Herald* on 17 August 1841 reported that Willis had mentioned a popular magistrate 'with peculiar emphasis' the tipstaff sought out its publisher, George Cavenagh and in court Willis said the phrase 'peculiar emphasis' was 'wilfully, knowingly and grossly false', that Cavenagh 'must have known that I used no 'peculiar emphasis' … I will not endure that any individual shall publish wilful and malicious reports merely because he has the use of press and type. Let Mr Cavenagh be sent for.'

Cavenagh: 'I am here, your Honour.'

Judge Willis: Then sir, you have heard what I have been saying. You have been guilty of false reporting, which is a contempt of court; and I want to know, sir, if you are prepared to purge the contempt by swearing that you believed the report to be true.' Who was the reporter?

Cavenagh refused to answer. 'If any party is to be brought here for punishment, it must be myself.' He denied disrespect.

Willis: I accept your apology this once, Sir; but in future be more cautious.

Cavenagh: I suppose, your Honour, I am not debarred from fair and legitimate comment?

Willis: If you, sir, comment on my conduct, or the proceedings of this court, in an unfair and malicious manner, I shall take such steps as may not be agreeable.

After Justice Willis preached to a jury in the King Street courtroom on the evil of raffles, Arden wrote a letter to himself signed Scrutator:

> Who among the magistrates, barristers, attorneys, witnesses, suitors, even those unlucky enough to have their names mentioned in his court, had escaped the judge's censure? The Judge praised only those who flattered and cringed to him. His temper fomented litigation instead of suppressing it. Was this a fit and proper person to fill the

highest judicial chair in the province? 'Judge he is not, nor ever will be.' The inner judge fed on 'ignorance and self-conceit'. The independent press might 'ere long' remove him.

Willis swore that the letter contained scurrilous and untrue statements. They could incite his friends to a breach of the peace. Willis asked the Police Magistrate, Major Frederick St John, sitting next to him in the courtroom, to issue a warrant for Arden's arrest. St John made it out. Willis said he would withdraw, leaving the hearing to St John and honorary magistrates J.B. Were and Dr Farquhar McCrae.

When Arden entered the court in the custody of the Chief Constable, Willis, yet to withdraw, told him he was there to answer for criminal libels in Scrutator's letter. Major St John said the magistrates required Arden's recognisance of £400 and two sureties of £200 each.

Arden asked if he might 'say a few words?'

Willis: 'Not one word! If you have anything to say, say it on affidavit.'

Arden: If I am not allowed to speak, why bring me here?

Willis: One single libel more published in your paper and your recognisances will be estreated [forfeited].

Willis told the magistrates he would withdraw 'rather than appear as judge in my own cause.' Major St John adjourned the hearing. As Arden left the court a crowd outside cheered. Hearing the eruption, Willis hurried back shaking with rage according to Edmund Finn and said: 'Tipstaff! Apprehend them all! Bring them before me! *All* — if I cannot keep other places so, I will at all events take care to keep the precincts of this Court free from insult.' As the astonished Arden watched, the tipstaff, swaying where he stood, did not move and 'His Honor's order fell impotently to the ground.'

Next morning Mr H.N. Carrington, for Arden said Arden was entitled to a jury trial. But since the affidavits failed to establish the breach of peace which the law stipulated was a necessary element of criminal libel, there had been no offence. No tendency to breach the peace was proven, in the magistrates' judgment. Arden walked free through a cheering crowd.

• • •

Herald reporter Joseph Byrne was talking to a lawyer in court in December 1841 when Magistrate St John abruptly ordered him to hold his tongue and said if the journalist spoke again he would have him put out. At the end of the hearing Byrne said he was surprised at the magistrate's discourtesy and presumed it was because of *Herald* criticism of Mr St John.

St John denied it and repeated the threat to order him out.

Byrne: Do so at your peril. If you insult me, I shall appeal to the Judge [Justice Willis] for protection.

St John: If I allow you to come into my court to report, I am not to be disturbed. I will not have it.

Byrne: You say I am *allowed* to come here; am I to understand that it is on sufferance?

Mr St John: Certainly. This is *my* court and I will not have it disturbed.

Mr Byrne: This is a court of justice open to the public, and as such I *claim* and do not *ask* admittance.

Mr St John: I tell you if you do not hold your tongue I will commit you for contempt of court.

Two weeks later Cavenagh sacked Byrne. Edmund Finn saw St John's 'underhand influence' in the dismissal.

The progressive Willis bought prisoners in Melbourne jail roast beef and plum pudding on New Year's Day 1842. In conservative eyes he pushed principles of humanity to the point where they became unsavoury. Could an abrasive liberal find favour with newspapers? Willis' irritating combination of partiality and thin skin made him a target for Arden and Cavenagh. In an arbitrated insolvency — Eddy Finn thought insolvency suited Willis's temperament — on 9 February 1842 when the judge required Cavenagh to produce a deed, Cavenagh asked for time to consult his attorney.

Judge Willis: I will not wait a moment. If you refuse, I can commit you.

Mr Cavenagh: Will your Honor grant me an hour for that purpose?

Judge Willis: No, sir.

Mr Cavenagh: Half an hour then?

After the arbitrators said they would wait till tomorrow, Willis said they were indulging a person who did not deserve favour. Cavenagh said he was not ashamed of anything in his life.

Judge Willis: I dare say you are not, for there is no shame in you.

When Willis suggested Cavenagh would disobey a court order, Mr Lock, an applicant said 'on our first applying to Mr Cavenagh for a sight of the deed, he said he would obey any order of the court and referred us to your Honour.'

Judge Willis: Oh yes! But there are ways of referring to His Honour. He may have said 'Go to His Honour if you like, what do I care?'

Adjudicating common-law in Australia Felix Willis had the impartiality of a scorned lover.

A week later Arden appeared before Willis charged with criminal libelling Willis on 12 February in a comment on Cavenagh's case. Arden said the judge's 'exhibition of passion' had been 'equally disgraceful to himself and the Government.' Mr Cavenagh had 'dared to have an opinion different from [the judge].' Because of this the judge had put onto the record suggestions that

Cavenagh was dishonest, lacked shame and character, was selfish, impious and a prevaricator.'

The Crown Prosecutor, James Croke, said on 19 February that the case was supported by affidavits by J.D.Pinnock, H.F.Gurner and H.H.Kitson, officers of the court, who deposed to the propriety, demeanour and dignity of the judge, their boss. (Next day the *Herald* said 'a hundred affidavits to the contrary could be found.')

The judge interrupted Croke.

'Of no action in my life am I ashamed. I care not if my whole life is laid bare and fully scrutinized.' When Croke mentioned compliments Arden paid Willis, Willis said: 'His reason is apparent: he was afraid, Mr Croke.' There was 'no shadow of excuse' for the article.

The issue for Willis, truth being irrelevant, was whether Arden had criminally defamed his good self.

When Croke asked Arden at the Court House in King Street, crowded with Arden's supporters, whether he was the editor, printer, publisher and proprietor of *The Port Phillip Gazette,* Arden, believing a truthful answer would send him directly to jail, made a bush-lawyer's evasion: 'On my oath I believe that there is no legal proof existing as to the personality of the editor, printer and publisher of the said paper.'

Judge Willis: 'Miserable man, I pity you. I will leave a prosecution for perjury to the Crown Prosecutor I dismiss from my mind all personal feelings in this case, as I trust I do in every case I adjudicate.'

Arden had been posing as a proprietor of public morals and tried to evade his oath. He had published 'a violent and contumacious libel, tending to bring the administration of justice into derision and contempt' 'It would be better to live under the most despotic law than submit to the unlicensed tyranny of the Press, which would spare neither private nor public character. No man, no matter how worthy, was safe should he incur the resentment of an editor such as Mr Arden'.

Willis said he did not fear scrutiny. He courted it.

He sentenced Arden to twelve months' jail and a £300 fine. Supporters followed the editor to the crowded prison. Next day *The Herald* suggested that Arden's delicate health and the state of the dungeon made the sentence 'little short of death'. The *Gazette*, now published by the printer, B.J.Jolly, said Willis had sowed 'seeds of dissatisfaction which alone can ripen into a thorough contempt for the administration of justice.' Even the *Patriot,* with a tone halfway between satire and melodrama, said Arden was so sick the sentence was 'equivalent to a sentence of death, and that too of the worst kind — a lingering death.'

In a few days Willis transferred the editor to the watch-house on the Eastern Market reserve where sympathisers visited daily, and released him on 15 April after a *habeas corpus* hearing. George Cavenagh stood surety for £150. Influential citizens petitioned Governor Gipps; he remitted the £300 fine.

The Governor walked a tightrope. When Gipps sought the judges' impartial advice on complaints against Willis on 18 October 1842 they could not give it 'as the judges are all parties against him.' So was the Attorney General. Among those learned in the law, a detached opinion on Mr Justice Willis could not be found.

Willis's partiality to the *Patriot*, and its partiality to him, had become notorious. The judge lent *Patriot* proprietor John Fawkner £1200 at 20 per cent per annum interest (the judge's salary was £1500). When the Sydney Supreme Court judges read the documents recording Fawkner's mortgage to Willis they said Willis had lent money to 'one of the conductors of the *Port Phillip Patriot*'. They required an explanation.

Willis said the statement was 'utterly false'.

When the judges drew his attention to the mortgage documents, Willis said he assumed their question was about the editor, William Kerr, the 'sole conductor' of the paper, not Fawkner.

Governor Gipps thought this specious, 'a quibble upon words altogether unworthy of a judge.' Mr Justice Willis had 'insultingly accused his fellows of a falsehood' while 'he himself suppressed the truth'. The executive council unanimously recommended his removal. Called from court on 24 June 1843 he was handed Governor Gipps removal order. The *Patriot* said he should not be sacrificed to satisfy the despicable clique from whose tyranny he had rescued them all, the *Gazette* that he had never administered one justice to the rich and another to the poor.

Chapter 15

Ned Kelly and Montague Grover

*1888–1914: **Monty Grover** on The Age, The Boomerang, The Argus and The Sun News-Pictorial.*

'Ah well, I suppose it has come to this.'

> Ned Kelly's last words reported by John Leach, *The Sydney Morning Herald*.

'Such is life.'

> Kelly's last words reported by John Middleton, *The Herald*, Melbourne.

As the hangman with the leather strap begins to bind Ned Kelly's arms behind his back, Ned says: 'There is no need for tying me.' The Melbourne gaol Governor, John Castieau, one of ten attending warders, doctors and priests says: 'It is indispensable.' Elijah Upjohn, 60, a white-haired chicken-thief who volunteered to hang Ned lacks familiarity with these tasks, lacks practice. He forces Kelly's wasted left arm behind his back and buckles the broad strap. A £5 fee is at stake.

Eight reporters look up from the stone basement floor beneath the scaffold. As always, they are pulled between hand and eye, between the note and the action. Their eyes catch Ned, walking from the condemned cell to the drop, preceded by two priests intoning prayers for the dead. Eight hands scribble into eight notebooks.

John Middleton has covered many hangings for the Melbourne *Herald*. The world-weary reporter is struck by the small number of witnesses standing quietly on coconut mats 'for a man who for so long kept half the colony in terror.' Middleton has an exact eye. The rope coiled around the main beam is 'about the thickness of a stout man's thumb.' Beneath the trap is a rope through a pulley with a 23-pound weight attached so the trap will not swing back and strike the hanged man. 'This is all the paraphernalia nowadays.'

With James Williams and E .C. Martin of *The Age*, Grant Oakley of the Anglo Australian Press Agency, J. D. Melom of *The Argus*, John Leach of *The Sydney Morning Herald*, M.Browne of the Melbourne *Daily Telegraph* and Alfred Wilson, representing the *Ballarat Courier* and associated papers, Middleton is reporting the voice of authority. As Ned walked past garden to the gallows he exclaimed, according to *The Sydney Morning Herald*, 'Oh, what a pretty garden!' The Sydney *Daily Telegraph* reported the remark as: 'What a nice little garden!' The *Argus* said he made 'only a single remark about the pretty flowers in the garden.'

On a big national story like this the reporters were under a microscope to editors, competitors and readers; accurate detail was the core to their standing — in their own eyes too. *The Argus*'s J. D. Melom said Ned's manner was 'jaunty' as he passed from brilliant sunshine to the shadows under the sombre walls. The Sydney *Daily Telegraph* found his manner at that moment 'very submissive'.

The eight write with complete confidence in their sources, who are the witnesses closer to the rope —the gaol Governor, six warders, two sheriffs, three doctors, two priests. The reporters have tickets. They are official witnesses with eyes to see the drop and ears to hear the last words and the prayers for the dead and the shudders in the beam. They have the evidence of their senses.

It is not enough. The reporters want more than sources and senses can give them. As Ned awaited Dean O'Hea in the cell by the gallows a few minutes before the drop, he sang 'snatches of songs'. Part of the *Herald*'s cynical John Middleton wrote as a prissy critic: 'Although the songs he sang were not sacred, they were of the better class of secular composition and contained nothing in themselves offensive.' The *Sydney Daily Telegraph* special correspondent knew the inner reason: Ned did it 'to while away the time.' During his last night Ned had 'endeavoured to drown his thoughts' by dictating a statement to a fellow-prisoner. At half past one 'he went to bed but not to sleep.'

The journalists, skilled, experienced, well-regarded, are working as novelists. Taking fact from authority and trying to think their way into Ned's inner life, they imagine narrative detail. When Ned told warders a few days ago that he faced execution with no fear, J. D. Melom of the Melbourne *Argus* reported — source, the reporter's reasoning — that Ned hoped for reprieve.

As Ned walks to the trapdoor under the noose he glances down at the row of reporters with their notebooks open. The hangman, guided by gestures from Dr Edward Barker, carefully places the knot of the slip-noose under Ned's left ear. Ned said, according to John Leach: 'Ah well, I suppose it has come to this.' Ned's courage had failed him; he had 'intended to make a speech.' The reporter saw 'a frightened look in his eyes.'

According to John Middleton, standing within a few metres of Leach, Ned glanced at the witnesses and reporters beneath, saying 'in a low tone: "Such is life."' It is impossible for noises to sound to one reporter close by as three one-syllable words and to another as nine words of ten syllables. Both reporters wrote as if they had heard the last words, but they did not. They reported what a source — Governor Castieau, or Dr Barker — told them. (The Sydney *Daily Telegraph* reported Ned telling Castieau 'Such is life' when the blacksmith struck off his leg irons an hour before the hanging.)

No reporter named or quoted a source. They accepted the official version. Whatever they said about warders and priests after deadline over a sheoak beer, on the job the reporters extended them the ultimate trust: they reported what they were told as if they knew what the source said was true. They left the source out of it. If the source was wrong, the reporter was wrong. And the reporter was responsible.

Unattributed sources gave reporters conflicting versions of the most famous last words uttered in the ancient continent. Multiple eyewitness versions of the first draft of history yielded a story full of holes — patchy, incomplete and untrue.

What did Ned's life mean? *The Brisbane Courier* editor Gresley Lukin asked. As rockets for Guy Fawkes' night lit the sky over the Yarra on 5 November an estimated 4,000 people jammed the Hippodrome with another two or three thousand outside in Exhibition Street. The Melbourne *Daily Telegraph* quoted an unnamed detective who had 'never, in the whole of his experience seen such a number of known vagabonds, thieves and persons who had been convicted, gathered in one place.' The *Bendigo Independent* said these 'male and female beasts' shocked respectable people into realising 'upon what a fearful volcano society stands.'

Estimating the number who protested the hanging at 10,000 — the numbers involved in demonstrations the editor disapproves of tend to rise when the event is interstate — Gresley Lukin saw in the Kelly gang a descent to anarchy in Victoria, a move 'from order to disorder', a reckless disregard of tradition, the shadow of socialism. In the premier colony, proud of its enlightenment and wealth, ten thousand citizens had pleaded for the life of a desperate felon. 'What does it all mean?' The *Courier* took a traditional position: it neglected to answer its own question and trusted 'the contagion will not spread to us.' As I read the *Courier* my subconscious reminded me of anonymous: '*All newspaper editorial writers ever do is come down from the hills after the battle is over and bayonet the wounded.*'

Outside Melbourne Gaol that day Monty Grover heard demonstrators denounce the 'degeneracy' of modern hangings behind the bluestone. One man had seen three executed on the wall in the old days, with 'all the town looking on.' Another had seen seventeen swing 'in one act' in Hobart. A soldier said that was nothing — sixty or seventy a day was the Indian Mutiny average.

'Like all Melbourne boys,' Monty said, he was for Ned. He went to lunch with his father Harry and the witnesses, the gaol chaplain, the Reverend Charles O'Hea, and the doctor, Edward Barker, at Barker's house in Latrobe Street.

Carving the turkey, Dr Barker praised the hangman. He talked with a surgeon's cellular understanding of asphyxiation. Dean O'Hea, born in France, now speaking a rich Irish brogue, described 'in graphic detail' three decapitations he had seen in Paris. They chatted about the technicalities, where the hangman's knot should touch the neck, the exactitude of the triangular blade on the guillotine, how the Italian weighted semi-circular knife could stick on the vertebra. Monty wondered if any adult noticed the connection between the conversation and the doctor's hands dismembering the turkey. He was ten.

Born on 31 May 1870 to Jesse Grover, a part-time journalist on the short-lived Melbourne *Bulletin*, and Harry, a part-owner of the *Bulletin*, an adventurer from an English establishment family who travelled to the Bathurst goldfields as a 20-year-old in 1851, Montague Macgregor Grover attended art school for two years after grammar-school education.

Training as an architect in 1888-92, Monty wrote for the Sydney *Bulletin*. The editor, J.F.Archibald, sent an encouraging letter. Monty, surprised and delighted, found the praise opened the wide world of journalism. Excited by the romance of writing, living on his wits, drawn to the fire of fame, he cherished the 'furtive' thought of making a name as a storywriter or poet. He thought journalists 'supermen'. When the architect sacked him in the depression of 1893, he was making 15/- to £1 a week from *Bulletin* contributions.

He ran into a 'capable' reporter, Herbert Power, who told him newspapers did not require literary genius, they wanted journalists with good all-round education and common-sense. Men who knew what was going on. That night at Cole's Book Arcade Monty bought Pitman's *Shorthand Teacher* and transcribed the system's lines dots and curves. He practiced twelve hours a day for a month.

His mother Jesse dropped a word to David Syme, who asked Monty to call. Quaking inside, he felt it would be fatal to show nervousness to King David, so faked chutzpah in the great man's office. When Syme asked about his university studies, Monty's heart sank. He wasn't interested in academia; he saw the door closing. He quickly reminded Syme that the Saturday *Age* had published two of his stories. Syme called the chief-of-staff, G.F.H.Schuler, introduced Monty and instructed Schuler to try him out with casual work.

Reporting a North Melbourne presbytery meeting in an early assignment, he caught the anger behind the theological exchanges — 'each sentence seems likely to start violence' — but could not follow the jargon. Nervous that a rival might be scribbling notes out of sight, Monty wrote outlines till his fingers couldn't move: he was trying to take every word. A cocky *Argus* man sauntered by his table and asked if Monty had written anything. Monty started to explain the theological detail. The reporter cut him off: 'We don't want any of that tripe.' He scanned the notice paper, said a few words to the clerk, wrote two and a half slips in longhand, signed them and handed them to Monty. 'That's all the thing's worth. It's no good our waiting here tonight; there's a [hot] girl at the Opera House now, I don't want to miss her turn.'

Monty read the story. 'The skilled reporter who wasn't there had translated into sense the whole proceedings which were utterly unintelligible to the unskilled reporter.' He paraphrased *The Argus* report for *The Age*. 'I had received my first lesson in practical journalism.'

As he tried out for *The Age*, Monty wrote for *The Boomerang*, a left-wing weekly published by a brittle coalition of the Fabian Society, middle-class intellectuals Monty thought of as drawing-room socialists, trades hall men headed by George Prendergast, later leader of the Victorian Labor Party, and progressive Collins-street stockbrokers. Each faction, Monty said, believed the others had substantial financial backing. Each was mistaken: *Boomerang* capital was £30. Before they published the first issue, the office boy issued a summons for his salary. After the third week Monty's thirty-shilling salary, was 'paid in hope'; so was the editor Alf McKain, a former *Age* reporter, and his associate Leslie Norman, *Argus* shipping reporter. A dilatory distribution deal with Gordon & Gotch meant writing theatre reviews days in advance; Monty wrote a rave review of actor Dan Barry's 'masterly' performance as Ned in 'The Kelly Gang', and discovered too late the play had been cancelled. He wrote stinging attacks on conservative politicians and 'contradicted the lying capitalist press' in which he was launching his career 'on every point'.

He never worked harder; twice a week he worked through the night. Folding the last copies at 5am, he permitted himself the hope the meagre circulation would never increase. He started a 'missing horse' competition modelled on the popular 'missing word' contests. Instead of picking a word, readers would pick the winner of the next big race and send in a shilling. 'It was a tote, pure and simple and I had some fears of the law intervening.' One solitary reader sent in his shilling. After eleven issues the board sacked McKain and appointed Grover editor. 'I wasn't so deliriously happy as I would have been eleven weeks previously,' he said. *The Boomerang* closed with the next issue.

He joined *The Age* in November 1894 working as general reporter till May 1896. He was having fun, expecting the world to give him what he wanted. Claude McKay, another young reporter Schuler hired, saw Monty breeze into the newsroom in a ribboned straw hat, pick up a pen and, as the nib malfunctioned, dip the handle into an ink-bottle, scrawl his name 'over three starred stories', toss the pen into a waste-basket and stride out. The breezy self-confidence made McKay nervous.

Grover at first resented Labor orators shouting that he was a toady of the lying capitalist press. Then he grew a shell, ostentatiously leaving his pencil untouched on the table as trades hall speakers reviled him as if he were John D. Rockefeller. The best part of the joke, said Monty, was that he was a 'bitter and uncompromising enemy of capitalism'. In fact he voted Labor, but only because the international socialists had no chance. He switched to *The Argus*, whose editorials he thought 'mediaeval—hopelessly out of touch' for a salary rise to marry Ada Goldberg, persuading himself that even readers who detested *Argus* Toryism bought it for its 'excellent, up-to-date and thorough' news.

At *The Argus* from May 1986 to March 1907, he found news reporting 'the most fascinating form of big-game hunting known to man.' In his mind the ideal reporter had a novelist's eye for detail and could deduce from whisky-stains on a politician's shirt-cuffs that he had been sacked from Cabinet, or suspect from a glimpse of a Rolls-Bentley in St Kilda that a trusted accountant had swindled a corporation. 'In ninety-nine cases out of a hundred he disproves his bizarre theories by investigation; but if he can score one in a hundred, he is content.'

Grover hoped to make readers and peers smile. When *The Argus* editor, Edward Cunningham, an honorary doctor of laws, insisted that a medical practitioner with a bachelor of medicine must be 'Mr' in *The Argus* unless he had a doctorate in medicine, requiring reporters always to have a medical register on hand, Monty, reporting a lecture on Africa, made the famous 'Dr Livingstone, I presume?' 'Mr Livingstone L.R.F.P.S., I presume?'

What is news? For Monty Grover the answer was as difficult as Pilate's 'What is truth?' Recognising hard news was the hardest part of journalism. After 24 years in the craft, he applied this principle: If the Sydney University Chancellor made a learned speech on constitutional law, the reader would quickly turn away. But if the Chancellor punched a professor on the nose, 'all

Sydney' would talk of it, while in Melbourne, Brisbane, Adelaide and Perth people would congratulate themselves they were not like that.

Grover could catch the reader's eye.

As founding editor, he promised in the Sydney *Sun*, of 1 July 1910 that in the rich southern land designed by nature for a great and prosperous democracy the paper would live by 'greatest good of the greatest number'. It would be progressive, wholesome and fearlessly democratic. Its pictures would recognise how important illustrations were to modern journalism and its independent cable service would focus the globe for readers.

News, being of human-interest, was elastic. Were an MP thrown out of the Victorian parliament for swearing or assault, it would be a lead story, but in the New South Wales bear-pit, ejection of a member, being as common as the day was long, rated a few lines.

When he was becoming the legend who created the *Sun-News Pictorial* in Melbourne, shaping a new journalism, new ideas of news, new newspapers, new readers, making vast circulation gains, giving the phrase 'human interest' its twentieth-century meaning, peers thought the gap between Monty Grover, editor, and Monty Grover the bloke was slight. He was a natural. He did not have to mould himself to the job. Monty Grover, bloke who swam at Bondi was stopped watching his daughter swimming in races at the beach. Authority did not permit men and women together on the beach; even a father watching his daughter was a violation. Monty the *Sun* and *Sunday Sun* editor campaigned for mixed bathing. Monty gave front-page play to rescues, near misses, sharks, skin and surf lifesavers. From 1 July 1910, a capital city daily had news on the front page.

To journalists Monty was the Nellie Melba of the craft; he had the singer's ear, the artist's eye. When Monty was firing in editorial conference it looked effortless, news ideas, picture ideas, angles, the men for the job, ideas for series and promotions poured out of him. They loved him. In editorial conference he never sought to wound. He was secure in his talent. A teetotaller in an industry fuelled by booze, he found his rum in conversation.

He recognised front, the reporter as manipulator. When his *Argus* mate Peter Symmons, whom Monty thought a 'freak' with a 'supernatural capacity for work' entered the Commercial Travellers Club at 2am after the paper had gone to bed on 10 October 1891 he met a police sub-inspector who crowed that the press might think it knew a lot but little did it know what had happened that night.

Symmons faked it: 'Doesn't it? I've just been writing up that matter you refer to for the last half hour.'

The sub-inspector bought it, but he was curious. 'The messengers at parliament house must have told you. Not a soul knows about it outside our office.'

Symmons: 'Don't you believe it. It's all over Melbourne. We got it from two distinct sources.'

Sub-inspector: The Speaker? Symmons shook his head. In a few minutes he knew the mace, symbol of authority, had been stolen from the Victorian Parliament House. He hurried back to the *Argus* and wrote the story not neglecting the beat-up. The robbery, (never solved) was 'the most extraordinary ever heard of in the colonies'. It was 'probably without parallel in the constitutional history of the world.'

As for newspaper politics, Grover wrote in the *Lone Hand* in 1914, in every newspaper he worked for—*The Age, Argus,* Sydney *Sun,* Sunday *Sun, Boomerang*—the press had been 'absolutely fair'. The lying capitalist press was fairer to Labor than the Labor press was to capitalism. He told the story of *The Sydney Morning Herald*'s Bert Toy reporting the Broken Hill strike in 1908. Toy went to union headquarters with other reporters and approached the table where six union leaders sat. The radical Tom Mann cried: 'Here come the representatives of lying capitalism, intent on doing their utmost to vilify Labor and mislead the people with their lying reports.'

Toy said politely: 'Pardon me, Mr Mann. I've just arrived and I would like you to point out in what respect my paper, the *Herald,* has been incorrect.'

'I'm not going to argue,' Mann shouted. 'You're all in the same boat. You conceal the truth and circulate a mass of lies to deceive the people.' Then he turned to the unionists and said 'I suppose I'll have to give these fellows something.'

Mann walked down the hall with the reporters, took Toy by the arm and said 'Well boys, what is it you want me to tell you?'

There was a lot of that, Monty said, denunciations from the platform followed by friendly cooperation. When anyone said a story was a 'tissue of lies', he asked for specifics. Often the problem turned out to be not the whole story but one sentence, or a word, or 'nothing at all'. The complainer blamed the reporter in public. In private he dropped it.

No-one was more trouble, no-one complained as much as men in dog-collars. Politicians might be shameless in their lying denials, but they could not hold a candle to clergymen. 'When a parson is speaking, keep your notes' was the reporters' axiom.

Grover set up special cable arrangements for the Sydney *Sun* to cover the world heavyweight title fight between titleholder Jack Johnson, a black cotton-picker from Galveston, Texas and Jim Jeffries, a white boilermaker from

Los Angeles, in Reno, Nevada on 4 July 1910, retaining Hugh D. McIntosh himself to cover it. The story was so big it shaped advertisements. 'The question of the hour. Black or white, which will conquer?' asked one stockbroker's single-column ad. The athletics world was 'seething with anxiety'. A Sydney bookmaker said 'I don't mind taking six to four that the nigger wins.' *The Sun*, describing its flag system to speed the news across the city from the Pacific Cable Board four wavers, a black flag for a Johnson win, white for Jeffries said it had copies in readers' hands three minutes and thirty seconds after the teleprinter stopped its tic-tac. It was a record. Hugh McIntosh reported that by round fifteen most spectators were 'hoping against hope' that Jeffries could 'recover the championship for the white race.'

Monty Grover remained high-minded. 'Pugilism is useless as all art is useless, all literature is useless. In the work of inspiring the world, the boilermaker of Los Angeles and the cotton lumper of Galveston are more than the poets; they are the poems,' he wrote before the fight. (Johnson won in the 15th round.) He used a novelist's technique in journalism two generations before Tom Wolfe. Sales swelled from 15,000 in 1910 to 120,000 in 1914. Not because of the style; because of the war.

Freedom Lost: A history of newspapers, journalism, and press censorship in Australia.

Chapter 16

The Tabloid School

1884–1923 John, Ada and *Ezra Norton*, the *Evening News, Truth, Daily Mirror, The Sun, Jack Muir*.

Here shall the Press the People's right maintain
Unawed by influence and unbribed by gain:
Here patient Truth her glorious precepts draw;
Pledged to Religion, Liberty and Law.

John Norton, Truth 10 January 1909

Tormented to the core, a saint and monster, John Norton followed Jesus and the Emperor Napoleon, passionately loved his wife and children, bashed his beloved, fought for battlers against sweating bosses, defrauded partners, created a national newspaper, drank like a lizard, threatened to kill his infant son Ezra, carried a revolver and spoke for the national subconscious.

Truth, The People's Paper, Conducted by John Norton poured out abusive editorial alliteration, projecting his inner torments; his pen was compulsive, often writing 5000 words a day. It did not stop there: from Melbourne, Brisbane and Perth he would write his wife Ada twelve letters a week, some of fifty pages, followed by months of silence.

His father, stonemason John Norton, died before his son was born in Brighton, England, on 25 January 1858. His mother, Mary Margaret, then married Benjamin Herring, a puritanical Bible-basher — the gifted Cyril Pearl called him a 'canting sadist' — birched the boy, locked him in his room and shaped him.

Migrating on impulse to Sydney at 26, he joined *The Evening News* in 1884, quickly becoming chief reporter, was a delegate of the NSW Trades and Labor Council to international trades union congresses in 1886 and two years later published and contributed to *The history of capital and labour in all lands and ages,* an Australian edition of an erudite US book. At 31 he edited *The Newcastle Morning Herald*; his tart, cheeky journalism increased circulation.

The monster, sacked for repeated drunkenness, returned to Sydney to join *Truth*, started on 3 August 1890 by politician-journalists of the larrikin left, William Willis, Adolphus Taylor and William Crick, a trio steeped in words, rebellion and whisky.

After a disturbed associate editor, James Crouch, posing as an author and clergyman with the name of Reverend Doctor Oswald Keating, sexually violated editor 'Mudgee' Taylor's under-age servant girl, Norton and Willis swore an information. Sentenced to five years, Crouch killed himself in his cell; Norton took his place.

Four months later the editor, Adolphus Taylor, a gangling alcoholic dubbed 'the giraffe' was disabled by syphilis (he died in Callan Park asylum). Norton stepped up to editor: he was living a *Truth* story. In 1891, when the NSW population was 1.1 million and Australia's 3.2 million Norton described himself as 'sole proprietor and publisher', a statement Crick contested in court for five years.

When he worshipped at the Unitarian Church in Elizabeth Street, Norton caught the eye of Ada McGrath, a comely daughter of dirt-poor Irish-born farmers, in the company of a man. One night they talked after the service. He asked her why she was at the Church; she told him that though she was Anglican, she liked literary sermons. 'What are you doing here?'

Norton, a Christian activist whose biographer Michael Cannon says suffered 'personal religious agonies' said 'I come to see you.'

As they strolled Elizabeth Street, John asked Ada who was the man he had seen with her? Ada : 'He was my fiance.'

John: He won't get you. I am going to marry you.

Ada: I have something to say about that.

John: No, you are just as much in love with me as I am with you.' Then he asked her name and walked her home.

After 'four or five' church encounters, they had sex under a bush in Centennial Park. Ada said she knew it was a sin; she knew she would pay.

While they lived at Watsons Bay in 1896 Ada fell pregnant and male paranoia began to torment Norton: a woman loose enough to make love in a public park might offer herself to a stray sailor. He smacked her across the face at home. Ada, strong-minded, short-tempered, decked him with a broomhandle. When she found John the monster too much she left, heavy with pregnancy but he begged her to return and she did. 'I was very much in love with him.'

When Queen Victoria became the longest-serving British monarch in September 1896, Norton ran the headline *God Save the Queen* and wrote that she was 'flabby, fat and flatulent', a 'semi-senile old woman' whose predecessors comprised madmen, lechers, bastards and blackguards; his desire for God to save the Queen was 'only to keep her rascal of a turf-swindling, card-sharping, wife-debauching, boozing rowdy of a son, Albert Edward, Prince of Wales, off the throne'. Readers loved his cheek. The abuse provoked authority to a prosecution for sedition but the jury could not agree.

The couple wed at St James Church on 29 April 1897, three weeks after their son Ezra was born. Ada, weak from labour, barely able to walk, left her bed for the service.

Saint John promised to 'wage war against class privilege' in his campaign for the Sydney Municipal Council in 1898; at a Surry Hills rally when as hoisted Ezra in his arms as a symbol of 'the new Australia' a boisterous crowd applauded. He won a Legislative Assembly seat at a by-election in June 1898, and a seat at the July general election that returned free-trade Premier George Reid.

Criminal barrister Richard Meagher, angered by *Truth* calling him 'premier perjurer' and 'champion criminal', phrases in which there was more than a grain of truth, waited with cronies and a horsewhip On 21 September 1898 in Pitt Street for John and Ada, attending a matinee of Gilbert and Sullivan's *The Gondoliers* at Her Majesty's Theatre at 2 pm. Meagher struck Norton from behind about the head with a whip handle 'eight or nine times' an eyewitness said, and turned to flee. Norton reached for a revolver in his hip-pocket but 'by the providence of God' it snagged on the pocket. But for that Divine intervention, Norton testified, 'I would have shot him point blank.' Meagher fled, dodging carts and cabs. Norton, in pursuit fired — at the big man's ankles, he testified. The editor said he always carried a revolver for self-protection because he walked home to Watson's Bay late at night. The shot missed Meagher and the passers-by. The barrister was convicted of assault and fined £5 and Norton found not guilty of assault with a deadly weapon.

Though his father's voice made Ezra shriek, the little boy also responded to the good John, rushing to the door to hug his dangerous Dad. At the *Truth* office in August 1901, Norton tried to force Ada to sign a confession of adultery with Nicholas Coxon, a swarthy *Sportsman* editor Ada was said to have dubbed 'liquorice' because he was black and sweet.

Ada said she wouldn't sign it. Norton walked around the table and said a woman who loved her husband would make sacrifices for him. He only wanted her signature as proof of her love.

Ada: One would almost think you believe I committed adultery.

Norton: Not at all… Ada started to cry. Norton, forehead glistening, picked up the four-year-old and screamed: Sign it, or I will bash this little bastard's brains out.

Ada: Put the baby down Jack and I will sign anything.

A *Truth* staffer witnessed the signature. Norton kissed Ada, saying he only wanted to be sure she loved him. He loved Ezra and always had loved him; he was passionately fond of the boy.

He felt a gap at his centre. Lucid with brandy he called the Duke of Edinburgh, who had visited in 1868 — at Manly a demented Fenian shot him in the back — a 'prurient-minded, lecherous-living, brothel-bilking, tradesman-tricking rascal.' Near the end of a lifetime of abuse he said the young Winston Churchill was a 'witless wild ass … a demi-demented decadent … the blatant, mad-brained bounder … this sybilating shyster.'

He kept the world at bay with words, used them as a shield and sword, he feared and abused rivals in politics, churchmen, authority figures, journals. *The Bulletin* was The Boodletin; *The Sydney Morning Herald* the 'saintly Smerald', *The Daily Telegraph* the 'Telegraft'; for the Melbourne *Argus* he coined 'Ah-goose'. He sneered at the 'daily Sup-press'. David Syme of *The Age* was 'saturnine Syme', one of the 'monopolistic mob' 'shrieking against socialism'.

He lacked shame, desired no privacy: details of his drunkenness and wife-bashing filled columns of the *Truth*. Led by religious who saw daily that drink had its part in wife-bashing, child-abuse, unemployment and the collapse of the self, the temperance campaign for prohibition was a major issue throughout Norton's editorship, reaching its peak in the 1890s.

Lurid abuse made a fence around him; no-one could get in. He conveyed, and provoked, rage, a rage that drew 60 libel actions. Cross-examination in a Melbourne suit in 1904 traversed his flaws:

> They have charged you with seduction? — Yes.
>
> Perjury? — Yes.
>
> Blackmail? — Yes.
>
> Habitual drunkenness? — Yes.
>
> Obscenity? — Yes.
>
> Improper conduct in a public place? — Yes.
>
> Scores of times? — Yes.
>
> Hundreds of times? — I won't say that, but I will say scores of times.
>
> By scores of different people? — Yes, hundreds.

All the charges made against you were false, of course? — I don't say that they were, all of them.

Take that seriatim. What about the seduction charge? — Well ...

You don't want to answer me, eh? Why? — I have never seduced any woman in my life. They have seduced me.

As he pushed against the confining law Norton revealed what gentlemen of Vaucluse feared: without the law of libel to protect reputation, men with John Norton's sense of restraint would publish what they pleased and make gentlemen afraid to have another tot of whisky or a few hours' relaxation in a whore-house. Without the gag-law, radical journalism would do what the *Truth* was doing.

To Norton words were words only, sounds, incantations, prayers. In January 1902 in an open letter in *Truth* to the first Prime Minister, Edmund Barton, 'concerning his disgusting drinking habits' Norton pushed Barton to sue him for libel, or prosecute for criminal libel. The Prime Minister did not take the bait. For Barton, Norton was sunk so deep in the mire he was not a man, he was a creature of the sewer. 'Toss-pot' Toby could afford to remain silent; it would grubby him politically to sue a journalist whom the establishment thought had the morals of a cockroach.

Some saw the gap at the centre and hurried to judge. Some lost perspective. Cyril Pearl, sensitive, intelligent, insightful, a man who had edited *The Sunday Telegraph* for Sir Frank Packer and knew the compromises of journalism, wrote in the last paragraph of *Wild Men of Sydney* (1958) that Norton was a ranting psychopath with the intuition of a rat, he was like Hitler.

In all his journalism the man penning the words is a ghost. Norton, bald, short, a pipe-smoker with a shrill voice who never spoke in a whisper, the alcoholic to whom hospital nurses brought brandy for the sake of keeping the peace, never saw how his abuse wounded. He let fly: where the words landed, how they hurt, he was not aware the barbed-wire words defended his psyche against a world reflecting the pain of Benjamin Herring's birch.

A portrait of Norton at thirty shows a strong-faced young man with short-cropped hair, handsome, intense. At forty, photographed for *The Sydney Mail*, his arms are folded protectively, his face puffy, his body pudgy; the eyes stare intently beneath an almost-bald skull, giving the impression of a man who has seen the world and found it ugly.

Insomnia made nights wretched. He would go to bed drunk and get up five times for brandy. In hospital he wanted nurses to sing. Frank Hill, a journalist who was Norton's secretary from 1906 to 1909, saw that Norton could not drink, a single glass of port wine changed him, but thought too that if he abstained he would go mad. Ada told the court hearing her petition for judicial separation in September 1915 that when he wanted brandy 'I know to give it to him is bad, but to keep it from him is also bad. He gets violent fits of screaming if he is refused the brandy, and we are afraid he will burst a blood-vessel.'

He reported from memory. He reported rumour. He got it wrong. His journalism was a dialogue with his stepfather. He could never rid himself of Herring; anger itself called Herring to Norton's mind, triggering further rage, more anguished, contagious alliteration.

Elected to the NSW General Assembly as a protectionist in 1898 and an independent in 1899, 1904 and 1907, Norton lost campaigns for the Senate in 1901 and 1906. Still he tapped a nerve. A digger waiting for the doctors to patch him up in the general hospital, Cairo, wrote home that at the Gallipoli landing on 25 April 1915 'the boys were shouting "Come on Johnny Norton's tourists" and go we did, right into the jaws of hell.' For Norton freedom shrieked at the Conscription Bill; it made schoolboys responsible for the defence of Australia, it was political cowardice.

Truth milked divorce courts and homicide squads, it created for a mass audience stories of infamous harlots and gunmen and laid out their vivid details as it struck moral poses. In 1900 Norton founded the Brisbane *Truth*, in 1902 Melbourne *Truth*, in 1903 *Truth* in Perth; on 21 November 1903 the Perth edition promised advertisers in the Commonwealth Advertising Medium access to one million readers; by 1909 there was *Truth* in New Zealand.

He was fierce on oppression. Why not institute fair-rent courts to deal with vampire landlords? Sydney *Truth* demanded on 23 September 1911, beneath headlines excoriating the rack-renters' exorbitant demands 'draining the life blood of the people'.

Saint John denounced the Colonial Sugar Refining Company as 'the greatest monopoly ever established in Australia' which bled cane farmers for profits reaching 16 per cent. A timber combine in Western Australia stole much of the high wages it paid its sawers through the inflated prices at combine stores, in Norton's view a 'system of robbery' imposed on men, isolated in the bush and tied to the combine stores, doing 'some of the most dangerous work known.' He exposed the racket.

When the Reverend J.C.Kirby, president of the Council of Churches of South Australia, proposed sterilisation of 'the unfit', Norton, quoting Havelock Ellis' *Psychology of Sex*, noted that castration did not stop sex offenders. On 27 April 1912, the founder of mass-circulation crime-based journalism in Australia said: 'There is abundant historical proof that hanging does not deter … Australia, this young nation … should be able to show that it can maintain order without the gallows and the lash.' He denounced flogging as if he were a bleeding-heart: 'flogging does not deter' and wowserism, a word he invented — as sadistic: harlots were being harassed with an ardour resembling that of the fox-hunt; Wowsers found a 'sly subtle sport' in 'hunting down human creatures instead of the lower animals.'

Consistency did not confine him. When *The Age* reported women dressing as bushrangers as a summer joke at a seaside resort, Norton put on the Wowser's hat. The report was 'somewhat sensational'; women dressing as men, and vice-versa, was 'becoming far too common'; it was 'decidedly immoral'. Railing against the 'prevalent pernicious practice' of abortion he recommended hanging or life imprisonment for abortionists. The premier larrikin journalist announced the death of larrikinism *Killed by Civilisation: Not many mourners either* on 10 January 1914. He sneered that knights were as thick in the capital cities as rabbits in the backblocks, but what he really stood for none of his million readers could say. Some thought him a village idiot. By then, his chauffeur Thomas Webb said, when he was binging he drank a half-dozen quart bottles of sauterne a day. Dr Henry O'Hara, who treated Norton for alcoholism in Melbourne from 1902, said that by 1913 'I thought he was dying.'

His news columns were for sale: an ad for Dr William Pink Pills to 'make the blood rich and red' and effect 'rapid and permanent' recovery from indigestion' promised that the adjoining stories about recovery from indigestion had been 'taken down word for word by reliable reporters'. He was accused of sending blackmail proofs of exposure stories to the exposed public figure, with the suggestion that a contribution would kill the story. But in public *Truth*'s public principles were high-minded:

> Here shall the Press the People's right maintain
>
> Unawed by influence and unbribed by gain:
>
> Here patient Truth her glorious precepts draw;
>
> Pledged to Religion, Liberty and Law.

Sometimes 'fraternity' replaced 'religion' among the glorious fundamentals. The moment in Centennial Park when eros overwhelmed him continued its torment. After a brandy or two, Ada was a fucking whore, a phrase he shouted in hotels, on the street, at home while neighbours froze or giggled. Every man who visited St Helena, his Marboubra mansion, from the stable-boy to the doctor to Norton's solicitor was her paramour. He sacked Frank Hill for helping Ada to a cab, saying 'I pay you as my secretary, not as her damned flunkey.' Fidelity was women's business. Norton had an affair with Sarah Burgess, wife of a groom he employed; he had prostitutes available under Ada's eyes; once she flung a flowerpot at Norton and a call-girl, showering them with wet soil. He travelled for weeks with Eva Pannett, whom he met in London in 1908 and paid £500 into her bank account.

Ada, John, Eva, Ezra and Joan had dinner in 1915. Norton helped Eva to chicken, then scraped her leavings onto his plate and began to eat them.

Ada looked at Norton, looked away, said nothing. Ezra looked at his mother.

Norton: What the hell is the matter with you? What have you got your nose stuck in the air about?

Ada: I don't know it is any higher than before, but I don't see the necessity for you to eat the scraps off Eva's plate.

John: Don't you? It's not the first time, by hundreds. If you don't like it, you know what to do — get out.

A waiter called him to the telephone. She had known many instances of Norton's adultery, she later told the court, 'but I have shut my eyes.' She opened them when she saw Eva laughing at her from the body of the court.

Ada: I have seen her leaning over the back of his chair with her head on his face kissing him.

Mr Windeyer (counsel for Ada): He kissed her in the court today.

Ada: Did he?

Windeyer: Of course he did. I suppose the jury saw it.

Norton: If I sneezed, would that be an offence?

Ada, the first witness in the 17-day hearing, took the stand trembling; asked where she first lived with Norton, she shook with sobs. Norton, representing himself, cross-examined her. 'I shan't irritate you,' he said. 'I shall ask you plain questions, and you give me plain answers.'

'Have you charged me with endeavouring to drag you down into the gutter? — Do you mean physically, or as far as my reputation goes?

Did you use those words? — It is quite possible …

What did you mean by it? — I understood that you would lead me such a life at home that I would be glad to go on the streets as a bad woman, and I told you it was not in your power, or the power of anybody else, to drive me to do that …

What is the first occasion when we actually cohabited? — One night when I had been out with you four or five times.

Where? — In Centennial Park. (hotly) You are twenty years older than I, and should be ashamed of yourself for asking such questions.

Judge Gordon: If anyone chooses to blacken the character of his own wife, he is entitled to do it, that's all.

Ada was tough-minded under pressure.

Norton: Have you said, when you first knew me, you were a pure and honest girl? — I never said such a silly thing. It is a term I don't use; (contemptuously) *Pure and honest!*

On the first day before the ice-cool barristers, the partial judge, the scribbling reporters and the gallery voyeurs, Norton asked Ada about an incident in a cab when, she said, in drink he had kicked a dog named Barney.

Ada: I can't remember. I tried to forget these things. You ought not to blame me for not remembering.

Norton: I am not blaming you. Your position is more painful than mine.

Ada: I don't think you should do this yourself. You should get a barrister.

She called him Jack and Dad; he called her Ada. 'They were there before the crowded court,' Mr Windeyer, for Ada, remarked to the jury, 'oblivious of everyone's presence but their own.'

At dinner at St Helena, on the night in November 1912 when Ada and John slept together for the last time, Ada objected to a remark John made to Joan at the dinner table about regularity of the bowels, she wished he would not speak about such disgusting things, couldn't he think of his son, a growing man?

Norton: You are shocked, you injured innocent.

Ada: I am not shocked because I have been your wife a great many years … but you ought to restrain yourself.

Norton jumped to his feet. Ezra rose and moved to his mother's side; Norton told him to sit down.

Ezra: No, I will stay by mother.

It was the first time Ada heard Ezra answer his father back.

Eva: Oh Ada, it is only plain English, uncle John has a habit of speaking plain English.

Norton said to Ezra: If you give me any back answers, I will come round and knock you down.

Ezra: No you won't. I have made up my mind about that. You won't punch me or knock me down, and you won't touch mother again, or I will punch your damned head.

Norton walked from the room. 'You needn't be afraid, mother, he won't touch you again,' said Ezra. He was fifteen.

When Ada petitioned for divorce in 1914 she took the papers with Ezra to the *Truth* office. Norton shouted to her to get out, pushing her shoulder. Ezra told him to take his hands off his mother. Norton threatened Ezra: 'If you interfere with me, I will give you in charge.'

John seized Ada's shoulder. Ezra punched him. John ran from the building and returned with a police constable, who arrested Ezra. When they went home that night, policemen barred Ezra's way. Ada, allowed in, found Norton lying on his bed 'very drunk', the insomnia anaesthetised. Ada and Ezra stayed at the Coogee Bay Hotel.

Norton was a policy kaleidoscope, a free-trader who kept a good word in for the arch-protectionist Sir Henry Parkes, then became a protectionist. He was a lush roaring denunciations of drinkers, a believer who snarled at Methodists, Catholics, Anglicans and Jews, a disciple of the brotherhood of man who was no-one's brother, a campaigner for socialism who called his house 'St Helena' and crowded it with busts, statues and portraits of the Emperor Napoleon. In print, in parliament, in his head, he was a hostile self-contradiction: Norton disintegrated in weeks-long binges of champagne, stout, sauterne, brandy. As he turned yellow from kidney disease the struggle between the two Johns reduced him in March 1916 to a month-long coma; he died on 9 April, *The Bulletin* remarking that no-one could write John Norton's life story, not even John Norton.

His will disposing of the *Truth* empire left Ada and son Ezra nothing: he left it all to his eleven-year-old daughter Joan. The NSW parliament then chivalrously made the Testator's Family Maintenance Act retrospective to the time it was introduced in the lower house, before Norton's death, and in 1920 the Supreme Court altered the will giving Ada a life income and splitting the estate equally between Ezra and Joan, with Ezra a trustee. When he turned 25 in 1923, Ezra had his father's position, sole control.

Ezra bore marks and memories of the two Johns. Over dinner in 1954 he told Hugh Cudlipp, visiting editorial director of the London *Mirror* group 'mind you, he knocked me about a bit'. On the other hand, Cudlipp saw tears in Ezra's eyes as Ezra said that one Sunday morning John pointed to church-goers in their finery, called them 'bloody hypocrites' and told Ezra that when he continued John's work at the *Truth*, keeping up its traditions without fear or favour, he would be in the same position of trust as his father: he would always be 'able to pour a bucket of shit over the lot of them.'

In Jack Muir's eyes, Ezra was a most peculiar man. An enigma. An oddity. *Truth* hired Muir in 1928 when he was 14, a kid from Tempe who beat 'a thousand other kids' for the job. He became Norton's 'white-haired boy', *Truth* circulation manager, then the *Daily Mirror* circulation manager. He thought of himself as Ezra's little brother.

Ezra was a gambler. After weekends at the track, the familiar voice would rasp into the cracking intercom: 'Jack, I want you to go down to city Tatts and settle for me.' He would give Jack a roll of £1, £5 and £10 notes with a list of settlements, but it was never clear to the youngster whether Norton owed the bookie or the bookie owed Norton.

The teenager, earning £1 a week, knew nothing about racehorses or book-makers except that there were *Truth* tipsters paid £20 or £30 a week and on Saturday nights they would borrow 2/6 from him to buy their tea. 'I thought there couldn't be much future in the racehorse business.'

He would go to city Tatts ante-room and tell the bookies' clerk: 'I've come to settle for Mr Norton.' The clerk would say 'Righto you owe me £440' or 'I owe you £220.' He'd finish up with a roll of 'maybe a thousand pounds in the 1930s', take it back to Norton and he'd say '"righto Jack" and stick it in his pocket without looking at it. Most trusting.'

Accompanying Norton around the city, Muir found 'he was like the Queen: he didn't carry money, and he didn't pay — and there I'd be in the taxi' — he pulls out empty pockets. Finally, Muir arranged with the *Truth* accountant to have a £20 note permanently pinned in his suit coat to cover Norton's taxi fares.

Ezra had his office sound-proofed. Even so, Muir sometimes found it 'eerie — he'd just stay there and [the office] reverberated. He believed in the trilogy of Christ, Caesar and Napoleon' and he had the three images 'all round the place in his office.' Once, Muir saw Ezra shouting at a man at the top of the stairs outside his office. 'I don't know what the bloke said to him, but [Norton] hit him and the bloke rolled from the top of the stairs to the bottom, blood coming out his mouth. He got up and scurried away. '[Norton] turned to me and shouted 'clean that [the blood on the stairs] up, Jack.' 'Being the depression, you dare not ask for a rise. The only way you could get a rise would be to threaten to leave. If you were game enough, you could say to *Mr Norton* that *Mr Packer* had talked to you. About once every eighteen months I'd pull the old trick that I was going to the *Telegraph* and I'd get a £1 or 10/- rise.'

Muir went to enlist in the RAAF in 1938. Asked what his job was he said without thinking 'circulation manager'. The interviewer said: 'We can't take you. You need a release from your employer.'

He went back and told Ezra: 'Mr Norton, I went down today to enlist.'

Norton: No bloody way. You're not going.

Muir: It's like this. Either you sign it and I go as Jack Muir, circulation manager, or you don't sign it and I go as Jack Muir, unemployed.'

Norton: All right, bugger you.

Norton picked up his pen and said: 'Have you ever thought what's going to happen to your family?'

Muir: Well, my mother will have to do the same as everybody else.

Norton: Don't worry. I'll pay her your salary while you're away

Betty Riddell, who started the New York bureau for the *Daily Mirror* in 1942 — Ezra hired her from New Zealand — said he never swore in her presence, he was always polite. Well-behaved. When he took her to lunch in Sydney 'he told me what to eat. He told me what I shouldn't eat (fat). And we would have one glass of wine. At Princes restaurant he would order 'a beautiful little bit of steak like that — 'she encloses the imaginary sirloin in slim fingers — 'with no fat on it at all, and some green vegetables and a glass of wine.' Sometimes lunch with Jack Muir would be one hard-boiled egg.

To establish *The Daily Mirror* Norton applied to the Menzies Government for a licence to import newsprint; the Government agreed 'in principle' on 29 March 1940. After Fairfax, Associated Newspapers and Consolidated Press protests that, while the Government was proposing to reduce newsprint consumption of all newspapers by 35 per cent, it was, as Fairfax general manager R.A.G.Henderson told Prime Minister Robert Menzies on 4 April, 'outrageously unfair to restrict the [newsprint] consumption of existing newspapers in order to permit a competitor to start'. On 31 May the Government revoked *The Daily Mirror* import licences. It reversed the decision in January 1941, allowing the *Mirror* to start on 12 May.

The year's delay was a disaster, Muir said. Journalists had been hired interstate, then put off; some lured from *The Sun* could not get their jobs back, a blow to Norton's credibility.

The Sun offered Muir £5000 for a dummy *Mirror*. He said he never thought of taking it. 'I'm not saying' — he lifts his hands like a cheerleader — "Rah rah, I'm a wonderful person." I just never thought of taking it. You know, why would I? I'd only ever had one job in my life, and that was working for Ezra Norton.'

Ezra was sober for 360 days a year, Muir said, but on the other five he was 'so drunk he couldn't scratch himself'. On Saturday mornings the two would talk about publishing. Ezra would grill Jack about *Women's Weekly* sales, *Sunday Sun* sales, asking 'all manner of questions' about the figures. They would sit drinking milk and eating ham sandwiches for two hours, the men disturbing the suburban subconscious; if Ezra had 'had a bad night' he would leave the milk alone and be quiet. Then he would go to the races.

He forbade beer at the *Mirror*, but turned a blind eye when he saw a lateshift printer with a couple of bottles. One night he saw Jack's brother Ian, a publishing hand, with the unofficially tolerated two bottles, turned to Jack and said: 'Sack him.' No explanation, just the order. Sack him. Jack didn't want a fight with the union and didn't want to sack his brother, so he moved Ian around, keeping him out of Ezra's way. One day when he was working at the *World* Ezra walked up and said 'I know you.' The boy said quickly: 'Oh no sir, you don't.'

When Jack returned to Sydney after four and a half years in the RAAF on one of seven ships returning just after VJ [Victory over Japan 15 August 1945] day, the Captain called him to the bridge and said he had a special request that Flight-Lieutenant Muir be taken ashore immediately.

Muir, said 'Shit, what have I done?'

'I don't know,' the captain said. 'Special request.'

Chapter 16 — The Tabloid School

The reporters were streaming out for interviews with the returning heroes. Muir asked the *Mirror* man what was up. 'I don't know — the young fellow wants to see you.' They all called Ezra the young fellow.

Jack went straight to Ezra's office. Ezra didn't say 'how're you going Jack?' He didn't say 'what's happened?' He grunted 'Gidday Jack' then said 'I want you here tomorrow.'

Jack said: 'Mr Norton, I haven't been in Australia for four and a half years. I've got no clothes.'

Norton: 'You've got a uniform haven't you? We're having trouble with the union. I think you can fix it.' Muir had no idea of Sydney wages rates. He didn't know how much he'd get himself, but he complied.

Norton appointed a circulation director above Muir, a man Muir thought knew nothing, he interfered for the sake of it and 'was no bloody good.' It wasn't working. He talked it over with Mark Gallard, first *Mirror* editor-in-chief and 'one of the finest blokes anywhere' and Gallard suggested 'writing a letter to the boss.' He did. (Gallard had taken knocks for Norton: in May 1935 he was fined £50 for the contempt of court of having published in *Truth* a picture of the killer in the famous shark arm case.)

Ezra telephoned. 'Do you mean what you say in the letter, Jack?' Muir had seen people back off fights with Ezra; he thought it was fatal, if you took a step back with Ezra he'd kick you to death. 'Yes, I do,' he said. 'Well you'd better reach for your hat,' Ezra said. There was no conversation. Ezra hung up.

Muir, bewildered, tried to get details of his sacking. What notice? What severance? Norton wouldn't take his calls. He stayed on the job as Norton gradually removed his functions. He drew his salary. After three months Muir spoke to the general manager, saying this couldn't go on, he had to see Norton. Norton refused to see him, but sent word he could write his own severance pay. Muir calculated that after 22 years and the missed vacations, the *Mirror* owed him a year's pay. Norton, hearing the demand, growled 'Yeah, that's alright.'

He called on *The Daily Telegraph*. Frank Packer would not see him. *The Telegraph* circulation manager told him: 'You've been blackballed. There is no newspaper job for you anywhere in Australia.' A Packer ban stretched from Broome to Byron Bay.

Around a big oval wooden table Norton would take senior *Mirror* staff over their failings. 'He was absolutely nuts about the fact that we had to beat *The Sun*,' Muir said. Beating *The Sun* meant survival; missing a story, coming out late, put the *Mirror*'s existence at risk. The conferences were not pretty. Norton would pick on an editor and (Muir's voice drops, recalling it fifty years later): 'He would really go for him. He would ride him into the ground. He was shocking.' To old hands like Muir the insults were water off a duck's back, it was just Ezra going over the top. But for some, having the proprietor who could sack you at any moment calling you 'imbecile' and 'bloody idiot' in front of your peers was more than they could take. 'When he wanted to be particularly insulting,' Betty Riddell said, 'it would be "Mister", and he would tell them what he would like them to do to themselves. Ezra was a gangster of course, but they're all gangsters and they look after their own.' She thought Ezra pushed one chief sub-editor to a stroke. Muir says he rode Frank McCoy, a 'marvellous machinist' with a natural stammer, to the point where McCoy could barely speak, then offered him use of Norton's private rooms at St Vincent's Hospital.

To Betty Riddell, Ezra was not charming. He was not heroic. When a cartoonist drew a cricket match with the Japanese batting against the Aussies, falling to our deadly attack, heads rolling on the pitch, Ezra pulled it from the paper and pinned it on his office wall. He wouldn't have it. He told Betty the slogan 'Get Your Grip on the Nip' reflected the mood in the country: *'You know, we might be working for them. We mustn't be rude to them.'* Betty thought he was 'getting his mind into the groove that he might have to publish a paper for the Japanese. He was getting ready for it.' When she came back to Sydney Betty told him the British were going to vote Winston Churchill out, the great wartime Prime Minister would lose the general election.

Ezra didn't get it. Betty said 'We [journalists] knew damn well Churchill was going to lose, because he wasn't offering the British public anything. The women had had the pleasure of the very free French, of the Poles, the Australians, the Canadians and the Americans. They were not going to go back to do what Churchill wanted of them.' Ezra told her he believed her, he had to believe her and he had to let her write it 'but I just don't understand it.' (On 26 July 1945 the Labor Party beat Churchill's Conservatives in a landslide.)

Chapter 17

News and Lies: The Capricornia School

1873–1996: Richard Wells, William Bednall, Charles Kirkland, George Mayhew, Louis Solomon, Joseph Skelton, Frederick Thompson, and The Northern Territory Times; *Jessie Litchfield*, first Australian woman editor, *R.D.Beresford* and the *North Australian; Administrator,* John Anderson Gilruth; Justice David Bevan; *Michaael O'Halloran* and *The Northern Standard; Lieut. Alex Baz* and *The Sunday Army News; Jim Bowditch* and *The Northern Territory News.*

The worse it is, the better it is, transcribing life in printer's ink. For your true journalist is little more, or a little less, than human, a child taking notes. He knows no partialities, no class-distinction, no creed distinction, nor colour-line, nor bias, nor loyalty, save to the story.

Ernestine Hill, The Great Australian Loneliness, 1937.

If readers cannot take their daily paper seriously they will not take it at all. Factual inaccuracy is an editor's principal nightmare. ... Although the struggle for perfect accuracy is hopeless it must be ceaseless.

Sydney Deamer, editor, The Herald (Melbourne) 1932

The very blood and semen of journalism is a broad and successful form of lying. Remove that form of lying and you no longer have journalism.

James Agee, then a Fortune magazine journalist, in Let Us Now Praise Famous Men, 1936

Visionaries flourished under the turquoise sky, husbands on the lam, drunks, scribblers, madmen, camel-thieves. Editors. Aboard the Gothenburg steaming from Adelaide with four compositors a press and type, Richard Wells' subconscious boiled with images of doom for the Aborigines: the 'white man's bitter hate', would sweep them from the earth as red gums wept tears of blood. Wells, a poet and *South Australian Register* journalist, planned publication of the first North Australia newspaper, *The Northern Territory Times* on 7 November 1873. When the Gothenburg docked on 2 November 47 passengers raised their glasses to the experienced, sober and popular Captain R.G.A. Pearce, toasting his vigilance and ability and wishing him a long life.

Wells met the deadline and published a lyrical leader in the next issue saying the population of 1,200 to 1,400 would have credit for starting 'the long career of prosperity that lies before it.' (Poet-journalist Ernestine Hill, reflecting scepticism as pervasive as saltbush, quoted the editorial in *The Territory*: 'the word *lies* was prophetic.')

Writing amidst monsoons and lightning, Wells, who had worked for a surgeon after leaving school in England, sought a calm tone: abuse, he believed, 'could achieve nothing more than temperate language'. An introvert in an extrovert's profession — the *Register* said he had 'a remarkably retiring disposition' — he turned on 2 January 1874 to his dominant theme: that Darwin was not an echo, hybrid or clone of Adelaide. Mining companies might 'call this place the Northern Territory of South Australia as long as they please; but it resembles South Australia in nothing and never will.'

Adelaide gentlemen might wear paper collars and waistcoats in the noonday sun 'but we are in the tropics and India and China are our neighbours.' Reproducing Adelaide's 'stereotyped English customs' on the shores of the Arafura Sea would be 'forcing nature backwards.' (Wells, who had shipped from Adelaide to London three times, left Adelaide less than a month before.)

The poet who lamented in *The Gum Tree King* in Adelaide in 1857 that the 'ruthless hand of fate' would sweep Aborigines from 'the joyous earth' became an editor who gave readers what they wanted. Should a white man shoot a black, the troopers would arrest him in a moment, 'but if a nigger spears a white man, no notice is taken of it,' a stringer 'reported' from Yam Creek on 15 December 1874. The stringer 'reported' that 'provocation is entirely on the side of the niggers.' How so? They are continually told to go away, but unless they see a revolver they refuse to do so.' Standing still till a white-feller pulled a gun was provocation. (Wells was also a Territory JP and Magistrate.)

When monsoons stopped newsprint ships the *Times* appeared on 'blue, beige, brown, green, pink, mauve or jaundice-yellow' paper, according to Ernestine Hill, who thought the yarns matched the yellow. But Wells struck a chord: in June 1874 a public meeting chose five men for the first local-government council, including Wells and an energetic storekeeper and liquor licensee, Joseph Skelton, whose page-one ads offered silk coats, galvanised iron, mosquito nets, and moleskin trousers from stores at Southport and Palmerston.

Returning to Adelaide in 1875 with gold, mail and Richard Wells aboard, a cyclone grounded the Gothenburg on the Great Barrier Reef near Holbourne Island, Queensland on 24 February about 7pm; passengers returned to their cabins expecting to refloat at high tide, but refloating failed. When Captain Pearce ordered a hard engine reversal the ship holed; about 3am three lifeboats, one crowded with women and children, were swept away and 100 people, some wearing gold belts, drowned in less than 15 minutes. Wells, Pearce and all the officers were among 98 to 112 (records vary) who died, some eaten by sharks (22 survived). From a hard news perspective, Wells died as a detail in what would have been his biggest story. The victims included a former S.A. Premier, judges, businessmen, the French Vice Consul.

When the catastrophe bell rang at the Darwin telegraph office on Wednesday 3 March, William Bednall, *Times* acting editor, ran in and read a cable from the *Register*: *Gothenburg wrecked in cyclone on Flinders Island. Two boats with passengers rescued. Three boats with 90 passengers still adrift. Telegraph immediately full list of passengers.* (Accuracy, perpetually elusive in tragedies, was astray: Flinders Island off Cape York is about 700 kilometres north of Holbourne.)

The Times editorial said many could not believe their friends were the sport of the ocean; everyone in Darwin mourned.

The tropical North might evoke dreams of plenty and myths of more, and its boundaries, elastic at the behest of distant authority, would embrace then exclude territory three times the size of France, but editing was not all beer and skittles, Bednall reckoned in February 1877. A printer's devil had put his foot through a page. People who complained did not subscribe; when they subscribed they did not pay. He sympathised with a Yankee editor who reckoned that when he published jokes, people said he was rattle-headed and when he didn't he was an old fossil; when he worked in his office, people said he was too proud to mingle. When he went out they said he never attended to business. When he wore a frayed shirt they said business was bad; when he wore silk they said he never paid for it. '*What are we to do?*'

Because he couldn't afford staff reporters, Bednall relied on casuals with an eye for detail and poetry in their subconscious. Readers should understand that the *Times* depended largely on themselves.

When twelve men with warrants set out to arrest four blacks for murder, Bednall reflected a brutal street view: 'The only things that have hitherto proved of any value in bringing the niggers to their senses have been dogs and the revolver. We trust the party now gone out will not be afraid to use them.'

Inside the *Times* office he had a different view: as it shrank from four to two pages, advertising, circulation, readership and staff diminished and by 28 July 1877 the staff comprised 'one man and a lad, and last but by no means least in his own estimation, a blackfellow.'

You couldn't please everyone; then there were the insults 'more easily imagined than described.' He was glad he kept his temper. Some readers imagined all an editor had to do was 'get a lot of type, shy it into a machine, turn a handle' and there would be a paper. It was not like that. Every week he sat trying to write an editorial with 'not a single item of news or public interest' available. This would be his last issue. He uttered a cry from the frontier to the future: as the Territory went ahead 'editing, like everything else, will become easier.' In the worst of times, things must get better. He had no doubt the *Times* would again become a four-pager, even an eight-pager.

Joseph Skelton heard opportunity knocking. Born in England about 1823, he arrived in Adelaide in 1856 and prospered as wholesale draper. A protectionist with fairness in his blood, he moved to Palmerston in September 1873, bought two stores selling horse-feed, gin by the case, potatoes, oranges, boots and bellows. He thrived, bought the *Times* in August 1877 and promised to inject capital and publish interesting general reports of minerals and still more interesting reports of gold.

In his *Times*, letters violating civility would find the wastebasket. But on editorial standards, balance and political bias, he was as hard to read as the winds that whispered in the Great Sandy Desert. 'We will endeavour to promote the true interest of the Territory to the utmost of our ability by truthfully reporting the state of the country.'

The truthful reporting Skelton promised covered another Chinese menace: when not bludging, they worked like dogs. 'The European goes to the wall, utterly unable to compete with the Asiatic, who can keep up his stamina and do a fair day's work on nine-pence a day,' Skelton wrote on 22 December 1877, reporting street gossip. In less than two months Chinese would outnumber whites. They could live cheaply. In the free port of Darwin they did not have to pay heavy Queensland duties on spirits, rice, opium and 'other commodities largely consumed by Chinese.' Chinese hordes were picking out the eyes of the infant Territory. They did not think for a moment of settling permanently. They would search for gold, pay nothing for roads, hospitals and jails and return to China laughing at 'the stupid liberality of our South Australian legislators.' Skelton's public persona believed in free expression: 'our motto is "Everyman is entitled to his own opinion."'

Another self within Joseph Skelton believed in human perfectibility, that all men were created equal and that Darwin storekeepers were responsible for their fellows in humanity, the street drunks.

Seeking money and tobacco, blacks from the Kakadu and the Adelaide river arrived in Darwin on a public holiday, 20 June 1881 offering women and children for prostitution. 'The old women were offered at sixpence,' young women for a shilling, children under ten for two shillings. What did southern Christians, who spent so much on missionaries, think of this? At noon on Wednesday the Inspector of Nuisances was told and the police cleared the mendicants. Skelton thought the answer to the problem was to 'give them a few bags of flour and tobacco and start them off to their own country' 150 kilometres away. Had any part of the Territory been set aside as Aboriginal reserves? The colonial surgeon, the blacks' protector, should see to it.
Eight prominent citizens cancelled their subscriptions on 25 June:

> Sir, — In consequence of the disgraceful articles and indecent allusions in your paper of today's date, and its general mismanagement, we, the undersigned, request you to erase our names from your list of subscribers. V.L.Solomon (later Times owner); Paul Foelsche (coroner and JP); Robert J.Morice (colonial surgeon); D.W.Gott; J.W.Bull; S.S.Moncrieff; L.Webster; Frederick Becker.

Skelton admitted reporting 'very plainly' but 'desperate diseases require desperate remedies. It was his duty to 'call a spade a spade'. As for indecency:

> we would ask our readers to take up any of the leading [interstate] metropolitan papers, on the table of every householder, and glance at that column (so dear to women) in which the proceedings of the divorce court are chronicled, with details far more plain than anything we have written. The day has gone by for hiding these matters from the female mind.' Such reports tended to induce feelings of 'horror and disgust. It is this feeling we wish to inspire in the minds of our readers. Is the article in question the true cause of this sudden burst of indignant virtue?

When an old subscriber offered to give Skelton particulars of 'the vilest conduct' by some of the signatories, he loved transparency. He would be glad to receive information about any of 'the octagonists' vile conduct. Seven casual buyers offered subscriptions to offset the loss. A reader said in a small town where everyone knew the rectitude or otherwise of every married man, 'I could give particulars to which your so-called offensive article were as skimmed milk.' Up and down the waterfront men and women mocked The Octagonists for reading the *Times* when no-one was looking.

When Adelaide barrister R.D.Beresford started the *North Australian* in 1883 the *Times* sneered at 'the reptile in our midst brimful of spite and personality'. Charles Kirkland came to Darwin in 1878 and bought the *North Australian*, then the *Times*, in 1890 with George Mayhew, 'amalgamating' the papers and closing the reptile. Mayhew served on the jury of six that convicted a pariah trader, Rodney Spencer, of the murder of Manialcum, an Iwaija man who Spencer shot in the head as he knelt on the ground, pinned by two tribesmen. After voting for the conviction as juror, Mayhew attacked it as editor. Why had only Spencer been charged, the *Times* asked, when the evidence showed two others participated? 'Let us not have it said that our mistakes release Aborigines and hang white men.'

• • •

Louis Solomon, 19, moved from Adelaide to Darwin in 1873 seeking gold. Practical, energetic, handy with words and numbers, he worked briefly for his uncle then started a company as merchant and agent. Bearded Louis, who dared to blacken himself as an Aborigine and walked naked through Darwin, dubbed 'black Solomon' quickly networked gossip into respect and became the most influential man in the Territory and from 1885 to 1890 owner-editor of the *Northern Territory Times*. A free-trader who saw in Chinese immigration more threat than opportunity, Solomon was a still more gifted politician than journalist. When the Territory won parliamentary representation in 1890, he campaigned on a railway trolley through the goldfields and topped the poll as Territory representative in the South Australian parliament. Elected to the convention framing the federal constitution in 1897, he tenaciously pushed free-trade and the rights of small states, becoming Premier of South Australia for a week in 1899 and elected Federal MHR in 1901. Defeated in 1903, elected again as Territory member in the South Australian parliament in 1905, he held the seat till he died in 1908.

• • •

The power of the press could be abused, Charles Kirkland told roaring supporters at Darwin Town Hall after his release from Fannie Bay jail on 29 April 1913, but 'on the whole it was the strongest, most incorruptible champion of the right, and fearless redresser of wrong, possessed by the people.' As conservatives mingled with 'rabid socialists', White Australians with Chinese, entrepreneurs with labourers, 200 had donated £115/15/- to cover a fine and costs. Kirkland told them he had often failed to live up to the ideals of the free press. He had tried his best. But the 'very existence' of *The Northern Territory Times and Gazette* depended on printing the Government Gazette. (Economically he was as free as George Howe had been in Sydney in 1803.) He hoped that 'in future the *Times* may prove itself more of a people's paper. ... Momentous events (the Australian Workers' Union general strike started by members' secret ballot the day before) were taking place' against the first Commonwealth administrator, Dr John Anderson Gilruth, who desired to 'eliminate all traces of unionism' from the Territory.

When Dr Gilruth, a veterinarian, arrived in April 1912 the *Times* reported that he was tall, fine-looking, neatly dressed, eloquent and cultured; Mrs Gilruth gave a garden party where the guests used the phrases the *Times* and the times and Dr Gilruth expected of them: it was the dawn of a new era; the garden city was blessed with inexhaustible fertility. Giddy with fine wine, they spoke of magnificent opportunities; the word 'bonanza' passed several wet lips.

The problem, Kirkland discovered in his first interview, where he told Dr Gilruth that he had invested in plant and type-setting machines at considerable cost, was that while Dr Gilruth hoped to be a creator, he was naturally abrasive, he couldn't help it. The Government 'arbitrarily and unnecessarily' pulled type from the paper, mutilating two issues. With money in the Estimates to establish a Government Printing Office; Gilruth proposed a Government daily newspaper. After the *Times* published errors in a notice of the Railway tariff, Kirkland said a negligent Government official failed to deliver the proofs. Gilruth issued a memo: 'this must not happen again' and threatened to end the Gazette subsidy.

Kirkland published the threat. A Government daily newspaper was 'wildly stupid and impractical. ... Surely a better use can be found for the expenditure of public money than in wantonly crushing private enterprise?'

When Gregor Manikov, a decorated Russian soldier, arrived in Darwin in December 1912 on a Brisbane-bound steamer with his wife Tatania and two young daughters, he was experimenting with change, looking for a new life. On an experimental farm in Batchelor, he was a hard, sober labourer. After Tatiana and Pasha Manikov, 16, complained that the farm manager, Charles Woolley sexually assaulted them on separate occasions, Gregor signed statements setting out the details of the rapes, committed on February 13 and March 20 1913. In response the police charged him with criminally libeling Woolley.

Both trials were before Justice David Bevan of the Territory Supreme Court. Bevan was a friend of Gilruth's and his associate in a scandal-ridden syndicate running the Daly River copper mine. After witnesses sought to suggest Pasha's sexual looseness, an attempt the judge acknowledged failed (no trial report exists, only the *Times*' journalistic summary) he said:

> But these episodes necessarily imply a knowledge of life, of the seamy side of life, on the part of this young Russian girl which one would not expect to find in a young English girl of the same age.

Kirkland, reporting for the *Times*, thought Bevan's thinking sex 'seamy' was not his only imperfection: his summing up was 'markedly biased' toward the accused. The jury returned a verdict of 'not guilty' in an hour. Bevan said he thoroughly concurred, and discharged Woolley 'without a stain upon his character'. The jury acquitted Woolley in a few minutes in the trial for Tatiana's rape after a summing-up Kirkland said was 'wholly in favour' of Woolley. Three days later, Gregor Manikov's trial for criminal libel came before Judge Bevan. After proof Manikov had published the statements, his counsel Donald Roberts said he would bring evidence to show the statements were true. The jury asked to retire and returned after 15 minutes; the foreman said they had decided. Judge Bevan warned that he could 'accept no verdict at this stage.'

Foreman: We have made up our minds, your Honor.

Judge Bevan: 'You have heard no direction from me as to what a libel is, or as to what publication is. You cannot decide at this stage.'

Foreman: We are satisfied on the facts. We don't want to hear any more.

His Honor: I am afraid, gentlemen, you must hear more.

The foreman, defying the judge's instructions, gave the verdict of the street before a full public gallery: 'I wish to state, your Honor, that we find the prisoner not guilty.' The judge warned that the remark was improper and threatened to charge him with contempt. The prosecutor formally asked for the jury to be discharged. The judge made the order and remanded the case for the next criminal sittings.

The cases shocked and angered people from drovers to preachers to nurses. Kirkland wrote an editorial, *Peculiar Trials,* for the *Times* of 24 April 1913 saying in more than thirty years as a journalist he had never heard such 'unanimous' public indignation. Pasha had been cruelly cross-examined for three hours. Her testimony had not been shaken.

> Since settlement was first started in this far north of Australia we do not think any legal proceedings have ever aroused such general public interest as the two [rape] cases. It is with the greatest reluctance that we make public comment ... but expressions of indignation have been so loud and persistent that we feel the duty cannot be honourably evaded. His Honor throughout both trials showed a bias in favour of the accused. This was markedly apparent in his summing up and directions to the jury.

Charged with contempt, Kirkland appeared at 10am on Monday 28 April before Mr Justice Bevan and a crowded public gallery to show cause why he should not be punished for scandalising Bevan and prejudicing the minds of the public in the case of *R v Manikov*, still pending.

After Mr R.I.D. Mallam, for the crown, proved publication and proprietorship, then read the piece, citing 'numerous authorities' that the judge had been scandalised and public opinion prejudiced, Kirkland asked Bevan if there were any appeal.

The judge declined to answer.

Kirkland read his address. He was the editor and proprietor of the *Times*, 'solely responsible' for *Peculiar Trials*. 'I deny most emphatically that I was actuated by feelings of malice toward anyone.' The published reports of the Woolley cases were fair and impartial. They contained 'none of the disgusting details in the evidence which I might have published had I been maliciously inclined.' His report of *R v Manikov* was based solely on a written statement Mr Mallam gave him, saying Judge Bevan had approved it. Mr Mallam told him there must be no comment on the case, which was still sub-judice. He had followed the direction.

> The comment in Peculiar Trials was only a feeble reflection of the bitter public indignation I have heard on every side following those trials. During the whole of a long experience in this Northern Territory as a journalist I have never heard so strong or so unanimous an expression of public indignation.

He did not wish to hide behind the idea that he was a mere reporter of public opinion. Had he remained silent he would not have been a man. 'I call God to witness that I wrote with reluctance, from a strong sense of duty and the interests of British justice and I have no wish to recall one word I have written.' Being prosecuted for contempt was abhorrent. 'I feel the procedure is cruel, unjust and unwarranted ... I leave my case in your Honor's hands.'

Before a packed public gallery at 3.30pm, Judge Bevan read a 'long judgment' very quickly, finding Kirkland guilty of contempt, fining him £100 and confining him to Fannie Bay jail till he paid.

Kirkland: I will not pay the fine, your Honor.

The judge: Then you will remain in Fannie Bay until you do, Mr Kirkland.

He awarded the prosecutor 15 guineas' costs.

As Kirkland climbed into the police trap to take him to jail a friend whispered: *we are raising the money*. He was driven to prison under a purple sky; men and women on the street cheered; Kirkland said he was dazed felt when he heard the prison gate clang shut and the bolts shot home and padlocked, the sounds triggered a psychological change; his mind was not free.

Relief was at hand. What offence, the prisoners asked, had given them the pleasure of his company? He tried to explain, he was under sentence for writing, sentenced for contempt, but the prisoners understood him too quickly: forgery! A dud cheque! At 5am next day a visiting friend told him 200 people had contributed the necessary £115/15/- in a few hours. Protest organisers refused banknotes, limiting contributions to silver coins, to widen the base of support. Astonishingly, on the street supporters grumbled about this: had he needed £500 he could have raised it.

On his way back to town after his release he saw bunting and fireworks and as he joined hundreds of demonstrators in Cavenagh Street it felt as if he were in a high-class joss-house. It was great to be a popular idol, a kind of god, for a few hours; he was proud and glad but also troubled. How could a 'poor devil of a journalist' who had only done his duty be an idol? He tried to convince himself the real cause of the outpour of public feeling was the principle, not the man.

Kirkland appointed Frederick Thompson, a gifted, orotund professional, an angry comedian from the Port Douglas *Record* as editor and manager in 1914.

Thompson coined the name Korupsha (he liked the sound) for the Gilruth administration and wrote in his column *Prickly Pars* that under Gilruth the Territory was an Augean stable; it would take Hercules to clean it. There were riots under the bullying veterinarian. Not even protectors of Aborigines troubled to conceal their immoral intercourse with Aboriginal women. The State owned the hotels and George Close, a barman in the Club Hotel swore in a declaration read to the House of Representatives in Canberra that the manager had told him on 8 December 1917 to pour slops containing flies, straw and the leavings of bottles of beer, stout, lager and soft drink into a cask of Carlton beer on tap. When Close told the manager the slops were not fit to drink, the manager told him to do as he was instructed 'as I was only the paid servant of the Government.' Some Club drinks, Thompson said, should be shunned like bubonic plague.

In a few months, by 30 July 1914 Thompson was driven to revolution in his editorials, a revolution of style, a poetry-leader:

> God give us men! A time like this demands
>
> Strong minds, great hearts, truth faith and ready hands;
>
> Men whom the lust of office does not kill;
>
> Men whom the spoils of office cannot buy;
>
> Tall men, sun crowned who live above the fog
>
> In public duty and in private thinking.
>
> For, while the rabble with their thumb-worn creeds,
>
> Their large professions and their little deeds,
>
> Mingle in selfish strife, lo freedom weeps,
>
> Wrong rules the land, and waiting justice sleeps.

Chapter 17 — News and Lies: The Capricornia School

Imprisoned with others in 1921 for declining to pay tax as part of a campaign against taxation without consent when the Commonwealth took over on 1 January 1911 — it stripped Territorians of their votes — Thompson started the *Jayle Journal*, slipped weekly to the *Northern Standard*. In Fannie Bay jail, where Ernestine Hill heard tragi-comedy, Marxists singing The Red Flag to the didgeridoo, Thompson saw 'the Riviera of the Northern Territory'; magistrates who unfairly deprived big businessmen of a break at 'the seaside resort' should give themselves a spell to open their eyes. When the Federal Government agreed to a non-voting Territory MHR in 1922, Thompson ran, one of six candadates. In Darwin and Parap, where he was best-known, three voted for him.

• • •

Jessie Litchfield, poet, mother of seven, Reuters correspondent, the first woman editor of a metropolitan newspaper, was a dreamer under the electric heaven. Appointed *Northern Territory Times* editor in 1930, she imagined a Territory jammed with wharves and docks, hundreds of factories, thousands of mines pouring out riches, white-winged planes linking great cities, farms 'granaries of the world.' Asphalt and the iron rail would end Territory isolation and neglect would be a pain of the past.

Jessie ended her memoir *Out With the Diamond Drillers* in 1930 with a song to 'the workers whose hearts have not grown faint, whose muscles are not slackened through sloth and evil-living, who through doubt and danger still FOLLOW THE GLEAM!'

Born in Sydney on 18 February 1883 to Jean Sinclair and John Phillips, a surveyor, Jessie formed a bond with the writer Mary Gilmore who taught her at high school. In 1907, sailing to China to visit relatives, she met a mining engineer, Valentine Litchfield and married him in Darwin on her return. They lived in a hessian hut on the West Arm diamond field, following the miners to Anson Bay, Brock's Creek and Pine Creek until the drilling stopped and Val got a job with Vestey's meatworks in Darwin.

She believed in the word, taught herself the speed and exactitude required for a wire-service, and reported for Reuters for six years. A *Times* owner and manager who Jessie said was 'about the size of a bull-ant, with a bull-ant's courage' appointed her editor early in 1930. A two-finger typist with the speed of a concert pianist, she found the typewriter 'not so apt to be misread' as handwriting. She wouldn't be without it. (When Ernestine Hill saw the paper to bed one night that year, a Larakia leader who sought time off to organise corroborees was printer's devil; two Wagait men in shorts and red headbands fed the ink roller.)

She affected to despise her predecessors' editorial standards on the paper, then selling 300 copies bi-weekly: her first job was to make it 'readable'. The job-printing was bread-and-butter. Without the paper there could be neither ads nor jobbing. Val died in May 1931 after a few days' illness.

Since newspapers in labour's eyes sided with the police, the state and the squatters, labour hungered for a press that would speak for strugglers, even strikers. *The Northern Standard*, published from 19 February 1921 by the Australian Workers' Union (Darwin branch), edited, printed and published by Michael Conlan O'Halloran, supported 'Peace, Progress, Patriotism, Freedom, Fraternity and Fair Play.' With the wonder of the twentieth century, the linotype, installed, Darwin would equal 'the more pretentious Southern cities' in serving 3,000 Territory whites and 20,000 Aborigines.

O'Halloran promised advertisers a bona-fide circulation reaching 'practically every unionist,' home and resident. The *Standard* favoured freedom of religion, democracy over imperialism, reason over prejudice, and sought to end privilege and monopoly.

Readers, he said, cried out for literature, not wastepaper. The *Standard* would go back to first newspaper principles: maximising useful reading, limiting advertising. Having sprung from the people, it would uphold ideals; it had no place for guttersnipe scribblers or spiteful slanderers. 'A large circle of genuine readers' would notice advertisements.

Among the menaces the *Standard* denounced was a controversy in the London press: Indians were agitating for the right to come and go from Australia in the same way as ordinary Britons. Japan too was clamorous. Australia's British connection was 'a standing menace to the fixed and necessary policy of a White Australia.'

When Reuters' London office appointed Jessie Litchfield Darwin correspondent for the 1934 London–Australia air race she told a friend she felt like jelly inside; she would have given anything to wriggle out of it respectably, but 'wasn't game to say I was funking the job.' Her cables reporting the arrival in Darwin of C.W.A.Scott and T.Campbell Black, on their way to setting a new London–Melbourne record, reached London 15 minutes ahead of the competitors, eight young reporters. She told her friend, understating the point — speed is the essence of wire-service reporting — 'That counts a lot with Reuters.'

When she heard a wounded man with information about a murder was on the train to Darwin she went to a loco-shed four kilometres out, boarded the train, found her man, 'got a nice little interview, just in time for the Saturday afternoon papers,' and scooped the men waiting at the Darwin station; their stories were not published until Monday. For Jessie there was Schadenfreude in the scoop: 'I rather like getting ahead of the other chaps. I do enjoy showing them I can hold up my end with them,' for they were specially trained and 'young enough to be my sons.'

She walked the literary track, writing seven novels, and found publishers frustrating. One would turn a manuscript down because the north was so little-known that people were not interested; another would say readers had heard so much they were tired of it. 'If you don't advertise,' Jessie advertised, in and for the *Times,* 'you are like the man who winked at a pretty girl in the dark: he knew what he was doing, but no one else did! Don't imitate him! Advertise! Let your goods be known!' She published an essay on boxing, how the world loved a clean fighter, whether in the ring or politics. Ladies, once were rarely seen at fights, but now there was no doubt a victorious gladiator 'wins the lady's heart.'

The Northern Territory could claim to be the oldest Australian state, she wrote on 25 July 1930, for according to legend Magellan had first sighted it in 1511. The Federal Government had spent £5 million sterling subsidising iron, steel, wire, oil, sulphur, meat, wine and canned fruits, but when it was suggested that £5000 be set aside to encourage Australian literature, there was no support. It should try to build up literature, the threshold of better things.

Jessie Litchfield was among the women and children evacuated from Darwin in 1942 after the Japanese attacked. When she died on 12 March 1956 visiting Melbourne, she left manuscripts and an estate of £3000 to the Bread and Cheese Club, Melbourne, for a literary award.

• • •

When the *Sunday Army News* was first published on 26 October 1941, Brigadier Frank Lind of the AIF believed 'the portrayal of all the truth, and the concealment of none' would help the war effort. Brigadier D.V.J.Blake said the Commonwealth Government established the paper 'to provide troops serving here with the amenity of a newspaper of their own.' The *News*, printed and published by Captain W.H.Sellen of 'the Press Unit, 7 M.D., Darwin', edited by Lieutenant Alex Baz, later a Sydney television executive, was the only Darwin newspaper from 19 February 1942, when Japanese bombers closed the Friday *Northern Standard*. On Thursday 19 February when stories had already been set for Friday publication, editor Jock Hector was worrying about next day's page one when the biggest story he would ever have, Japan Bombs Darwin, deprived him of the power and staff to print it, according to Douglas Lockwood. (It resumed publication in 1946 and closed in 1954.) Brigadier Lind's promise that *Army News* would portray all truth and conceal none revealed a stranger to both journalism and truth. Baz told Lockwood, the recently posted Melbourne *Herald* correspondent, that army censorship stopped him publishing his eyewitness account of the bombing and strafing which killed 15 and wounded 24, according to the Minister for Air, Mr A.S.Drakeford, and which according to the Royal Commissioner, Mr Justice Lowe on 27 March, killed about 250 and wounded between 300 and 400.

Douglas Lockwood, who saw the bush, the traditional owners and the squatters with the eye of humanity and a new reporter's energy, became the best-known Territory journalist. His report of a Timorese boy stowing away after the war in an aircraft wheel-housing in a flight to Darwin (he survived) won a London Evening News competition in 1957 for 'the world's strangest story'. Of his thirteen Territory books the ground-breaking *I the Aboriginal* won the *Adelaide Advertiser* 1962 Festival of Arts literary award.

Led, fed and inculcated by U.S. journalists after World War Two, 1950s newspapers in the West reflected and generated readers' anxieties about aliens and cold war paranoia. Suppressing fears of meretricious narrative, reporters and editors reasoned from the governing principle of Western journalism — to be first with the story — that if you withheld a flying saucer story on the grounds that it was specious, the opposition would publish and you would look like a newshound who couldn't sniff out a story until it applied Man Bites Dog and bit you.

While no God-bothering sky-pilot could prove flying saucers existed, neither could a theoretical physicist or existential philosopher prove they did not. Besides, since many readers looked into the purple night around the Southern Cross and perceived rockets, saucers and aliens, flying saucers were as big as the sun in yellow journalism. There were sources for saucers in the smallest camp on the Nullarbor Plain. George Adamski, a Polish American, claimed to have interviewed, by an extrasensory means he dubbed telepathy, a man from Venus in the Mojave desert in California. The Venusian, according to Adamski, had travelled on a cigar-shaped UFO which shed a silver disk carrying him, dressed in a one-piece suit, into the desert strewn with the gold ghost towns of the old West such as Leadfield and Darwin and Dublin Gulch; Adamski, who had audiences with European royals and the Pope, led UFO research and publishing.

No reporter believed you could interview a man from Venus. That was axiomatic: believing would define you as lacking scepticism, the essence of an Aussie journalist. In January 1954, after four Aborigines heard a 'strange and sinister noise hiss across Harts Range field' and next day six Alice Springs residents saw 'a strange craft' streaking across the early-morning sky, Jim Bowditch, editor of the Friday *Centralian Advocate*, thought he, the paper and the town needed a flying saucer story. The witnesses Bowditch tracked down were bashful. If he reported their names they would deny the whole thing. Bowditch knew the sceptics in the Advocate's audience would read the story as he did himself, like an atheist in a cathedral. In the red centre as in coastal capitals since an authentic UFO yarn was necessarily a fairy story, the word 'fake' had to appear somewhere.

On 5 February Bowditch published a photograph of what looks like a garbage-bin lid above jagged Mount Gillen, 15 kilometres west of Alice Springs, captioned 'fake' or 'flying saucer' (no question mark) with a page one story quoting a note signed 'Unknown'.

> Men from Venus, secret flying machines from Russia, meteorites, optical illusions or just plain fakes and lies — what are these "flying saucers" reported to have been seen in many parts of the world, including Alice Springs?Below we have published a photograph claimed to be that of a "flying saucer".

With the picture, this note was pushed under the door of the *Advocate* office:

> For several reasons, one of which is because I can hardly believe it myself, I refuse at this stage to come forward and allow my name to be used. But study this picture of a flying saucer yourself.
>
> I was taking a picture of Mt Gillen on the day that a number of Alice Springs people said they heard something strange pass over the town (Friday, January 15). Suddenly an enormous round-looking object appeared from behind Gillen. It went high, then dropped to come quite low between the mountain and the town it was not travelling fast at this stage in fact it appeared to be almost hovering. That was when I took this picture almost automatically I focused and clicked the camera. It would have been possible to take more shots, but I just looked, then suddenly the thing moved off very fast, it gained speed until it must have been travelling at terrifying pace, going high and to the West.
>
> I did not hear much of a whistling sound. The saucer looked to have been anything up to 50 feet across. I don't know. Maybe Adamski had something about those men from Venus.

Bowditch wrote: 'The only comment the *Advocate* is prepared to make at this stage is that the picture could easily be a fake. On the other hand one would have to go to considerable trouble to make it up. If genuine, the saucer looks to be a very large affair, although distance would make all the difference in this.'

The note was the sole source for the story. In the phrase 'could easily be a fake', the editor added the last essential detail for authenticity. Mockers who believed the bold, gifted Bowditch to be capable of faking news now had this problem: the editor himself drew attention to that possibility on page one.

'We tried to find out who was having the joke with us, but couldn't,' Bowditch wrote in his column for Darwin's *Northern Standard*. Some readers thought the picture was of the wheel of a toy car, some a button, a washing-machine agitator, a blown-up rubber cushion. It didn't look good to him.

Born in London in July 1920, in a working class family of seven, Bowditch left school in the depression at 15 to labour in a canning factory. He worked his passage to Sydney on a cargo ship, arriving with his family and £4 in his pocket. After training at an experimental farm at Glen Innes, he worked on a sheep station at Cunnamulla, fossicked for alluvial gold on the Macquarie River, ring-barked wattle and ironbark trees for 1/7d an acre, tramped and train-jumped. When he discovered Aussie farm hands were paid £1 a week and Poms 10/-, his mate Douglas Lockwood said, he shed his London accent and told anyone who asked he was 'from Cunnamulla'.

He fought at Tobruk and Milne Bay in the AIF, joined the Z special force, worked as a spy, in demolition and sabotage behind Japanese lines, winning a Distinguished Conduct Medal and killing a teenager with a knife in Borneo. 'I still have nightmares about it,' he told Darwin historian Barbara James in 1980. After the war he sold iron stands door-to-door and for 17 months was Moreton Island lighthouse keeper.

Believing he had an affinity for the land and the inner Jim was a farmer, he went to Alice Springs, searching with a migrant's focus for the Australian core, enticed, he said, by the prospect of a land grant under the Federal Government's soldier resettlement scheme. Instead he became paymaster at the Works Department and, quick with clerical chores, found time to write for the *Centralian Advocate*, first published on Saturday 24 May 1947, edited and part-owned by a friend, Alan Wauchope, and to string for *The Age* in Melbourne. 'I took to reporting. I liked finding out what was going on around the place. I was also developing some strong attitudes.' When Wauchope fell seriously ill in 1950 the manager and co-owner, Ron Morcom, asked Bowditch to step in as editor and sole reporter. 'There's nothing like starting at the top,' he told Lockwood dryly.

He was 30, 'knew nothing about newspapers' apart from a bit of freelancing, and couldn't type. He was a radical humanist and one of his attitudes, in a culture sold on the White Australia policy, was that the black Australians who crowded Gap Road in the town centre but were rarely seen behind a counter were unjustly treated. He had a 'completely free hand' on the paper, loathed bullying and tried to expose violations of the fair go. He believed 'you don't legislate to end discrimination, you educate'; he was a teacher-editor, a wiry squash obsessive, and a big drinker. 'Everyone lost patience with Jim eventually,' said author and journalist Kim Lockwood, Douglas's son, who was a *News* reporter and leader-writer with Bowditch from 1968 to 1971. 'In drink he'd push me in the chest: "What would you know?" What did the words 'Jim Bowditch' conjure in Lockwood's mind? 'The day he tried to strangle me. I asked him in my office after 43 beers if he'd ever killed anyone in Z force and in one bound he was behind me, pulling me backwards off the chair in a stranglehold.'

As he honed his eye for the angle, reporting a 'world record' in an Alice Springs Country Women's Association competition to fit the greatest number of objects (no sand-grains) into a matchbox (140, including tobacco, glass, peppercorn, a nib, needle and bobby pins), where locals spoke casually of cattle properties bigger than Belgium, he hoped to become a literary figure; in his heart Bowditch believed he could write stories of miners, stockmen and black-trackers as if he were Henry Lawson. But when a member of the MacDonnell Nickel Copper Syndicate released a survey showing a 4200-square-mile prospecting area showed geological formations 'similar to that of Rhodesia' which included 'one of the richest copper belts in the world' he knew his duty. The story led the paper and asked, as if Bowditch were a corporate spin doctor: 'Will Alice Springs become the centre for one of the world's really big copper producers?'

By mid-February, he found an expert prepared to vouch that the flying saucer photograph was authentic. A member of the South Australian Astronomical Society, Mr F. Churchman, told Bowditch: 'these cartwheel pattern saucers are not uncommon.' He knew of eight similar sightings dating back to 11 June 1855. 'I for one do not think for a moment it is a "fake" and would like to get in touch with the man that took the photo privately, through your paper, and will keep his name a secret if he wishes.'

Bowditch wrote (in bold) in the *Advocate* of 19 February 1954: 'Mr Churchman is not alone in wishing to contact "unknown", so in the words of the poet we ask "come out, come out wherever you are." The photographer has nothing to fear, but may have a considerable amount to gain; there are rewards for this picture.'

Beneath the headline WHAT IS IT? he published the photograph again on 5 March asking whether it was 'genuine, as one South Australian observer believes,' or a button, meteorological balloon, bottle top, or part of a washing machine, as mentioned by the cynical?

Curious about the picture, two young men found a box with the word 'radiosonde' a radio and set of meteorological instruments carried by a balloon at the base of Mt Gillen and brought it to the *Advocate*. English author Harold Wilkins, writing *Flying Saucers on the Moon*, said two boys in the Westmoreland Lake district had photographed a similar saucer. The British, French, American and possibly the Australian War Department knew 'certain facts' about flying saucer reports dating from 90 BC. Some saucers were 'definitely hostile'.

Bowditch published the letter on 12 March, saying his mind was open, but he would appreciate readers' reports.

The whole story was an exemplary fabrication.

Bowditch wrote the letter from 'Unknown', pushed it under his own office door, then acted as if it were from a reader. (He briefed a local woman photographer who took a picture of an object on a string, and superimposed it on an image of Mt Gillen.)

It opened the door to a legendary career. A few weeks later Canberra journalist Don Whitington hired Bowditch as editor of the Darwin afternoon bi-weekly *Northern Territory News*, policy 'truth, decency and a fair go' published since 8 February 1952 by the public relations company Eric White Associates. He drove 1600 kilometres up the Stuart Highway through what looks from a passenger-jet like a red, white and purple sand abstraction; when he arrived the retiring editor, Mac Jeffers, mourning his own loss, was lifting a glass to 'the death of the *News*'. Bowditch, whose gift was hard news, not stylistic nuance, thought the start less than ideal but he had the crier's obsession. On his way home after a waterfront strike stopped a newsprint shipment — and therefore the next day's paper — he called by a butcher for roast beef and when the apprentice wrapped it in clean newsprint, bought thirty reams and kept the paper on the street.

Mick Daly, a rangy good-looking drover, 33, telephoned from the Katherine police station 320 kilometres south of Darwin. He had been convicted of the offence of 'cohabiting' with his lover, Gladys Namagu, 20, from the Kimberley in Western Australia. The couple, taking a herd of 1500 cattle to Queensland, stopped in Katherine to get married. That was the story. Was Bowditch interested?

The editor quickly saw a story with romance, race and international potential. It emerged that tiny Gladys, about 150 centimetres and 36 kilograms, had been sung to sterility at five because tribal elders feared the sickly girl would bear sickly babies. She had been married as a child to a tribal elder, Blind Billy, who, suspecting her of infidelity, shoveled embers on her nightdress while she was sleeping. Severely burned, she was flown to Wyndham Hospital.

Now as a young woman she had two problems. As a ward of the state, the Welfare Department, headed by director Harry Giese, controlled her as legal guardian. She required Giesee's permission to marry. Another complication: she was married under tribal law to a 'tall sophisticated' Nyoongar, Arthur Jumala.

Bowditch the editor saw a great story. Bowditch the man was sympathetic: he had married his wife Betty, an Arrernte woman in Alice Springs a few years earlier and when he first met Gladys he saw a 'wafer-thin young woman with one leg crippled at birth by cerebral palsy, bright intelligent eyes and what seemed an unbreakable spirit.' Bowditch the radical humanist thought Welfare power over blacks was a fundamental denial of human rights. The Welfare argument that the law was not discriminatory because any person, black, white or brindle, could be declared a ward was a sham: 'While almost all tribal Aborigines and many part-Aborigines were so classified, not one white person was ever listed.'

When Bowditch questioned the Welfare Director, Giese was cool and distant. Field officers had told him Gladys was married under tribal law. She could not marry the Catholic drover. He had made his decision: that was the end of it.

Bowditch shouted that he would make sure the story was told overseas. When the world got to hear of it the department's name would 'stink internationally'.

With Mick Daly staying at Bowditch's home in Fannie Bay, Bowditch next morning climbed the fence to the dusty Bagot Aboriginal housing compound, found Gladys, took her home and — part of the struggle with Welfare — obtained a permit to employ her as his housekeeper.

Giese wrote to Daly refusing permission to marry; Mick and Gladys became an international story, lovers star-crossed under the Southern Cross, Romeo and Juliet outback. When Bowditch interviewed Gladys on 16 August with her tribal husband Arthur Jumala, who met Gladys at Hall's Creek and lived with her for five years, Arthur said: 'She fell in love with Mick Daly. I told Gladys she could go with Mick. That's all right — I got another girl at Montejinnie.' He thought Daly 'not a bad sort of fellow —good man.'

Daly, under contract to deliver 1500 cattle to Queensland, was back on track east of Wave Hill when Labor MLC and lawyer Dick Ward wired Robert Menzies' Minister for Territories, Paul Hasluck asking for a 'thorough investigation'. Hasluck, who became convinced while reporting for *The West Australian* that the people need the guidance of elites, suggested Daly wait six months. As Ward pressed Giese for details of Arthur and Gladys' tribal marriage — at least when and where — Giese was evasive. In reply Ward quoted the English Satirist Samuel Butler: 'Some men love truth so much they seem in continual fear lest she catch cold from over-exposure.' As Mick Daly neared the Queensland border, Dick Ward moved in the Legislative Council on 28 October that Harry Giese MLC be required to table all papers relating to the Namagu-Daly case. Giese said they contained confidential information. Ward: 'The two persons who really matter want everything disclosed.' After Territory administrator J.C.Archer ruled that Giese was entitled to vote on the motion it was defeated 6-7 by that single vote. Next day after the administrator ruled Giese was entitled to vote on Ward's motion censoring Giese it lost 6-7 to cries of 'Shame! Shame!' Finally, because Gladys could not remain a ward of the state beyond December 31, the couple married in a Darwin Catholic church on New Year's Day; Dick Ward gave the bride away and Giese — Bowditch thought 'to his everlasting credit' — attended as guest. The newlyweds flew to Mount Isa to join Mick's brother Steve at Wolgra station.

Part of the strategy driving 'objectivity' in journalism is that it keeps the journalist's profile lower than a snake's belly. The doctrine rendered print journalists as close as practical to invisible on the public stage. The cost of the journalist's privileged position is tremendous: reporting is all, reporting is the end of it. But the rules that governed journalism in Adelaide, Melbourne and Sydney evaporated along with propriety, civility and law under the North Australian sun.

After the pearl-shell market collapsed in 1961, three Malayan pearl workers lost their jobs and Alexander Downer, the Immigration Minister, ordered them deported. Jaffa Madunne had worked in Australia for twelve years, Daris bin Saris and Zainal bin Hashim five years (they could stay only while employed). Bowditch had the *News* say: 'The indentured labour system is a shocker. These innocent men who have worked well for Australia are being made to suffer.' He knew his readers: 2500, one white in five, signed a petition against the deportations. After a packed public meeting at Darwin Oval hundreds marched to Government House as police reinforcements rushed to protect the Administrator, Roger Nott, who agreed to meet a delegation on the veranda. Bert Graham, president of the North Australia Workers' Union, told him: 'I don't want this to sound like a threat, but I would not want to be responsible for what may happen if an attempt is made to deport these men.' Nott promised to tell Downer the feelings of the people. Bowditch, an activist on the citizens' Anti-Deportation Committee, hid Saris and Hashim at his house after Madunne came out of hiding on the promise that his case would be reviewed. Police searched Bowditch's house three times under warrant without finding anyone (men in blue could look the other way). Supporters donated £3000 and briefed barrister Frank Galbally in Melbourne. Saris and Hashim surrendered to the Administrator in September; Downer stopped deportation proceedings in October and allowed the three to stay.

On December 10 three sailors on the Portuguese frigate Gonzales Zarco jumped ship seeking political asylum from the dictator Antonio de Oliveira Salazar. Promising to report daily to Robert Meldrum, an ASIO official, Norberto Andrade, Jose da Costa and Joaquim Teixeira were freed while Downer considered their applications for asylum. When he announced they would be returned to Portugal they hid in the bush at Fannie Bay.

Bowditch, president of the Anti-Deportation Committee and one of its biggest donors, urged the Government not to shame Australia in the eyes of the world. 'Will we give asylum to these men or send them to their deaths?

That is the choice.' With the three working in an ice-cream factory, Mr Justice Bridge in the Northern Territory Supreme Court in March found the minister's discretion unassailable and dismissed an application to overturn Downer's order. On 30 April the High Court dismissed an application for leave to appeal. Hearing the news in Darwin, Andrade took a cord from his pocket and in a gesture induced or created because journalists were watching, wound a noose round his neck and shouted: 'This first, this before Portugal.'

Next day Downer reversed the order.

The Darwin street said he could turn an enemy into a mate over a cold beer, but in news reporting Bowditch did what he had to. Kim Lockwood said Bowditch once chartered 'everything that floated' to keep Douglas Lockwood behind on a big sea story. Though the US would not let the old radical visit, it awarded him a Bronze Star in 1995 for his courage in Z force behind enemy lines. He died of pneumonia in October 1996.

Chapter 18

The Black Swan

1829–1993: *Charles Macfaull* and *The Perth Gazette* and *Western Australian Journal*; *Frances Lochee* and *The Inquirer*; *John Winthrop Hackett, Charles Harper, Griff Richards, Jim Macartney, Paul Hasluck* and *The West Australian*.

It's enthralling and you think you are having influence and you have gratifying social standing, but it consumes your soul. It consumes your soul. You have to commit yourself to it. There's no room for anything else. The editor has to be absolutely the creature of the newspaper and those who sail in it. It takes it out of you.
   Frank Devine, editor, The Weekend News, Australian Reader's Digest, Chicago Sun-Times, New York Post, Australian.

Pretend to be dumb. That's one of the first things I learnt in reporting politics. Always ask dumb questions. Never let on you know things.
   Don Smith, managing editor, The *Sunday Times* (Perth) 1995

Penetrating the void and mystery of the Southern Land, Dutch adventurers made news on the West coast more than two centuries before print began its work, 151 years before Captain James Cook 'discovered' Australia. Pushed by the roaring forties, the Dutch East India Company's Dirk Hartog landed on the island off Shark Bay named after him on 25 October 1616, using the medium of a pewter plate to report the visit to passing explorers and indigenes, but nothing enticed or interested him in the harsh deserted north-west coast and they sailed to Batavia (Jakarta). In 1619 Dutch sailors reached a spot on the unknown land inshore from Rottnest Island. The Gilt Dragon, wrecked when it struck a reef off Ledge Point on 28 April 1656 lost most of its crew of 193; 75 made it to shore and 13 'seeing certain death on all sides resolved to expose themselves to the mercy of the waves ... at least the death they found there would be swifter,' a French account published in Amsterdam in 1708 reported. Thirteen reached Jakarta but Dutch navy searches failed to find survivors or retrieve the Dragon's casks crammed with silver bullion, pieces of eight, off a country where mountains were rocks, valleys desert and plains sand. After spear-fishermen discovered the wreck in 1963 the frontier drama continued: looting prompted protective legislation and one discoverer hanged himself in prison. (The 'Gilt Dragon Research Group' of 'volunteer scientists' was researching the mystery from Cranbourne, Victoria from 2010 and seeking crowd-funding in 2017.)

When British settlers arrived in June 1829 to start what would become the most isolated city in the world they were hungry for news. As naval surgeon T.B.Wilson walked the planned St George's Terrace on 18 October he saw a hand-written newspaper pinned to a gumtree. That there was no 'opposition tree' pleased him. While a free press might nourish a community 'at a certain state of perfection', in a raw new colony private affairs would be jealously noticed. Matilda Bay might not yet be stained by convictism but that did not mean it was ready for a free press.

Charles Macfaull, first editor of *The Perth Gazette and Western Australian Journal* first reported a shipwreck mystery on 12 July 1834. A Nyungar said 'white man's friends are sitting on the ground sorrowing — the ship which has walked with them over the sea now lies dead, broken on the rocks.' The reporter of this extraordinary news was reliable: George Moore, a devout lawyer and farmer researching Nyungar languages.

Moore, who studied law at Trinity College, Dublin, was torn when he heard the story from a black named Weeip. Delay would inflict suffering on shipwreck survivors, but was the news right, had there been a wreck? Weeip said 'white man says if one black man spears a white man and another black man see, both black men are bad.' Weeip's son had been accused of spearing a soldier. He struck a bargain. If he took Moore's letter to the shipwrecked men, would the Governor say to the white men 'Weeip is friend?' He would walk fast: fifteen days to Shark Bay — about 850 kilometres. Moore wrote a letter instructing survivors to look out for a rescue ship, make large fires, raise flags and beacons, wrapped the papers in oiled silk and tied it in a 'roll as thick as a finger'.

The Government Resident, John Morgan, believed whites with bleeding hearts would ruin Nyungars. In a Public Notice in *The Perth Gazette and Western Australian Journal* on 2 March 1833 Morgan argued that 'plunder and violence must, and will, follow' when the natives discovered money could buy food. There were 'sixty stand of arms, with a full supply of ammunition' for those 'ready to inflict a prompt and heavy punishment.' When the notice arrived, the Journal editor, Charles Macfaull, had written an editorial hoping for friendship between settlers and natives, who were becoming such accomplished beggars that soon 'force must be used'. When he read Morgan's notice, Macfaull retorted that the natives' 'treacherous methods of revenge' meant recourse to arms would be 'as futile as ridiculous'. In Macfaull's newspaper, do-gooders wrestled muscular men of action, as they did in his heart.

Optimism coloured his editorial on 13 December 1834. 'With a view to try the experiment of civilising the Natives,' it said, the Governor had been pleased to appoint an interpreter, Mr Francis Armstrong, who would explain the scheme to recipients. 'The natives are to understand that they are to procure their own means of subsistence … It does not form any part of the intended plan to maintain the natives at the public expense, or support them in a state of indolence.' Mr Armstrong would live with the Natives at Mt Eliza Bay; when they were sick Mr Armstrong 'will take them to the doctor to be cured.' They would be shown how to build huts. The Governor would provide a boat for fishing and Mr Armstrong would help dispose of spare fish for flour or money. If they did not procure enough for themselves 'they must go without.' As long as they behaved well 'they shall not be molested by any one, whether black or white; and if they are, the Governor will take their part.' Finally, while at the bay, 'they must behave well and do as Mr A. directs them — if they are not well conducted Mr A. will not let them remain there.' Macfaull thought it was the Aborigines' responsibility to understand the Governor and the *Gazette*. He was silent about the responsibility of the Governor, interpreter and *Gazette* to convey meaning. Communication between the voice of the Swan River colony and the Aborigines was the responsibility of the powerless. When Nyungars murdered a young settler Macfaull called on 26 July 1834 for 'severest chastisement ☐ a summary and fearful example'. Killing blacks would prove 'in the end an act of the greatest kindness and humanity'. It would be merciful to put a quick end to the illusion that black resistance had a future.

When *The Inquirer, A Western Australian Journal of Politics and Literature*, appeared on 5 August 1840, Macfaull said the public would decide whether or not there was room for two journals; personally he though not. An *Inquirer* piece 'Chinese English', about misunderstandings between Cantonese and English drew this from The *Gazette*: 'The article on Chow-chow, At-chow and Chow-ee — Chinese literature — we should hope, is not to be a specimen of future productions…'

Frances Lochee, the *Inquirer* editor, printer and publisher, was not a man to take that lying down. Naturally the *Gazette* was malicious, he said: it had been scooped in a news story from York in the wheat-belt. The *Gazette* was so embarrassed it had asked the *Inquirer* for details. Lochee allowed his taste for mockery to show on 12 August 1840: 'How is it that our contemporary was so reduced as to be forced to apply to us?' The *Inquirer,* desiring to report the York meeting to its readers, had 'made some little exertion to procure [a report]; the same means were open' to the *Gazette.* The *Inquirer* had better sources or else the *Gazette* had been idle.

Lochee was an argumentative, some thought a brazen, journalist, but in this second issue he had gone too far. Born in London on 8 March 1811, Lochee, barrister John Lochee's son, was cared for by a guardian with his elder sister and identical twin brother after his parents' death in his early childhood. He studied law but his stammer turned him away from advocacy and he sailed for the Swan River Colony in the *Britomart* under Captain William Macdonald in July 1838.

Lochee and the abrasive Macdonald did not get on. Late in July Lochee, who never suffered in silence, said he would as soon eat the breadbasket as the 'rocks' inside it; the Captain snarled that he deserved to starve. Three weeks later Captain Macdonald said he would provide better biscuits if the gentlemen would leave them for the ladies. At the breakfast table next morning, Lochee, not knowing the arrangement, took a ladies' biscuit.

The Captain stared at him, picked up a biscuit and said a man who could not eat it deserved to starve, in fact should go straight to hell.

Lochee: I beg to differ.

Captain Macdonald: You are no gentleman.

Lochee: You are a liar!

The Captain seized a knife from the table and advanced on Lochee shouting 'Damn your liver.'

Lochee picked up a knife: 'Two can play with knives.'

The Captain paused; both sat down. Macdonald said Lochee was a rogue and sharper who showed the society he was accustomed to by leaving his boots outside his cabin door.

At Capetown in October Lochee wrote to the *Commercial Advertiser,* mentioning 'a report current in town' that the *Britomart* crew had been encouraged to mutiny by the passengers. He could not speak for the crew, but on behalf of the passengers, the author of such a report was guilty of base and malicious falsehood. Macdonald found the letter 'inflammatory'. When Lochee returned the mate told him he had orders not to let him on board. Lochee confronted Macdonald: was this so?

Macdonald: 'Yes. You are an audacious scoundrel, capable of committing murder.' Next day Macdonald refused to allow Lochee's goods on the ship;

Lochee thrashed him with a stick. A day later both were bound over to keep the peace and Lochee fined £1.

There was also a teacher and visionary in Francis Lochee. By 1855 he believed every man in the new, progressive colony hoped to see his children occupy the highest offices and would insist on education to fit them for the tasks of leadership. He took another step. The time would come when men would be respected not for their positions but their brains.

The gulf between *The West Australian,* which believed in the status quo exemplified by the Anglican Church, the Government and St George's Terrace, and the Chief Justice, Sir Alexander Onslow, who believed in socialism and human perfectibility, was as wide as the Nullarbor Plain. For its part, the *West* never permitted its distaste for Onslow's politics to sully its columns: the *West* would not be so overt. Nor did it report Onslow's socialism. In Perth in the 1880s where nothing was said directly, abuse flowed like the tide.

On 15 December 1883, the *West* criticised the conduct of the case *Davies v Randall* by Attorney General A. P. Hensman, who had just arrived. Because the case was over —only a chambers hearing on costs remained — the *West* thought it could not prejudice the hearing and ran no risk of contempt of court. Hensman and the Chief Justice thought otherwise: Hensman prosecuted the *West* for contempt. In the hearing on 19 December 1883, the Chief Justice said the editorial writer had disregarded 'any sense of justice, honesty and fair play' for the Attorney General. The writer was 'an utter quack' and 'a charlatan'. The *West*'s reproaches to the Attorney were 'unwarranted, libellous and unjustified'. The *West* said the Chief Justice would be in a difficult position if he had to determine whether its words were libellous.

For Onslow that was enough: having been on cordial terms with that pillar of the Perth establishment, the *West* editor John Winthrop Hackett, he now declined to speak to him. Hackett read rage into the disdainful silence. Born in Ireland in 1848, Hackett migrated to Melbourne in 1875 and moved to the Gascoyne to manage a sheep station in 1882, acquiring co-ownership of the *West* with a farmer-educator, Charles Harper, in 1883.

They were an odd couple. Harper, born on 15 July 1842 near Toodyay, the only son of a barrister turned clergyman, was an experimenter. He tried pearling in Roeburne, spent a year building a boat, patented a food extracted from grass-trees, invented a shearing machine and a process for treating sceptic tank effluent. The first classes in what became Guildford Grammar School were taught in the billiard room of his house. Harper had the money, Hackett the newspaper skills.

After the *West* sneered at auctioneers' puffery in a land advertisement in August 1885, few attended next day's auction. The auctioneers sued for libel for damages of £3000. When Hackett and Harper heard that the Chief Justice intended to try *Fienberg and Rogers v the West Australian,* they felt 'the utmost anxiety', knowing his 'hostility for their journal.' That Attorney-General Hensman was counsel for the auctioneers did not make Hackett and Harper's minds any easier. On 14 November 1885 Hackett, not at all mollified by the jury's verdict of a farthing's damages, wrote of the Chief Justice:

> From the moment he takes an interest in one side of a case, the other side literally ceases to have any existence for him, save in so far as parts of it can be brought in to support that side fortunate enough to win his interest. And this unique incapacity to look at two aspects of a question, coupled with a disposition to hold all who support a side to which he may happen to take a dislike, as traitors to justice, hostile to right, and personally offensive to himself, are qualities which tend to confirm every unsuccessful suitor in the belief that he is not receiving justice. Such we admit remains our own conviction and remains so more than ever after reading once more the judicial harangue we publish to-day.

The Chief Justice did not respond. Mr Justice Stone, said that if Hackett and Harper found the Chief Justice partial, they could appeal to the Full Court. Hackett scoffed that since the Chief Justice had two votes 'an appeal would have been useless.' The jury's award of a farthing was 'contemptuous' of the auctioneer's case, but the Chief Justice required the newspaper to pay costs.

The West Australian frowned on Friday 16 September 1887. The Chief Justice had published correspondence between himself and the Governor, Sir Frederick Napier Broome, and the Secretary of State for the Colonies, Sir Henry Holland, in the *West's* competitor, the *Inquirer and Commercial News.* The letters revealed that relations between the Governor and the Chief Justice had deteriorated so far that Broome was on the point of suspending Onslow. But what enraged the *West* was the *Inquirer's* publication of communications 'of a character which never, except in the case of a public inquiry, leave the secret drawers of officialdom.' Opening the secret drawer the *West* thought a serious error, manifest indiscretion and a grave and startling public act. In publishing the facts Onslow 'set at naught some of the most sacred rules of the [public] service.'

At times in that remote city, the most isolated on earth, men lost perspective, as if the treeless plain stretching endlessly to the East moulded their psyches as well as their geography. On 25 July 1887, the prickly Broome sent Onslow papers on convicts' appeals for mercy, requesting advice. Onslow refused. The 'prerogative of mercy lies with the Crown alone; and the Judge having once passed sentence has nothing further to do with the case.' Broome went to the Executive Council, which as he expected took his side, saying Onslow refused to give advice 'out of obstinacy'. Broome and Onslow asked the Secretary of State, Sir Henry Holland, for a ruling. When Broome a few weeks later returned four prisoners' petitions to Onslow again asking for advice, Onslow did nothing, awaiting Holland's response.

Then on 30 August 1887 Broome asked Onslow to return the petitions, with advice attached. Onslow replied next day that he would give advice when he learned Holland's views. After two more requests Broome charged Onslow with detaining official papers, the property of Her Majesty's Colonial Government.

Onslow returned the papers saying he was shocked the Governor had taken the very serious, unprecedented and illegal step of 'making charges against me which are altogether unwarranted.' He wrote Sir Henry Holland: 'Is it possible for me to satisfactorily carry on the administration of justice if I am perpetually to be exposed to the harassing and insulting treatment which for so long a time I have met at the hands of Sir F.N. Broome?

> I ask you to consider whether Sir F.N.Broome is a man in whose hands may safely be trusted the very large powers which are vested in the Governor of a Colony?

Shortly after he wrote those words, at 3pm on 8 September, a reporter with a nose for news asked Onslow was it true that the Governor had inhibited him? Onslow said only that disputes had arisen between himself and Broome, but he thought the reporter's question meant 'the mischief was out'.

There was in Broome, a father of democracy in the West, a compulsion to bend others to his will that caused him to focus on the personal and petty and lose perspective on his vision. Born on 18 November 1842 in Canada, Broome was a sheep farmer in New Zealand and a poet and journalist in London; he wrote regularly for *The Times* and published a book of poetry *The Stranger of Scriphos* before he was appointed Governor of W.A. in 1883.

Onslow, born on 17 July 1842 in Surrey, England, was appointed Attorney General of Western Australia in 1880. Arriving in Albany in December 1880, he suffered sunstroke playing cricket shortly afterwards, an incident to which magical thinking attributed his want of discretion. Onslow thought humanity perfectible; a contemporary described him as believing in 'the highest form of constructive socialism.' He wanted to bridge the gulf between the haves and the have-nots; he believed exploiting labour degraded both master and servant.

The *Daily News*, the liberal afternoon paper, called attention to the extraordinary powers the Queen's representative had in Western Australia. British judges could only be removed on a petition to the Crown from both houses of parliament. This, the *News* observed, would be the law in Western Australia when the colony obtained self-government.

On Saturday night, after the Perth Workingman's Club assured the Chief Justice of sympathy and support, a packed Perth Town Hall — the *Inquirer* reported 2,000 present — heard Mr A.P. Hensman MLC propose that they considered that the Governor's course 'a gross interference with the independence of the Bench and an attack on the liberties of the people.' Loud cheers. After two hours of speeches, denunciations, cries of 'shame', hisses and laughter, they formed a torchlight procession, swelling to what the *Inquirer* estimated as 3,000 or 4,000 people, accompanying an effigy of Governor Broome, dressed in an expensive suit, standing on a trolley supported by two costumed clowns.

Laughing, jeering and groaning within earshot of Government House they wended down Hay Street, turned into William Street, stopped at the Governor Broome Hotel and asked the effigy to 'have something to drink'. A demonstrator brought the drink out; the lead clown swallowed it.

His assistant called for silence.

The clown sentenced the effigy to death.

As he spoke something caused the effigy's head to move; the clown scoffed that the Governor was begging for mercy and smacked his face. In a vacant block opposite they planted a circus pole, affixed a yardarm and hanged the effigy; it fell to the ground. The Chief Justice's supporters, some refreshed from the Governor Broome's bars, drenched it with five tins of kerosene. As the flames consumed it the clown said: 'Gentlemen, it is a disgrace to be burnt in effigy by anyone, but for a Governor to be burnt in effigy by a clown, why — it's just too much.'

Three days later at Fremantle Mr Hensman was again the chief speaker and again they burned Broome's effigy. More was to come in the tempest of insults between Hensman the robust liberal and Hackett the granite conservative. On 23 May 1888 the *West* said Hensman, 'in two short years' as Attorney General 'had put himself outside the pale' of the Colonial Service. 'Then came his precipitate publication of a scandalous pamphlet in the Eastern Colonies' which had been just as 'precipitately suppressed'. If there was one thing more upsetting to Winthrop Hackett than a scandalous publication, it was a scandalous publication about the Western colony in the Eastern Colonies. Hensman made Hackett very angry. On 28 May 1888 the *West* reported: 'Misrepresentation, misquotation and false insinuations are weapons of which Mr Hensman, whether rightly or wrongly, has been very generally accused.' That was the last straw for Hensman. On 7 June 1888 he issued a writ for libel claiming £5000 damages.

Chief Justice Onslow heard the case; the jury awarded Hensman £800. That was the last straw for Hackett and Harper. Onslow had suddenly reordered Supreme Court business to hear the case himself, with the plaintiff 'his intimate friend' and the defendant the journal he had regarded with 'unrelenting asperity' ever since he quarrelled with 'his old friend, its former Editor, over Mr Hensman nearly five years ago.'

After the verdict, Hackett and Harper petitioned the Legislative Council. 'Our business, our properties, our reputations are imperilled. The baser kind of journalist and public speaker assails us confidently and with impunity. We cannot obtain justice in the Supreme Court. Persecuted, plundered and insulted, we are helpless and without relief before the chief tribunal of our Queen. To your Honourable House we appeal to aid in ending a state of things which is a scandal to the Bench, a menace to the welfare of the colony, and a dishonour to the Crown.' They asked for a third judge.

The most powerful voice in Perth, speaking for St George's Terrace, the Church of England and the Government, required protection against base journalists and public speakers. In the Legislative Council on Friday 19 October 1888 Hensman said he should be sorry to see the day when the judge of an English Court descended to 'answer the petition of two disappointed … litigants,' the gallery drummed their feet. Hensman thought Hackett and Harper were smarting because a jury of twelve had punished them for a series of libels. 'It shocks me to think that a Judge is to have mud thrown at him in this way, and by whom? By disappointed litigants.'

Septimus Burt mocked Mr Hensman. He had won £800 damages for libel and 'must find it a good paying speculation to go before the Supreme Court and a jury. If all business succeeded like that I can only say it would be a payable business.'

Stephen Henry Parker, the 'people's Harry', presented the *West's* petition; the ayes numbered nineteen and the noes four. The petition went to the Secretary of State; Mr Secretary said the matter was for the colony to decide. In April 1889 the Council declared by ten votes to seven that the Chief Justice's language against Hackett in *Davies v Randell* was 'highly intemperate', it would have been better had Mr Justice Stone heard *Hensman v Harper and Hackett*, the community was divided into hostile camps and harmony was not to be hoped for while Mr Onslow was Chief Justice. Nothing had been resolved. Onslow diplomatically took leave for twelve months, returned in 1891 to a 'conciliatory' *West* editorial and retired in 1901. When Harper died in 1912 Hackett acquired full *West* ownership for £88,000, dying four years later on 19 February 1916 and leaving the estate to his wife, son and four daughters, the State Library, charities, the University of Western Australia and the Church of England.

• • •

A student at Boulder Central School in 1923 drawn by crowd and colour, Griff Richards went to the Kalgoorlie spring racing carnival. A moment, in his telling, caused his career. He looked up to the grandstand and saw Jack Hocking, reporter for the *Kalgoorlie Miner*, in the press box at the back of the stand and thought 'this is the life for me. You are up there looking over the world, you are not trapped in an office doing a limited job, the whole world's your baby.'

He enrolled in shorthand and typing at Boulder Technical School. When he moved to Perth, enrolling in arts at W.A. University, he 'haunted' *The West Australian* office, went on jobs with reporters, watching how they worked, hoping that one day the *Front Page* cliché would come true: he would be the reporter on the spot, get the story and make his name.

When the day came, the chief of reporting staff, Charlie Frost, assigned Richards to cover the Children's Court. There was no *Front Page* or front-page story, just a maintenance application by a single mother — against a journalist who had taught Griff reporting. The old man, a long-serving *West* editor, 1956 to 1972, chuckles dryly: 'I had a good laugh.' But no dilemma: the paper did not use names from the Children's Court. (When Frost hired Richards he said: 'Mr Richards, I've taken the liberty of putting you on the staff. Is that alright?')

He talks like a wire-service at 86 in his Dalkeith garden in the afternoon sun overlooking the glittering river, spilling detail, names, times, phrases from conversations sixty years ago, the memory precise as if he's editing every phrase for publication. The moment feels right for the anecdote that explains it all or James Thurber's cackle of 'that glee known only to aging journalists.'

It's not there. Richards is cold. Of Jim Macartney though, the most gifted journalist of his generation, a colleague from student journalism to retirement, his recall is acid.

Richards was first editor of the W.A. University undergraduate newspaper *Pelican* in 1929; Macartney followed. At West Australian Newspapers, Macartney was editor of the *Daily News* at 24, the managing editor who appointed Richards editor of *The West Australian* in 1956 and the managing director who emasculated him in 1969, giving him the bogus title editor-in-chief as consolation for retaining responsibility only for editorial and op-ed pages, *trapped in an office doing a limited job.*

From 1952, when the symptoms that Macartney was in Richards' phrase 'a lost-forever alcoholic, a hopeless case', not just a hard-drinking journalist surfaced, to 1969 when the WAN Board sacked him, precipitating a takeover by the Herald and Weekly Times, Macartney took periodic dry-out leave. Richards said that after he noticed' 'cigarettes on my table disappearing and the papers in disarray,' he locked his door. Next morning Macartney was 'on the doorstep, furious, shuffling his feet as he did when he was agitated.' Richards said JM had been lifting the boardroom keys from Richards' table for access to the board's liquor bar. (Macartney did not smoke.) I always left the door unlocked.

'You'd see him one night out to it on the floor. He couldn't even get up to go to the lavatory. He couldn't get up to open the door.' Richards says — he is pleased with the phrase and repeats it — that Macartney would lie '*in his own filth*' all night. Richards would not say *he pissed himself*; he was a gentleman with words. *Filth* implied the loathing he felt for his oldest colleague. After he unexpectedly heard Macartney's voice on an office intercom, Richards persuaded himself that Macartney had wired him for sound. The morning after one of these nights, Richards laughs, Macartney would 'be round the office as bright as a button', writing insulting memos, detailed story ideas, long-term plans. He had an athlete's physiology in middle age. Richards draws a blind against the afternoon sun and consults his inner gossip columnist. 'Do you know Ian Bessell-Browne? Ian was in the Army [in World War Two] and he was captured and put into a German prisoner-of-war camp for the rest of the war. And he had a beautiful young wife and Jim got together with her and as a result his [Macartney's] name stank around town.' (Macartney served in the RAAF from 1942 to 1945 and married Margaret Bessell-Browne, his second wife, on 15 February 1946. He kept his name out of the papers and into this void right-wing businessmen whispered until the 1960s that Macartney had not volunteered and *stole a prisoner-of-war's wife*. The hatred along the river for a non-conformist who controlled the microphone was visceral.)

Demons drove the restless, mercurial Macartney, born in Coolgardie on 15 July 1911. His father died when he was 18 and Jim felt he had to replace him, to be his equal and to do that he had to be perfect. Mistakes woke the ghosts. Alcohol anesthetised them.

Appointed *Daily News* editor at 24 in 1936, he quickly transformed the lacklustre afternoon broadsheet into a focused tabloid, pushing circulation in a week from 23,000 to 36,000. When as managing editor friends and acquaintances sought to keep their divorce out of the West's list, 'JM' pointed to a clipping on the wall reporting his divorce from his first wife Edith Flanagan in 1942.

A humanist, realist and progressive, he also mocked aspiring progressives. Their line was 'I would love to vote for the Labor Party but I couldn't, because *The West Australian* gave me advice to the contrary.' Emotionally intelligent, sensitive to news impact, he told reporters with a wry smile in 1967 even an engagement notice could break hearts. When John Slee a skilled *West* industrial roundsman asked Macartney, who after he was sacked described the paper's editorials as 'feebly reactionary' 'how much pressure were you under from the board?' he did not reply. He thought foreign-affairs editorials wasted space.

The *West* could change nothing in Hanoi or Washington: it should write about events it could influence, events in Perth, Canberra occasionally. Richards, influenced by the security and status of the British Empire, enjoyed supervising editorials about events 'East of Eden' and thought the paper's status enhanced by international perspective. He said off-hand in an editorial conference on Apartheid South Africa in 1970: 'the blacks are barely down from the trees.' Bush pubs excluding Aborigines 'were not imposing a colour-bar: it was a hygiene bar.' Eloquent in ridiculing censorship, consistently pro-choice on abortion, he supported conscription and the war in Vietnam from the beginning, then in 1971 when the waste and futility were evident uttered the remark 'We should never have been there.' After all the editorials urging on Johnson and Nixon, his conservative associate editor Bill Loh said, the turn-around was 'outrageous'.

Macartney died of throat cancer at 66 on 21 September 1977, Richards on 14 September 2004 at 96.

• • •

Don Smith, managing editor of *The Sunday Times* in Perth, wanted to be a journalist when he was eight, at primary school in Kalgoorlie. Greying when we talked, he spent his life as paperboy, reporter on the *Kalgoorlie Miner*, police, political roundsman and editor of *The West Australian*, managing editor of the *Times*.

What drew him? Don, a tattooed grandfather, genial storyteller, pauses. 'I don't know. It was something I always wanted to do, and I don't know why.' He reminisces aloud for a minute, then says emphatically, hand thumping the table: 'I think it was the desire to be first to tell something, like a town gossip, the desire' — the hand descends again — 'to be first to tell somebody something. And they would say: "*Is that right?*"'

After delivering the *Miner* as an eleven-year-old, Don worked for two summer holidays as assistant proof-reader. The *Miner*'s Jack Hocking told Don's father there was a cadetship coming up; did Don want it? His father said well, the boy hasn't got his Leaving (high school) certificate yet; Hocking said 'there won't be another cadetship for four years: he can get his Leaving and wait another four years, or he can have the job now.' He didn't hesitate. He was 16.

At the Eastern Goldfields Technical School on Friday nights he attended shorthand lessons, discovering to his dismay that he had thirty-four classmates, every one a girl. That was more than young Don could cope with: instead of shorthand, instead of chatting up the girls, in the romantic tradition of journalism he practised at Colgan's Billiard Saloon.

Chapter 18 — The Black Swan

In the romantic school shorthand was for pedestrians: real talent did not depend on Pitmans. Real talent got by on front. Real talent could do what was technically impossible such as reviewing a book without reading it. Real talent, in the romance school, could turn up late at a Premier's press conference, ask a single question to which the answer was *no comment*, and write in twenty minutes a 300-word page-one lead in which there were no factual errors. Real talent could report what ministers said at a secret Cabinet meeting, the tone in which each word was uttered, the skin tone of the speaker; real talent had the capacity to report what politicians thought but didn't say, even–especially–when it contradicted what they said.

A real reporter in the romance school could pick a fake when he said gidday. If a man who had never been inside a newsroom tried to pass himself off as a reporter, he wouldn't last two sentences. If he tried to fake a persona as editor, especially in the practical, hard-nosed culture of goldfields journalism, he would be laughed out of town.

Malcolm Cook was hired as editor of *The Kalgoorlie Miner* in 1947. He was a toff with a Cambridge degree and a way with words. An English gentleman. After Cook spoke at the Hannon Club, the resident magistrate, Tom Draper, asked Percy Hocking, the *Miner* owner: 'Tell me Percy, how did an insignificant rag like *The Kalgoorlie Miner* acquire the services of such a distinguished scholar?'

Don Smith, awed by Cook, one day was surprised to see the polished exterior crack. Cook telephoned the telegraph office and blistered the operator about a page missing in a foreign story. The angry operator, a man who normally couldn't say two words without stuttering, ran to the *Miner* office and snarled at Don, no pause between the words: 'Where is the Pommy bastard?' He spotted Cook, who was immediately placatory, murmuring 'settle down, my good man.' Don saw a cloud of dust as Cook retrieved a bottle of Scotch hidden in his files. What stuck in his memory was Cook's crumbling, how quickly the shouting bully became the drinking mate.

Cook's real name was Murray Beresford Roberts and his talent was the con. Born in Wellington New Zealand, where he attended medical school, Roberts in Australia impersonated a cancer specialist, a plastic surgeon, an English judge, a schoolteacher, a neurosurgeon, counsel assisting the Petrov Royal Commission. He posed as 'Lord Russell, Governor-General designate.'

'I can talk sensibly and adequately on many subjects. Even in prison I get the daily newspapers and keep up with contemporary news,' he wrote in his autobiography, *King of the Conmen*. He served 'a dozen' jail sentences. He reckoned he had more press than Ned Kelly. On a good day he would check into a posh hotel, approach a well-frocked matron explaining that he desired to remain incognito but his wig was torn — he was the Chief Justice of New

Zealand — and would she be kind enough to help? Shortly the whole hotel would know of the shy Chief Justice and targets would present themselves to the king of conmen, who looked reassuringly elderly. He had the chutzpah, knowing no law, to engage magistrates in debate about legal points. (He invented common-law precedents: who would confess ignorance to a judge who sounded English?)

On a bad day his confident exterior did not convince Roberts himself. Depression engulfed him. In a hotel in the Darling Range he took a new razor blade, slashed his left wrist, then his neck. A guest entering the wrong room saw Roberts lying on blood-stained sheets and called an ambulance.

Recollecting Roberts pleases Smith; his tone is admiring. 'He would be without doubt the greatest conman ever known,' he says, 'and he was my first editor, mate.' The friendly, talkative Smith's tone is flat when he speaks of young Don, but mention of Roberts injects animation into the sandpaper voice.

• • •

Given a sympathetic ear, most enjoy talking about their work. In two hour-long interviews with Frank Devine I watched with fascination verging on alarm as Frank, chatting about his brilliant career, slumped lower and lower in his chair as some ghost leeched animation from his voice. Finally he perked up: 'This is boring: let's have lunch.'

That ghost hides much journalism from scrutiny. Devine is right. The mechanics of reporting — the mechanics, not the information — tracking sources, milking the telephone, attending a staged conference, scribbling notes indecipherable by the end of the week, is often less interesting than staring at a clear blue sky.

After five weeks on night police rounds at *The West Australian*, Peter Ewing, the editor who recruited him said: 'Don, what about politics?' Smith said: 'Christ mate, I couldn't tell a left-winger on a sports field.'

Ewing: 'Give it a go.'

He was state political roundsman for thirteen years when Charles Court was the dominant WA politician, hyperactive, over-ruling colleagues, looking for his name in the paper.

Macartney disliked Court's dominance, his authoritarian manner and hard conservatism. It was a reflexive dislike, little to do with policy, though the policy differences reinforced it. Once, on Macartney's instructions, Smith went three times to a dinner Court was addressing at the University of WA, each time with new Macartney-inspired questions on a story too dull to detail now. When he made it home after a thirteen-hour day, Smith, invariably amiable, no deadline pressure could crack his geniality, told his wife 'when that bastard [Macartney] dies I'll dance on his grave.'

He turned that placidity into his professional strategy. 'I still don't know what it's all about,' he said late in 1995. 'You get more stories by pretending to be dumb than you ever do by pretending you know it all. *Pretend to be dumb*. That's one of the first things I learnt in [reporting] politics. Always ask dumb questions. Never let on you know things.'

• • •

When he joined *The West Australian* as a cadet in 1923, the romantic Paul Hasluck dreamed of writing a great Australian novel; the realist learned shorthand. Born on 1 April 1905 to E'thel and Patience Hasluck, dirt-poor Salvation Army believers whose principle of life was 'trust and obey", Paul rejected that faith. He found a substitute: the bush. Stretched out on a granite rock as a young man he had the feeling that under his spine was 'the pulse of creation.' The bush possessed an 'almost demoniac power.' He felt a mystical connection. 'I did not own the land; the land owned me.' In a long life in journalism, academia, diplomacy and politics he kept in mind that his peers might think him barmy and so held his tongue and 'sustained an appearance of normalcy'. When he was an old man and nothing mattered any more he spilt the secret in his autobiography, *Mucking About*.

Driven by intellectual curiosity, Hasluck turned journalism into higher education. At 18 he would go anywhere. The Presbyterian General Assembly. A rowing club social. A six-hour Baptist Hall debate about the meaning of Jesus' death yielded only six column-inches, but Paul the budding Dickens was satisfied.

Sometimes the would-be novelist displaced the journalist. Posing as vice-squad detectives Paul and another reporter joined a detective sergeant checking East Perth brothels and opium dens. 'He trusted us,' Hasluck wrote. 'We were not in search of copy and had no intention of writing anything.' Working reporters *not in search of copy?* Hasluck: 'I was still occupied with thoughts of writing my novel and had the younger writer's illusion that anything to do with the sordid side of life was more realistic than the normal.'

He was surprised how easily doors opened; strangers liked him. He drafted a resolution for a meeting of striking milkmen and then, reverting to objectivity, reported their adoption of it. He punched into bullies threatening a cop who was protecting two girls from harassment, surprised at his own exuberance, feeling 'I could fight any man in the house.' His literary career comprised half-finished first chapters; he reproached himself for lacking even rejection slips.

Drawn to our most unfairly reported story, Hasluck in 1934 wrote a series on the treatment of Aborigines, taking an original view that Nyungars were not dying out. He travelled with Royal Commissioner H.D.Moseley for three months. Hasluck recommended calm examination of the facts, and 'steady and unsentimental but boldly idealistic thinking.' He enjoyed Moseley's confidence and 'repaid it with discretion' in the news stories he filed from Derby, Noonkanbah and Fitzroy Crossing.

Tragedy and squalor did not push him to challenge the status quo generally. He thought 'any strong assertion of political views' was 'a sign of prejudice and hence of an unintelligent method of reaching a judgment.' 'I never saw that the French Revolution ... or the Russian Revolution ... had done much to make people happier and more useful.' He believed in hierarchy. He wondered in the 1930s whether democracy meant disintegration. On the *West,* he noted that circulation was becoming the yardstick of journalism. 'The rewards did not go to the man who knew more about the subject but to the man who could make a good story out of it, and a good story was not necessarily the one that would have been fair, clear and exact, but rather the one that helped to sell papers.' At 20 he thought journalism wonderful. At 30, he was interested in historical research, producing drama and starting a publishing house, Freshwater Bay Press. The *West* gave him a year's leave in 1938 to lecture in history at the University of Western Australia. He did not return. A suggestion by John Curtin, a fellow-activist on the Australian Journalists Association, led to the External Affairs Department. After working as head of the Australian mission to the United Nations in New York, he returned to Perth and a telephone call from a Liberal and Country League official led to endorsement as LCL candidate for Curtin in the 1949 Federal election won handsomely by the politically reborn Robert Menzies.

Hasluck held the seat for 20 years. After Prime Minister Harold Holt drowned in boiling surf near Portsea, Victoria, in December 1967, he stood against John Gorton for the Prime Ministership, losing because the party felt he was a weak campaigner who closed his door to television crews and when he opened it a careful scholar, not a charismatic campaigner, emerged.

In a rare newspaper interview he told a reporter from his old paper of his passion for privacy. His public persona contained a Tory who felt the land owned him, an intellectual politician, a journalist who missed a big prize because he drifted far from journalism and thought reporters should tell the important story, not the one for which people would queue around the block. In public he was a rational academic, hiding a tormented inner self. The rational man loathed the passionate poet who was troubled by the boundaries confining the thinker. Governor-General of Australia from 1969 to 1974 he died on 9 January 1993 having requested no eulogy at the State funeral and memorial service in St. George's Cathedral.

Chapter 19

The Act of Creation

1895–1949: revolution: news on page one; the world's first labor daily, *Jack Lang* and *The Daily Post*; *Alfred Deakin* and *The Age*; *Hugh Denison* and *The Sun*; *Hugh D. McIntosh, Robert Clyde Packer* and *The Sunday Times*; *James Joynton Smith, Claude McKay,* Smith's Weekly and *The Daily Guardian*.

A great newspaper [like The Age] is not an accident; it does not come into existence by spontaneous generation; it has to be explained.

Rev. W.H.Fitchett, Australian editor, The Review of Reviews November 1892

The man most subject to press influence may be the one who think he is least. And exercised as it constantly is upon mass mentality, the influence of the press is the Archimedean lever which moves the world.

The Daily Telegraph 1909

Driven by the market, as business saw it, or moguls as labour saw it, newspaper ownership peaked in 1923, the year that faith in print and political division among newspapers also peaked. Twenty-one proprietors owned twenty-six capital-city daily newspapers in a population of 5.7 million, one owner for 271,112 people. Six Melbourne dailies, five in Sydney, four in Adelaide, Brisbane and Hobart, two in frontier Perth.

If the peak had a name it would be *Mount Warning*. Had the ratio to population remained stable, in 2019 we would have 112 dailies with ninety owners in the eight capitals. Compared to reality — twelve dailies with two principal owners, News Ltd and Fairfax, and one single city independent, *The West Australian,* one owner for every eight million people — the figures seem a hash-induced fantasy. The proportion of proprietors to population has shrunk in 85 years to *one ninetieth* of the 1923 peak.

How come? A common answer is three words: radio, television, Internet.

It has not been all drought and dust since we passed Mt Warning. *The Canberra Times* started in 1925, *The Daily Mirror* (Sydney) in 1941 *Northern Territory News* in 1951; *The Australian Financial Review* went daily on 21 October 1963 and Rupert Murdoch started *The Australian* on 15 July 1964. But apart from these Australian crawls against the tide, the main themes of newspaper history for the first and last quarters of the twentieth century were merger, closure and insolvency. (The last, *Business Daily,* launched in Sydney on 6 July 1987, closed six weeks later on 18 August.)

When our first paper, the *Sydney Gazette,* went daily for six weeks from New Year's day 1827, there was one capital city daily owner, Robert Howe, to 39,000 people. Since then Australia has published 67 capital city dailies; on average a daily started every three years. Between 1880 and 1920, before, during and after the great strikes that took the country near civil war, with the press seen as an enemy of organised labour, five dailies started which were owned by labour and five sympathetic or committed to the cause. (The average life of a labour-owned daily was 12 years against the average of 38 years.) In the turmoil of the 1890s with its 'short-lived parliaments and yet shorter-lived ministries' the Rev. W.H.Fitchett, editor of the Australian *Review of Reviews* believed that in perilous colonial society the great dailies were the main social steadiers after the eternal comforter of faith.

The questions in 1923 were: would the capitalist press with its status-quo bias prevail? Or would labour owners who believed in fairness governing wealth and income find the advertising to pay for a place on the public stage? Magnates, journalists, printers, copy-boys, advertisers, hot-metal typesetters, illustrators and photographers ascended the volcanic rainforest of Mount Warning.

The orthodox explanation in newsrooms for Mount Warning has not been subtle; gross advertising revenue is said to account for both climb and fall. In 1923 radio was the original intruder on print, the first medium to leech advertising, distract readers and, slow as a glacier, start to undermine the fundamental of print, the basis of its magic and power — its (24-hour) permanence. Reporters understand the medium. When a printer's devil causes us to omit a word such as 'not' or disfigure a clergyman's Christian name, every letter whinging about the mistake underlines the fact that print is permanent although the paper is also — *who wants yesterday's papers?* — obsolete the day it is published.

Some in the labour movement believed in print as preachers believed in faith; news in eight-point Roman was the way, the truth and the life. Jack Lang, New South Wales Premier in 1925–27 and 1930–32, who was a newsboy at seven, ran copy on an underground Labor paper at nine, edited the weekly *Century* till he was ninety and worked in journalism for more than sixty years reckoned newspapers 'became almost a religion' with labour men.

On the other side some transcended labour faith and hope. Alfred Deakin, the liberal Prime Minister who began public life as an *Age* reporter in 1888, thought newspapers Homeric as he anticipated the first Federal election on 29 March 1901: 'The Press will be mainly responsible for the start we are making in our new national life and probably the path we pursue in the future.'

> Our Commonwealth, reposing on the broadest suffrage, rests on the Press, which controls its exercises; it consists of States whose chief voice and influence are those of their principal journals; and it is therefore in almost as absolute a fashion a Federation of newspapers as of Colonies. Between the electors, from whom all authority comes, and those whom they elect to execute their behests is interposed a power which moulds both. … In the political world [the Press] is often the maker of Premiers and the destroyer of Cabinets. The Federal election is being fought by and in the journals rather than on the platform.

As long as only big-business newspapers caught readers' eyes, the voice of labour reached the people as a whisper, echo or lie. 'You can't expect *The Evening News* to whoop for you any more than the fat man can expect the *Worker* to barrack for him,' the Sydney *Worker* said on 28 October 1893. As the Australian Workman Company, chaired by Chris Watson, former compositor on *The Daily Telegraph, Sydney Morning Herald* and *Australian Star*, later Prime Minister, planned *The Daily Post*, disciplined labour men believed that without direct control, the poets, drunks and preachers who inhabited the ranks of journalism — or worse still, an ideologue of a different stripe — would debauch the ideals of working men.

When the shearers, sailors and miners of the Australian Workers' Union climbed the first step to Mount Warning in 1895 they asked a different question. How could men hear the truth when the money-press was loud with the voices of special-interests, squatters, police, government and big business? If workers read the truth printed in their own newspapers, the world would grow quiet and reasoned; prophets like William Lane and Henry Lawson would be heard in their own land.

The world's first labour daily sought Sydney readers on 9 January 1895. *The Daily Post* believed that honest work spoke for itself, required no explanation. While the editors and reporters asked to be judged on performance, not promise, they also hoped readers would not cry 'shame!' over the errors and omissions which afflicted all first issues.

The newspaper said nothing about the revolution it had just begun: *there was news on page one*: with three men injured, one batsman out-of-form and another unable to play, the chances were against Australia in the third cricket test against England starting in Adelaide next day.

Reasoning that labour journalists did not know what they were doing and the page-one news revolution would not last, capitalist newspapers did not panic: the last capital city daily to do so, *The West Australian*, moved news to page one fifty-four years later on 10 December 1949.

As they switched the front page from advertising to news, proprietors and editors were comedians. Twenty-nine years later on 8 October 1924 *The Daily Telegraph* changed saying it had always led, 'others may follow'. In an industry governed by the primal urge to be first, where *faster* means *better*, the technologically easy switch to front-page news did not evolve at leisurely speed; *glacial* was more like it. When *The West Australian* switched on polling day in what the *West* thought 'the most fateful [federal] election since federation' it seized the day and raised the price from 2d to 3d. Readers called the tune: not one switch to news on page one caused a sudden surge in circulation. In 1943 *The Sydney Morning Herald* news editor Angus McLachlan weighed whether readers would think page-one news signified lack of restraint by the oldest Australian newspaper. Full of anxiety, he hoped readers would feel better pleased with the paper 'without quite noticing why'. Fewer than a dozen protested.

Back in 9 January 1895 the *Daily Post* said it would give 'temperate expression to the industrial and political aspirations of the workers. It will strive to purify the ideals of the people; encourage their legitimate desires; strengthen their just demands; and guard their liberties against every form of encroachment.' A newspaper aspiring to rewrite the laws of psychology and politics would also suspend the laws of commerce. On 13 January the chairman, Sam Smith, confessed to shareholders that 'the organizing work has been neglected.'

Shearers who had been fleeced muttered over schooners about the Daily Ghost. In the eyes of true believers, the paper was not political, not unionist enough. But for readers more interested in news, sport, gossip and froth than in ideology, it was too dull to be worth a glance; a man's eyes would glaze over.

Bean-counters saw the laws of journalism and commerce had not evaporated. The last issue appeared on April Fools' Day and the six directors were prosecuted for conspiracy to defraud a creditor. Four were convicted and W.A. Holman, later NSW Premier, and Sam Smith were sentenced to two years' hard labour, the other two to 18 months. (They had served two months in Darlinghurst Gaol when the full court quashed the convictions.)

The press could turn a street-sweeper into a poet, a banker into a visionary. Anything was possible. The Australian Workers' Union started Labor Papers Ltd in 1910 to establish a Sydney daily as the first in a national chain which came to include the Brisbane evening *Standard*, (1912-1936) Adelaide *Daily Herald* (1910–1924) and Hobart *World* (1918-1924). Donald Macdonell, the gun shearer from Tinapagee elected general secretary in 1899, initiated a £1-a-head *Labor Daily* levy in 1910; the movement had 'a continent to win and a newspaper to win it with.' Levies raised paid-up capital of £250,000 by 1925, newsprint [paper] stock, a £30,000 press from England competitive with the best at the capitalist dailies, and a modern eight-storey building in Pitt-street. Firemen and engine-drivers, draymen and tanners, boilermakers, plumbers, sign painters, blacksmith and bricklayers paid the levy; printing workers kicked in £2,250, miners £3650, the mighty AWU £120,000.

Between idea and action fell the shadow. The rangy Macdonell — Henry Lawson thought him 'the tallest, straightest and best' of the bush unionists — died of cancer a year later in 1911. Labor Papers Ltd directors appointed D. J. Gilbert, *Herald* leader-writer, editor and Keith Murdoch, Melbourne correspondent of the Sydney *Sun*, associate editor of the planned evening *World*. The Great War stopped the press shipment and Murdoch, who saved £500 from 1d-a-line contributions as *The Age* Malvern correspondent afflicted with a nervous stammer, moved to another brilliant career.

For proprietors and reporters as well as the men and women they quoted, described and encouraged to leak, print was a faith. When *The Sun* owner Hugh Denison on 7 July 1910, *launched* the new afternoon paper on the glittering harbour by motor boats, with yellow posters cruising from Circular Quay to Kirribilli Point, reporters used the language of gods: 'Today the golden-haired Apollo sped through the metropolis of the South ' But they were still Aussies. There had been a difficulty with the police: 'in these modern times even a God has to observe traffic regulations.' A King-street florist's window 'heralded the rising of *The Sun*,' which beneath the masthead called itself 'the only daily paper in Australia.' The word 'stunt' went walkabout; newspapers describing themselves draw portraits with the head missing.

Born on 11 November 1865 near Forbes in the New South Wales bush, Denison was educated in Melbourne, Adelaide and London; he worked on the transcontinental railway in Western Australia, returning to work in Adelaide for his father, a tobacco manufacturer involved in the formation of the British-Australasian Tobacco Company Limited. Courteous, easy to talk to, he owned the Melbourne and Caulfield Cups winners in 1906 and 1907 and founded Macquarie Broadcasting Services Pty Ltd.

The Sun directors, H. A. Russell, E. P. Simpson, William Stuart and Herbert Easton debated its politics with Denison over dinner. After five-hours' circular discussion they said the paper would be 'unique in its freedom from party issues' and 'exemption from political entanglements'.

It would sit on the fence.

Denison did not look over editors' shoulders. In launching the Melbourne *Sun News-Pictorial* in 1922 with Montague Grover as editor, he fostered one of the most successful owner-editor relationships of the century.

Hugh D. McIntosh — journalists dubbed him 'Huge Deal' — was another ready to stick his neck out. Born in Sydney on 10 September 1876, as a boy he was an itinerant jeweller's assistant, ore-picker, tarboy, stage-hand, farm-labourer, pie-seller and waiter. When he married Marion Backhouse, a painting teacher, on 10 November 1897 he said he was a barman. He supplied pies to racetracks and prize-fights, ran a physical culture club, raced as a cyclist and ran the League of Wheelmen of New South Wales; adaptable and energetic, never short of self-esteem, he would have a go at anything.

McIntosh staged the world heavyweight title fight between the champion, French-Canadian Tommy Burns and Australian Bill Squires in 1908. Burns won and defended his title at Rushcutter's Bay against American Jack Johnson on Boxing Day. McIntosh, in referee's whites, appeared more agile than Burns in the early rounds. He stopped the fight in the 14th and Johnson became the first black world heavyweight champion. McIntosh produced a film and next year toured Europe and the U.S. with the movie. In May 1916 he bought a controlling interest in *The Sunday Times* (Sydney) started in 1885 by William Bailey, an English gentleman who had fought with Giuseppe Garibaldi to unify Italy and wearing a monocle, established the gold-boom *Cooktown Herald* in 1872.

As *Times* circulation, lifted by the big story of the century, World War One, climbed from 30,000 in 1909 to more than 100,000 in 1915, reporters with an eye for the story behind stories saw another reason for the rise: the new editor, Robert Clyde Packer.

Born in Hobart on 24 July 1879 to Arthur Packer, a customs official, and Margaret, Robert Clyde, affectionately dubbed 'Pack', less affectionately 'RC' impressed one editor as a 'reporter possessing the true journalistic instinct'. Bob Packer knew what interested the reader. He left for Sydney in 1902, worked as a labourer, married Ethel Maude in Paddington, staff-reported for papers in Dubbo, Coffs Harbour and Townsville. As he trawled for stories and jobs through a thousand miles of bush, he knew where he was going. When he joined *The Sunday Times* in Sydney in 1908 the editor, T. R. Roydhouse, chairman of the Scout Committee of Control, recruited Packer as chief scoutmaster of New South Wales.

Packer believed the new movement could create 'a sound boy, mentally, morally and physically'. Scout work tested patrol leaders. 'If he is a born leader, then his scouts stick to him like glue,' he wrote in *The Lone Hand*, 2 August 1909. Scouts valued honour as life. Scouting was democratic; there was no such thing as 'class' in the mind of a true scout. Scouts would respond like the heroes of Waterloo when the time came. Packer's vision for scouts was his picture of himself.

When his time came he applied to join the Australian Imperial Force. Life broke the narrative: the AIF turned him down on medical grounds (sinus trouble).

When Hugh McIntosh bought the controlling interest in *The Sunday Times* McIntosh, knowing he could not control Packer and, his employment contract making sacking expensive, tried instead to make his job intolerable, to force RC to self-sack. As Packer put the paper to bed one Saturday night McIntosh abused him. Instead of cowing the scoutmaster, the abuse awoke his inner animal. The next time McIntosh appeared, Packer, metal rule in right fist, said 'If you enter this room I'll brain you.' McIntosh paid out the contract for £500.

As *Sunday Times* managing director, McIntosh loaned himself £85,000 and leased Lord Kitchener's castle at Broome Park, Kent. Owing a small fortune to the paper, he sold it in 1927 and bought the Tivoli Theatre; it went into liquidation in three years. He sold Angora rabbits and ran a Derby sweep. When he started the Black and White Milk Bar in Fleet Street, London; it thrived but the next huge deal, a Black-and-White chain, was a dream. He died broke in London on 2 February 1942.

• • •

Born in London on 4 October 1858, James Joynton Smith travelled to New Zealand as an ocean-liner cook, made money as a Wellington hotel licensee, married Ellen McKenzie, an illiterate farmer's daughter in Auckland when he was 24, returned alone to London in 1886 and gambled his savings away. He returned to Wellington that year, was founding secretary of the Cooks' and Stewards' Union, went to Sydney, managed a hotel, divorced Ellen and married Eloise Parkes.

Reflexively anti-Semitic, he repeated stories caricaturing greedy Jews as if he believed he originated the bigotry. Once in Naples he threw bacon-rind on an ash-heap by the ship's galley and watched as 'twenty Italian labourers fought like dogs over the scrap.' The entrepreneur thought it 'one of those glimpses of man the naked animal that one doesn't readily forget.' Joynton Smith was a hater.

Smith, Claude McKay and Packer published the first *Smith's Weekly* on 1 March 1919. McKay, born in Kilmore, Victoria, had reported for *The Age*,

Argus, Courier Mail and *Daily Telegraph*. His colleague George Blakie thought he had the presence of an English gentleman; when Blakie told a racetrack stranger McKay was a 'stunt man' the stranger scoffed: McKay, he said, looked like a High Court judge.

Smith thought the war brought out people's 'best impulses'. An 'all-Australian newspaper' would keep up fighting spirits: the diggers would save Australia. Smith thought McKay, a talented pen-for-hire who as PR for Wonderland Circus contrived a Brisbane controversy about whether a toothless, hairless, tired lion was 'really the oldest lion in captivity' and Packer, a relentless organiser who knew what people wanted before they knew it themselves, would make the paper.

Did Packer run on money or principle? Smith says they met in George-street and outside the Town Hall he wrote a cheque for £500 and handed it over.

Packer: 'What's this for?'

Smith: 'For the work you did in the war loan for me.'

Packer: 'But the Commonwealth Bank paid me.'

Then he dropped an elliptical remark to which Smith, an entrepreneur from the same mould, a hard man not famous for insight, made no response. 'Besides, you may not have known it, but *you* were actually working for *us*.' Packer said he could not think of taking the money. Next day Smith offered McKay a £500 cheque; McKay too turned the money down. Smith said in his autobiography *My Life Story* he thought *'that'll do me.'* Two young men with drive and ability had turned down significant money with no strings attached.

When Smith, Packer and McKay, each owning one-third of Smith's Newspapers Ltd, the company owning Smith's Weekly, started *The Daily Guardian* on 2 July 1923, iconic *Manchester Guardian* editor C.P.Scott wrote in a special cable that *'a newspaper's first duty is to give news* and give it whole, without suppression or half concealment and without bias.' In an aphorism quoted in newsrooms for generations, he said: 'The most insidious and wicked thing a newspaper can do is to suppress or pervert facts essential for readers' judgment. *Opinion is free, but facts should be sacred.'*

For him it was all a game, the stories, the owners, the advertisers, the boys in the reporters' room, writing, calling contacts, all boisterous fun. Claude McKay, the kid from Kilmore, Victoria, a founder and editor of Smith's Weekly, and editor of *The Daily Guardian*, was poking his finger in the eye of the world and getting away with it. He cocooned himself in the fun and smiled, the smile often a shield against frightening things. In his autobiography *This is the Life* he said that late in 1924 when the *Guardian* was 18 months old, he was 'on deck from ten in the morning until midnight, seven days a week. The result was a nervous breakdown and under doctor's orders I had to take a complete rest. With my wife I went to California.'

Chapter 19 — The Act of Creation

Concealed in the blokey heartiness was a reporter's ear which heard a steward gasp when Claude offered to pay for the Prince of Wales' cocktail in a gentlemen's club in London and a man who 'more than once in my life as a newspaperman ... realized a truth of our trade — that the greater the integrity of a paper, the smaller its sales.'

The first *Daily Guardian*, on 2 July 1923, disappointed him: over-compressed and under-displayed news, too much type, too little space, a 'false start'. C. P. Scott sent a cable. A newspaper's

> first duty was to give news and give it whole, without suppression or half concealment, and without bias.
>
> The most insidious and wicked thing a newspaper can do is to suppress or pervert facts essential for readers' judgment. Opinion is free, but facts should be sacred.
>
> There are other duties. A newspaper is apt to be more or less of a monopoly. Power thus given should not be abused.
>
> Not every crank has a right to run his hobby or air views, but a newspaper should, as far as possible, be an open platform. Every honest and competent opinion should be allowed expression, within reason, in its correspondence column.
>
> Then there is the larger duty. A newspaper has no right to be merely an organ of the private opinions of its owners. Truth is said to live at the bottom of a well. In any case, it cannot be discovered without some searching, and some competence in the searcher.
>
> Naturally, a newspaper will have a point of view, as we all have our points of view, but that does not absolve it from the duty of care, impartiality, sincerity and a constant eye to public good. That may be an ideal. All rules of conduct are ideals, but all the same we have to plod away along the path they mark out. There is the question also of the newspaper writer. He ought not to be a hireling or treated as such. Unless he is in substantial accord with the opinions of his paper, he had better not write for it, or at least not write matter wherein he is in definite disagreement. For it can't be done well and thus he degrades both himself and his paper. Especially is this true of literary and artistic criticism. Criticism is essentially individual, and to be of any value it must therefore be free. It goes without saying that it is the business of a newspaper to make itself efficient all round. That is an obvious duty to itself, as well as to the public and is perhaps less likely to be neglected than some of the sterner prescriptions.

Adjoining Scott's high-minded paragraphs was a single-column sketch of the bearded editor, Scott as prophet. But Claude McKay kept righteousness under wraps. He wanted dirt. A placid epoch in journalism, he said, 'ended yesterday'. In principle *The Daily Guardian* idealised Scott's principles; in practice it sought the beat-up. On the Parramatta bus they called it the Flappers' Daily. Its reporters included a 16-year-old cadet expelled from Turramurra College when he was nine — he took his father's revolver to school — and lost nine-tenths of the vision in his right eye to a packing-case splinter a year later: Frank Packer.

McKay kept playing games. The *Guardian* offered journalists salaries higher than *The Daily Telegraph* and *The Sydney Morning Herald*. When scribes from rivals approached, McKay told them 'sorry, no vacancies' — then handed them a written offer of a bigger salary. The scribe returned to his office, showed the offer and brazenly invited a match. Invariably, he said, there it was. As they 'believed they were thus putting a nail in our coffin, everyone was satisfied! The working newspaperman in particular was happy.'

Copying U.S. originators, (the lacklustre *Lone Hand*-sponsored Miss Australia quest of 1908 had disappeared from cultural and corporate memory) *The Daily Guardian* started the Miss Australia quest for 'the perfect woman of a continent'. An outsider among a thousand entrants, 19-year-old Beryl Mills, a WA swimming champion whom bookmakers priced at 25 to 1, won a trip to the U.S. accompanied by Claude McKay, 49, Frank Packer, 19, and chaperoned by her mother. The day of the final the *Guardian* sold 275,000 copies against its standard 150,000. While the four explored San Francisco, Chicago and New York, Robert Packer introduced free insurance for readers. After the free-insurance giveaway the paper outsold the dominant *Sydney Morning Herald*'s 180,000 a day. The *Labor Daily* sneered at the 'Daily Girlie'; readers should buy 'a man's paper'.

• • •

When the Empire Press Delegation arrived in 1909 'the eyes and ears of the Empire were on Australia,' *The Daily Telegraph* reported. Pressmen from all the King's Dominions were 'specially trained in the science of analysing human affairs'. News mirrored the Kaleidoscope of life and was the greatest educator of modern times. A man too busy to balance the pros and cons of every public question could use the services of a journalist, who had time for nothing else.

> As this is seldom done consciously, the man most subject to press influence may be the one who think he is least. And exercised as it

> constantly is upon mass mentality, the influence of the press generally is the Archimedean lever which moves the world.

Toward capital or labour? The Daily Telegraph did not answer that question.

Albert Willis, general secretary of the Miners' Federation, told the All-Australian Trades Union Congress in July 1921 that unionism would only be permanent when it had 'great daily papers in all cities of Australia, voicing its wrongs and fighting its battles for supremacy.'

Harbour-side Tories looked down on reporters and editors whose eye for the public pulse made them vulgar, whose staccato language implied inferior education and whose sexual imagery implied that they were men, even women, whose standards derived from the out-house rather than the drawing-room. For reformers such as Albert Willis, that Sir Hugh Denison and Sir James Joynton Smith and R.C.Packer and Huge Deal McIntosh were enemies of the movement was so axiomatic that to say so in print was a waste of space. Everyone knew it. It was not news that Mr Fat Man's money-press was at war with the workingman, as it was not news that the sky was blue.

Willis, a Welsh miner from Balmain, was a hungry reader in whose fertile brain, Jack Lang thought, the idea of One Big Union evolved. The means of production and distribution would not be transferred to the community, but to trade unions, which would own banks, factories, shops and mines; craft unions would be displaced by industry unions, then One Big Union would absorb all. It would replace the parliament; the state would wither away and the golden wattle stand for socialism under the Southern Cross. When Willis, *Labor Daily* managing director, offered Roy Connolly the editorship in April 1924, he had his fingers crossed.

Connolly started in journalism at fifteen, worked on the Sydney *Sun* and *Daily Telegraph* and Brisbane *Truth* and was editor in 1923 of the Sydney *Daily Mail* at £22 a week, with rises promised for increased circulation; he was thirty and believed in reporting the news as if the news had shaped him to its purposes. He did not soften hard news for owners or advertisers. He believed in the fair go and had a clear eye for what miners, sailors, printers, carpenters, barmen and jockeys liked to read. Norman Lindsay nudes in a Collins-street window dislocating traffic, 'the funny trams in Melbourne' running up to a mile without stopping. Connolly thought himself 'a temperamental man', calmed his demons at Trim's Hotel, and was certain of his capacity to give workers the paper they wanted. He did not delude himself that they hungered for details of ALP fiscal policy over their porridge. After four months editing the *Mail* he discussed a job with Bob Packer at *The Daily Guardian*, then moved to *The Labor Daily* at £25 a week.

When he suggested Willis ask the directors to promote him to managing editor, he knew he was pushing his luck. Willis told Connolly the ALP wanted a paper, 'with a policy laid down by the All-Australian [ALP] Conference, as modified by the New South Wales State ALP Conference.' Connolly replied as if he had not heard a word. He told Willis he knew what was wanted: circulation. The one way to get it was sensational stories. Willis said he would sooner stop the paper than stoop to capitalist sensationalism. What was the point of a Labour paper if it mirrored the lies of bosses' journalism?

After another parallel conversation, neither taking in what the other said, Connolly asked Willis to give him a chance. When Willis telephoned saying he didn't want the *Labor Daily* 'run as a detective agency' Connolly told him: 'If you want circulation, my plans will get it.'

Willis: 'Cut it out.'

Comrades who both believed the economic system 'insane' were as far apart in journalism as Broome from Byron Bay.

The board appointed Thomas Gurr, who had been advertising manager on the New Zealand *Herald*, advertising and business manager on the Melbourne Herald and Weekly Times and general manager of Hugh D. McIntosh's *Sunday Times,* as general manager. Willis told Connolly Gurr would be 'in complete control'.

Connolly: 'You will be sorry.'

Willis: 'Don't get excited. You will have to work with him.'

When Gurr rang Connolly at home on 3 June 1924 about a letter to the editor he told Connolly he had been appointed manger.

Connolly: 'I don't know you.'

Gurr: ' have been appointed manager.'

Connolly: 'I have not been apprised of the fact.'

He hung up.

The boundaries between management and editorial were as clear as the Parramatta river after a summer downpour. Through July and August the parallel conversations grew more heated; neither changed position. When Gurr asked the editor to run news paragraphs with advertisements, they did not appear. Because of this breach of faith the paper would get no more business from an important advertiser.

Gurr told Connolly he had a legal opinion that the use of the word 'gangster' (in the era of Chicago's 'scarface' Al Capone) was dangerous. It was an instruction: *don't use the word.*

Connolly said he was editor, free to say what he liked and use any words he pleased. Interference from Gurr or directors was not in the paper's best interests. Gurr told Connolly that if he used the word 'gangster' he would 'report it to the board as insubordination.' The paper was in the hands of a gifted journalist who knew how to catch a reader's eye, a managing editor who thought those gifts a threat and a manager who was a stranger to editorial autonomy. At a policy meeting on 24 September, Willis said the paper had to apply the policy of the All Australian Trades Union Congress.

Connolly baulked: how was an editor was supposed to run a newspaper applying the phrase 'the socialisation of industry'. What did that mean? How could anyone do it? He meant that a newspaper 'reporting' events through the lens of the way the world should be would quickly find its traditional place, the trash-can.

Trades Hall condemned the paper as sensational; Communists denounced it as not militant enough. The editor inside every man was having his day. The meeting adjourned. When it resumed on 30 September Jack Baddeley, the Miners' Federation president, made the remark: 'This sort of thing [fights between Gurr and Connolly] has got to cease.' Connolly left the meeting.

When he returned Baddeley said: 'We have decided to suspend you.'

Connolly baulked: 'When?'

Baddeley: 'Immediately. We are determined you will never write another line in the paper.'

Connolly left the room, told the news editor, packed and left. He wrote asking for reasons.

Gurr asked him to resign.

He refused, again asked the reasons and on 17 October sued for wrongful dismissal. After working on *The World* as news editor, he freelanced in London, wrote a novel and in 1946 became press secretary to Sir Arthur Fadden, the Country Party leader, Treasurer and deputy Prime Minister from 1949 to 1958. Fadden in 1946 called for the Communist Party to be banned; it was 'a venomous snake — to be killed before it kills.' Another radical turned reactionary deepened labor mistrust of scribblers: they were men for sale.

Labor papers like the *Daily Herald* in England published material for the zealot but disregarded the rank-and-file who were its real objective, the *Labor Daily* reported on 28 January 1927. Australia had the knack of discarding such ideas. The paper realised early that it must 'function as a newspaper first, if it expected to win circulation and advertising support.' 'The workers must realise that they can expect the militancy of a Labor newspaper to be tempered by the necessity of getting a daily sustenance from [advertisers] not always conspicuously friendly to its ideals.' It reported 'average' circulation at 21,000 in 1924, 60,000 in 1925 and 70,000 in 1926 with peaks of 27,000, 102,000 and 90,000 each consecutive year. In 1925, advertising doubled that of 1924 and in 1926 increased by half over 1925. The editorial said 'in three years foundations of sand have become foundations of granite.'

Mr Willis thought it the age of publicity. Publicity dominated social and industrial life. It was a powerful employers' weapon. A workers' press was indispensable. With the power of numbers, the workers 'could make the *Labor Daily* the largest and most powerful newspaper in Australia and the most vigorous exponent of that new social order which is the shining goal of the Labor Movement and the ideal of every lover of humanity.'

Elected Premier in 30 May 1925, Jack Lang told a Newtown crowd of ten thousand that his government would mean 'better times for the toilers, better times for shopkeepers, better times for manufacturers.'

The real aim of the movement, said Lang, was to produce its own daily newspaper. That was the only way to counter the loud voice of vested interests in commercial papers. Public debate was newspaper debate. Without newspapers, the movement would be as fecund as the desert back of Bourke. This was an 'article of faith' with the Big Fella.

He had run copy and turned a flatbed press mangle on an underground Labor paper in the 1880s. Though business hated him and some in the movement thought of another 'big feller, 'the Chicago mobster Al Capone, others believed he was greater than Lenin. As gentlemen in the Wentworth Hotel and the Melbourne Club dreamed uneasily of a report in eight-point Roman converting a laundryman into a revolutionary, shearers and flappers had other ideas. Men and women could break the mould.

In Melbourne Hugh Denison's *Sun News-Pictorial* Monty Grover sought to catch the reader's eye with pictures from the four corners of the earth and to match the pace of the roaring, booming Twenties. It contained 'All the News that's Fit to Print', (a slogan borrowed from *The New York Times*), but the comprehensive coverage need not cause a busy executive to waste a moment. He could read the Sun-Pic in half the time it took to read the other papers 'and still be just as well informed'. On the St Kilda tram, on the Moorabbin bus, it was the most popular paper.

For *The Evening Sun*, motor cars were moving more than drivers, families, passengers and dogs. They were breaking down barriers of class, wealth and income. The motor car had displaced the horse-drawn gig in the popular imagination. Because it carried 'no special prestige' it was the vehicle not only of democracy but also of the White Australia policy. 'The more thoroughly the country is opened up, the better are the prospects for populating it with people of our own race.'

For letter-writers to the new popular press, more was less. The market inverted the male subconscious: 'The shorter the letter the greater the chance of its insertion,' *The Evening Sun* told readers on 2 July 1923. Was the stage immoral? Could chorus girls advance 'without a personal sacrifice of the things most women hold dear?' *The Evening Sun* asked that day.

In marvellous Melbourne a long struggle between wowsers and drinkers — some thought it a struggle between men and women of high standards and still higher anxiety against tosspots who did not care if the bars in Flinders Street remained open till the end of the *World* — was at tipping point. When North Carlton church leaders protested to the city council that children were playing in Princes Park on Sundays, *The Evening Sun* pulled out the stops. Melbourne was alone among the great cities of the modern world in tamely surrendering to 'the spirit that was driven out of Massachusetts long ago.' It was time for freedom-lovers to 'snap the chains with which intolerance has fettered their lives' on Sundays. Cartoonist Jim Banks drew a black-clothed Puritan dropping a black book of gloom, smiting his brow at the sight of a ring of children dancing in the grass. Photographs from Tamworth showed the leaves of the year's tobacco crop being sun-dried, stacked and carted. Pictures were telling of a struggle for the souls of the people. In Sydney as subsidised British migrants, some wondering whether the seed of culture had yet to germinate under the Australian sun, poured off ocean-liners through *Circular Quay* — were these colonials not acquainted with circles, or quays, or dictionaries? Associated Newspapers, seeing the future in photographs, started *The Daily Pictorial*.

• • •

Jack Lang put the argument for a newspaper tax quickly as Premier and Treasurer, in the House of Assembly on 22 December 1926. If a tax of a halfpenny now threatened to stifle the press and the spread of knowledge, he said, how was it that when circulations rose during the war, the proprietors did not hesitate to charge an extra penny? When the proprietors slipped their hands into people's pockets, there had been no question of taxing knowledge or stifling the free press.

The tax was 'a simple little matter.' To exempt county papers, it would apply only to those with a circulation of more than 10,000; if he was wrong in that, the exemption could extend to circulations of 15,000. He could not conceive of it reducing the circulation of the great metropolitan newspapers. It was light. It was small. The revenue would be applied to education.

He expected newspaper criticism. The metropolitan press criticised 'everything this government does, just as it has criticised everything any Labour Government has done.' The leader of the opposition, Thomas Bavin: 'The Premier is going to tax his political opponents in the city and exempt his political opponents in the country.' Mr Lang thought he could hit his political opponents and at the same time conciliate the country press. 'That is the whole explanation of this measure.' The Government had 'had as fair a run from the metropolitan press as any Government has ever had.'

The Sydney Morning Herald said Lang was an 'apostle of reaction. He takes his stand among the inveterate Tories.' Before the High Court in March, Robert Gordon Menzies argued for the Lang Government that the tax was valid; Herbert Vere Evatt argued for newspaper proprietors that it was unconstitutional because it imposed an excise, an exclusive power of the Commonwealth.

Lang was surprised voters so quickly forgot about the progressive Evatt appearing for the magnates, the round-vowelled Menzies for a labour visionary. Menzies, Lang said 'collected on his brief to defend a Labor Government against the Press Nabobs. Fancy Menzies appearing for a Red-ragger Government trying to collect money from those long-standing defenders of freedom, the newspaper proprietors.' When Associated Newspapers directors published a notice that they would not accept advertising from the Australian Labor Party during the campaign he thought that was the way men run by profit defended freedom of the press.

• • •

The question the law framed on appeal to the High Court was simple: was the payment of £86,500 by Robert Clyde Packer's Associated Newspapers to Sydney Newspapers, chaired by his son Frank to stop publication of a cheaper newspaper competing with the Sun *tax deductible*? (Sir Hugh Denison, chairman of directors of Sun Newspapers Ltd authorised the payment; R.C.Packer was managing editor of the *Sun* and E. G. 'Red Ted' Theodore a director. Frank chaired Sydney Newspapers Ltd.)

The facts of the agreement, made on 9 November 1932, said the Chief Justice, Sir John Latham, were not in dispute. *The World* afternoon newspaper, started on 26 October 1931 with Montague Grover as editor, was to close next day. Frank Packer agreed not to publish a daily or Sunday paper within three hundred miles of Sydney for three years. Frank's proposal to publish a daily evening paper, the *Star*, at 1d1/2d cheaper than the *Sun* was dead. Justice Owen Dixon thought the chief object of the £86,5000 was to protect *The Sun* against lowering its selling price and losing circulation and revenue. Justice McTiernan agreed. All judges, including Justice Rich who heard the first appeal from the Commissioner of Taxation's ruling that the sum was capital expenditure, not income against which the owners could deduct costs, made no mention of readers' interests in newspaper price-reduction or advertisers' interests in newspaper competition which could drive rates down. Newspapers' only competition for advertising revenue was from direct-mail catalogues and billboards. That readers, advertisers or the public had no interest in a deal closing one newspaper down and preventing the most likely competitor starting another was so clearly the case, so obvious, so axiomatic it was unnecessary to say it. Two hundred and forty joined the unemployed of the great depression.

Company names told the story of shrinkage from the heights of Mount Warning. The Sun Newspapers Company, publishing the evening *Sun, Sunday Sun, Daily Telegraph Pictorial, Sunday Pictorial, Newcastle Sun, Wireless Weekly* and *World's News*, merged with Samuel Bennett Ltd, the publisher of *Evening News, Sunday News, Woman's Budget* and *Sporting and Dramatic News*, on 1 October 1929 forming Associated Newspapers, proprietor: Hugh Denison, principal executive: R. C. Packer. The merger would cut waste. It would save thousands of pounds a year.

Smith's Weekly had another perspective. *The Evening News* had exposed corruption in the City Council which led to the Council being replaced by a Civic Commission. Now *The Sun* might influence, it might control, the *News*. Was this because the Council was about to pay *The Sun* £345,000 compensation for resumption of its Martin Place land? Journalists would suffer. *The Sun* and *News* editors and executives would no longer bid against each other for sharp reporters and talented editors. If a reporter fell out with one editor, the doors of the group would shut against him.

The misgivings multiplied. Hugh Denison closed the *Sunday News* on 26 January 1930. In October the Smith's Newspapers annual meeting resolved to distribute half the 400,000 Associated Newspapers preference shares to Joynton Smith, 145,000 to R. C. Packer, the remaining 65,000 split equally between Frank Packer and an associate. On 17 March 1932, Lang suddenly introduced the Companies Amendment (Preference Shareholders) Bill. Retrospective to 1 July 1929, it stopped ordinary shareholders disposing of assets without the consent of preference shareholders.

R. C. Packer had 'committed the most glaring act of robbery that could be discovered in the commercial life of the city.' After the abrupt suspension of standing orders, the bill, which would have bankrupted R.C. passed all stages in the Assembly before midnight. The Council heard attorneys for R.C. and Frank Packer arguing against it. Lang, who said the old man wept in a parliament house corridor while this was going on, saying the bill would ruin him, counted councillors and found 'Packer snr. had won.' Lang did not have the numbers. He let it lapse. On 13 May Governor Sir Phillip Game dismissed Lang's Government for repudiating debts to international banks.

Lang said Associated directors had 'robbed and despoiled more people than any of the picturesque London swindlers who have found their way inside the English gaols. The manner in which the *Evening News* and *Sunday News* were acquired and then closed down, and their shareholders robbed, is well-known.' There was more infamy, immorality and corruption under the golden dome of the Associated Newspapers building, the whited-sepulchre of Elizabeth Street, than in any other place in Sydney or New South Wales.

> These swindling humbugs, by the use of their newspapers, destroy the character of men whose shoes they are not worthy to black. They have been fattening and battening because of their control of powerful newspapers. The newspapers would be glad to see the last of me; there is no doubt about that. But by the living God, as long as I am here, if they want a fight they can have it.

C. P. Scott asked on 5 April 1928: How far does the increasing concentration of newspaper ownership in a few hands tend to weaken or destroy this instrument [a free and independent press] and thus to impair the security we at present possess for the free play of public opinion and the wise control of public affairs? The movement towards aggregation and the concentration of power is young at present, and any dangers involved in it are as yet largely undeclared. But it is growing and may yet attain to vastly greater dimensions. And what then?

Australia had an answer to Scott's question. In Sydney from 1803 to 1824 and Hobart from 1816 to 1825, Australian editors, advertisers and readers endured maximum ownership-concentration, with one newspaper in each colony and the government the dominant partner, able to jail or bankrupt the editor-owner, shut the paper down or publish a Government competitor. In the struggle for a free press six capital city editors suffered 83 months in sandstone cells for true, substantially true or stories such as Andrew Bent's Gideonite where no-one could say what was true. The cost to readers in stories unpublished, incomplete or unfinished, chances forgone, bargains not struck or insights forgone were not considered. The cost of thirty years of gagged journalism was invisible. Silence reigned; in the culture created by Australian journalism no-one dwelt on what it meant.

Newspaper accounts of newspapers, why they are started and how they are run, can be comic. John Fairfax thought in 1869 that the prospects for another evening daily to compete with the thriving *Evening News* were 'sufficiently bright' for the firm to have a go. On Monday 3 January 1870 the penny *Afternoon Telegram* made its first appearance with four pages each of six columns. The editor was Samuel Cook, a gregarious parliamentary reporter. 'We think we see before us a course of usefulness, and we shall endeavour to pursue it with unflagging zeal,' the new editor, later an innovative Fairfax general manager, told baffled readers in characteristically opaque prose in the first issue, also promising that 'Its news will be tersely written.' Confined by clotted style, Cook could not see readers yawning.

A Fairfax historian saw prophecy in an aphorism in the first editorial that tears invariably followed smiles, as well as a first-issue poem, *Thoughts on Suicide*. Cook edited the *Telegram* as if news no longer had to be new, the *Herald* did not exist, and the readers shared his fascination with full-page reports of cliché-suffused parliamentary speeches. On April fool's day the editor declared himself well satisfied with the paper's 'large and increasing circulation' but the advertisers did not believe it. Mr Cook did not believe it himself. The paper never attracted more than two columns of advertising and survived for four months, closing with the 101st issue on 30 April.

The gap in the afternoon market was real. On 1 May 1875 Fairfax published the first penny *Echo*, edited by Sam Cook. With that combination of faith, hope and inertia that characterised his management, the newspaper genius John Fairfax did not hold the *Telegram* catastrophe against Cook. He hoped an afternoon paper, catching trains to Cowra, Goulburn or Lithgow would catch country readers for whom *Herald* news was mouldy, at least a day, often a day-and-a-half old when they read it. *The Echo* reached Cowra readers with today's news. Fairfax was not looking to sell the *Herald* in the morning and *The Echo* in the evening to the same reader: it wanted the men and women who baulked at 2d for the big *Herald*, but would fork out 1d for a quick afternoon read. After an uncharacteristically quick (for Fairfax) editors' turnover, four in 18 years, it folded in 1893 leaving the field to *The Evening News*.

Chapter 20

The Press in Utopia

*1836–1973: **George Stevenson, Robert Thomas** and* The South Australian Gazette *and* Colonial Register; ***John Brown, Charles Mann** and* The Southern Australian; *Resident Commissioner **James Hurtle Fisher** and Governor Sir **John Hindmarsh**; **John Stephens**,* The Adelaide Observer; ***John Henry Barrow, Langdon Bonython, Catherine Spence, King O'Malley**, Prime Minister **Billy Hughes, Lloyd Dumas**,* The Advertiser.

George Stevenson and Robert Thomas believed in London in 1836 that frontier Adelaide would be a new society. Next to deserts the size of Europe, men and women who knew what was what would abolish poverty applying the theories of Edward Gibbon Wakefield. The new civilization — Stevenson thought of a 'radical Utopia' — would require a newspaper that Stevenson and Thomas would write, edit and publish. (Wakefield, who believed the 'dissemination of knowledge' to be essential, also thought that teachers and libraries would be sufficient for that purpose; news and the new were not part of what he knew.)

Wakefield thought little of, and about, the Press, writing wildly in the visionary *A Letter from Sydney* in 1829, when there were no newspapers in Melbourne or Adelaide: 'the newspaper press of New South Wales, Australia Felix and South Australia is as coarse, as violent, as unscrupulous, often as brutal, as that of the representative Colonies in which the democracy is constituted by law. Of course there are exceptions to this as to every other rule.

There have been colonial newspapers, though I do not recollect one that lasted long, noted for moderation and forbearance. In the *Letter* the gifted scribe wrote from Newgate prison, where he was serving three years for abducting a 15-year-old heiress, as if he were familiar with everyday life in Sydney, including its irritants — 'the conversation is all wool, wool, wool' — with novelistic detail still convincing today. He had a turn of phrase. Bushranging was 'a kind of land piracy'. He derived all his convincing checkable-in-principle facts from documents. When it came to the Press he made it up.

As the first ships left England for South Australia in 1836, Stevenson was joint editor of the London *Globe*, a Whig newspaper owned by Robert Torrens, a marine, economist and publicist, who would become a South Australian founder.

Practical and visionary, Stevenson had farmed in Canada, worked before the mast on voyages to Central America and the West Indies and co-authored a book on France. An extroverted Presbyterian, he felt the contempt of a black-and-white thinker for those either one degree more liberal or one degree more conservative than himself. Words were weapons, his tone angry and his mode attack. He and Thomas, a law-book seller, published the first issue of *The South Australian Gazette and Colonial Register* on 18 June 1836 in London, 'the capital of the civilised world', and planned the second in accordance with the ordinary logic of distribution in the 'city of the wilderness' in South Australia. Ten days later Robert Thomas set sail on the *Africaine* with an iron Stanhope Press, a wooden press and a half-ton of type.

Stevenson, offered the job of private secretary to Governor Sir John Hindmarsh, resigned from the *Globe*, married Margaret Gorton, the journalist daughter of the previous *Globe* editor, and, in debt for £365, sailed on the *Buffalo* with Hindmarsh on 4 July. (When Hindmarsh's daughter Mary published a manuscript ship's newspaper, the *Buffalo Telegraph*, the Stevensons presciently sneered at 'a dead failure'.)

The *Buffalo* docked at Glenelg on 28 December, but sailed for Hobart with most of the type still aboard; no-one noticed. With a skerrick of landed type, Thomas, appointed Government Printer, printed a proclamation of the Government in a hut of rushes quickly built for his daughters on Glenelg beach, calling on settlers to treat the natives as citizens.

Even before the hut was finished, flames of idealism ignited. Wilderness democrats accused Hindmarsh of 'trespass and depredation'. They meant cutting the rushes. When he retrieved a dispatch from a mailbag, they accused him of violating private letters. The resident commissioner, James Hurtle Fisher, convened hostile public meetings; the faction complained to London of Hindmarsh's mean table and tight hospitality; milk and honey were not flowing in progressive Adelaide.

As editor and reporter, Stevenson hoped to expose jobbery and humbug, keep a sharp eye on every Jack-in-office, protest against all secret transactions of public business, 'in short to speak truth and shame the Devil' (an aphorism reported as 'common' in England in 1555.) Aligned with authority as Governor's secretary, Protector of Aborigines, Registrar of Shipping, Postmaster and Customs Officer and Agent for Lloyd's, he believed from the first Adelaide issue of the *Register* on 3 June 1837, after the type returned from Tasmania, in the work ethic, transparency and plain speaking. He would not confine himself by old-world boundaries, language or law.

> The Governor and his Council must be watched here as elsewhere and if they act rightly so much the better for us all; if wrongly we can tell them of it when we know what they are doing. What we want in this colony is not the transcript of an English Statute Book, but well considered laws applicable to the state of society existing in our infant colony, unfettered by precedent, expressed simply, distinctly and with no more words than necessary.

While Stevenson had a dangerous view for an editor depending on real estate advertising — no man should own land 'who is not prepared to obey the divine command and labour on it permanently' — he also had an investigative eye and was ready to apply transparency even to the intimate trust patients gave doctors. On 13 October 1838 he reported the Adelaide hospital was 'a disgrace to humanity.' A man would be ashamed to see his dog kennel in such a state of filth. A man admitted with a hand shattered in an explosion waited *four days* to see the Colonial Surgeon. Stevenson called on the authorities to notice and punish such conduct.

With a pragmatic eye he thought Adelaide intellectuals 'delude themselves and their silly followers by extravagant dreamings of some republican Utopia — "the freest of the free" — which has never existed but in their own distempered imaginations.'

Robert Thomas had brought a journeyman printer, Robert Fisher, from London — one printer among a thousand settlers. But Fisher resented his place in both life and the newspaper office and sought to exploit the print platform. Seeking to undermine Stevenson and strike at the Governor through him, in October 1837 Hindmarsh's enemies induced Fisher to stop typesetting. For three weeks the *Register* did not inform entertain or irritate a single reader. Utopian journalism had high ideals, low circulation and still lower earnings. Then Thomas' son, 16-year-old William, who had briefly worked in a Fleet Street printery, took his place and Fisher was jailed for two months with hard labour for conspiracy.

The emigration agent John Brown and Advocate-General Charles Mann published a Manifesto for *The Southern Australian*, a weekly newspaper-antidote to Stevenson's partisan journalism, a newspaper which would give a fair go to Governor Hindmarsh's rival for authority and influence in the colony, the Resident Commissioner James Hurtle Fisher.

The question dividing the colony into rancorous factions was whether Hindmarsh or Fisher ranked higher, a matter which the Colonial Office, precedent and the South Australia Act all left ambiguous. Now what Stevenson called 'the dirty Fisher faction' was to have a newspaper. 'A few half-witted gentlemen have found their way hither and not contented with scribbling lying nonsense for the gratification of their private friends are ambitious to see their lucubrations in print.'

For his part Fisher found the *Register* 'a perfect bane to the colony'. Departing for England, one of the faction, Paddy Kingston, expressed his 'surprise and regret' that Hindmarsh had tried 'to restrain the free expression of opinion by those who hold office in the colony' a policy which was 'at all times unwise and oppressive and decidedly opposed to that liberal system of government which all those who understand the principles on which the colony is founded hope would have been adopted here.' A split of personalities over control was clothed in fundamental principles.

Charles Mann the Advocate-General, republican and founding editor of the *The Southern Australian*, believed democracy was the driving force of emigration; it sent forth the burning democrat 'to the wilderness of nature with a Bible in one hand and axe in the other'. He believed Wakefield's system of using the proceeds of crown lands sales to pay for the labour needed to farm it would annihilate distance. It would become as easy to migrate from London to Adelaide as it was to Wales. In the first issue on 2 June 1838 he denounced the *Register*'s party bias, despotic use of monopoly, and disgraceful insinuations and falsehoods.

Stevenson responded that though he scarcely thought it necessary to pollute his columns with 'trash doled out by the persons who club their wits to rake together a weekly sixpence worth of scum' his stomach was strong and he ventured 'a few specimens out of the nauseous and disgusting puddle'. Stevenson's style was courting attention and punching noses.

Mann, convinced that Hindmarsh, 'that colonial autocrat, John the first,' was seeking to undermine the law and expecting Hindmarsh to dismiss him, resigned as Advocate-General on 13 November 1837 saying South Australia was not the free colony they all hoped for. 'We have been defrauded. The contract has been broken. We must be given self-government instead of the rottenness of absolute power.'

Mann said of Stevenson: 'It is as impossible to follow a liar through all his twisting as it is to grasp an eel.' Stevenson was a 'prince of charlatans and a paragon of sycophants'. Stevenson of Mann: 'This lame, impotent and miserable shuffler.' Of Mann's journalism: 'dull plodding as much out of place as jests in a sermon.' Even a woman joined the dung-throwing. Writing as *Colonist*, Margaret Stevenson accused Fisher of partiality to big landholders. Both men could barely remember the time three years ago in London when they had enjoyed each other's company, friendship and respect.

Hindmarsh, recalled, left Adelaide on 14 July 1838. His replacement, Lieutenant-Colonel George Gawler arrived on 17 October 1838 with instructions to act as both Governor and Resident Commissioner. He also brought a proposal to separate the *Gazette* and its revenue of £1500 a year from the *Register*. Charles Mann in the *Southern Australian* quickly found Gawler vain, empty-headed and meddling, a land-jobber but while Stevenson defended Gawler in the *Register*, Gawler delayed emasculating *Register* revenues.

Early in 1839 Mann wrote that while the words *liberty and peace* on South Australian banners had brought thousands to her shores, the words were lies. 'She is ruled by one man only and her government in no respect differs from the government of penal colonies.' An angry Gawler wrote to the Colonial Office that his authority would certainly be less steady if chained to a party led by Mann holding principles for which there was no legal authority and which did not spare him public insult and misrepresentation. On 20 June 1839 Gawler separated the *Gazette* from the *Register*, cutting its revenue by £1500 a year.

Gawler's friend, the ambitious Colonial Secretary George Milner Stephen, had been acting Governor between Hindmarsh and Gawler. (Stephen was a distant relative of the influential James Stephen in the Colonial Office and brother of Alfred Stephen, Chief Justice of New South Wales.)

In a colony of 5,800 driven by intellectuals brawling over control, land, symbols and the principles of democracy, Stephen was a problem. A settler described him: 'a good-looking dapper little man with light curly hair and whiskers and *small* in every way, who wore ladies' No. 4's in boots and possessed various strange accomplishments. He danced well and sang soft sentimental ditties to the accompaniment of a guitar adorned with a blue ribbon.'

Fisher refused to pay Stephen's salary as Governor. With Mrs Hindmarsh's help in February 1839 Stephen bought 1619 hectares on the Gawler River for £4000. In March, real-estate gossip said he had sold 800 hectares for £20,000. The *Southern Australian* said the sale was a hoax. Stephen successfully sued the printer Robert Thomas for libel, declaring on oath that the price was £10,000 and denying that he had ever claimed it was £20,000.

Thomas prosecuted Stephen for perjury and produced a letter from Stephen to George Stevenson in which Stephen said the land had been sold for £20,000. Justice Sir Charles Cooper, who was Stephen's house-guest while Cooper's house was being built ruled the letter inadmissible since it had not been produced at the earlier trial. Stephen was acquitted. Several magistrates declined to sit on the bench with him. When Stephen again sued the *Register* printer for libel, he lost the case and his implausible claim to have written £10,000 and that the '2' in the £20,000 was a forgery, was revealed as false. No-one was astonished. Stephen had committed perjury before all Adelaide.

He resigned all public offices, helped edit the Wednesday *Adelaide Guardian* from 7 September 1839 and after more real-estate deals married Mary Hindmarsh, the Governor's daughter, at Trinity Church on 7 July 1840. From 10 December the paper became the *Adelaide Chronicle and South Australian Advertiser.*

A thousand miles away in Albany Western Australia, George Grey replaced the King George Sound resident magistrate, Sir Richard Spencer, in June 1839 and married Spencer's daughter Eliza Lucy in November. He published a vocabulary of the dialects spoken by the Aboriginal races of South-Western Australia and proposed to bring Aborigines under British law, convert them to Christianity and dilute the authority of tribal custom by compulsory assimilation. Ordered home in 1840, he visited Adelaide with Eliza and for three weeks Gawler entertained them; Grey 'met everyone and saw everything' a woman said. In London in October he was appointed Governor and arrived on 10 May 1841. He started cutting official salaries and allowances, disallowed 2s. 6d. for office-window glass, refused 8d. to an office boy for pencils, queried the emigration agent for using mustard at public expense, suspended work on public buildings and reduced government relief hoping to force the unemployed to the farms. Demonstrators twice invaded Government House grounds. A letter to the editor suggested burning him in effigy.

• • •

A London Baptist minister, James Allen, switched to a print pulpit and shipped to South Australia in 1839, edited the *The Southern Australian,* founded the short-lived *South Australian Magazine* and in August 1842 bought the money-losing *Register* from Thomas and Co. He experimented with twice-weekly, briefly daily, publication. In October 1842 he started the weekly *Southern Star*, with a logo from Shakespeare's Richard the Third: *Think upon Grey and let thy soul despair.* Mr Allen did not accept the convention that newspapers publish fact or, when publishing fiction, identify it. *The Southern Star* published what the historian George H. Pitt described as 'a long and circumstantial account of a trial of Governor Grey by a special commission'. The account was invented. It reported Grey's recall; that too was untrue. In June 1845, with creditors wearing a path to his door, Allen sold the *Register* to John Stephens a Methodist teetotaller. Stephens had edited the *Christian Advocate* in England, joined the Register in 1843, could not get on with Allen, quit and started the weekly *Adelaide Observer* on 1 July proposing to promote 'peace and goodwill among men' and therefore not report politics. In free South Australia he had Happy George Howe's vision from the convict days. Poems, essays and light literature congenial to rural readers took the place of political roar and insult. In the *Register* that roar and insult attracted suits for libel.

John Henry Barrow and his wife migrated to Adelaide in 1853 where John Henry kept accounts at the *Register*, becoming a leader-writer in 1854 when Andrew Garran, the co-editor, later *Sydney Morning Herald* editor, moved to Sydney. Barrow had the gift of the word. Born in England, he preached in Congregational churches in Shropshire and Leeds and published fliers urging temperance and denying the Pope was St Peter's successor. He too sought print pulpits, contributing to the liberal *Bradford Observer* and other newspapers. While still at the *Register* he became pastor to a congregation in Kensington; Sarah died. In 1856 with the Adelaide Press all in favour — 'intelligent human beings, not lands, not houses, nor cattle' was the basis of the right, the *Register* thought — South Australian adult males acquired the right to vote, 'universal suffrage'; Great Britain achieved it 62 years later in 1918.

Barrow left the *Register*, resigned the ministry and was elected member for East Torrens in the House of Assembly in August 1858. Several gentlemen, believing a second newspaper desirable and Barrow would deliver, formed a company and appointed him editor and manager. The daily morning *Advertiser* first appeared on 12 July 1858. 'A newspaper published by a joint-stock company has many difficulties,' the *Advertiser* said. 'In conducting a paper, as in carrying on a war, there must be one ruling mind.' Barrow was the ruling literary mind but on the business side several minds did not think as one. 'The company was not a financial success.'

When the penny evening *Telegraph* started on 16 August 1862, financial success was under yet more pressure; every advertising £1 spent on the *Telegraph* was £1 the *Advertiser* could not have. The reasoning also applied to the *Express*, a 1d evening *Advertiser* paper started on 30 November 1863 but, with the *Advertiser* presses being used twice a day the laws of economics expected the *Telegraph* to prevail over the *Express*. In 1864 Barrow's joint-stock company was dissolved and control of the papers passed to a syndicate of eight, with Barrow editor and literary manager and Thomas King business manager. From 1 July 1865 the paper was *The Daily Telegraph*; the Barrow-King syndicate bought it in December 1866 and next month 'combined' it with the *Express*.

The stronger publisher had eaten the weaker competitor; visionary South Australia had yet to detect the menace in monopoly.

• • •

Born in Melrose on the Tweed, Scotland, in 1825 to David Spence and Helen Brodie, Catherine Spence said 'I account myself well-born, for my father and mother loved each other.' She remembered fondly that a glass of whisky in the 1830s cost less than a cup of tea. The only cloud in a happy childhood was the gloom of the Calvinist Presbyterians. She despaired of salvation: since few could be saved, God in her eyes appeared unlovely and since it was wicked not to love God, she was condemned.

When the Palmyra dropped anchor off Glenelg in November 1839 Catherine was dismayed at the dusty frontier, the drought-stricken town, the mangroves, the wind from hell off the plain. The red-haired 14-year-old 'had a good cry.'

She defined and discovered herself in the act of writing for newspapers. Cut off from books, intellectually frustrated, she shrank from bringing children into a world which offered them so small a chance of salvation, turning down a marriage proposal from a 'very clever young man', noting wryly that six weeks later he was engaged to another. 'It is always supposed that love and marriage are the chief concerns in a girl's life, but it was not the case with me.' She wrote letters and verse for the *South Australian*. She taught as a governess, earning three guineas a month. The payment made her proud. Her shyness disappeared. She felt mature at 17. 'I had seen things I had written in print.'

She saw that men were born free but women were in chains. 'Very few single women were free agents in 1839. We were hopelessly ruined, our place would know us no more.' Single women wore caps as an outer and visible sign of their inner state: they were spinsters; they were not available. Catherine did not wear the cap, but she accepted her fate. The 'number of lovers had been few' she said late in life.

Pouring journalism into the *South Australian*, hoping her stories would help keep it alive, she went with her brother John and sister Mary to a fund-raising ball for the *South*. They ran into John Taylor, the *Register* editor. Taylor told Mary people were pointing her out and talking of her as 'the lady who wrote for the newspapers.' Mary was indignant. Catherine 'did not like it even to be supposed of myself.' For a woman to write for a newspaper in Adelaide in 1853 was to be subject to demeaning gossip at a newspaper fund-raising ball.

Self-doubt rarely tormented her. She wrote a goldfields novel, *Clara Morison — A Tale of South Australia during the Gold Fever* and gave it to John Taylor to pitch to the London publishers. Taylor had not found a publisher when his trip ended, but gave it to another man from Saint Vincent's Gulf who placed it with J.W.Parker and Son which published it in 1854. The publisher offered payment of £40, then charged her £10 — a common manoeuvre — for abridging because the novel was published as part of a series.

In black-and-white photographs taken shortly before she died, she is not a gorgeous woman: wide hips beneath brocade, square jaw, nose in profile a bit like a Rosella's. But she also has generous lips, a cheeky smile, smoky eyes beneath that hair, flame-red when she was young, the eloquent hands, the long delicate fingers, the verbal bounce; when a superior male told her 'I don't mind if you do' when she offered to sign his copy she said coolly: 'Do you want me to sign it, or do you not?'

She urged equal representation on the electors in her 1861 *Plea for Pure Democracy*. South Australia could show the world how to protect minorities against the tyranny of the majority. It could build an Athenian city-state on the River Torrens, follow Giuseppe Garibaldi and George Washington on the path to independence and make democracy transparent, accountable and equal.

Catherine sought an interview with the dominant left-intellectual for her generation, John Stuart Mill, son of the Scottish philosopher James Mill, who shielded John from chiacking with other little boys, teaching him Greek when he was 3, political economy at 13. Mill sought to shake the branches. He was arrested at 18 for distributing fliers on contraception to the London poor. At 24 he suffered clinical depression. When Catherine interviewed him in London in 1865 his essay *On Liberty* was a shield for individual liberty against coercion by the state or society around the world. He was an intellectual reformer, like her. Their genes were Scottish. He too had an Adelaide connection: his first wife Harriet's brothers were Catherine's friends.

She thought the interview a failure; her questions did not induce aphorisms or eloquence from the world that teemed in Mills' mind. The Socrates of the liberals was short on answers, long on questions: how was the Wakefield experiment going? Women's suffrage? The interview reversed: the reporter became the subject. 'I didn't get as much out of him as I expected.' He alarmed and amused her when he said he was pleased to get information from such a good authority. She thought she had no special knowledge. Mill: 'You are observant and thoughtful and what you have seen you have seen well.'

Mill sparked her interest in proportional representation, which she pushed in *A Plea for Pure Democracy* regretting the idea 'did not set the Torrens on fire'. The young woman shaped by newspaper writing lived with her parents, raised three families of orphaned children, campaigned for the vote for women which was enacted for South Australia with the right to stand for parliament in 1894, the first jurisdiction in the world to do so. (New Zealand enacted the female vote the year before.) At 72 she was the first Australian woman candidate for office in the 1897 election for the constitutional convention. She died on 3 April 1910.

• • •

Scene from a press life: Lloyd Dumas purses his lips as President Franklin Delano Roosevelt adds a liqueur to a dry martini in the White House. Making small talk, he asks the president whether Mayling Soong, wife of the former Chinese premier Chiang Kai-Shek, then a White House guest, 'is staying long, Sir?'

Roosevelt: 'Thank God, the bitch goes tomorrow.'

Dumas, shocked, wants to draw the sting from the remark. In his autobiography says he is 'sure there was nothing personal' in it.

Born in Mount Barker in 1891, he knew as a toddler he had ink in his veins. His father Charles founded the *Mount Barker Courier* in 1880. One Sunday young Lloyd, excited when his fox terrier caught a rabbit, hurried home proudly clutching the animal by the ears. Charles thrashed him. He made this enigmatic remark: 'It [his father belting him] was not a repressive discipline as long as we played the game.' With an air gun he filled parakeet pies; at 12 his father gave him a 16-guage double-barrelled gun to hunt quail in the hills; at 16 Charles, looking to Lloyd taking over the *Courier*, arranged his cadetship with Sir Langdon Bonython, the Adelaide *Advertiser* proprietor-editor.

Bonython, born in London on 15 October 1848, joined *The Advertiser* as a reporter in 1864; John Barrow quickly made him chief of the literary staff. He had the Midas eye, bought into the paper with profits from mining speculation, rose to editor in 1884 and sole proprietor in 1893. He was by nature a member of George Howe's tucker-box school of journalism. He lusted to prosper. He was a snob, hoping, after his knighthood in 1898, for an hereditary title. He was a saint, distributing meal-tickets in the depression, donating £100,000 to complete Parliament House in 1934. His eldest son John Lavington Bonython, born in 1875, joined the *Advertiser* management in 1896 and edited *The Saturday Express* from 1912 to 1930.

Focused, intent, Dumas stood out as a fast shorthand writer. (*Advertiser* and *Register* reporters provided the Hansard service.) Specialising in sport, the mild-mannered young reporter discovered he could stay ahead in the news game by taking minutes for the Rowing Association, Tennis Association, even National Football Council meetings in Adelaide. The job gave him access to information and also meant the secretaries owed him.

At 24 on vacation he worked as a casual for the Melbourne *Argus*. The *Argus* offered him a senior reporter's job at £7 a week 'pretty attractive' since *The Advertiser* paid £5. He married stenographer Daisy Hall, Edward Smith Hall's great-great granddaughter, in November 1915 —'the wisest thing I ever did'—moved to Melbourne as town hall and trades hall roundsman and was quickly appointed Federal roundsman, the top-reporting job in marvellous Melbourne where federal parliament was sitting. King O'Malley, his father's colleague in the South Australian parliament, Minister for Home Affairs in the Fisher Government, an influential campaigner for the Commonwealth Bank and a wowser who loathed 'stagger juice' was a friend and contact.

When Dumas visited O'Malley on a quiet Saturday, King handed him a statement about a plan for a reservoir on an island 30 miles from Darwin. The idea was to pump water undersea to Darwin. When Dumas the old mate from Adelaide read it his alarm grew with every syllable. 'You can't publish this. Everyone will laugh at you.'

O'Malley said if people laugh at you they are thinking of you. The greatest fear of a public man was nobody thinking of him. 'You publish the paragraph.' Dumas found getting close to Billy Hughes easy. The Labor Prime Minister dubbed 'the little digger' loved publicity. He was always ready to meet Dumas more than half way. They were soon on what Dumas called 'friendly terms'.

The Prime Minister asked *The Argus* to second Dumas to his staff for the conscription campaigns of 1916 and 1917. Every capital city daily campaigned for conscription. *The Sydney Morning Herald* agreed with Hughes not to publish the resolutions of anti-conscription meetings, on the grounds that these meetings were 'generally violent and mostly intended to do harm.' Hughes characterised those against conscription as parasites lacking both principle and spine.

On 28 October 1916 voters rejected overseas conscription by a majority of 72,476 out of two and a quarter million. Hughes, the newspapers and the sunny *Argus* reporter, who was developing a 'tremendous affection and admiration' for his Prime Minister, did not give up. When the Labor caucus voted its lack of confidence in him, Hughes said 'Let all who support me follow me' and walked from the party room. Twenty-four of the 65 Labor MPs followed. Hughes formed the Nationalist Party with his ex-Labor colleagues and the support of the opposition. In December 1917 the anti-conscription majority was 166,588. Hughes told Dumas 'out of evil cometh good'; the defeat would but strengthen their resolve.

In 1918 Hughes asked Dumas to be his press secretary at the Imperial Conference in England. Dumas baulked — it would mean leaving *The Argus* — talked to his father and wife, then agreed.

With the Prime Minister in Washington, Mary Hughes in London tells Dumas Billy has forgotten to give her money. Dumas, thinking that sort of thing happens, especially with Billy Hughes, lends Mary £50 to tide her over. When the Prime Minister reaches London, he goes feral. Dumas should have known Mary couldn't be trusted with money. He should never have lent her that much. But Billy does not put his hand in his pocket.

Hughes and Dumas are on a southbound train after a tour of Scotland. Dumas is pleased with himself. He has supplied Fleet Street papers with paragraphs about Hughes. He wrote a piece for the *Daily Mail* about how Australia treated men caught trading with the enemy and the Mail had used it 'without alteration as its only leading article that day.' He was proud of his skills as a journalist and press secretary.

Hughes asked Dumas to show him the copy for the next morning's papers. Dumas handed him the story.

Hughes threw it to the floor. 'A schoolboy could have done better.'

When the train reached London Dumas cabled *The Argus* seeking his old job. He had thought his special relationship with Hughes would protect him. He threatened legal action in Australia, Hughes repaid the £50 and the 'old relationship gradually came back.'

He joined the Sydney journalists talking of forming the Australian Journalists Association when he was on vacation and was on the first South Australian committee. Reporting a Broken Hill strike in 1919 he found mining families living in iron shanties and resenting the absentee directors and managers in Melbourne. They were not Bolsheviks, he saw; they were not bomb-throwers. They were Aussie workers who wanted Collins-street executives to know what it was like to work a mine in Broken Hill and live in a town with no trees. His reporting reflected these views. People were surprised that an 'ultra-conservative newspaper like *The Argus*' would publish such journalism. Lloyd Dumas believed it made a difference.

Worried by the drain of talent to Sydney, he recommended salary rises for the best reporters and sought *The Argus* board's approval to hire two men from outside at higher rates. The editor, Edward Cunningham, said he would support it. Two days later the general manager, A.C.C.Holtz called him down and told him the board had rejected his recommendations.

Dumas accepted an offer by Herbert Campbell Jones, managing director of the Sydney *Sun* to be editor of the *Sun News-Pictorial* Sir Hugh Denison started in 1922. Montague Grover was editor-in-chief, but Campbell Jones told Dumas he would have 'complete control' of the picture-tabloid daily. Dumas liked the legendary Monty, founding Sun-Pic editor, whom he thought a brilliant writer, but he also chose the word 'calamitous' for his journalism. Grover understood readers wanted entertainment. He wanted colour.

Dumas wanted facts. A reporter handed him a brightly written story on a minister's speech, all atmosphere and interjections, nothing of the speech. Dumas asked what the politician had said. Reporter: 'We leave that sort of stuff to the *Age* and the *Argus*.' Dumas tore the copy sandwich in two in front of the astonished journalist and told him to report the speech. The word, Dumas said, spread quickly and in twelve months Sun-Pic circulation increased by 50 per cent.

In 1924 Sir Hugh Denison and Campbell Jones, managing director of the Sydney *Sun*, told him they were closing the evening *Sun* and selling the *Sun News-Pictorial* to the *Herald*. Dumas spent seven evenings in Keith Murdoch's flat identifying who to sack. 'It was a very unhappy time.' Nothing in NSW, Victorian or Federal law made swallowing a competing newspaper illegal. Readers were on their own.

When World War Two began on 1 September 1939 Dumas sold his double-barrelled gun, thinking of the parakeets in the Adelaide hills, and never deliberately killed anything again. Not a moth. Not an ant.

He looked in a photograph like a bloated press lord: short, tubby, in a dark suit, cigar between fingers thicker than the cigar, leaning back on his heels he stands with his lady on manicured buffalo grass, with full smiling lips and heavy spectacles. He had his aphorisms. 'It is a great secret of life,' he said when he was 78. 'If you can establish a personal relationship, it is often more effective than logic.' A dozen grasshoppers could make a hillside ring while thousands of cattle chewed in the shade of the British oak but 'pray do not imagine that those who make the noise are the only inhabitants of the field.'

He viewed the cold war gently. 'It is not hard to understand the appeal communism has for kindly people,' he wrote in 1968. 'The theoretical basis of communism is one for all and all for one. Christianity has the same guiding principles and some day the world may adopt them.' The world would be happier if this were possible, but that would need 'a change in human nature.'

Late in life he dined on Wednesdays with Adelaide peers calling themselves The Barbarians. After a 'relatively juvenile' knight of 86 proposed the toast to the Queen they took snuff. When a London *Times* editorial said in 1968: 'A generation ago the danger was that a student who had sexual relations should feel abnormal and unclean. Now it is the student who stays chaste who is more likely to be loaded with the neurotic burden of society's own sexual anxiety,' Dumas was shocked. 'Is the community to have no standards?' Raised Anglican, he said academics should not sneer at faith 'whether it be Christianity, Mohammedanism, Buddhism, or some other'. Without the anchor of faith the gales of passion that swept men, and women too, might wreck them.

He died on 24 June 1973 at Calvary Hospital, North Adelaide.

Chapter 21

Style, Stereos, Seers

Behold, the dreamer cometh. Come now therefore and let us slay him ... and we shall see what will become of his dreams'

Portrait of Martin Luther King Jr., King Street Newtown, Sydney.

Decision invariably involves renunciation: for every yes there must be a no, each decision eliminating or killing other options (the root of the word decide means "slay," as in homicide or suicide).

Irvin D.Shalom *Love's Executioner* 1989

In the New York Times for August 10, 1914, I read of the attempt by German officers disguised in British uniforms to kidnap General Leman at Liege. The reporter wrote that the General's staff, "maddened by the dastardly violation of the rules of civilised warfare, spared not but slew." This sentence had a tremendous effect on me. ... It led me back to do a book on the world before the war.

Barbara Tuchman, *Practising History* 1983

In the [Melbourne] Herald, the words to slay, slaying, slain do not exist. Never use them.

Stuart Brown, editor, 1 August 1967.

Newspaper style books are like fingerprints at a crime scene, evidence that the author-editor is guilty of offences to which later fault-finders including me are immune. In the minds of a resentful minority of readers, newspapers themselves are a crime, violating standards of grammar, taste and privacy, shouting when a whisper is appropriate. When it comes to murdering syntax, rhythm and nuance, newspapers are both perpetrator and evidence. But style books go to motive, the patterns of the suspect journalists' subconscious.

Resembling fingerprints, they are also like finger-paintings, implying child-like states of mind; the journalist in me wants to protect them, give the background, explain them away. '"Pregnant" can be used now; but it would be as well to avoid over-using it' says an editor's note in a Melbourne Herald stylebook of 1946. Then the hand-written note of another editor having a second thought: 'Don't use "Pregnant" or "Intimacy". If you can't find alternative term, ask Chief Sub to refer to Editor.'

These are skilled men and women and one of their most exquisite skills is judging readers' tastes. 'It's desirable to use only the correct form in naming a married woman, e.g., Mrs John Smith, not Mrs Mary Smith,' says a note of March 1953. In 9 February 1957 Cecil Edwards, later *Herald* editor, insisted: 'She isn't Mrs Lorraine Smith unless she's a widow.' Stuart Brown, editor on 22 June 1962: 'All too often in stories we use a married woman's Christian name — Mrs Jessie Jones, say — instead of the correct form, Mrs John Jones.' At a dinner in New York with me and Adele Horin in mid-1973 Mrs Keith Macpherson, wife of the Herald and Weekly Times managing director, defended the anachronism at length with Keith at the table.

Mocking poor dead codgers imprisoned by conventions which have disappeared is easy. Editors believe they're reflecting readers' tastes. But a more telling fashion — what to leave out — can be so culturally ingrained the style book itself leaves it out. The 201-page 2001 News Limited alphabetical stylebook governing all that vast organisation's Australian publications provides no guidance on the word 'fuck', for example, though under 'obscenity, profanity, vulgarity' it says 'If an obscene word has to be used *always* use the form f—- or c—- and so on. *Never* write the word out in full.' By 2001 women acting the Vagina Monologues provoked audiences to shout the word cunt — 'not in anger, not in anger' — and originating feminist author Anne Summers announced the re-birth of the 'c-word' in the opinion pages of the staid *Sydney Morning Herald*. In the *Herald-Sun*, *Australian*, *Daily Telegraph*, *Sunday Times* and *Courier-Mail*, in News Ltd papers from Perth to Brisbane, the word remained in shadow-land. It could be unambiguously implied. It could never be printed. The advance of liberalism since the 1960s, when swearwords drew jail sentences, to the Noughties, when a NSW magistrate decided that 'fuck' was no longer an obscene word, usage having made it part of everyday language, was for newspapers glacial. In their use of language, journalists evolved with a caution that made lawyers seem wild. Purse-lip puritans cast a censorious influence on journalism well beyond their numbers by the simple distortion of making swearwords their first issue.

For anyone not familiar with their content, format and reasoning — the readers for whom they are written, new staff reporters — style-guides, being hard to follow, contradict their purpose. 'Don't detail suicide methods' appears in the old Melbourne *Herald* loose-leaf guide — under 'M' for 'Miscellaneous'. 'We do not suggest the abolition of "nigger-brown" shoes' says *The Herald* style book of July 1951. 'Generally, avoid "black races," "yellow races," etc. "Native peoples" or "coloured races," and sometimes "Negroes (cap N) serve the same purpose. Never "niggers," please, unless there is a strong reason for using it in direct quotation marks. Certain latitude, of course, must be applied to this rule.'

'I think we should play down big betting stories,' Sir Keith Murdoch told an editor a few days before the 1947 Melbourne Cup. 'The community over-indulges in betting tremendously at this time of the year. To my mind the whole activity of the betting ring should be given *'rather briefer mention'*. Who could say if a betting story were 'rather briefer'? On the other hand no-one could say on that evidence that Sir Keith, whose father had a gambling problem, was trying to dictate content, or censor news, from the managing director's office.

The Herald worried as if their readers were their children. Names of poisons should not be published 'without strong reason' in 1951. The admonition remained unchanged till 1963 when the style book said under 'drugs': 'don't mention specific drugs in most reports of suicides or attempted suicides. For sodium Amytal, for example, "a barbiturate" would do, or we could speak simply of "an overdose of drugs". This remained till 2001, when 'avoid mentioning their brand names in non-medical contexts' was News Limited nation-wide style.

When defendants said police had threatened or bashed them the paper should treat the allegations 'with special care.' Unsupported allegations by 'publicity-seeking lawyers should be especially suspect,' editor Cecil Wallace instructed in 1957. Wallace, who had left school at thirteen, promised the Army *The Herald* would not play up hard-luck stories by men court-martialled for being absent without leave. 'The Army says [such stories] are often untrue.'

The teacher in Stuart Brown wanted the *Herald* to spell out — 'at least from time to time' — the derivation of the hallucinogenic LSD. (When I read the full name in his handwritten style-book note — lysergic acid diethylamide — his desire struck me as heroic. Asking a reader struggling in rush-hour with a broadsheet in a crowded tram to absorb a word such as diethylamide is the urge of an educator-hero.) Of the word 'intrastate' he thought on 21 August 1964: 'many of our readers probably don't know what this word means.' His solution was not to ban it but to 'explain it at first reference.'

He was annoyed and offended when readers wrote complaining about 'our abandonment of long-established standards of good grammar.' Three weeks after he instructed sub-editors not to use 'like' for 'as if', his eye fell on: 'More than 50 people sat in the City Square — most of them looking like they arrived by accident.' The news editor was cross. 'Someone is going for the big drop, unless this stops.'

But the frustrations of daily journalism rarely pushed Brown to take out the cane. He was a gentle man. 'Would everyone please be a little more careful to stop slang intruding unnecessarily into the *Herald*,' he wrote on 7 August 1968. 'Several times recently we have used in "formal" reports: "knocked back" for "rejected". And we often use "don't", "hasn't", etc. at times when we should not. One of these days, perhaps, usage will accept these words in all contexts. 'As things are, though, we must discriminate. Someone doing a racy, signed piece can take liberties we should avoid, for instance in court or parliamentary reports. 'I emphasise that I do not want to discourage colourful, down-to-earth writing in its place. 'As the Preacher said: To all things there is a season.'

He could be short. 'Please drop the horrible verb "schooled." The *Herald* used it twice last week,' he wrote on 6 January 1969. Sometimes he tried to make subs and reporters smile. 'Let's write "breaking" a law rather than "breaching it, please,' he wrote on 23 January 1969. 'Who would say that Ned Kelly was a "lawbreacher"?'

Editors did not always have the last word on a word. 'I have had a direction saying that the use of the word "abrasive" to describe a person, statement or a policy, is banned,' Stuart Brown wrote on 5 March 1971. Here was an essence of sloppy journalism: a factually accurate report which raised more questions than it answered. Did the memo ban the word 'abrasive'? It suggested Brown did not agree with it. Would he enforce it? Would it enhance authenticity to forbid using the word 'abrasive' to describe an abrasive person? Would *coarse* or *harsh* or *rough* do? Who gave the direction?

Style can shape political reporting. 'Would you remind subs, please, that we have agreed not to use the tag "National Serviceman" in casualty lists unless circumstances really demand it,' editor Stuart Brown told the news editor on 9 May 1967. He later described the issue in more detail: 'We accepted the Army's point that the National Service boys themselves and the "Regulars" resent any discrimination. Of course, it was vital at times to say "so many National Servicemen were killed or wounded."' He attached a *Herald* clip: Canberra. — Army Headquarters announced today two soldiers, one a National Serviceman from Victoria, had been injured during operations in Phuoc Tuy province.

The style books, a step removed from the action, suggest news is shaped by groups such as advertisers, the military and politicians. 'We have agreed to support the city retailers in their Downtown promotion. We have told them to contact the COS [chief of reporting staff] or picture editor direct with any story or picture ideas,' Pat Hinton, *Herald* editor, 16 August 1979.

The law diminishes the vocabulary of public debate. 'Beware of the word "confession" in court reports and especially in headings,' Stuart Brown said on 4 April 1967. 'Prosecutors sometimes use the word when they are referring to statements they allege were made to the police. Accused people can, and often do, repudiate these 'alleged statements,' even when they have been signed.' What the editor did not say — perhaps he was ashamed to — was that *The Herald* could be convicted of contempt of court for publishing a 'confession' which turned out not to be a confession, even if the prosecutor said it was. A Herald and Weekly Times lawyer formally advised *The Herald* editor on 7 June 1966 that under the Juries Act 1958 it was an offence to publish the name, address or occupation of any empanelled juror, or the photograph of any juror, 'even a picture with the face erased.'

In this culture words such as lush, liar, levitator, gangster, gorilla, goon, goof, godfather, bristle with defamatory imputations and come with red-light attached; much of the dictionary is illegal. When *The Argus* revised its style book in Melbourne in 1925 it advised its reporters to 'avoid words violating decency and good taste'. 'Female' for 'woman' was not in good taste. Neither was the word 'publican'. 'Adultery'— the word, not the deed — violated decency.

The style book slipped from taste to political censorship when it banned the words 'blacklegs' and 'scabs'. The leading Melbourne conservative newspaper would not permit reportage of standard union words for hated strike-breakers. While *The Argus* insisted: No bias should be allowed to creep into the report of any speech or meeting, it was proud of its long-standing reputation for fairness and accuracy and hoped reporters would 'never be afraid to ask anybody anything', it would not report that 'a militant wharf labourer screamed 'blacklegs! scabs! as strike-breakers crossed picket lines in South Melbourne.' Invisible lines about which there was no argument shaped reporting of *capital v labour*, the big story, as well as a minor issue such as the great Australian adjective.

'The editor-in-chief wonders if "bloody" is not getting into the papers too often said *The Herald* editor Stuart Brown on 11 June 1969. 'I'm inclined to think it is. We need to have strong reasons for using it.' *The Herald* should be 'restrained' in identifying motor cars in which people died, he said on 5 August 1969. 'Would you please refer things like this to the editor.' He did not say that car manufacturers advertised in *The Herald*. That would breach the wall between advertising and editorial. Besides, it was not necessary.

• • •

Our habits of thinking about newspapers are so coloured by technology they are ingrained in the language. We used to think of newspapers as 'the press' and the reflex obscures reality. After computerised typesetting started in Australia in 1980, enabling huge payroll savings through printing job losses, metropolitan daily newspapers atrophied: circulations, revenues and advertising shrank and eight daily or weekly papers, some trading profitably since the 1800s died in twelve years in Sydney, Melbourne, Brisbane, Adelaide and Perth.

The technology of printing excites newspaper executives — the size! the cost! the power! — and sometimes facilitates efficiency fantasies, or dreams of overwhelming the competition. It was the core of an ancient craft. For Peter Tyler, the first secretary of the Australian Society of Compositors, who hanged himself on a tree near Government House, Sydney, in July 1842 and for his peers before and since, the craft evolved through struggle, strikes and pain.

For readers, till computerisation and the Internet, photographs, graphics and colour were the only fundamental changes in two centuries of printing in Australia. Until electronic publishing in the 1990s they were the only fundamental changes since Gutenberg.

The flatbed screw-press George Howe worked on the *Sydney Gazette* in 1803 had not substantially changed for three hundred and fifty years; steam, coal and horse power contributed nothing; it ran on the power of hand, wrist and arm, manpower. A pressman inked the metal type from the ink board with two wooden-handled cups, dabbing one against the other and both against the type — the pressmen called it 'beating'; his mate fed the paper, ran the carriage of type under the press and screwed the press down. The work, hard, slow, repetitive, ate Howe's time and energy and the print was uneven; sometimes the look of the pages suggested a willy-willy had done the beating. He found ink-making difficult and disagreeable. In 1814 when *The Times*, London, printed on a steam press invented by Frederick Koenig the paper said it was 'the greatest improvement connected with printing since the discovery of the art itself.' The system was 'almost organic' it was an 'unconscious agent' operating at such a velocity it printed no less than 1,100 sheets in a single hour.

Compositors inhabited a distinct world. When Europeans first heard of ideas to set type mechanically they laughed, saying this would require a machine that could think. After nine years trying, a German-American clockmaker, Ottmar Mergenthaler, invented the Linotype in Baltimore in 1886; *The New York Tribune* first used it in 1896. In Sydney 1930 a Sun Newspapers historian thought Linotypes could do 'everything but talk'; they had 'fingers and minds'. A skilled operator could set a line-of-type with molten lead at 280 degrees centigrade, with tin for hardening and antimony, a white element, to link the two metals, at five times the speed it took a hand operator setting individual letters. The electric genius Thomas Edison called the Linotype 'the eighth wonder of the world'. A good hand compositor could set 2000 letters an hour. A machine compositor could set 10,000 an hour. When David Syme introduced the linotype at *The Age*, more than a hundred compositors lost their jobs. Those who had worked 25 years or more at the paper were pensioned for life. (Syme hired an agriculture expert to find land for printers who dreamed of putting down roots in the Mallee.)

It was not just the operators' distinctive skills, speed-reading mirrored type, quickly breaking words at the right syllable to justify the line without causing the reader to pause, fingers flying over two sets of alphabets, one lower case on the left, (black) one in capitals (white) on the right, in the middle (blue) punctuation, numbers and solid spaces.

They were making history: scribes had written for tens or hundreds of readers, never for hundreds of thousands, so the printers protected their culture in language setting it apart, organising themselves into Chapels led by the Father of the Chapel, implying that typographers deserved the protection afforded the Church. The Chapel comprised not only men of high status and wages; it also aspired high: to infallibility. 'The Chapel cannot Err' Joseph Moxon, an Anglo Dutch printer, a scholarly 'how-to' publisher, wrote in London in 1677, repeating an ancient aphorism.

Printing was a new mode of transmitting meaning; no-one could predict where it might take them. Even the shape of a letter could cause controversy, since anyone who made letters might proclaim his to be the 'true shapes'. This worried Moxon because neither the ancients from whom they had received the letters, nor any authentic authority had handed down rules governing letter shapes. Since there was no geometry of design there was no certainty. Moxon answered that letters comprising circles, parts of circles and straight lines 'may deserve the name of True Shape, rather than those that have not.' Having taken the mantle of this new authority, of the word, printers acquired its influence and status. (Moxon guessed the title 'chapel' was conferred by a Churchman as a reward of courtesy for printing Books of Divinity.)

The chapel also acquired some of the authority of the state. For offences such as fighting, abusive language, drunkenness or neglecting to snuff a candle, it could arbitrarily fine an offender between one penny and one shilling, punishments called *solaces*. When an offender refused to pay, his peers forced him to lie on his belly on the correcting-stone and struck him eleven blows on the buttocks with a paper-board, the severity limited only by the striker's mercy. 'Tradition tells us,' said Moxon, 'that about 50 years ago one was *solaced* with so much violence that he presently pissed blood and shortly after died of it.'

The word *solace*, comfort amidst chaos, implied that the chapel's authority resembled that of the Almighty: it transcended language. Penalties were decided by 'a plurality of votes, it being effected as a maxim that the Chapel cannot Err. When any controversy is thus decided, it always ends in the good of the Chapel.'

Following this principle, London printers' unions pushed feather-bedding and over-manning to the point in 1961 where had the *Daily Mirror* publishing and machine-room employees all turned up together, 'they would' the general manager said, 'have suffocated'. Newspaper printing houses in London had dozens of men drawing salaries for standing around. Lord Beaverbrook told the Shawcross Royal Commission in 1961 the union officials were 'much abler than our people' and the unions 'more powerful than the Newspaper Proprietors' Association'. 'Fat takes', typesetting carrying extra pay for work done by another, allocated by time-on-the-job, were common as breathing. The river would never run dry.

Of all the discoveries science had placed at man's disposal, the Sydney jobprinter J. Degotardi thought in 1861, none had been as important as printing. As a branch of art or science, printing might claim to be the fountain of civilisation. Its influence, increasing daily, was felt in every station in life. Man could not be deprived of the gift of printing, but if he could we would sink back into barbarism. The new horizontal Hoe press was rendering the Impossible possible, and in the wonderful discovery of printing by electricity, and by the aid of photography, he respectfully announced in *The Art of Printing in its Various Branches* his own attempts to advance this scientific art in Australia.

After John McDouall Stuart struggled through the vast country from Adelaide to Darwin where inland seas appeared and vanished, in 1859–62 an overland telegraph line was known to be possible. Charles Todd, an astronomer who feared no-one would ever marry such a dull fellow as himself, the Postmaster General of South Australia, supervised work on 'the singing string'. 'In the mosaic hills of Port Augusta [in July 1872],' Ernestine Hill wrote, 'wagons, horses, bullocks, carts, drays, poles, wire, insulators, tools and hillocks of stores were waiting. Newspaper advertisements called for men — and men they must be.' There were no award rates and union hours, no camps with water and light laid on with cooks, refrigerators, recreation halls, bacon-and-egg trucks and electric fans. These men were bound for oblivion with a packhorse and a swag.

Two questions were asked: 'Are you sound in mind and limb?' and 'Can you live on bandicoot and goanna?' Wages were '25s. a week and found'. If you were lost you ate what you found till you were found. If you were found.

The telegraph connected the bush to the cities and the world. Then, experimenting on the mechanisms of speech, an Edinburgh father and son discovered that when vowel sounds were whispered, each had a particular pitch, so just by whispering vowels a pair of lips could produce a musical scale. Then there were unexpected difficulties: some vowels seemed to possess a double pitch, one probably due to the resonance of air in the mouth, the other to resonance in the air in the cavity behind the tongue. Alexander Graham Bell pursued the research, he told the Society of Telegraph Engineers in London on 31 October 1877, and discovered that a mouth formed for an 'a' 'e' 'i' 'o' or 'u' caused different tuning forks on the lips to resonate. A German physicist, H. L. F. Helmholtz, hoping to find a physiological basis for the theory of music, had published a theory of tone in 1863. Professor Bell was then 'too slightly acquainted' with the laws of electricity to understand its implications, but by 1877 he thought it feasible to reproduce music through a telegraph wire to a distant city. The idea, which 'took complete possession of my mind' was a key to the electric telephone. Two years and seven months later on 12 May 1880 Australia's first telephone exchange, 44 subscribers, opened in Melbourne. After extended argument about the 'merits and demerits' of the system *The Sydney Morning Herald* reported on 7 August 1880 the first Sydney conversation, between Mr F. R.Wells, 'the local agent for the invention' at the Sydney Exchange and a Mr Cracknell at the General Post Office. 'This offers a great convenience to business men, and the project is likely to be taken up,' the *Herald* said. For journalists the telephone was a key to a core of the craft — speed — once it became widely used. Uneasy about status, drawing lines of education and class against men who worked in overalls, journalists thought little of technology. In *A Century of Journalism* in 1931 and the brilliant, ground-breaking history by Gavin Souter in 1981, *Company of Heralds*, journalist-historians on the oldest newspaper barely noticed the telephone, their most-used technology.

But the men who worked the hot-metal machines understood the fundamentals more deeply than quick, clever reporters, or stubborn investigative diggers or editors bubbling with ideas for all humanity or colour-writers with Henry Lawson's eye.

At Fairfax, computerisation was at the expense of what Gavin Souter said were 'the two most costly strikes in the company's history', a 25-day Printing and Kindred Industries Union strike in March-April 1975 and a 60-day strike in October-December 1976 by the PKIU and seven other unions, not including the Australian Journalists' Association (the Media, Entertainment and Arts Alliance predecessor). The PKIU with 52,000 members, took the long view. New technology had been with us a long time: the invention of the wheel was new technology, Ted Bennett, the Federal Secretary, said in March 1979. To set a page of broadsheet text would have taken a hand compositor 22 hours, a linotype operator 5.5 hours and a teletype setting unit 1.3 hours. A computerised photocomposing machine could do it in 15 seconds.

Nor was that all. New ink-jet printers could put an advertisement on the surface of a fresh-laid egg. The new technology was already a reality. There was no way of stopping it. The union sought retraining, no redundancies or wage cuts, fewer working hours and extended annual leave.

When journalists struck in May 1980 after asking $50 a week for working at monitors, then called video display terminals, and getting $5 from the Arbitration Commission's Justice Alley — 'Give us the real figure', members of the union's federal executive told John Lawrence, the federal president, when he hurried across town with the news. They thought he was joking. Twenty-eight *Australian* sub-editors and one at Fairfax were sacked for refusing to work the monitors for $5. The printers whose jobs they were taking naturally did not support the 31-day strike, the AJA's longest, and only national, action. It succeeded. Journalists working the monitors received an extra $12 to $25 a week; all received an extra three days' annual leave; the sub-editors were re-instated.

Fear still ran information in the ancient continent. The question 'what if' worried parents as much as Premiers and Prime Ministers as tormented widows discovered emails from lovers in the departed husband's computer and editors worried that the Web began to suck dry the resource that made digging, deep disclosure, possible: classified advertising. As blogs and Websites exponentially increased the number of news sources and pressure for government transparency, gossip flowed like rivers on texts and emails and reader feedback to newspapers became more comprehensive and faster than ever, but deadlines moved forward so far that morning newspaper journalists quipped that with one more technological revolution *The Sydney Morning Herald* would be an afternoon newspaper. In 1892 *The Age* could take copy till 2.45am. Now the first-edition deadline is 6pm, four hours earlier than in the 1960s; a big story in the electronic age can make the paper till midnight, even 1am during the 2008 Beijing Olympics.

The faith in print which reached its peak in 1923 thinned for the rest of the twentieth century as blokes and sheilas grew ears for radio and eyes for television and advertisers saw that essentials such as toothpaste, soap, detergent and breakfast cereals which ran like rivers out of both supermarkets and corner-stores flowed as in flood when advertised on television, as if in drought when pushed by full-page newspaper ads. Long before print-faith drained to the point where we paid more public relations practitioners to manipulate news than we did journalists to report it, before Google diminished thoughts to seconds and students thought research was pressing buttons, we slid to agnosticism. 'He who first shortened the labor of Copyists by device of Movable Types was disbanding hired Armies, and cashiering Kings and Senates, and creating a whole new Democratic world: he had invented the Art of Printing,' said the Scot Thomas Carlyle in *Sartor Restartus* in 1831. A century later Sun Newspapers Ltd acted out Carlyle's faith erecting its Gothic Elizabeth-street, Sydney building in 1929. When Associated Newspapers, the Sun predator, bought the building in 1939 the faith had ebbed under the wounds inflicted by the great depression. 'The air is full of the spoken word,' said Keith Murdoch at the Australian Newspapers Conference in 1937. Radio was a miracle ranking with the invention of print as a servant of humanity. In 1937, when radio was as new as digitization is in 2017. Murdoch knew some newspaper people felt threatened: radio was cheaper than print, it was quicker, it spread information more effectively: people didn't have to stop what they were doing to read it. Suddenly the centuries to develop print seemed ephemeral. Murdoch said newspaper people had no right, or wish, to repress the 'new, precious possession of humanity.'

While print thrived in the television age, trained its best reporters and producers as television expanded the taste, reach and audience for news, when the World Wide Web made information available immediately for nothing, vast print corporations failed to maintain their dominance of classified advertising, their lifeblood. The inertia infecting corporate giants exposed news revenues to brilliant '.com' kids. After two centuries of news gagged by judges and leaders who believed the Australian experience was not to be trusted, journalists remained stubborn believers, poets, preachers, story-tellers. Fairfax, News Ltd and the ABC joined for the first time in the cause of free speech.

• • •

The complexities of information explored first by Plato and Aristotle and millennia later by the imaginative Canadians Marshall McLuhan and Harold Innes quickly approach infinity. Our hunger to know what's going on is now being satisfied at the speed of light. The argument for suppression is the argument for ignorance. As printers evolved to print guns, bicycles and human organs, 86 per cent of the international Internet Society survey respondents agreed in 2012 that 'freedom of expression should be guaranteed on the Internet' and 71 per cent of the same respondents that 'censorship should exist in some form on the Internet.' The Aborigines' oldest culture on earth did not develop printing because they lacked population density and therefore guns, germs and steel but also because all koori ideas of property, particularly intellectual property, law and authority were radically different to the settlers. The Aborigines' rejection of print was forced by circumstance, but it's possible that underlying it was the collective wisdom that print could undermine parental and tribal authority. In a speech in 52 BCE Cicero used the phrase 'the thing speaks for itself" ('res ipsa loquitur') which evolved into a principle of common law, history and 'objective' journalism: *let the facts speak for themselves*, which everyone who writes journalism, (and history) and everyone who reads it, knows is impossible. The digital age and the universality of electronic media may enable us to evolve to trust communication. It's not a romantic hope. Once we were bounded by memory. Now we can check everything; if we evolve to trust communication we might outperform sea-eagles and bull-ants, even save ourselves.

www.ingramcontent.com/pod-product-compliance
Lightning Source LLC
Chambersburg PA
CBHW082032300426
44117CB00015B/2447